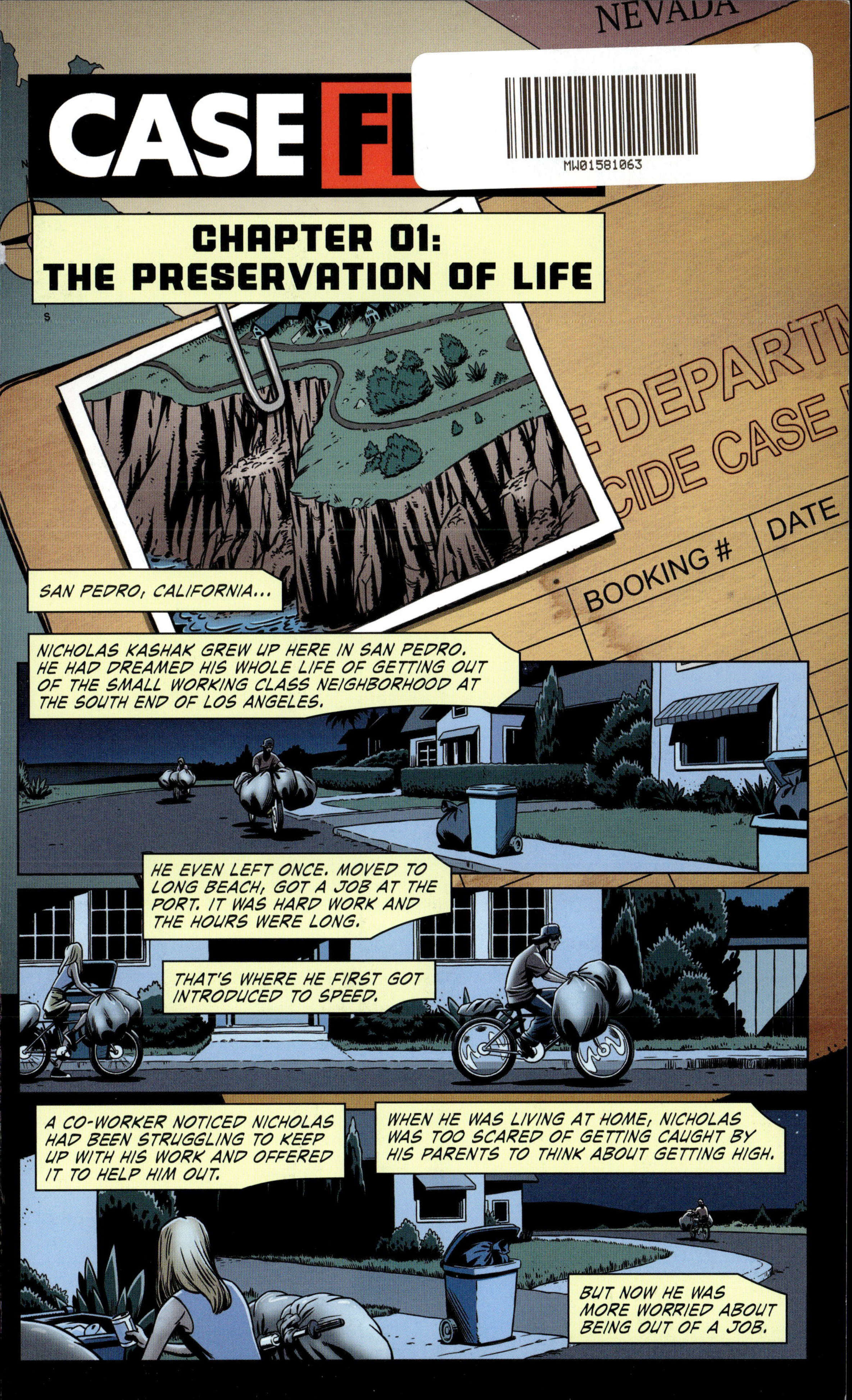
NEVADA
CASE FI
CHAPTER 01:
THE PRESERVATION OF LIFE
DEPARTM
CIDE CASE
BOOKING #
DATE
SAN PEDRO, CALIFORNIA...
NICHOLAS KASHAK GREW UP HERE IN SAN PEDRO. HE HAD DREAMED HIS WHOLE LIFE OF GETTING OUT OF THE SMALL WORKING CLASS NEIGHBORHOOD AT THE SOUTH END OF LOS ANGELES.
HE EVEN LEFT ONCE. MOVED TO LONG BEACH, GOT A JOB AT THE PORT. IT WAS HARD WORK AND THE HOURS WERE LONG.
THAT'S WHERE HE FIRST GOT INTRODUCED TO SPEED.
A CO-WORKER NOTICED NICHOLAS HAD BEEN STRUGGLING TO KEEP UP WITH HIS WORK AND OFFERED IT TO HELP HIM OUT.
WHEN HE WAS LIVING AT HOME, NICHOLAS WAS TOO SCARED OF GETTING CAUGHT BY HIS PARENTS TO THINK ABOUT GETTING HIGH.
BUT NOW HE WAS MORE WORRIED ABOUT BEING OUT OF A JOB.

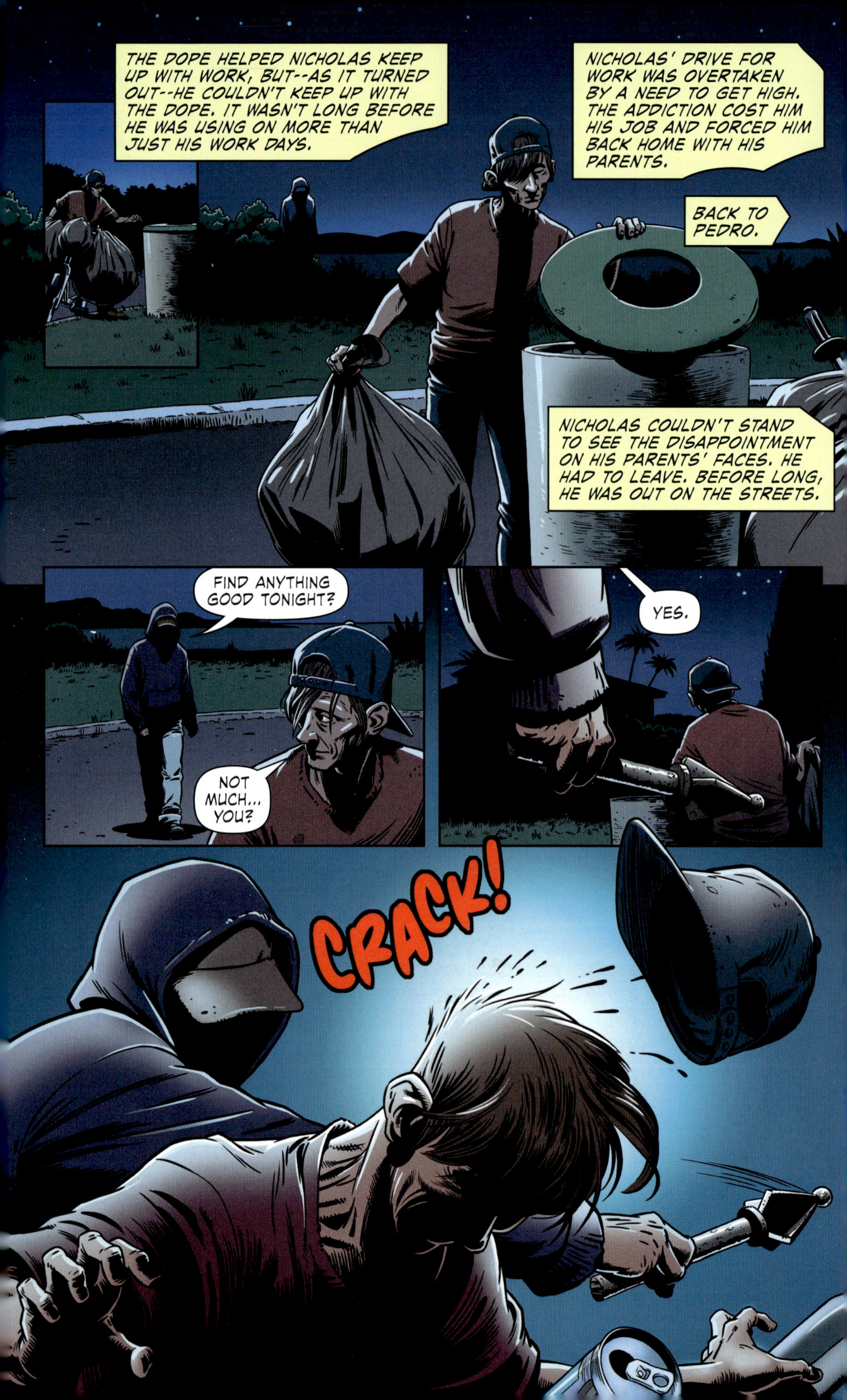
THE DOPE HELPED NICHOLAS KEEP UP WITH WORK, BUT--AS IT TURNED OUT--HE COULDN'T KEEP UP WITH THE DOPE. IT WASN'T LONG BEFORE HE WAS USING ON MORE THAN JUST HIS WORK DAYS.
NICHOLAS' DRIVE FOR WORK WAS OVERTAKEN BY A NEED TO GET HIGH. THE ADDICTION COST HIM HIS JOB AND FORCED HIM BACK HOME WITH HIS PARENTS.
BACK TO PEDRO.
NICHOLAS COULDN'T STAND TO SEE THE DISAPPOINTMENT ON HIS PARENTS' FACES. HE HAD TO LEAVE. BEFORE LONG, HE WAS OUT ON THE STREETS.
FIND ANYTHING GOOD TONIGHT?
NOT MUCH... YOU?
YES.
CRACK!

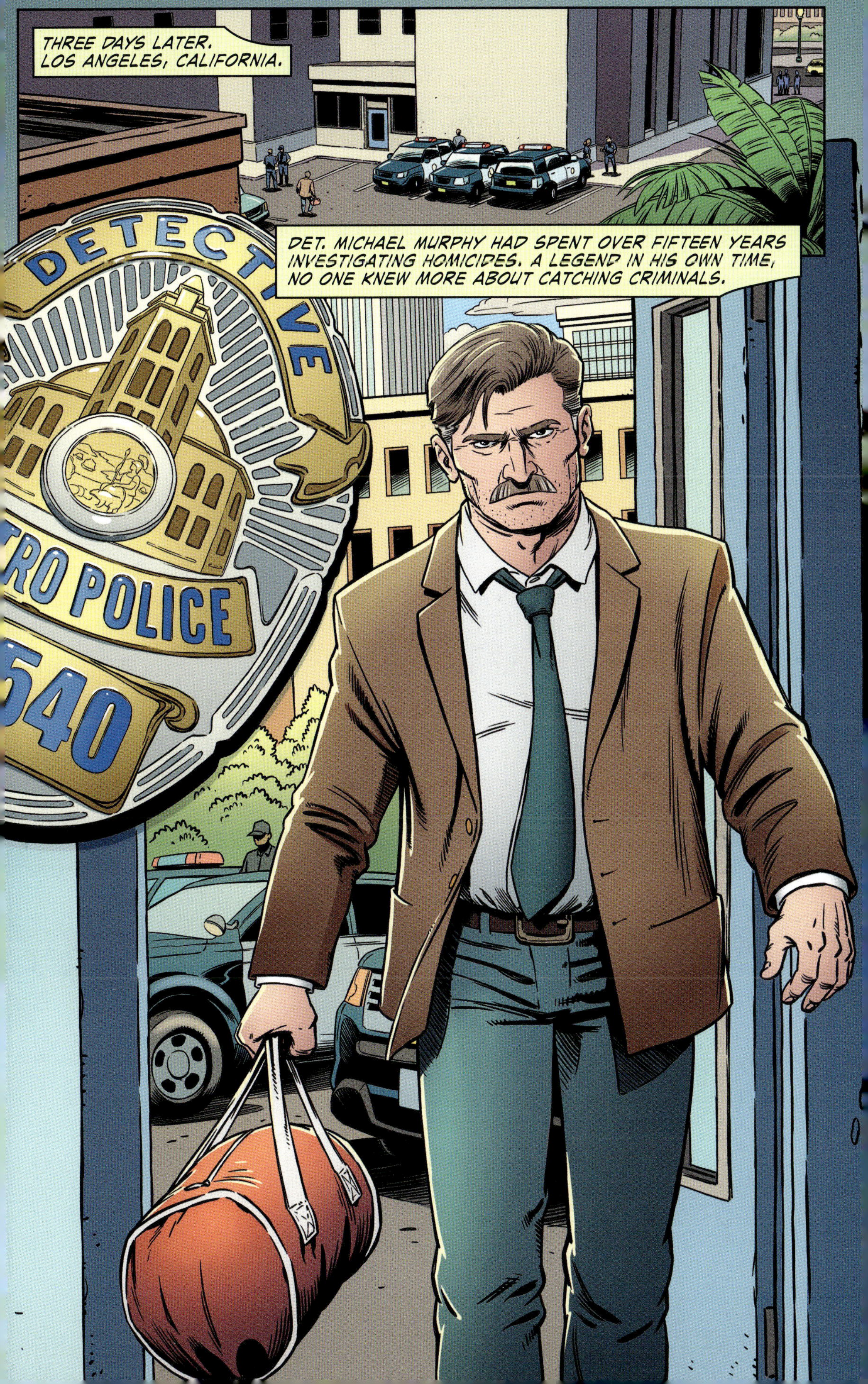
THREE DAYS LATER.
LOS ANGELES, CALIFORNIA.
DET. MICHAEL MURPHY HAD SPENT OVER FIFTEEN YEARS INVESTIGATING HOMICIDES. A LEGEND IN HIS OWN TIME, NO ONE KNEW MORE ABOUT CATCHING CRIMINALS.
DETECTIVE
TRO POLICE
540

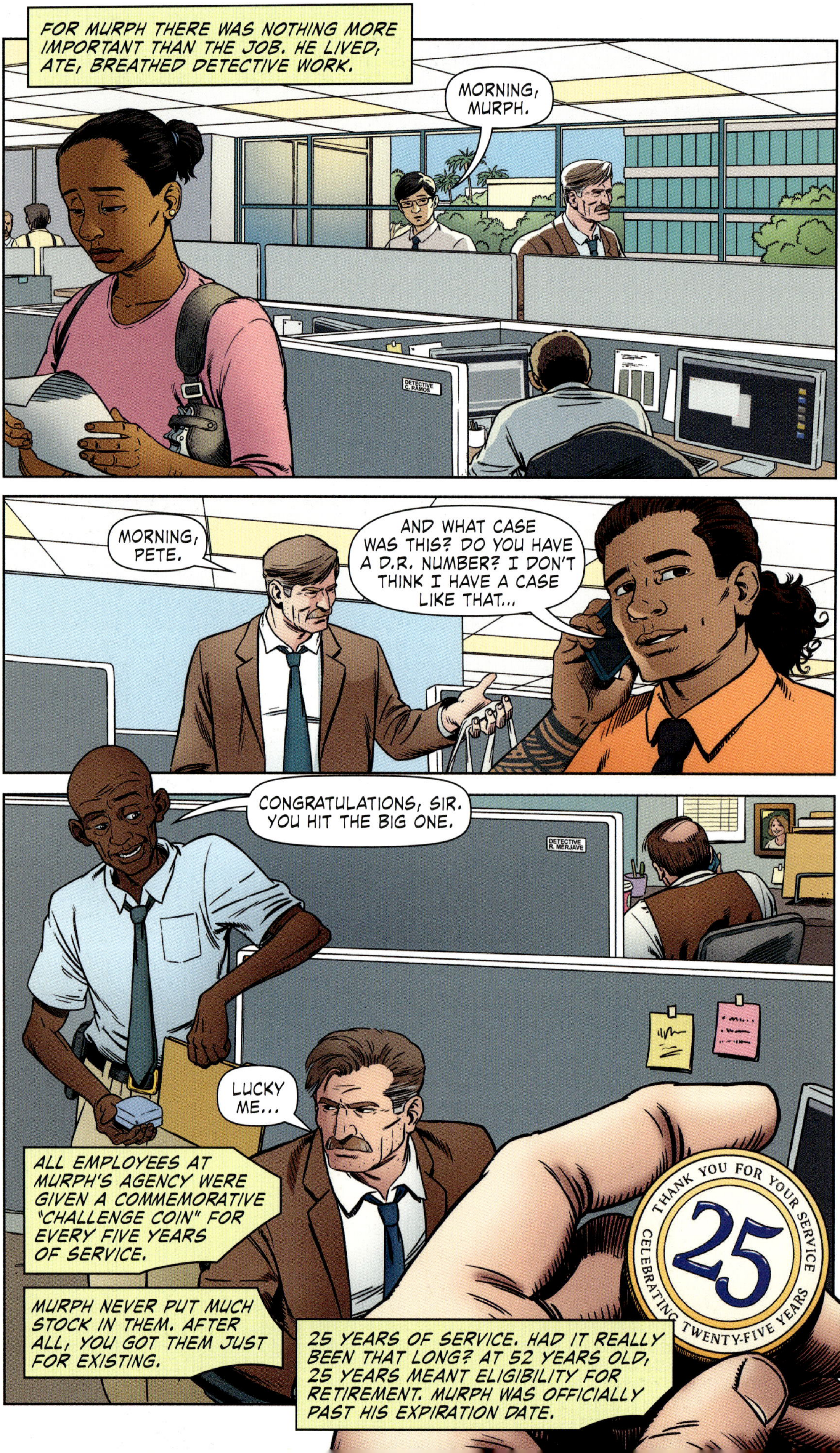
FOR MURPH THERE WAS NOTHING MORE IMPORTANT THAN THE JOB. HE LIVED, ATE, BREATHED DETECTIVE WORK.
MORNING, MURPH.
DETECTIVE C. RAMOS
MORNING, PETE.
AND WHAT CASE WAS THIS? DO YOU HAVE A D.R. NUMBER? I DON'T THINK I HAVE A CASE LIKE THAT...
CONGRATULATIONS, SIR. YOU HIT THE BIG ONE.
DETECTIVE R. MERJAVE
LUCKY ME...
ALL EMPLOYEES AT MURPH'S AGENCY WERE GIVEN A COMMEMORATIVE "CHALLENGE COIN" FOR EVERY FIVE YEARS OF SERVICE.
MURPH NEVER PUT MUCH STOCK IN THEM. AFTER ALL, YOU GOT THEM JUST FOR EXISTING.
THANK YOU FOR YOUR SERVICE
25
CELEBRATING TWENTY-FIVE YEARS
25 YEARS OF SERVICE. HAD IT REALLY BEEN THAT LONG? AT 52 YEARS OLD, 25 YEARS MEANT ELIGIBILITY FOR RETIREMENT. MURPH WAS OFFICIALLY PAST HIS EXPIRATION DATE.

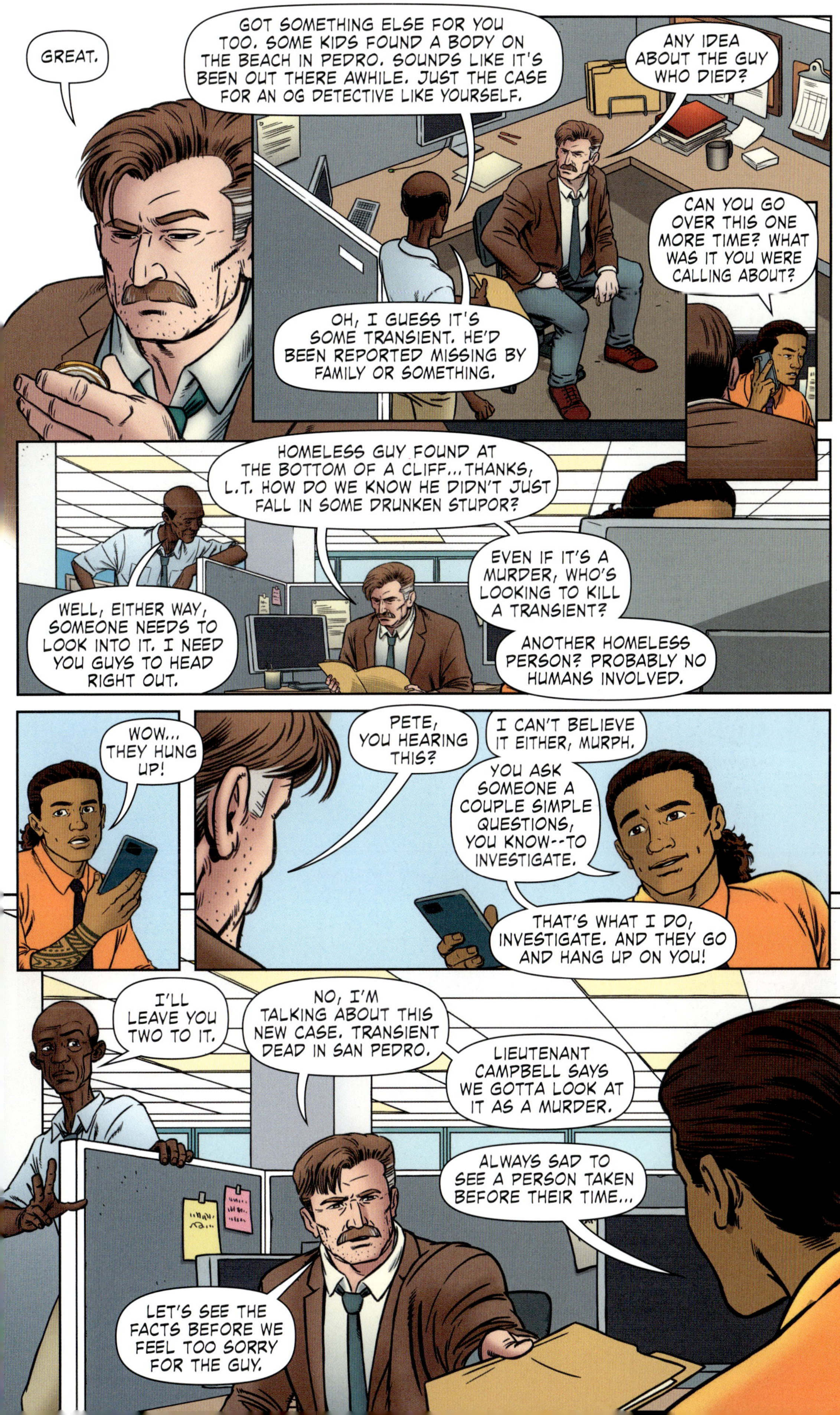
GREAT.
GOT SOMETHING ELSE FOR YOU TOO. SOME KIDS FOUND A BODY ON THE BEACH IN PEDRO. SOUNDS LIKE IT'S BEEN OUT THERE AWHILE. JUST THE CASE FOR AN OG DETECTIVE LIKE YOURSELF.
ANY IDEA ABOUT THE GUY WHO DIED?
OH, I GUESS IT'S SOME TRANSIENT. HE'D BEEN REPORTED MISSING BY FAMILY OR SOMETHING.
CAN YOU GO OVER THIS ONE MORE TIME? WHAT WAS IT YOU WERE CALLING ABOUT?
HOMELESS GUY FOUND AT THE BOTTOM OF A CLIFF...THANKS, L.T. HOW DO WE KNOW HE DIDN'T JUST FALL IN SOME DRUNKEN STUPOR?
EVEN IF IT'S A MURDER, WHO'S LOOKING TO KILL A TRANSIENT?
WELL, EITHER WAY, SOMEONE NEEDS TO LOOK INTO IT. I NEED YOU GUYS TO HEAD RIGHT OUT.
ANOTHER HOMELESS PERSON? PROBABLY NO HUMANS INVOLVED.
WOW... THEY HUNG UP!
PETE, YOU HEARING THIS?
I CAN'T BELIEVE IT EITHER, MURPH.
YOU ASK SOMEONE A COUPLE SIMPLE QUESTIONS, YOU KNOW--TO INVESTIGATE.
THAT'S WHAT I DO, INVESTIGATE. AND THEY GO AND HANG UP ON YOU!
I'LL LEAVE YOU TWO TO IT.
NO, I'M TALKING ABOUT THIS NEW CASE. TRANSIENT DEAD IN SAN PEDRO.
LIEUTENANT CAMPBELL SAYS WE GOTTA LOOK AT IT AS A MURDER.
ALWAYS SAD TO SEE A PERSON TAKEN BEFORE THEIR TIME...
LET'S SEE THE FACTS BEFORE WE FEEL TOO SORRY FOR THE GUY.

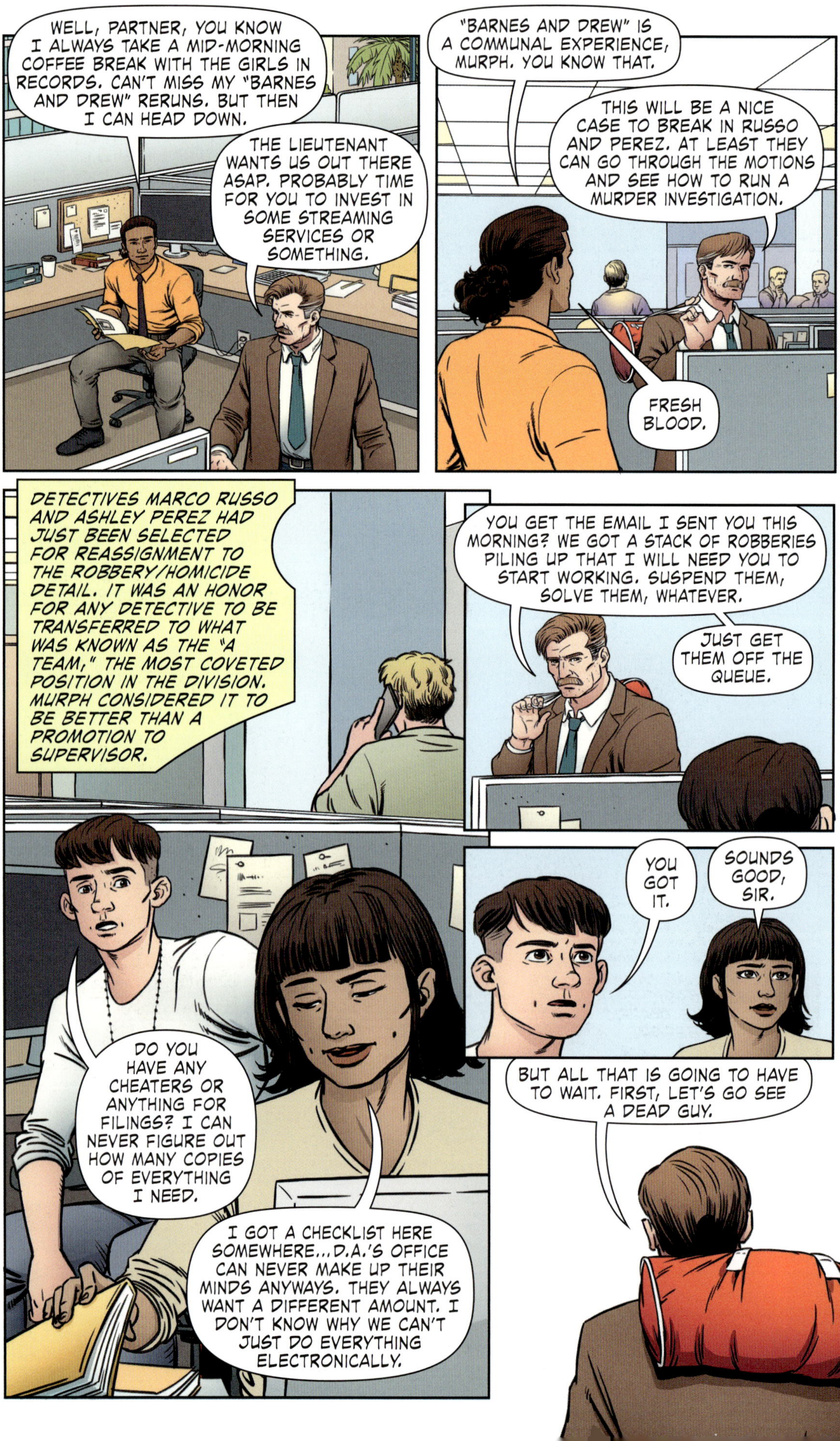
WELL, PARTNER, YOU KNOW I ALWAYS TAKE A MID-MORNING COFFEE BREAK WITH THE GIRLS IN RECORDS. CAN'T MISS MY "BARNES AND DREW" RERUNS. BUT THEN I CAN HEAD DOWN.
THE LIEUTENANT WANTS US OUT THERE ASAP. PROBABLY TIME FOR YOU TO INVEST IN SOME STREAMING SERVICES OR SOMETHING.
"BARNES AND DREW" IS A COMMUNAL EXPERIENCE, MURPH. YOU KNOW THAT.
THIS WILL BE A NICE CASE TO BREAK IN RUSSO AND PEREZ. AT LEAST THEY CAN GO THROUGH THE MOTIONS AND SEE HOW TO RUN A MURDER INVESTIGATION.
FRESH BLOOD.
DETECTIVES MARCO RUSSO AND ASHLEY PEREZ HAD JUST BEEN SELECTED FOR REASSIGNMENT TO THE ROBBERY/HOMICIDE DETAIL. IT WAS AN HONOR FOR ANY DETECTIVE TO BE TRANSFERRED TO WHAT WAS KNOWN AS THE "A TEAM," THE MOST COVETED POSITION IN THE DIVISION. MURPH CONSIDERED IT TO BE BETTER THAN A PROMOTION TO SUPERVISOR.
DO YOU HAVE ANY CHEATERS OR ANYTHING FOR FILINGS? I CAN NEVER FIGURE OUT HOW MANY COPIES OF EVERYTHING I NEED.
I GOT A CHECKLIST HERE SOMEWHERE... D.A.'S OFFICE CAN NEVER MAKE UP THEIR MINDS ANYWAYS. THEY ALWAYS WANT A DIFFERENT AMOUNT. I DON'T KNOW WHY WE CAN'T JUST DO EVERYTHING ELECTRONICALLY.
YOU GET THE EMAIL I SENT YOU THIS MORNING? WE GOT A STACK OF ROBBERIES PILING UP THAT I WILL NEED YOU TO START WORKING. SUSPEND THEM, SOLVE THEM, WHATEVER.
JUST GET THEM OFF THE QUEUE.
YOU GOT IT.
SOUNDS GOOD, SIR.
BUT ALL THAT IS GOING TO HAVE TO WAIT. FIRST, LET'S GO SEE A DEAD GUY.

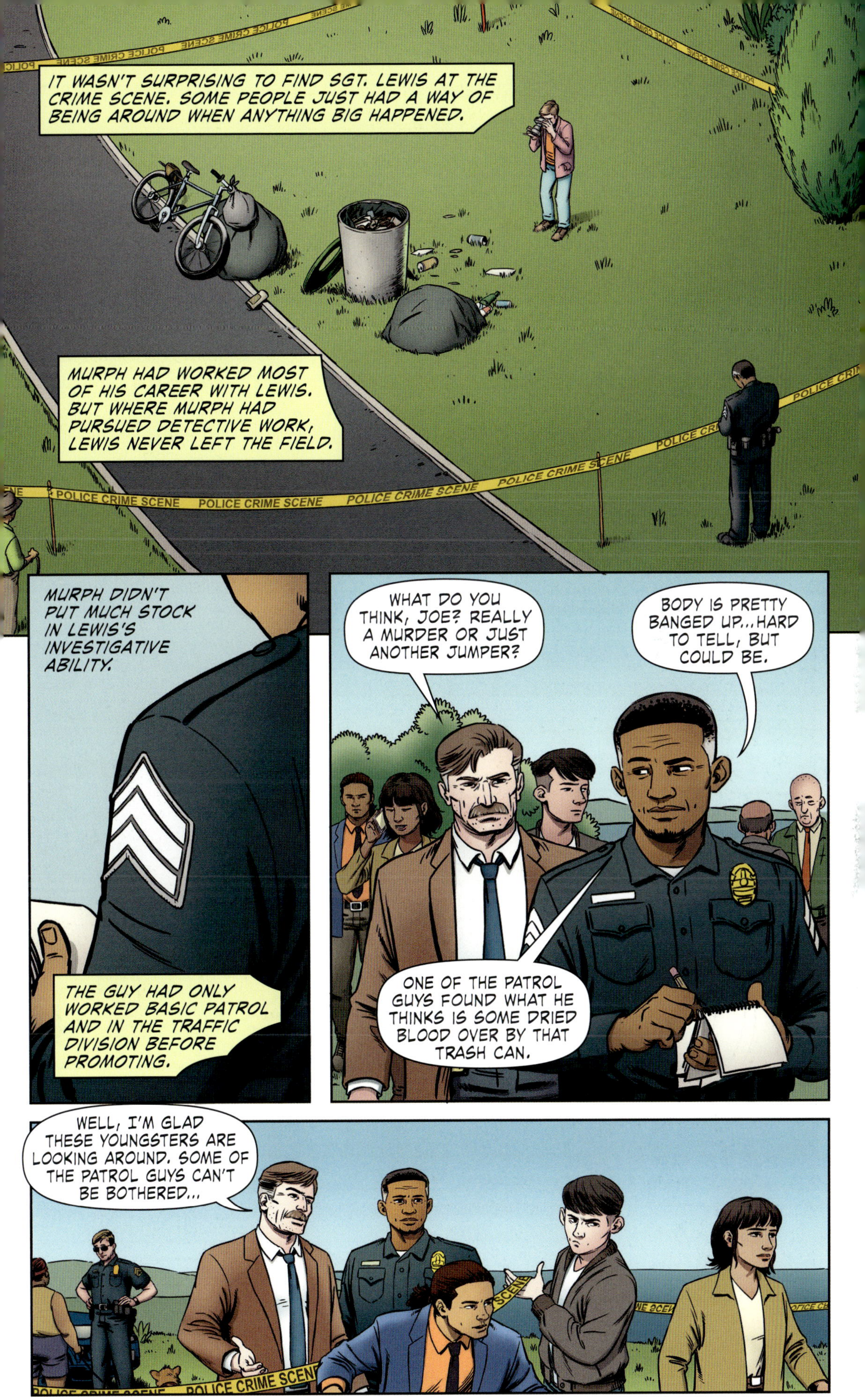
POLICE CRIME SCENE
IT WASN'T SURPRISING TO FIND SGT. LEWIS AT THE CRIME SCENE. SOME PEOPLE JUST HAD A WAY OF BEING AROUND WHEN ANYTHING BIG HAPPENED.
MURPH HAD WORKED MOST OF HIS CAREER WITH LEWIS. BUT WHERE MURPH HAD PURSUED DETECTIVE WORK, LEWIS NEVER LEFT THE FIELD.
POLICE CRIME SCENE
MURPH DIDN'T PUT MUCH STOCK IN LEWIS'S INVESTIGATIVE ABILITY.
THE GUY HAD ONLY WORKED BASIC PATROL AND IN THE TRAFFIC DIVISION BEFORE PROMOTING.
WHAT DO YOU THINK, JOE? REALLY A MURDER OR JUST ANOTHER JUMPER?
BODY IS PRETTY BANGED UP...HARD TO TELL, BUT COULD BE.
ONE OF THE PATROL GUYS FOUND WHAT HE THINKS IS SOME DRIED BLOOD OVER BY THAT TRASH CAN.
WELL, I'M GLAD THESE YOUNGSTERS ARE LOOKING AROUND. SOME OF THE PATROL GUYS CAN'T BE BOTHERED...
POLICE CRIME SCENE

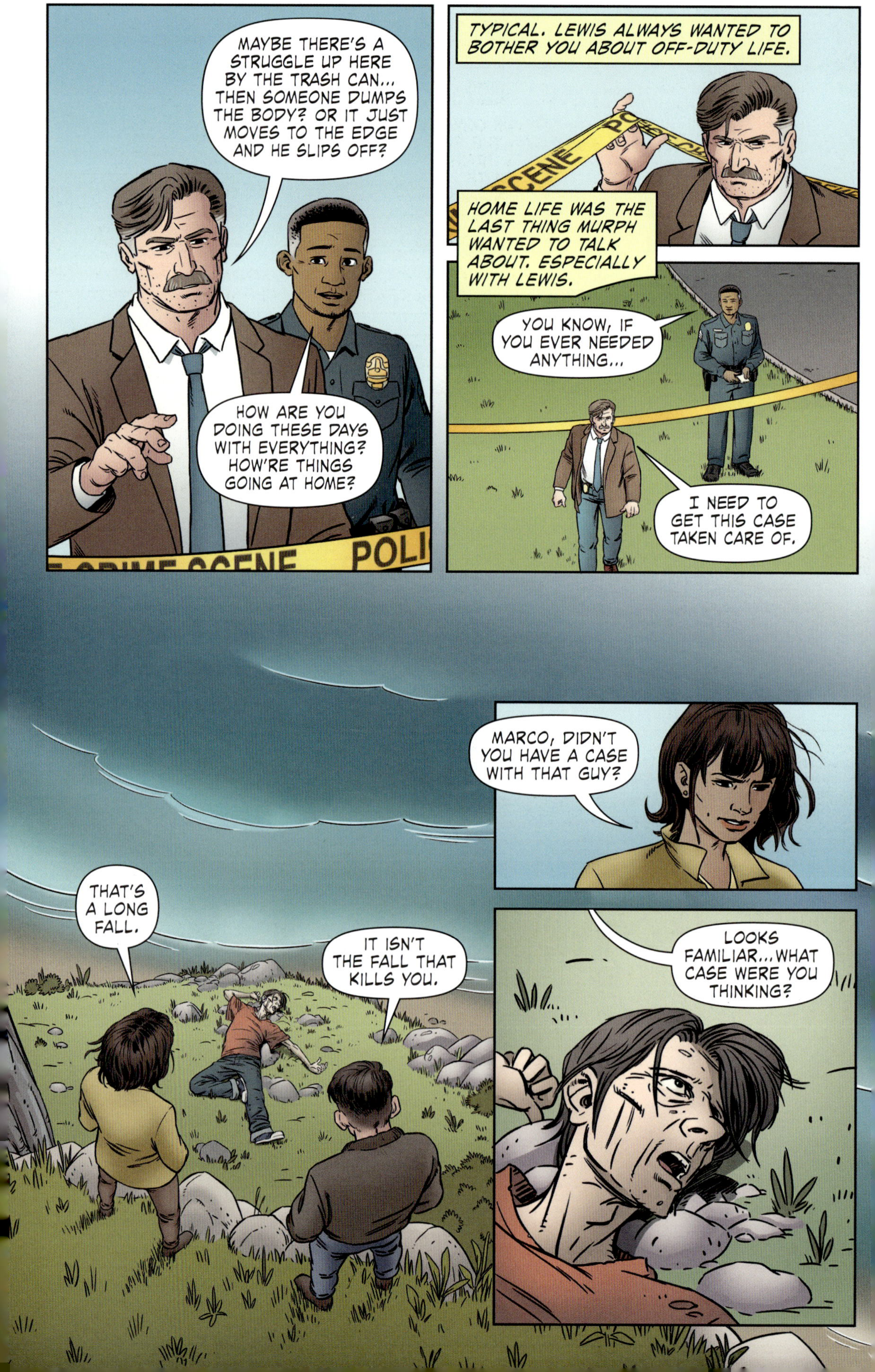
MAYBE THERE'S A STRUGGLE UP HERE BY THE TRASH CAN... THEN SOMEONE DUMPS THE BODY? OR IT JUST MOVES TO THE EDGE AND HE SLIPS OFF?
HOW ARE YOU DOING THESE DAYS WITH EVERYTHING? HOW'RE THINGS GOING AT HOME?
CRIME SCENE POLI
TYPICAL. LEWIS ALWAYS WANTED TO BOTHER YOU ABOUT OFF-DUTY LIFE.
HOME LIFE WAS THE LAST THING MURPH WANTED TO TALK ABOUT. ESPECIALLY WITH LEWIS.
YOU KNOW, IF YOU EVER NEEDED ANYTHING...
I NEED TO GET THIS CASE TAKEN CARE OF.
MARCO, DIDN'T YOU HAVE A CASE WITH THAT GUY?
THAT'S A LONG FALL.
IT ISN'T THE FALL THAT KILLS YOU.
LOOKS FAMILIAR...WHAT CASE WERE YOU THINKING?

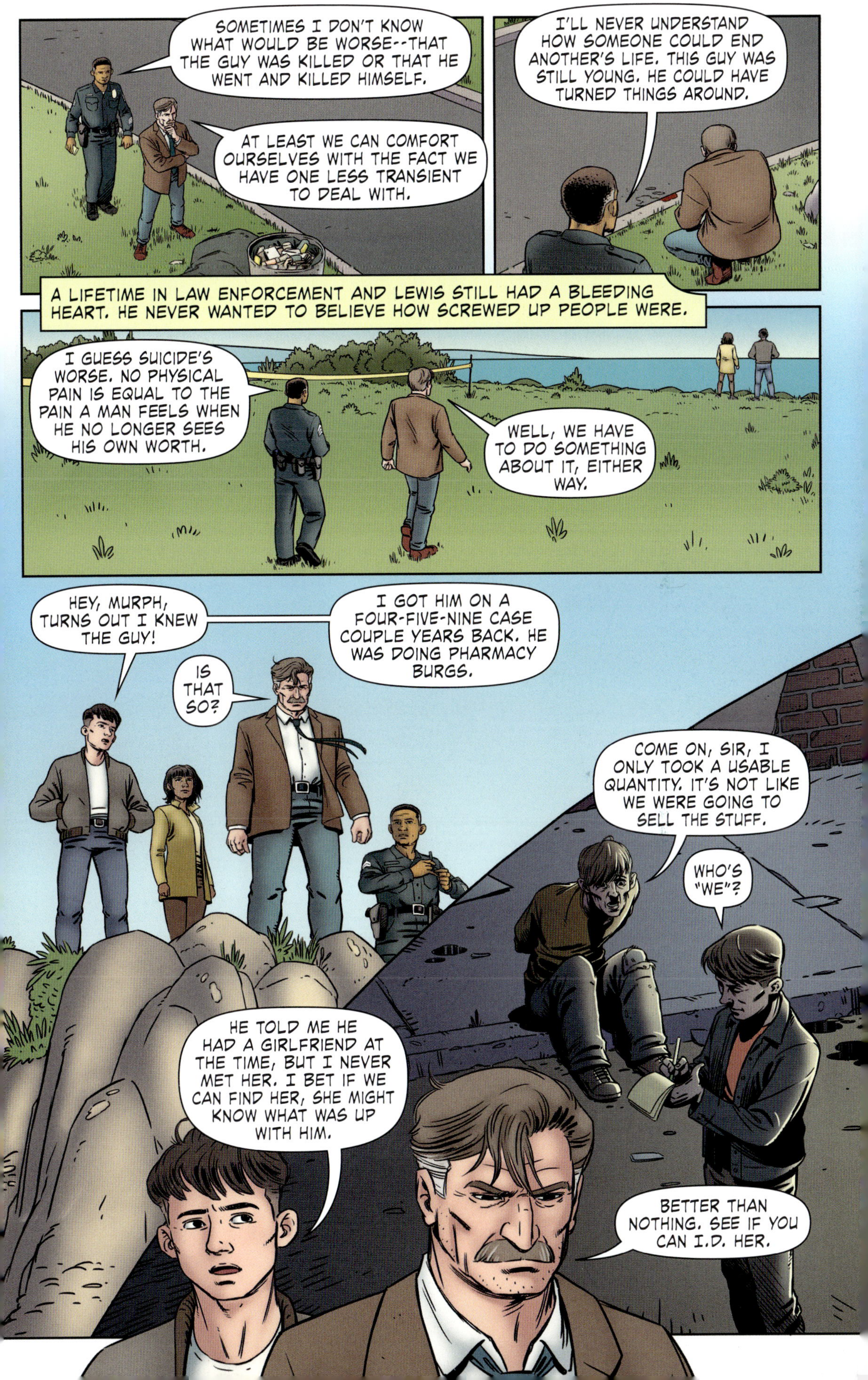
SOMETIMES I DON'T KNOW WHAT WOULD BE WORSE--THAT THE GUY WAS KILLED OR THAT HE WENT AND KILLED HIMSELF.
AT LEAST WE CAN COMFORT OURSELVES WITH THE FACT WE HAVE ONE LESS TRANSIENT TO DEAL WITH.
I'LL NEVER UNDERSTAND HOW SOMEONE COULD END ANOTHER'S LIFE. THIS GUY WAS STILL YOUNG. HE COULD HAVE TURNED THINGS AROUND.
A LIFETIME IN LAW ENFORCEMENT AND LEWIS STILL HAD A BLEEDING HEART. HE NEVER WANTED TO BELIEVE HOW SCREWED UP PEOPLE WERE.
I GUESS SUICIDE'S WORSE. NO PHYSICAL PAIN IS EQUAL TO THE PAIN A MAN FEELS WHEN HE NO LONGER SEES HIS OWN WORTH.
WELL, WE HAVE TO DO SOMETHING ABOUT IT, EITHER WAY.
HEY, MURPH, TURNS OUT I KNEW THE GUY!
I GOT HIM ON A FOUR-FIVE-NINE CASE COUPLE YEARS BACK. HE WAS DOING PHARMACY BURGS.
IS THAT SO?
COME ON, SIR, I ONLY TOOK A USABLE QUANTITY. IT'S NOT LIKE WE WERE GOING TO SELL THE STUFF.
WHO'S "WE"?
HE TOLD ME HE HAD A GIRLFRIEND AT THE TIME, BUT I NEVER MET HER. I BET IF WE CAN FIND HER, SHE MIGHT KNOW WHAT WAS UP WITH HIM.
BETTER THAN NOTHING. SEE IF YOU CAN I.D. HER.

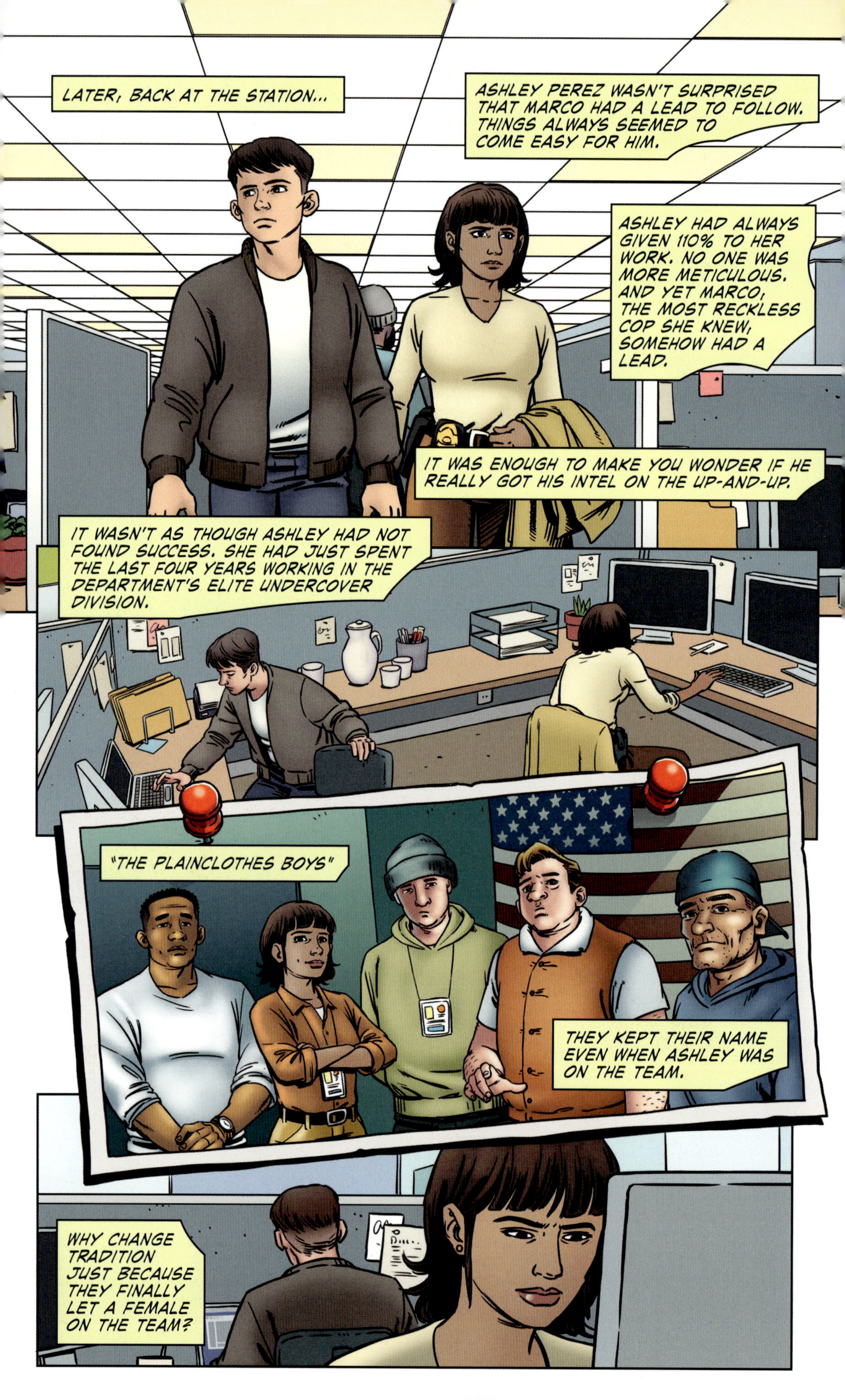
LATER, BACK AT THE STATION...
ASHLEY PEREZ WASN'T SURPRISED THAT MARCO HAD A LEAD TO FOLLOW. THINGS ALWAYS SEEMED TO COME EASY FOR HIM.
ASHLEY HAD ALWAYS GIVEN 110% TO HER WORK. NO ONE WAS MORE METICULOUS. AND YET MARCO, THE MOST RECKLESS COP SHE KNEW, SOMEHOW HAD A LEAD.
IT WAS ENOUGH TO MAKE YOU WONDER IF HE REALLY GOT HIS INTEL ON THE UP-AND-UP.
IT WASN'T AS THOUGH ASHLEY HAD NOT FOUND SUCCESS. SHE HAD JUST SPENT THE LAST FOUR YEARS WORKING IN THE DEPARTMENT'S ELITE UNDERCOVER DIVISION.
"THE PLAINCLOTHES BOYS"
THEY KEPT THEIR NAME EVEN WHEN ASHLEY WAS ON THE TEAM.
WHY CHANGE TRADITION JUST BECAUSE THEY FINALLY LET A FEMALE ON THE TEAM?

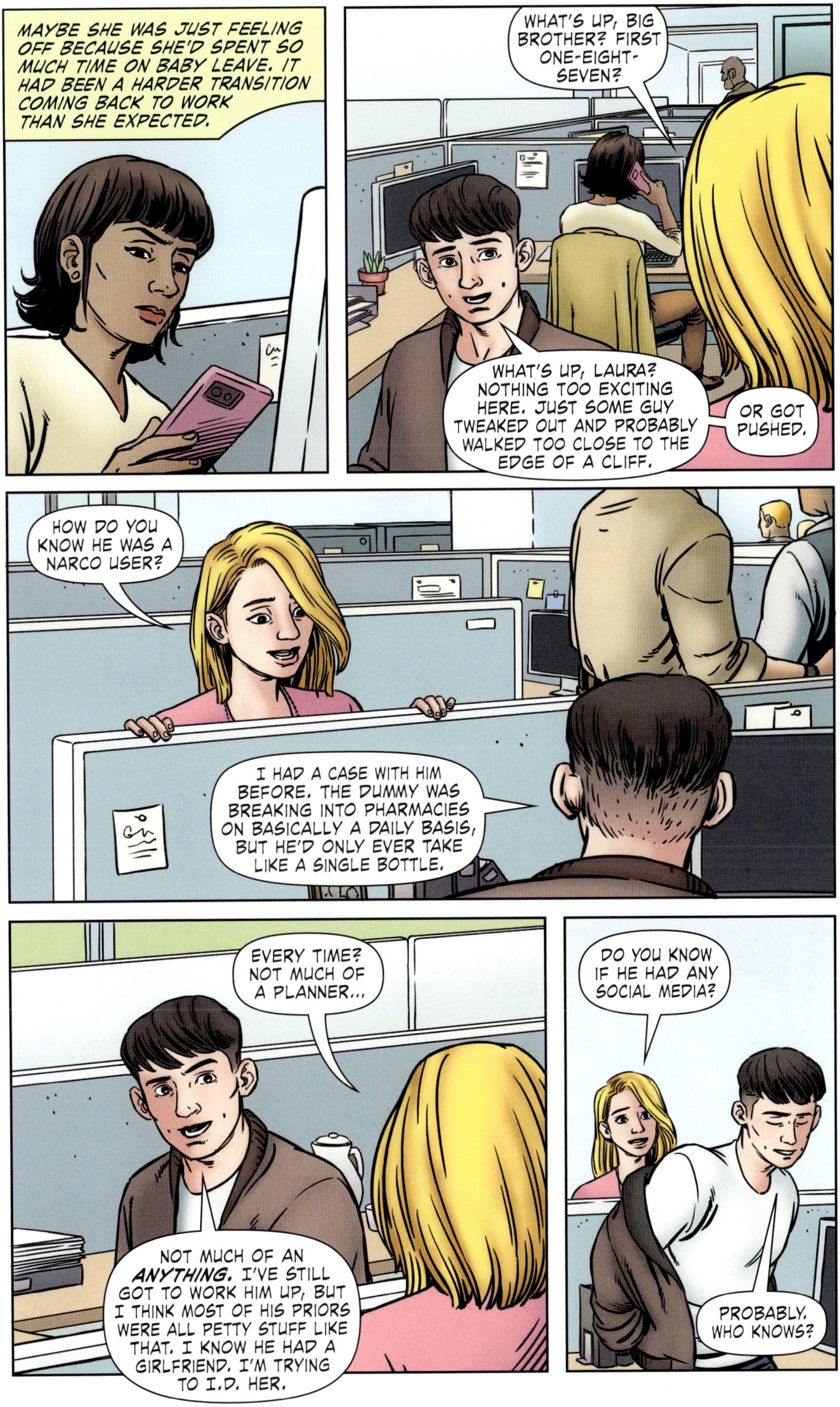
MAYBE SHE WAS JUST FEELING OFF BECAUSE SHE'D SPENT SO MUCH TIME ON BABY LEAVE. IT HAD BEEN A HARDER TRANSITION COMING BACK TO WORK THAN SHE EXPECTED.
WHAT'S UP, BIG BROTHER? FIRST ONE-EIGHT-SEVEN?
WHAT'S UP, LAURA? NOTHING TOO EXCITING HERE. JUST SOME GUY TWEAKED OUT AND PROBABLY WALKED TOO CLOSE TO THE EDGE OF A CLIFF.
OR GOT PUSHED.
HOW DO YOU KNOW HE WAS A NARCO USER?
I HAD A CASE WITH HIM BEFORE. THE DUMMY WAS BREAKING INTO PHARMACIES ON BASICALLY A DAILY BASIS, BUT HE'D ONLY EVER TAKE LIKE A SINGLE BOTTLE.
EVERY TIME? NOT MUCH OF A PLANNER...
NOT MUCH OF AN ANYTHING. I'VE STILL GOT TO WORK HIM UP, BUT I THINK MOST OF HIS PRIORS WERE ALL PETTY STUFF LIKE THAT. I KNOW HE HAD A GIRLFRIEND. I'M TRYING TO I.D. HER.
DO YOU KNOW IF HE HAD ANY SOCIAL MEDIA?
PROBABLY. WHO KNOWS?

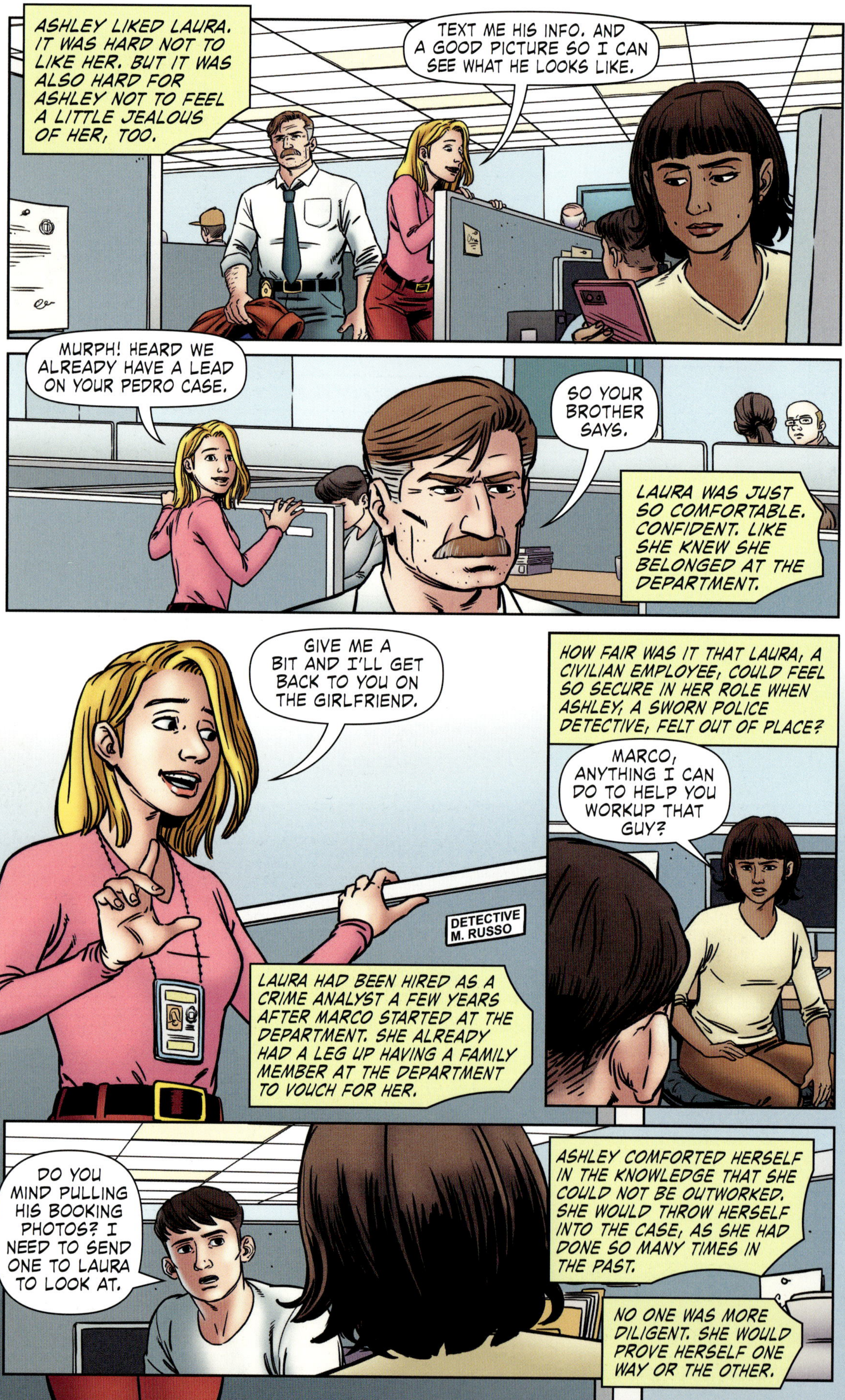
ASHLEY LIKED LAURA. IT WAS HARD NOT TO LIKE HER. BUT IT WAS ALSO HARD FOR ASHLEY NOT TO FEEL A LITTLE JEALOUS OF HER, TOO.
TEXT ME HIS INFO. AND A GOOD PICTURE SO I CAN SEE WHAT HE LOOKS LIKE.
MURPH! HEARD WE ALREADY HAVE A LEAD ON YOUR PEDRO CASE.
SO YOUR BROTHER SAYS.
LAURA WAS JUST SO COMFORTABLE. CONFIDENT. LIKE SHE KNEW SHE BELONGED AT THE DEPARTMENT.
GIVE ME A BIT AND I'LL GET BACK TO YOU ON THE GIRLFRIEND.
DETECTIVE M. RUSSO
LAURA HAD BEEN HIRED AS A CRIME ANALYST A FEW YEARS AFTER MARCO STARTED AT THE DEPARTMENT. SHE ALREADY HAD A LEG UP HAVING A FAMILY MEMBER AT THE DEPARTMENT TO VOUCH FOR HER.
HOW FAIR WAS IT THAT LAURA, A CIVILIAN EMPLOYEE, COULD FEEL SO SECURE IN HER ROLE WHEN ASHLEY, A SWORN POLICE DETECTIVE, FELT OUT OF PLACE?
MARCO, ANYTHING I CAN DO TO HELP YOU WORKUP THAT GUY?
DO YOU MIND PULLING HIS BOOKING PHOTOS? I NEED TO SEND ONE TO LAURA TO LOOK AT.
ASHLEY COMFORTED HERSELF IN THE KNOWLEDGE THAT SHE COULD NOT BE OUTWORKED. SHE WOULD THROW HERSELF INTO THE CASE, AS SHE HAD DONE SO MANY TIMES IN THE PAST.
NO ONE WAS MORE DILIGENT. SHE WOULD PROVE HERSELF ONE WAY OR THE OTHER.

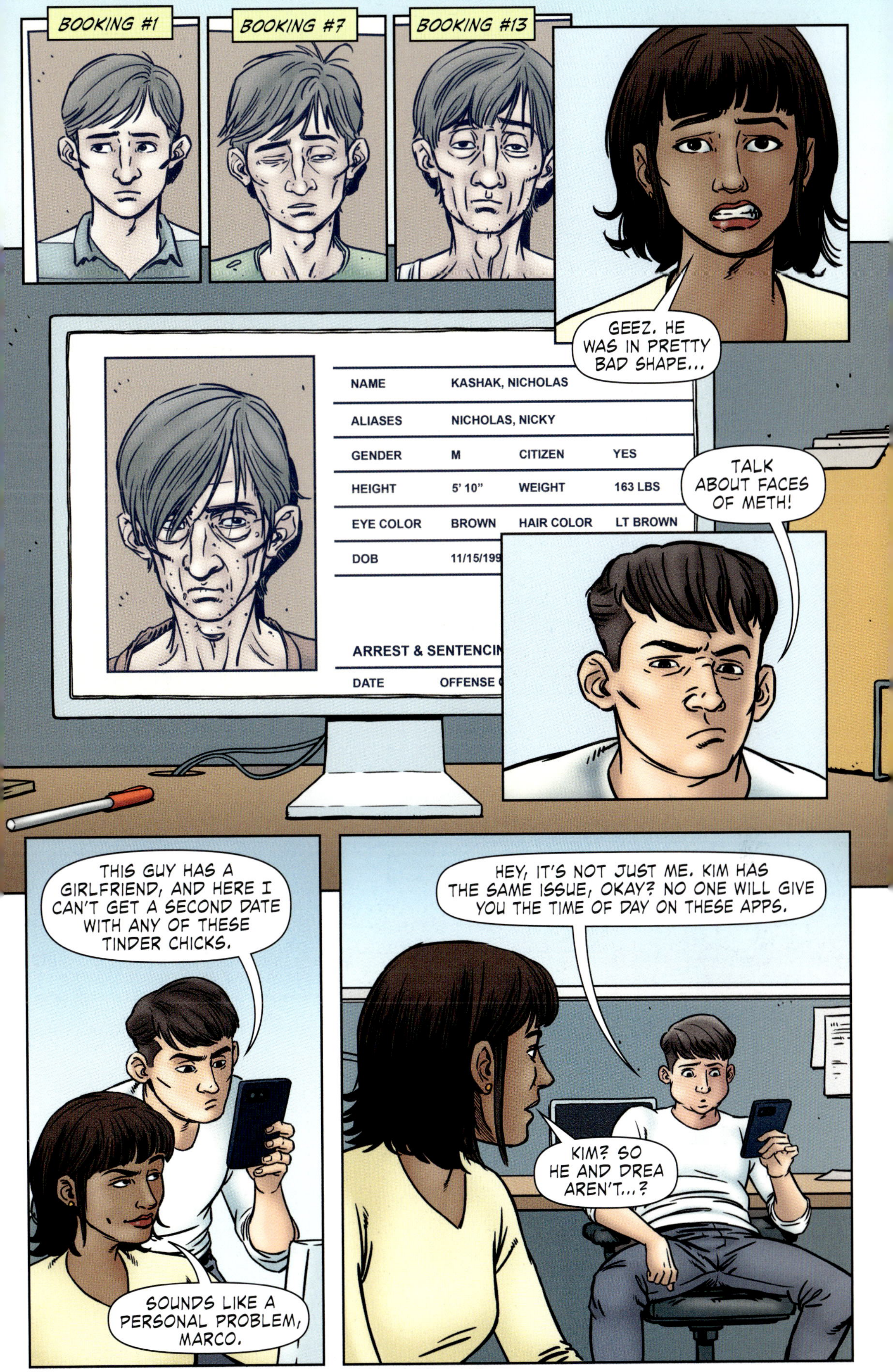
BOOKING #1
BOOKING #7
BOOKING #13
GEEZ. HE WAS IN PRETTY BAD SHAPE...
NAME KASHAK, NICHOLAS
ALIASES NICHOLAS, NICKY
GENDER M CITIZEN YES
HEIGHT 5' 10" WEIGHT 163 LBS
EYE COLOR BROWN HAIR COLOR LT BROWN
DOB
TALK ABOUT FACES OF METH!
THIS GUY HAS A GIRLFRIEND, AND HERE I CAN'T GET A SECOND DATE WITH ANY OF THESE TINDER CHICKS.
SOUNDS LIKE A PERSONAL PROBLEM, MARCO.
HEY, IT'S NOT JUST ME. KIM HAS THE SAME ISSUE, OKAY? NO ONE WILL GIVE YOU THE TIME OF DAY ON THESE APPS.
KIM? SO HE AND DREA AREN'T...?

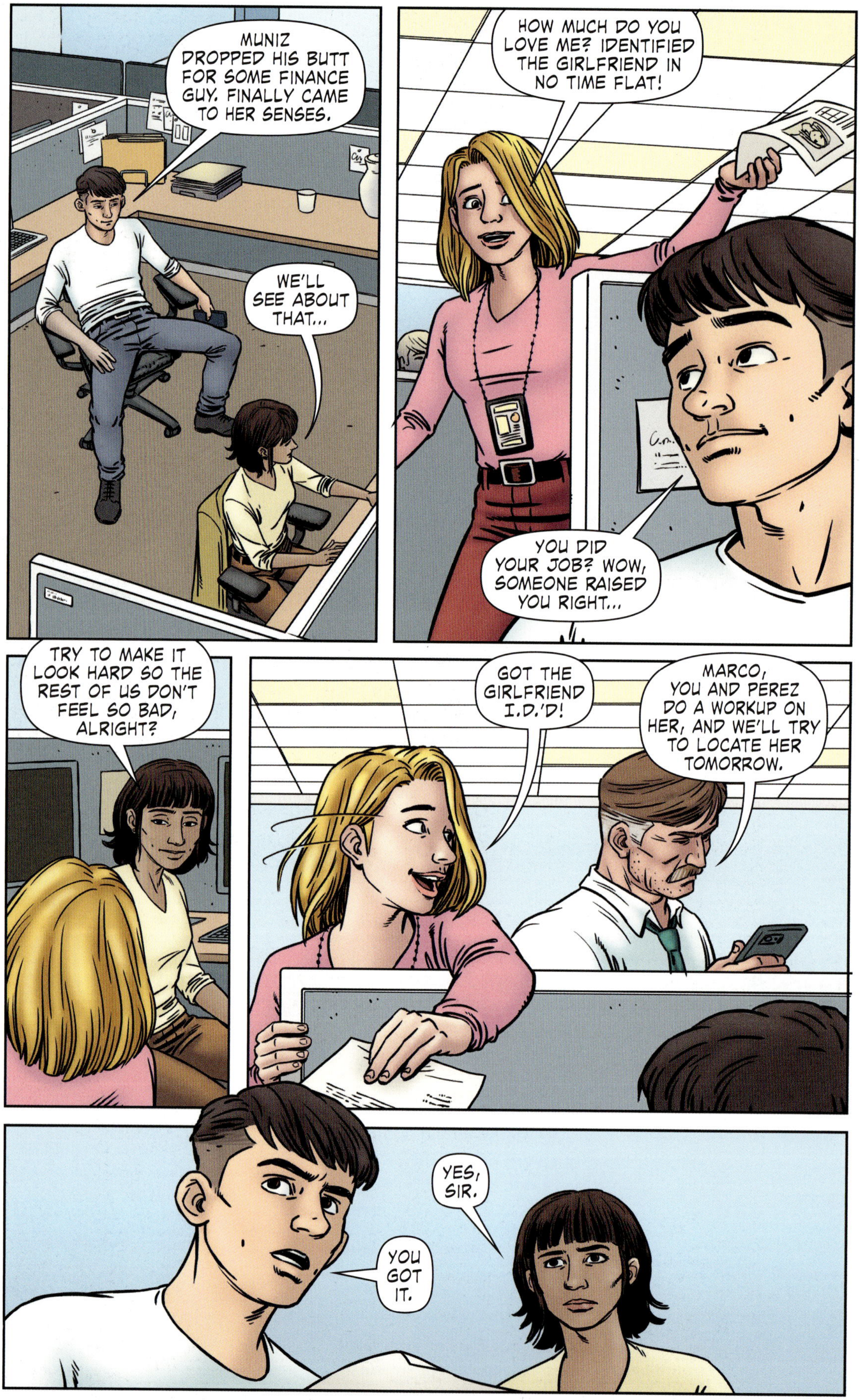
MUNIZ DROPPED HIS BUTT FOR SOME FINANCE GUY. FINALLY CAME TO HER SENSES.
WE'LL SEE ABOUT THAT...
HOW MUCH DO YOU LOVE ME? IDENTIFIED THE GIRLFRIEND IN NO TIME FLAT!
YOU DID YOUR JOB? WOW, SOMEONE RAISED YOU RIGHT...
TRY TO MAKE IT LOOK HARD SO THE REST OF US DON'T FEEL SO BAD, ALRIGHT?
GOT THE GIRLFRIEND I.D.'D!
MARCO, YOU AND PEREZ DO A WORKUP ON HER, AND WE'LL TRY TO LOCATE HER TOMORROW.
YES, SIR.
YOU GOT IT.

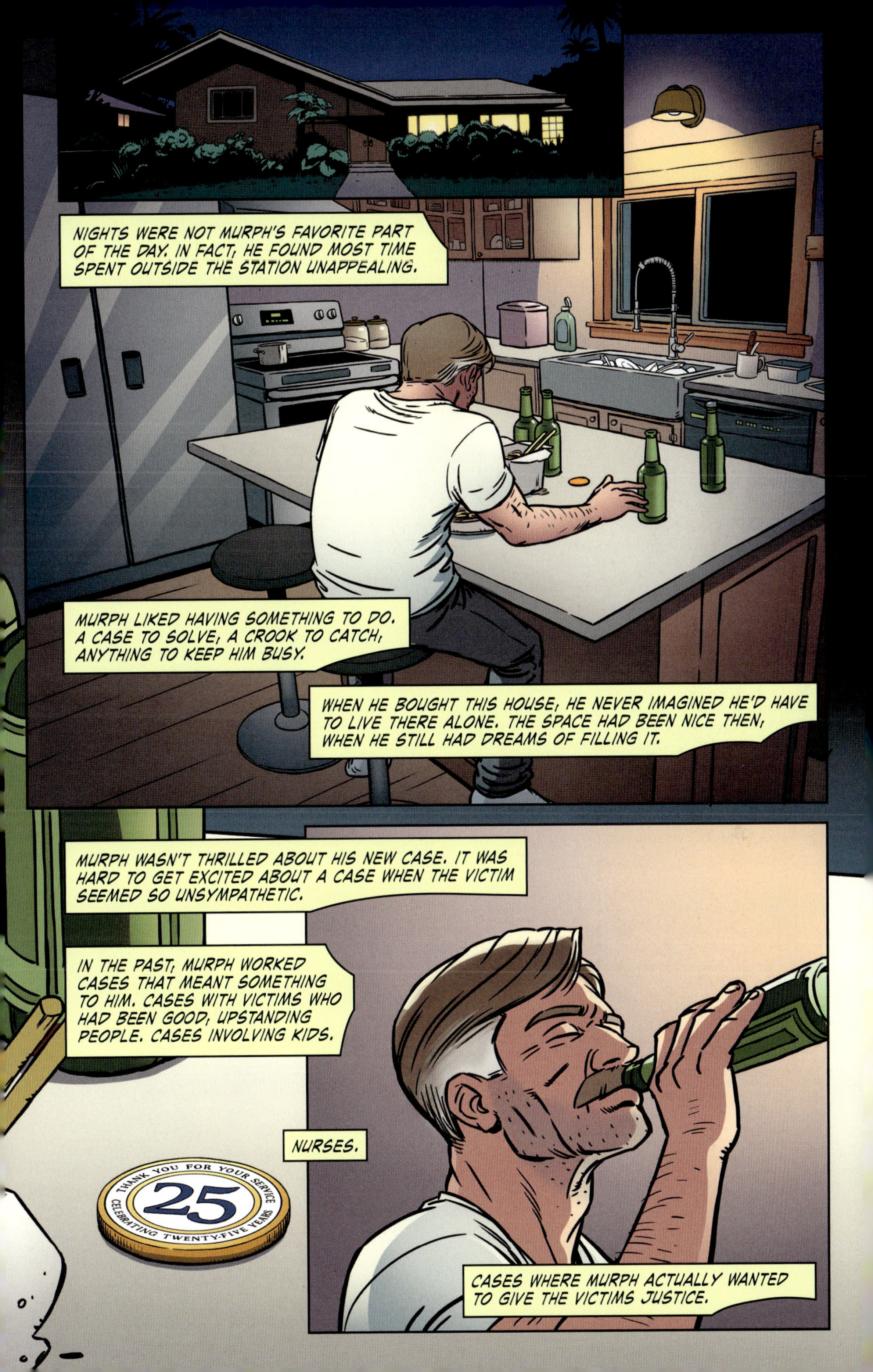
NIGHTS WERE NOT MURPH'S FAVORITE PART OF THE DAY. IN FACT, HE FOUND MOST TIME SPENT OUTSIDE THE STATION UNAPPEALING.
MURPH LIKED HAVING SOMETHING TO DO. A CASE TO SOLVE, A CROOK TO CATCH, ANYTHING TO KEEP HIM BUSY.
WHEN HE BOUGHT THIS HOUSE, HE NEVER IMAGINED HE'D HAVE TO LIVE THERE ALONE. THE SPACE HAD BEEN NICE THEN, WHEN HE STILL HAD DREAMS OF FILLING IT.
MURPH WASN'T THRILLED ABOUT HIS NEW CASE. IT WAS HARD TO GET EXCITED ABOUT A CASE WHEN THE VICTIM SEEMED SO UNSYMPATHETIC.
IN THE PAST, MURPH WORKED CASES THAT MEANT SOMETHING TO HIM. CASES WITH VICTIMS WHO HAD BEEN GOOD, UPSTANDING PEOPLE. CASES INVOLVING KIDS.
NURSES.
THANK YOU FOR YOUR SERVICE
25
CELEBRATING TWENTY-FIVE YEARS
CASES WHERE MURPH ACTUALLY WANTED TO GIVE THE VICTIMS JUSTICE.

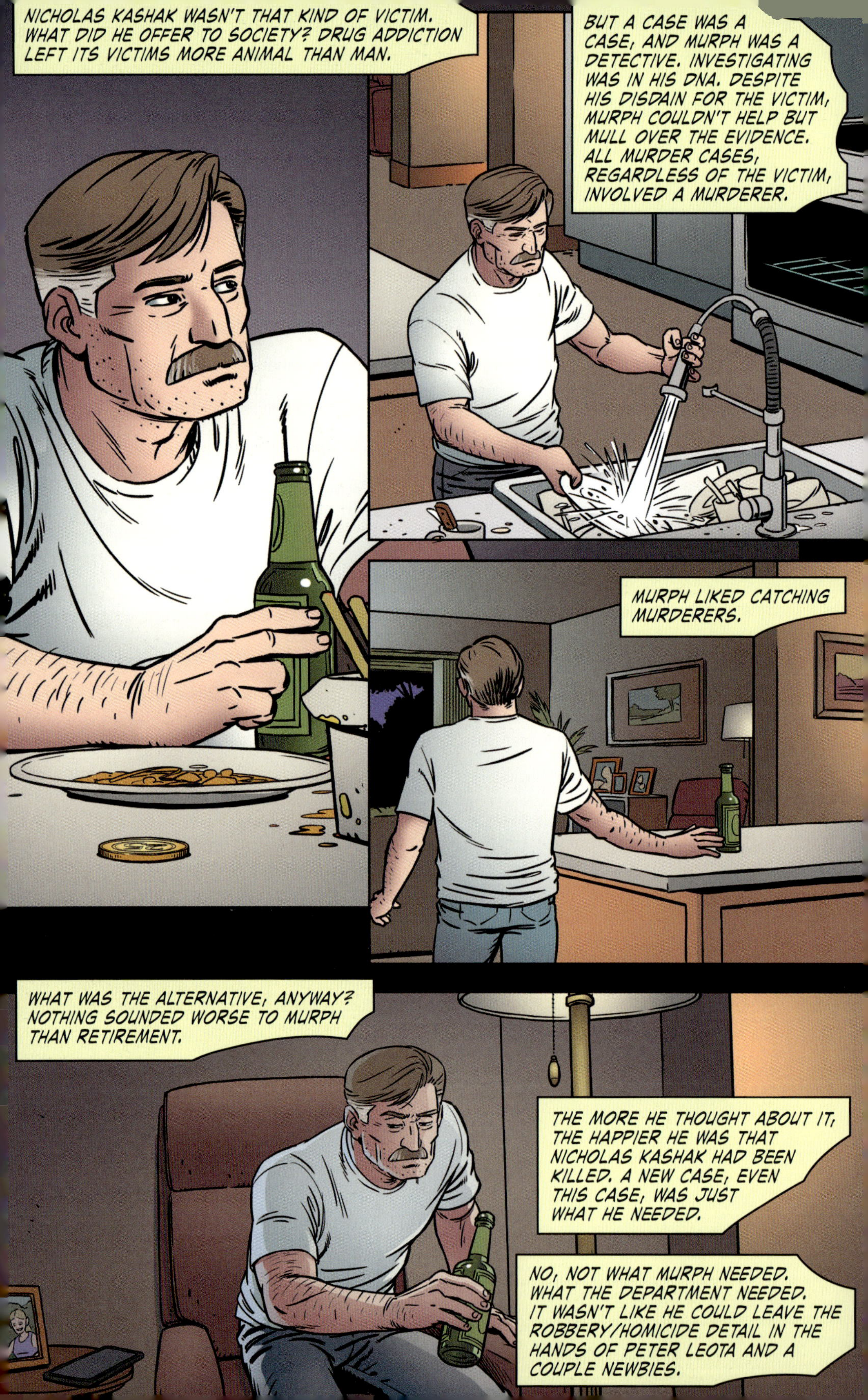
NICHOLAS KASHAK WASN'T THAT KIND OF VICTIM. WHAT DID HE OFFER TO SOCIETY? DRUG ADDICTION LEFT ITS VICTIMS MORE ANIMAL THAN MAN.
BUT A CASE WAS A CASE, AND MURPH WAS A DETECTIVE. INVESTIGATING WAS IN HIS DNA. DESPITE HIS DISDAIN FOR THE VICTIM, MURPH COULDN'T HELP BUT MULL OVER THE EVIDENCE. ALL MURDER CASES, REGARDLESS OF THE VICTIM, INVOLVED A MURDERER.
MURPH LIKED CATCHING MURDERERS.
WHAT WAS THE ALTERNATIVE, ANYWAY? NOTHING SOUNDED WORSE TO MURPH THAN RETIREMENT.
THE MORE HE THOUGHT ABOUT IT, THE HAPPIER HE WAS THAT NICHOLAS KASHAK HAD BEEN KILLED. A NEW CASE, EVEN THIS CASE, WAS JUST WHAT HE NEEDED.
NO, NOT WHAT MURPH NEEDED. WHAT THE DEPARTMENT NEEDED. IT WASN'T LIKE HE COULD LEAVE THE ROBBERY/HOMICIDE DETAIL IN THE HANDS OF PETER LEOTA AND A COUPLE NEWBIES.

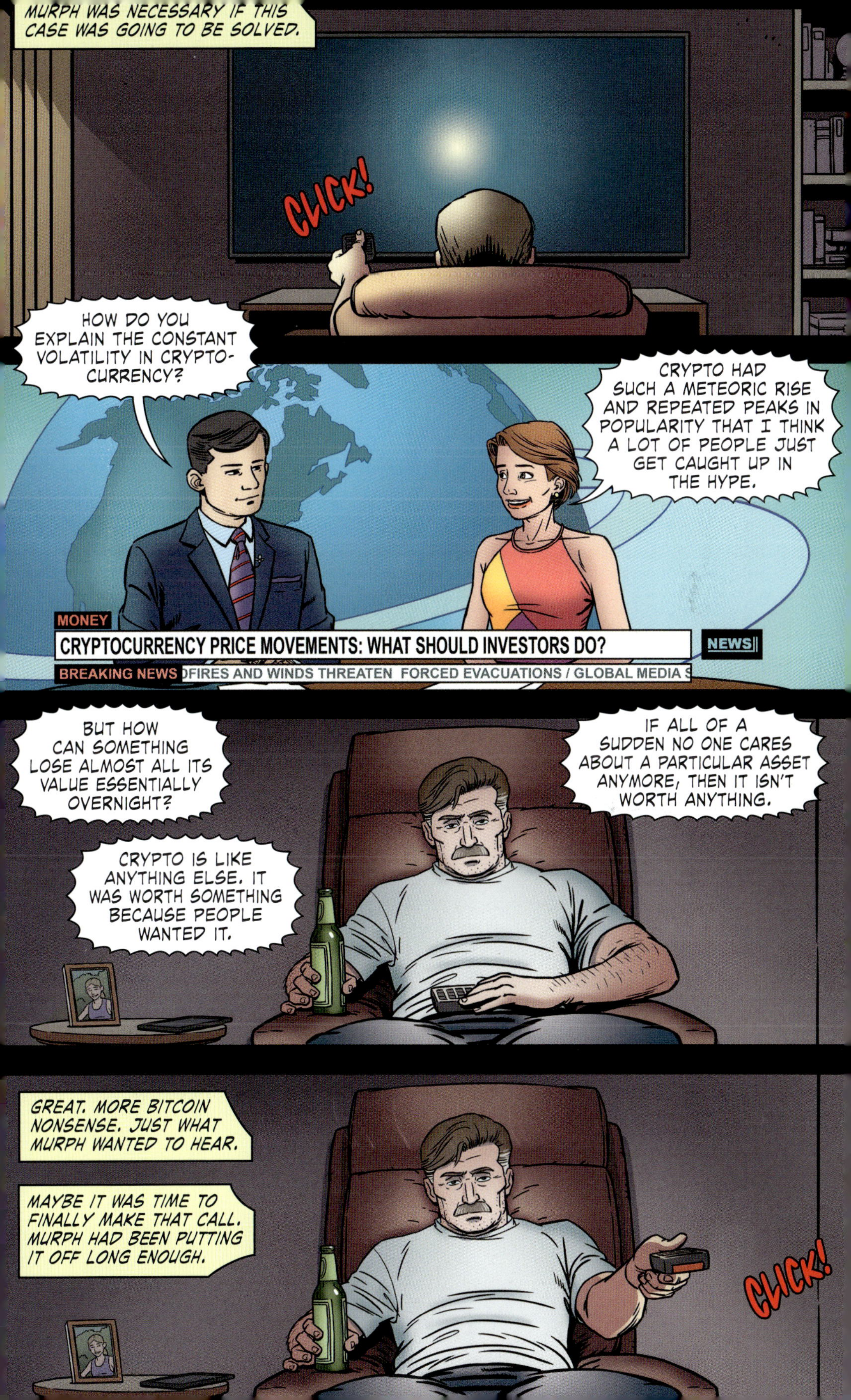
MURPH WAS NECESSARY IF THIS CASE WAS GOING TO BE SOLVED.
CLICK!
HOW DO YOU EXPLAIN THE CONSTANT VOLATILITY IN CRYPTO-CURRENCY?
CRYPTO HAD SUCH A METEORIC RISE AND REPEATED PEAKS IN POPULARITY THAT I THINK A LOT OF PEOPLE JUST GET CAUGHT UP IN THE HYPE.
MONEY
CRYPTOCURRENCY PRICE MOVEMENTS: WHAT SHOULD INVESTORS DO?
NEWS
BREAKING NEWS
FIRES AND WINDS THREATEN FORCED EVACUATIONS / GLOBAL MEDIA
BUT HOW CAN SOMETHING LOSE ALMOST ALL ITS VALUE ESSENTIALLY OVERNIGHT?
IF ALL OF A SUDDEN NO ONE CARES ABOUT A PARTICULAR ASSET ANYMORE, THEN IT ISN'T WORTH ANYTHING.
CRYPTO IS LIKE ANYTHING ELSE. IT WAS WORTH SOMETHING BECAUSE PEOPLE WANTED IT.
GREAT. MORE BITCOIN NONSENSE. JUST WHAT MURPH WANTED TO HEAR.
MAYBE IT WAS TIME TO FINALLY MAKE THAT CALL. MURPH HAD BEEN PUTTING IT OFF LONG ENOUGH.
CLICK!

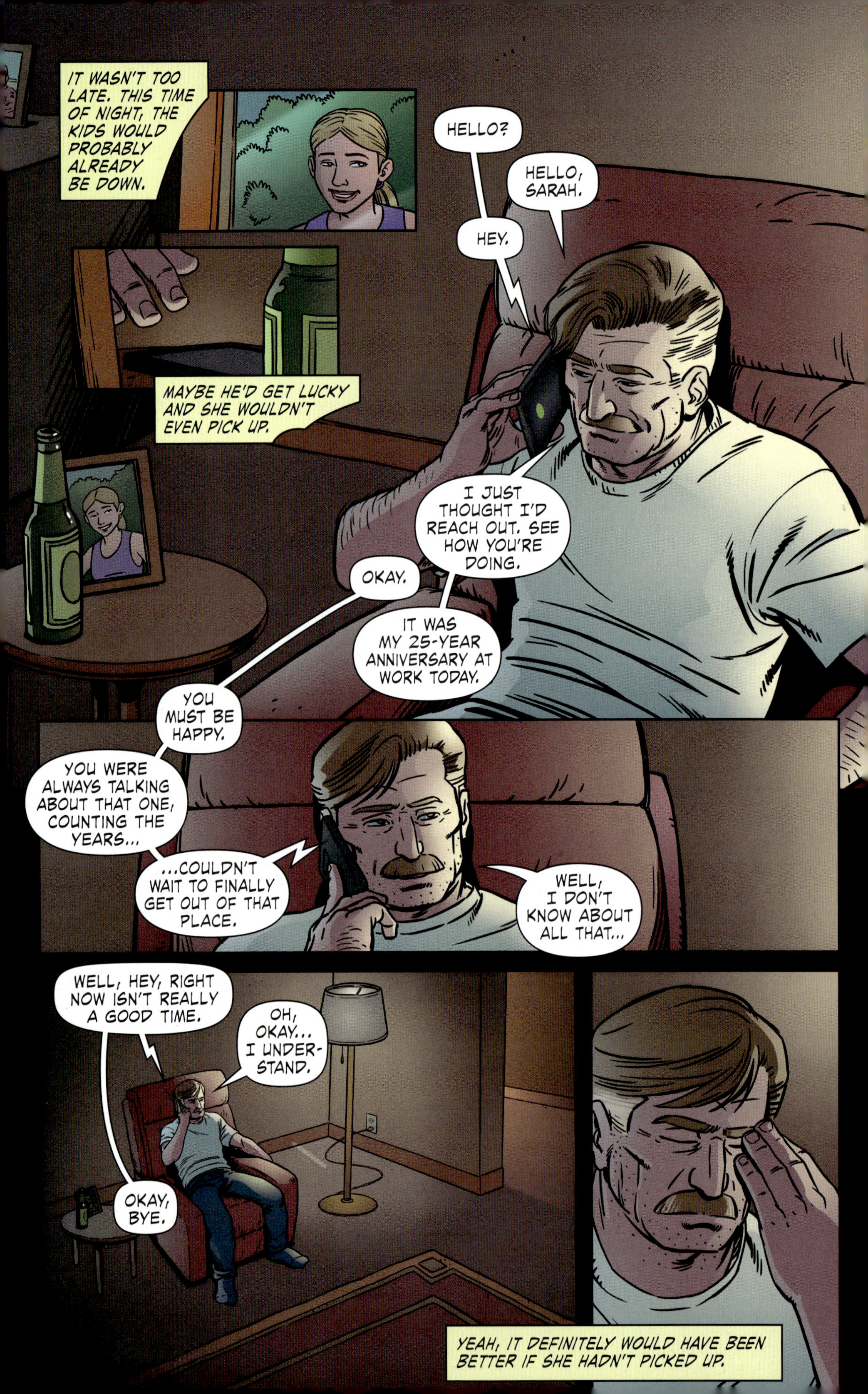

IT WASN'T TOO LATE. THIS TIME OF NIGHT, THE KIDS WOULD PROBABLY ALREADY BE DOWN.
HELLO?
HELLO, SARAH.
HEY.
MAYBE HE'D GET LUCKY AND SHE WOULDN'T EVEN PICK UP.
I JUST THOUGHT I'D REACH OUT. SEE HOW YOU'RE DOING.
OKAY.
IT WAS MY 25-YEAR ANNIVERSARY AT WORK TODAY.
YOU MUST BE HAPPY.
YOU WERE ALWAYS TALKING ABOUT THAT ONE, COUNTING THE YEARS...
...COULDN'T WAIT TO FINALLY GET OUT OF THAT PLACE.
WELL, I DON'T KNOW ABOUT ALL THAT...
WELL, HEY, RIGHT NOW ISN'T REALLY A GOOD TIME.
OH, OKAY... I UNDER-STAND.
OKAY, BYE.
YEAH, IT DEFINITELY WOULD HAVE BEEN BETTER IF SHE HADN'T PICKED UP.

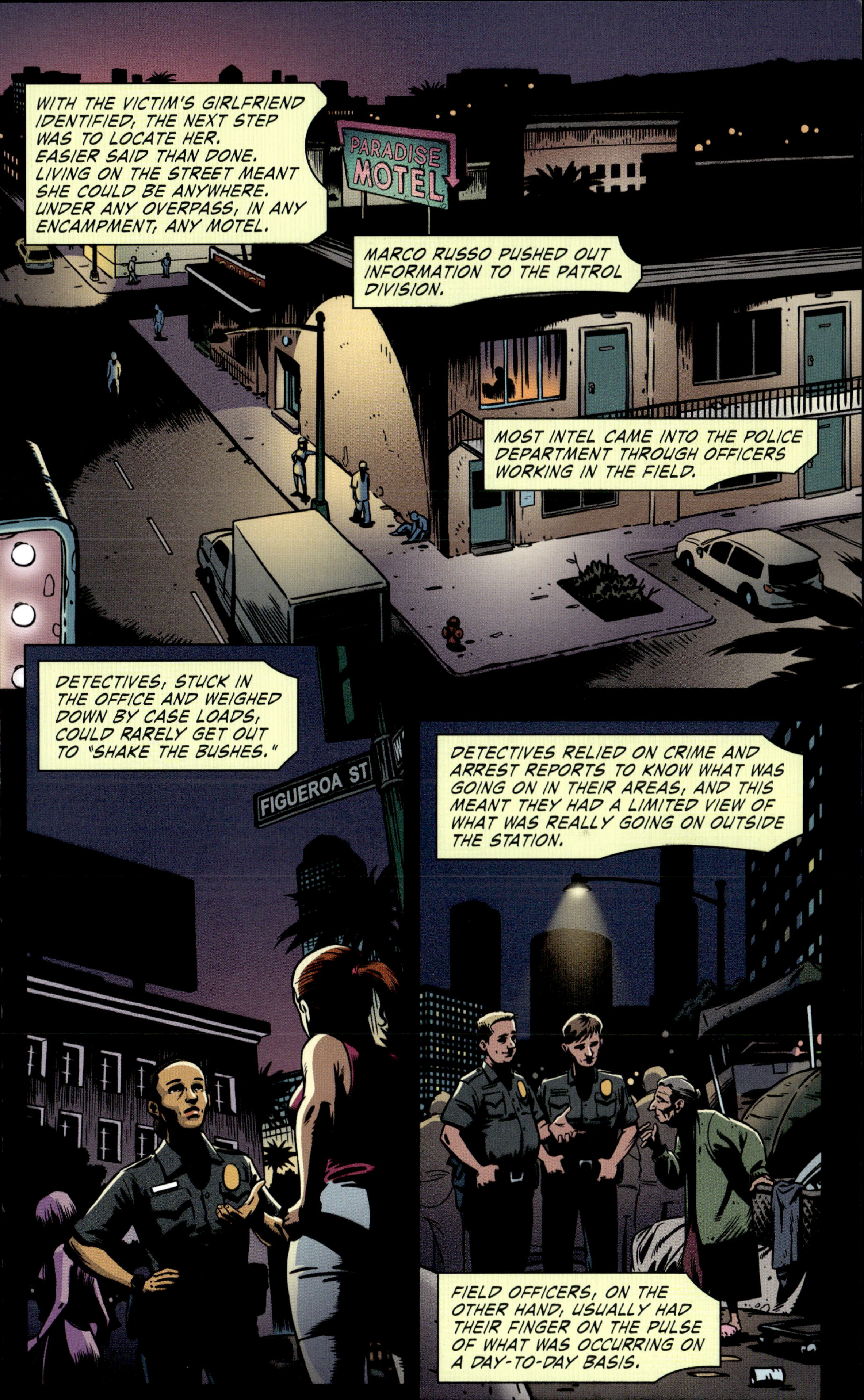
WITH THE VICTIM'S GIRLFRIEND IDENTIFIED, THE NEXT STEP WAS TO LOCATE HER. EASIER SAID THAN DONE. LIVING ON THE STREET MEANT SHE COULD BE ANYWHERE. UNDER ANY OVERPASS, IN ANY ENCAMPMENT, ANY MOTEL.
PARADISE MOTEL
MARCO RUSSO PUSHED OUT INFORMATION TO THE PATROL DIVISION.
MOST INTEL CAME INTO THE POLICE DEPARTMENT THROUGH OFFICERS WORKING IN THE FIELD.
DETECTIVES, STUCK IN THE OFFICE AND WEIGHED DOWN BY CASE LOADS, COULD RARELY GET OUT TO "SHAKE THE BUSHES."
FIGUEROA ST
DETECTIVES RELIED ON CRIME AND ARREST REPORTS TO KNOW WHAT WAS GOING ON IN THEIR AREAS, AND THIS MEANT THEY HAD A LIMITED VIEW OF WHAT WAS REALLY GOING ON OUTSIDE THE STATION.
FIELD OFFICERS, ON THE OTHER HAND, USUALLY HAD THEIR FINGER ON THE PULSE OF WHAT WAS OCCURRING ON A DAY-TO-DAY BASIS.

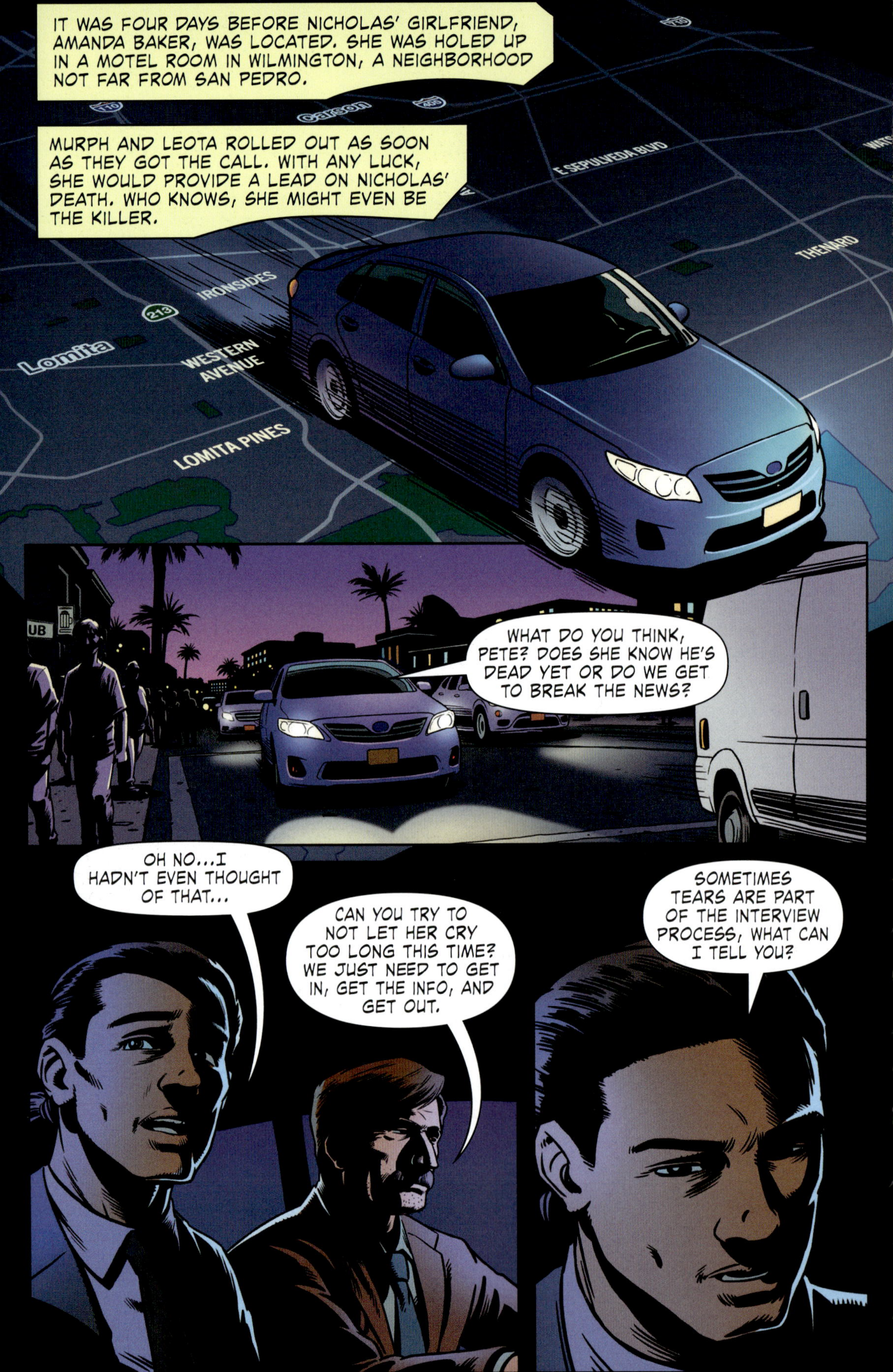
IT WAS FOUR DAYS BEFORE NICHOLAS' GIRLFRIEND, AMANDA BAKER, WAS LOCATED. SHE WAS HOLED UP IN A MOTEL ROOM IN WILMINGTON, A NEIGHBORHOOD NOT FAR FROM SAN PEDRO.
Carson
MURPH AND LEOTA ROLLED OUT AS SOON AS THEY GOT THE CALL. WITH ANY LUCK, SHE WOULD PROVIDE A LEAD ON NICHOLAS' DEATH. WHO KNOWS, SHE MIGHT EVEN BE THE KILLER.
E SEPULVEDA BLVD
THENARD
IRONSIDES
213
Lomita
WESTERN AVENUE
LOMITA PINES
WHAT DO YOU THINK, PETE? DOES SHE KNOW HE'S DEAD YET OR DO WE GET TO BREAK THE NEWS?
OH NO...I HADN'T EVEN THOUGHT OF THAT...
CAN YOU TRY TO NOT LET HER CRY TOO LONG THIS TIME? WE JUST NEED TO GET IN, GET THE INFO, AND GET OUT.
SOMETIMES TEARS ARE PART OF THE INTERVIEW PROCESS, WHAT CAN I TELL YOU?

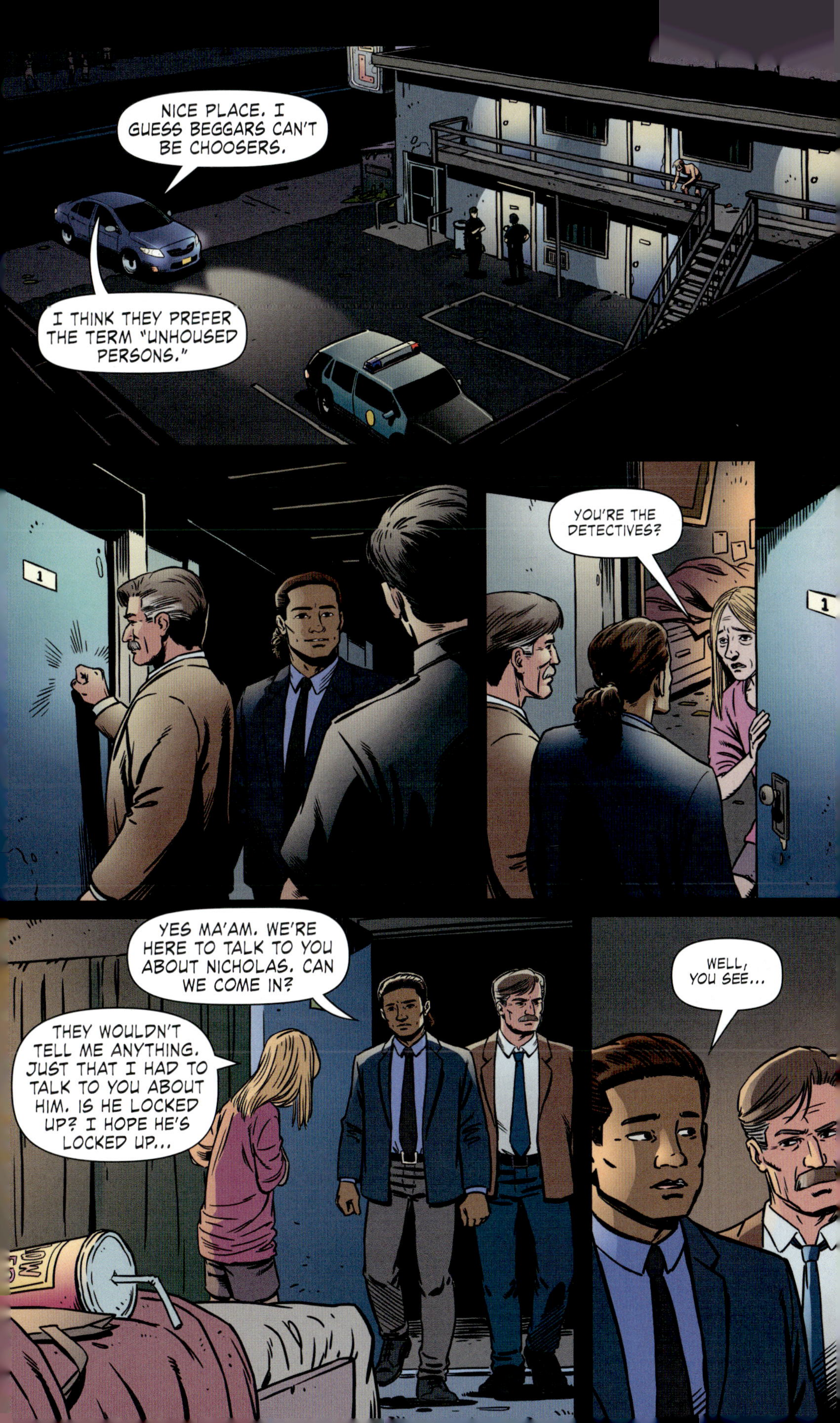
NICE PLACE. I GUESS BEGGARS CAN'T BE CHOOSERS.
I THINK THEY PREFER THE TERM "UNHOUSED PERSONS."
1
YOU'RE THE DETECTIVES?
1
YES MA'AM. WE'RE HERE TO TALK TO YOU ABOUT NICHOLAS. CAN WE COME IN?
THEY WOULDN'T TELL ME ANYTHING. JUST THAT I HAD TO TALK TO YOU ABOUT HIM. IS HE LOCKED UP? I HOPE HE'S LOCKED UP...
WELL, YOU SEE...

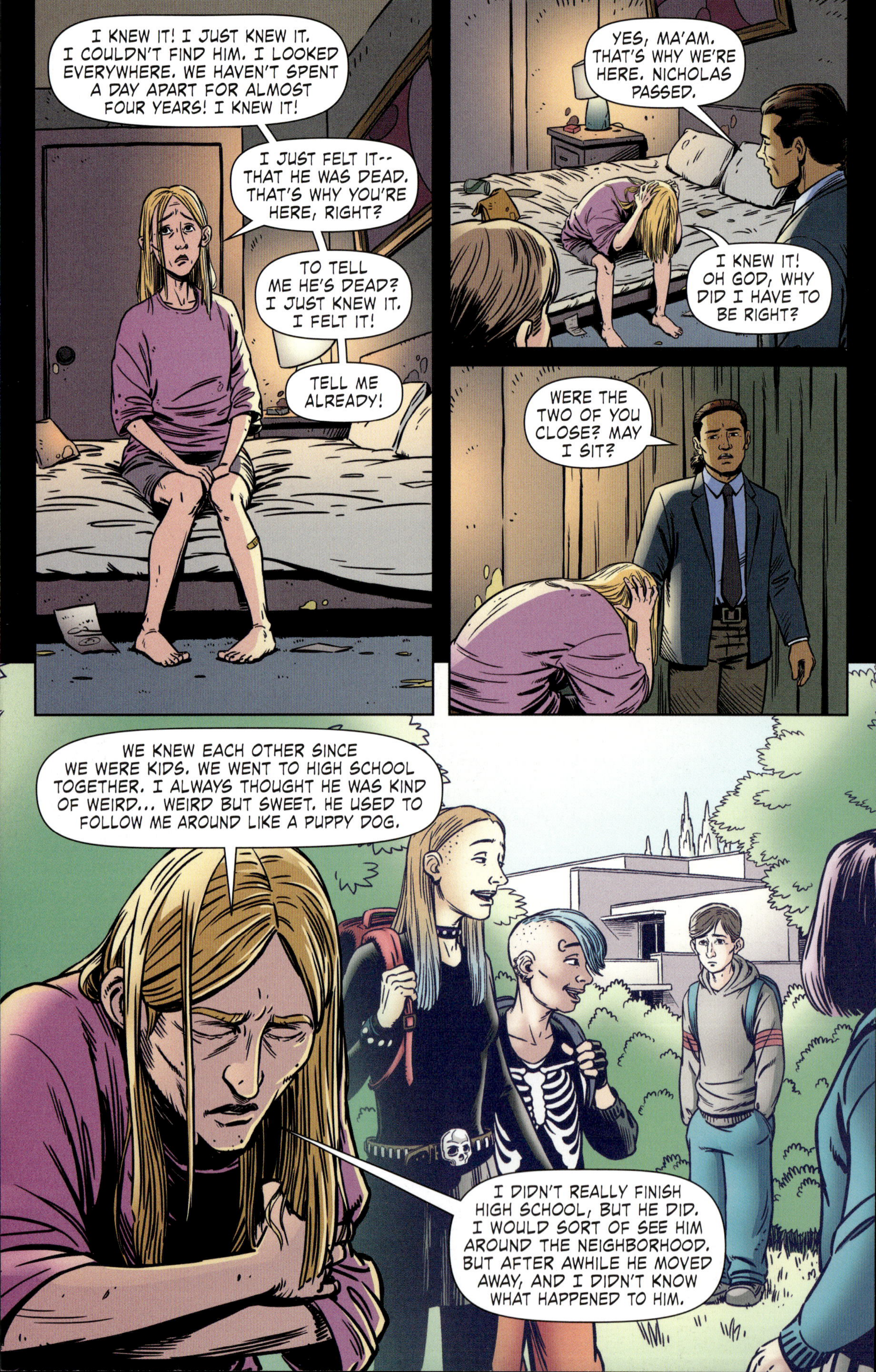
I KNEW IT! I JUST KNEW IT. I COULDN'T FIND HIM. I LOOKED EVERYWHERE. WE HAVEN'T SPENT A DAY APART FOR ALMOST FOUR YEARS! I KNEW IT!
I JUST FELT IT-- THAT HE WAS DEAD. THAT'S WHY YOU'RE HERE, RIGHT?
TO TELL ME HE'S DEAD? I JUST KNEW IT. I FELT IT!
TELL ME ALREADY!
YES, MA'AM. THAT'S WHY WE'RE HERE. NICHOLAS PASSED.
I KNEW IT! OH GOD, WHY DID I HAVE TO BE RIGHT?
WERE THE TWO OF YOU CLOSE? MAY I SIT?
WE KNEW EACH OTHER SINCE WE WERE KIDS. WE WENT TO HIGH SCHOOL TOGETHER. I ALWAYS THOUGHT HE WAS KIND OF WEIRD... WEIRD BUT SWEET. HE USED TO FOLLOW ME AROUND LIKE A PUPPY DOG.
I DIDN'T REALLY FINISH HIGH SCHOOL, BUT HE DID. I WOULD SORT OF SEE HIM AROUND THE NEIGHBORHOOD. BUT AFTER AWHILE HE MOVED AWAY, AND I DIDN'T KNOW WHAT HAPPENED TO HIM.

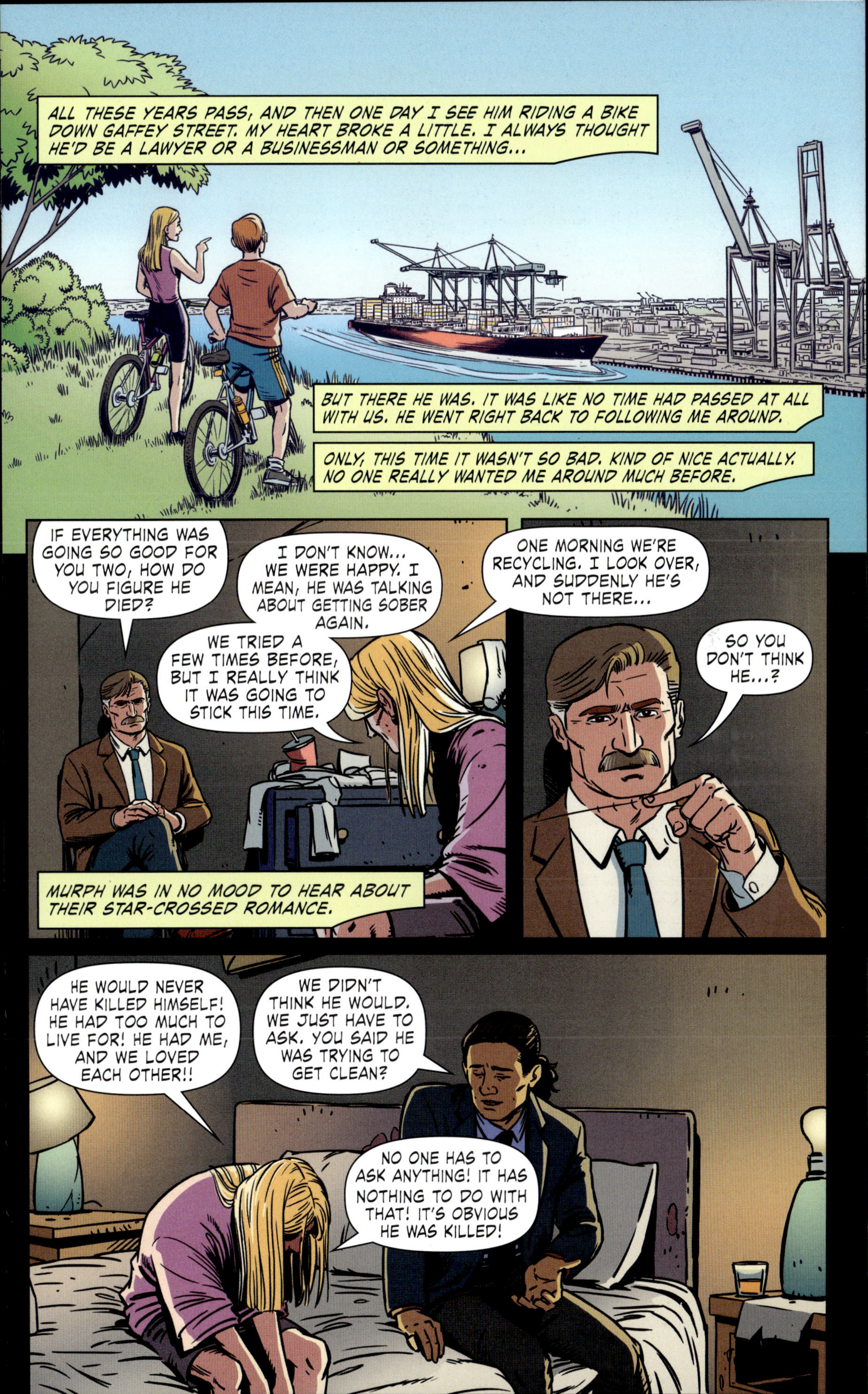
ALL THESE YEARS PASS, AND THEN ONE DAY I SEE HIM RIDING A BIKE DOWN GAFFEY STREET. MY HEART BROKE A LITTLE. I ALWAYS THOUGHT HE'D BE A LAWYER OR A BUSINESSMAN OR SOMETHING...
BUT THERE HE WAS. IT WAS LIKE NO TIME HAD PASSED AT ALL WITH US. HE WENT RIGHT BACK TO FOLLOWING ME AROUND.
ONLY, THIS TIME IT WASN'T SO BAD. KIND OF NICE ACTUALLY. NO ONE REALLY WANTED ME AROUND MUCH BEFORE.
IF EVERYTHING WAS GOING SO GOOD FOR YOU TWO, HOW DO YOU FIGURE HE DIED?
I DON'T KNOW... WE WERE HAPPY. I MEAN, HE WAS TALKING ABOUT GETTING SOBER AGAIN.
WE TRIED A FEW TIMES BEFORE, BUT I REALLY THINK IT WAS GOING TO STICK THIS TIME.
MURPH WAS IN NO MOOD TO HEAR ABOUT THEIR STAR-CROSSED ROMANCE.
ONE MORNING WE'RE RECYCLING. I LOOK OVER, AND SUDDENLY HE'S NOT THERE...
SO YOU DON'T THINK HE...?
HE WOULD NEVER HAVE KILLED HIMSELF! HE HAD TOO MUCH TO LIVE FOR! HE HAD ME, AND WE LOVED EACH OTHER!!
WE DIDN'T THINK HE WOULD. WE JUST HAVE TO ASK. YOU SAID HE WAS TRYING TO GET CLEAN?
NO ONE HAS TO ASK ANYTHING! IT HAS NOTHING TO DO WITH THAT! IT'S OBVIOUS HE WAS KILLED!

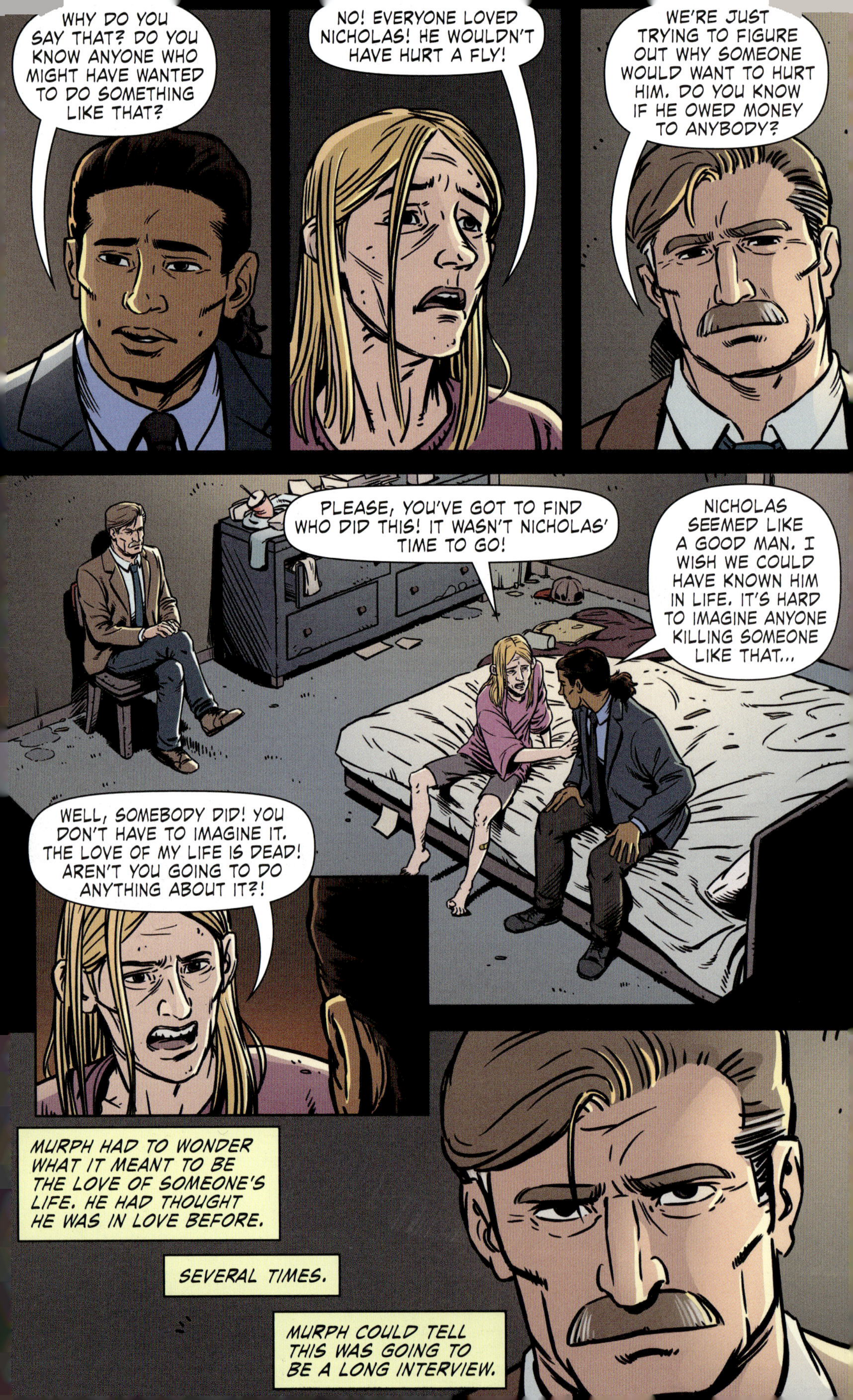
WHY DO YOU SAY THAT? DO YOU KNOW ANYONE WHO MIGHT HAVE WANTED TO DO SOMETHING LIKE THAT?
NO! EVERYONE LOVED NICHOLAS! HE WOULDN'T HAVE HURT A FLY!
WE'RE JUST TRYING TO FIGURE OUT WHY SOMEONE WOULD WANT TO HURT HIM. DO YOU KNOW IF HE OWED MONEY TO ANYBODY?
PLEASE, YOU'VE GOT TO FIND WHO DID THIS! IT WASN'T NICHOLAS' TIME TO GO!
NICHOLAS SEEMED LIKE A GOOD MAN. I WISH WE COULD HAVE KNOWN HIM IN LIFE. IT'S HARD TO IMAGINE ANYONE KILLING SOMEONE LIKE THAT...
WELL, SOMEBODY DID! YOU DON'T HAVE TO IMAGINE IT. THE LOVE OF MY LIFE IS DEAD! AREN'T YOU GOING TO DO ANYTHING ABOUT IT?!
MURPH HAD TO WONDER WHAT IT MEANT TO BE THE LOVE OF SOMEONE'S LIFE. HE HAD THOUGHT HE WAS IN LOVE BEFORE.
SEVERAL TIMES.
MURPH COULD TELL THIS WAS GOING TO BE A LONG INTERVIEW.

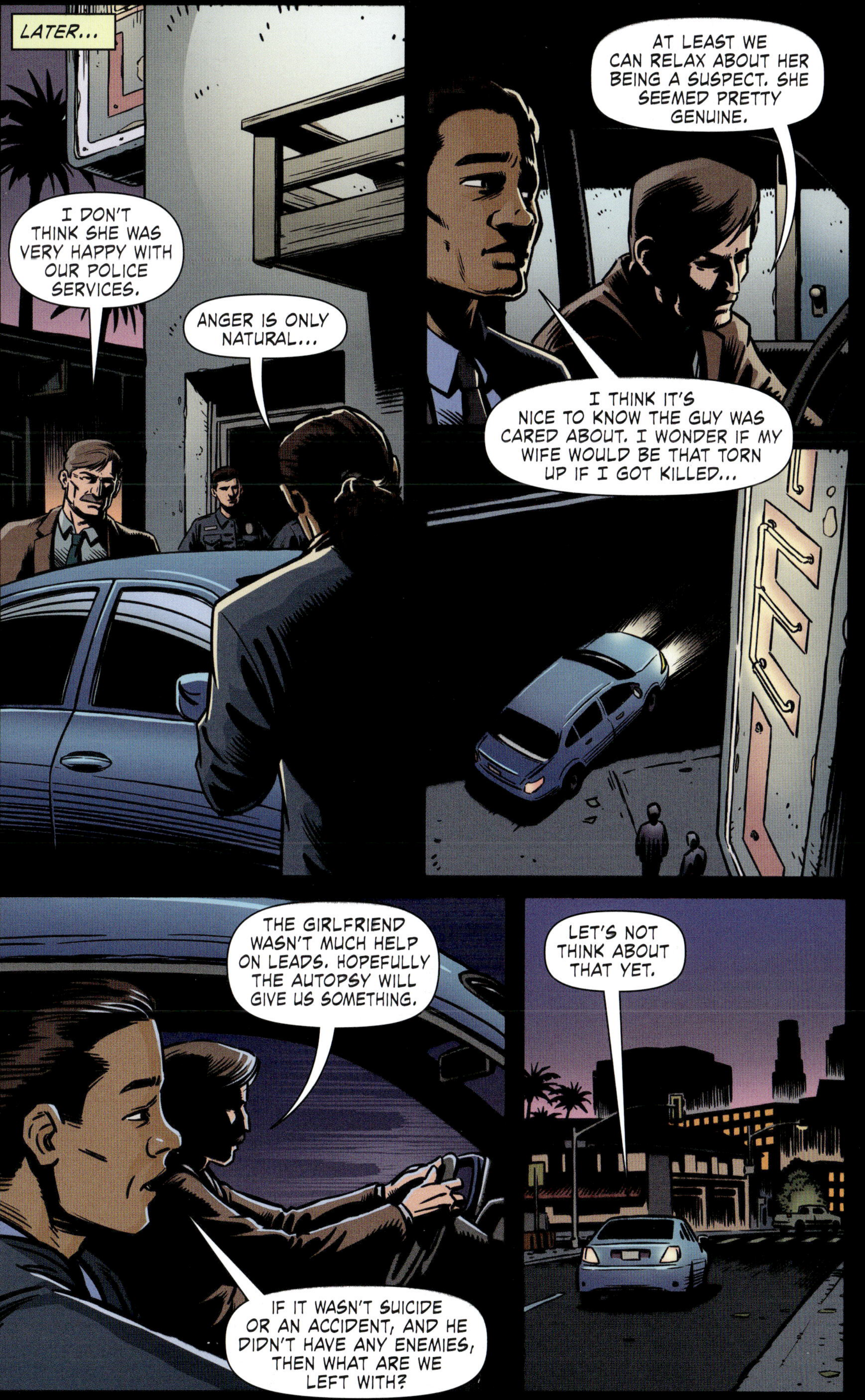
LATER...
I DON'T THINK SHE WAS VERY HAPPY WITH OUR POLICE SERVICES.
ANGER IS ONLY NATURAL...
AT LEAST WE CAN RELAX ABOUT HER BEING A SUSPECT. SHE SEEMED PRETTY GENUINE.
I THINK IT'S NICE TO KNOW THE GUY WAS CARED ABOUT. I WONDER IF MY WIFE WOULD BE THAT TORN UP IF I GOT KILLED...
THE GIRLFRIEND WASN'T MUCH HELP ON LEADS. HOPEFULLY THE AUTOPSY WILL GIVE US SOMETHING.
IF IT WASN'T SUICIDE OR AN ACCIDENT, AND HE DIDN'T HAVE ANY ENEMIES, THEN WHAT ARE WE LEFT WITH?
LET'S NOT THINK ABOUT THAT YET.

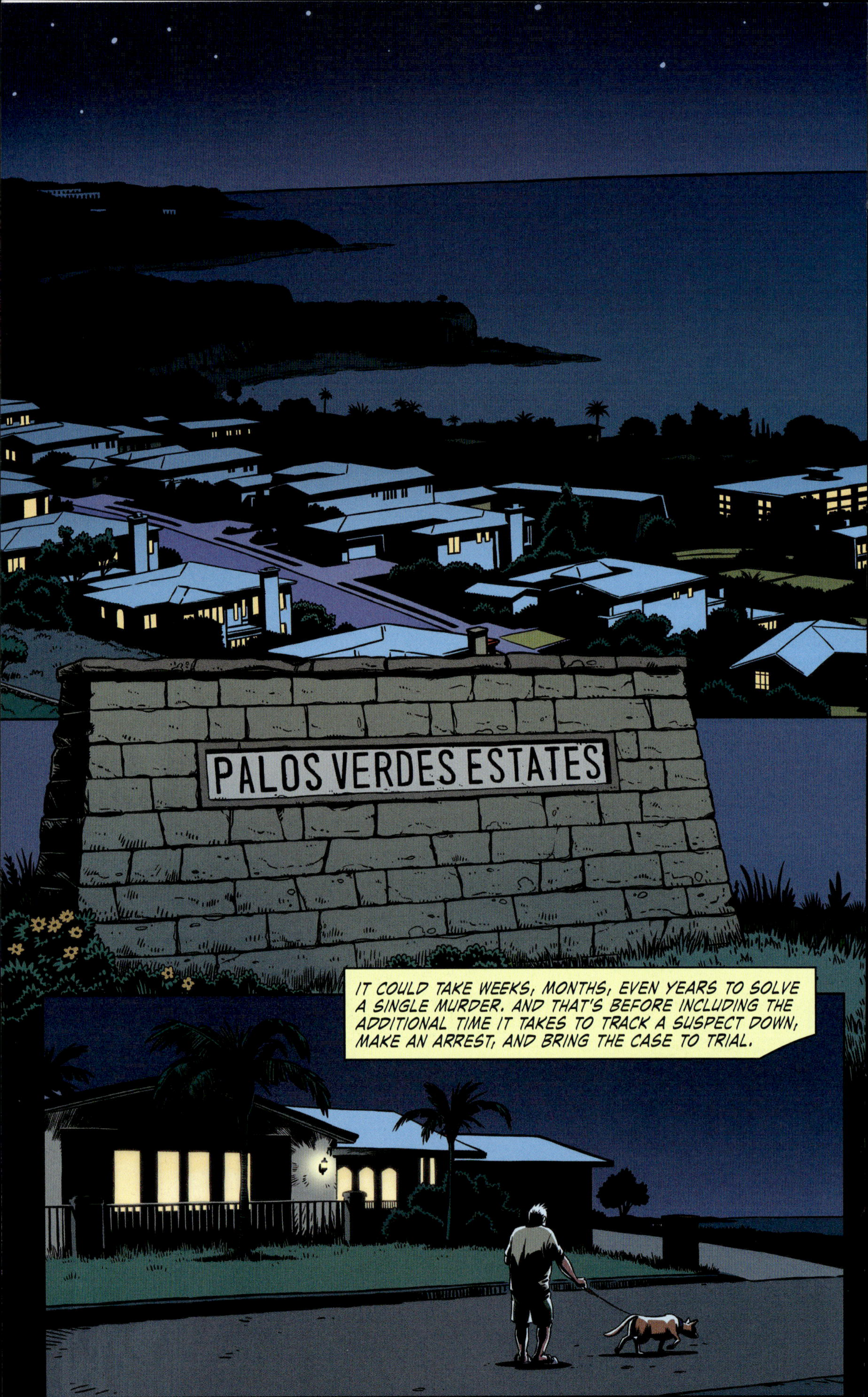
PALOS VERDES ESTATES
IT COULD TAKE WEEKS, MONTHS, EVEN YEARS TO SOLVE A SINGLE MURDER. AND THAT'S BEFORE INCLUDING THE ADDITIONAL TIME IT TAKES TO TRACK A SUSPECT DOWN, MAKE AN ARREST, AND BRING THE CASE TO TRIAL.

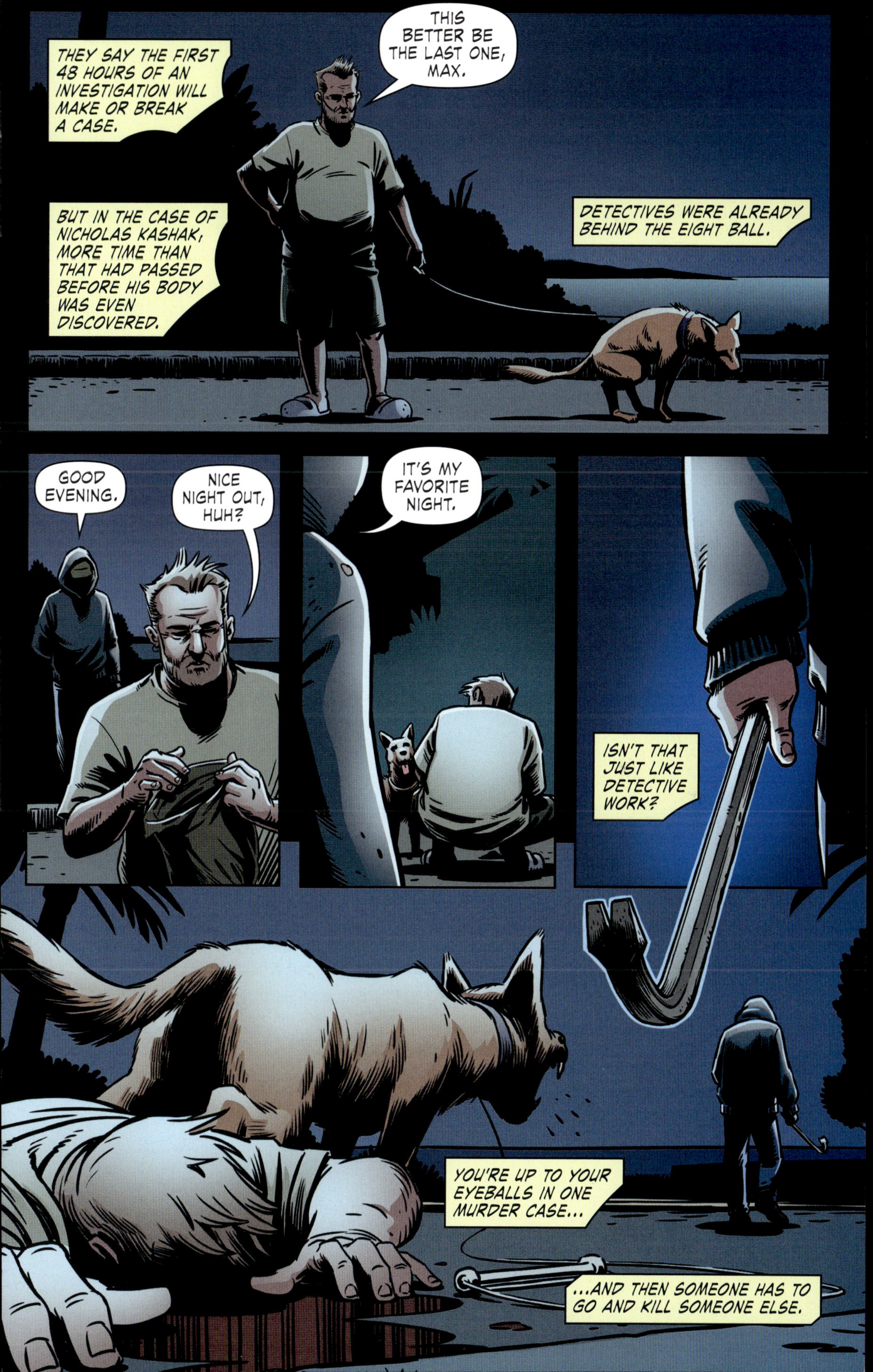
THEY SAY THE FIRST 48 HOURS OF AN INVESTIGATION WILL MAKE OR BREAK A CASE.
THIS BETTER BE THE LAST ONE, MAX.
BUT IN THE CASE OF NICHOLAS KASHAK, MORE TIME THAN THAT HAD PASSED BEFORE HIS BODY WAS EVEN DISCOVERED.
DETECTIVES WERE ALREADY BEHIND THE EIGHT BALL.
GOOD EVENING.
NICE NIGHT OUT, HUH?
IT'S MY FAVORITE NIGHT.
ISN'T THAT JUST LIKE DETECTIVE WORK?
YOU'RE UP TO YOUR EYEBALLS IN ONE MURDER CASE...
...AND THEN SOMEONE HAS TO GO AND KILL SOMEONE ELSE.

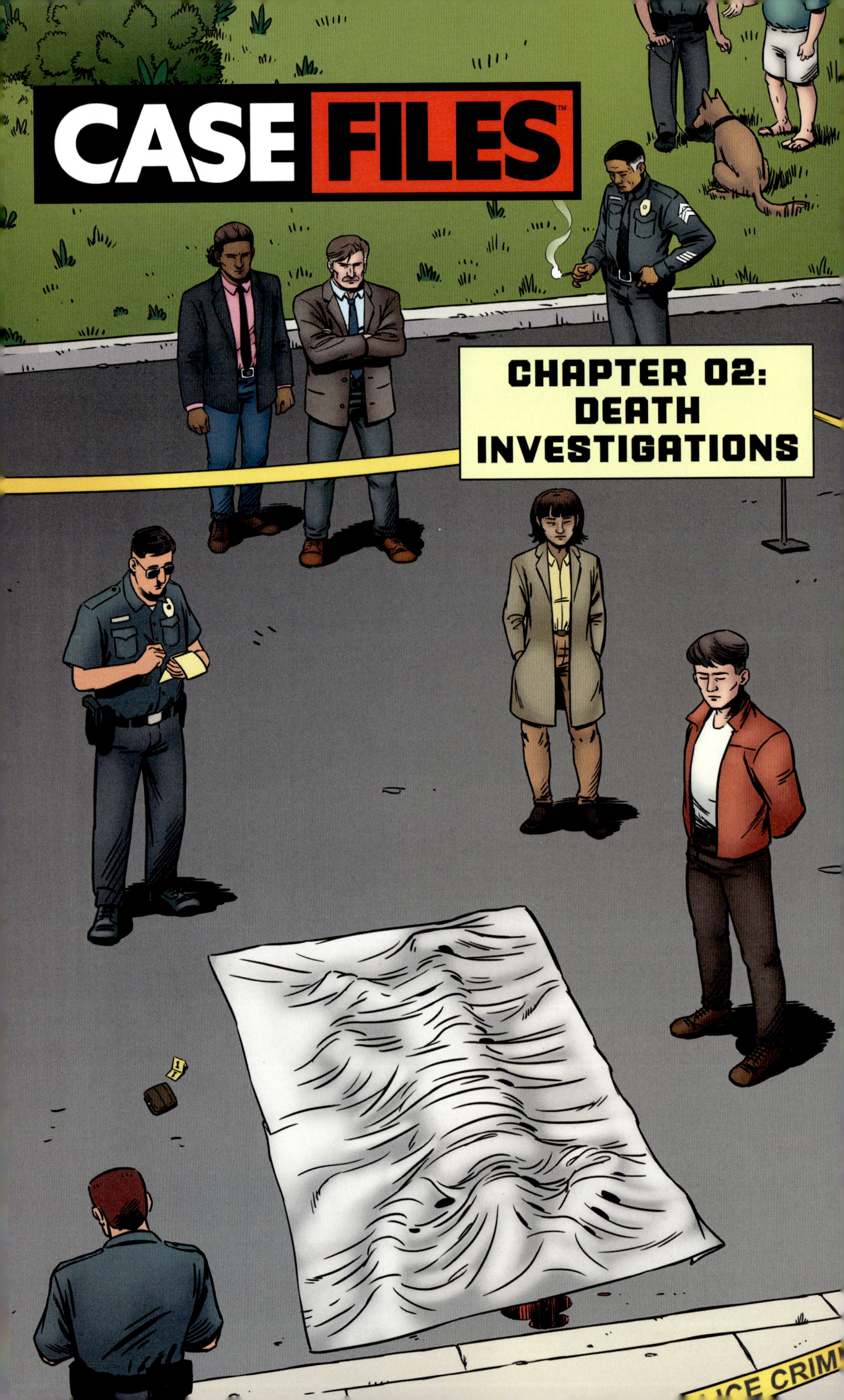
CASE FILES™
CHAPTER 02:
DEATH
INVESTIGATIONS
ICE CRIM

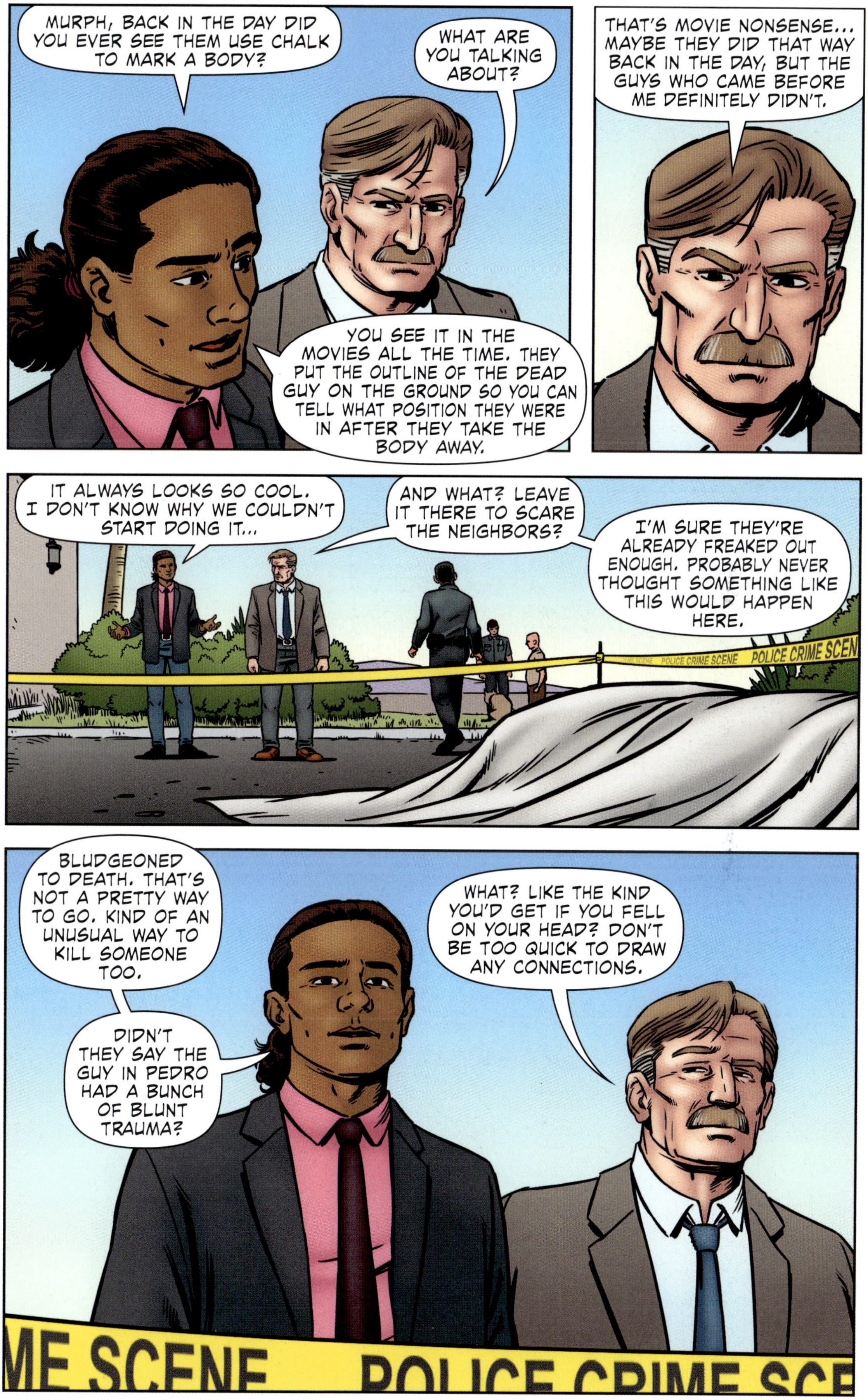
MURPH, BACK IN THE DAY DID YOU EVER SEE THEM USE CHALK TO MARK A BODY?
WHAT ARE YOU TALKING ABOUT?
YOU SEE IT IN THE MOVIES ALL THE TIME. THEY PUT THE OUTLINE OF THE DEAD GUY ON THE GROUND SO YOU CAN TELL WHAT POSITION THEY WERE IN AFTER THEY TAKE THE BODY AWAY.
THAT'S MOVIE NONSENSE... MAYBE THEY DID THAT WAY BACK IN THE DAY, BUT THE GUYS WHO CAME BEFORE ME DEFINITELY DIDN'T.
IT ALWAYS LOOKS SO COOL. I DON'T KNOW WHY WE COULDN'T START DOING IT...
AND WHAT? LEAVE IT THERE TO SCARE THE NEIGHBORS?
I'M SURE THEY'RE ALREADY FREAKED OUT ENOUGH. PROBABLY NEVER THOUGHT SOMETHING LIKE THIS WOULD HAPPEN HERE.
POLICE CRIME SCENE
BLUDGEONED TO DEATH. THAT'S NOT A PRETTY WAY TO GO. KIND OF AN UNUSUAL WAY TO KILL SOMEONE TOO.
DIDN'T THEY SAY THE GUY IN PEDRO HAD A BUNCH OF BLUNT TRAUMA?
WHAT? LIKE THE KIND YOU'D GET IF YOU FELL ON YOUR HEAD? DON'T BE TOO QUICK TO DRAW ANY CONNECTIONS.
ME SCENE
POLICE CRIME SCE

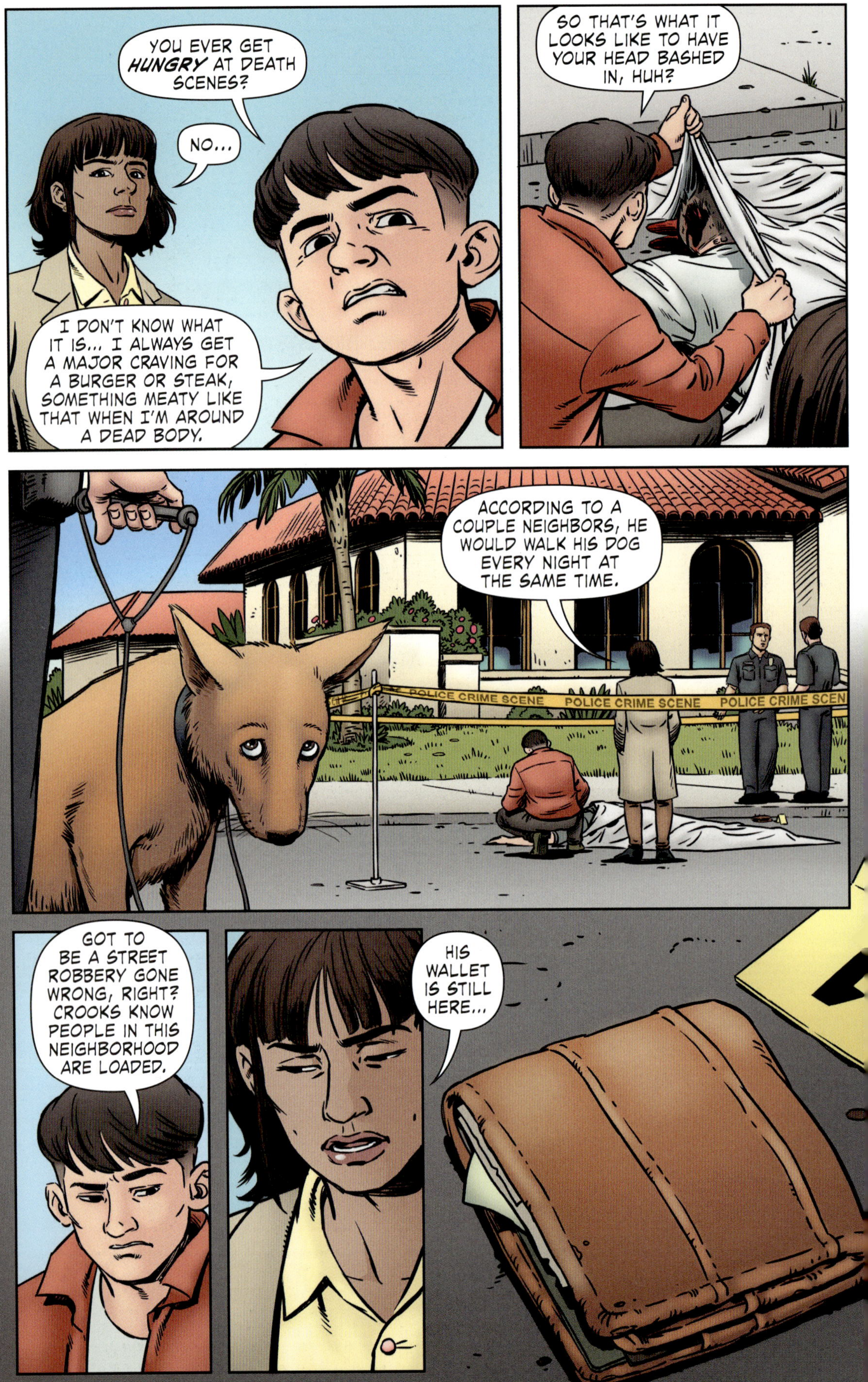
YOU EVER GET *HUNGRY* AT DEATH SCENES?
NO...
I DON'T KNOW WHAT IT IS... I ALWAYS GET A MAJOR CRAVING FOR A BURGER OR STEAK, SOMETHING MEATY LIKE THAT WHEN I'M AROUND A DEAD BODY.
SO THAT'S WHAT IT LOOKS LIKE TO HAVE YOUR HEAD BASHED IN, HUH?
ACCORDING TO A COUPLE NEIGHBORS, HE WOULD WALK HIS DOG EVERY NIGHT AT THE SAME TIME.
POLICE CRIME SCENE
GOT TO BE A STREET ROBBERY GONE WRONG, RIGHT? CROOKS KNOW PEOPLE IN THIS NEIGHBORHOOD ARE LOADED.
HIS WALLET IS STILL HERE...

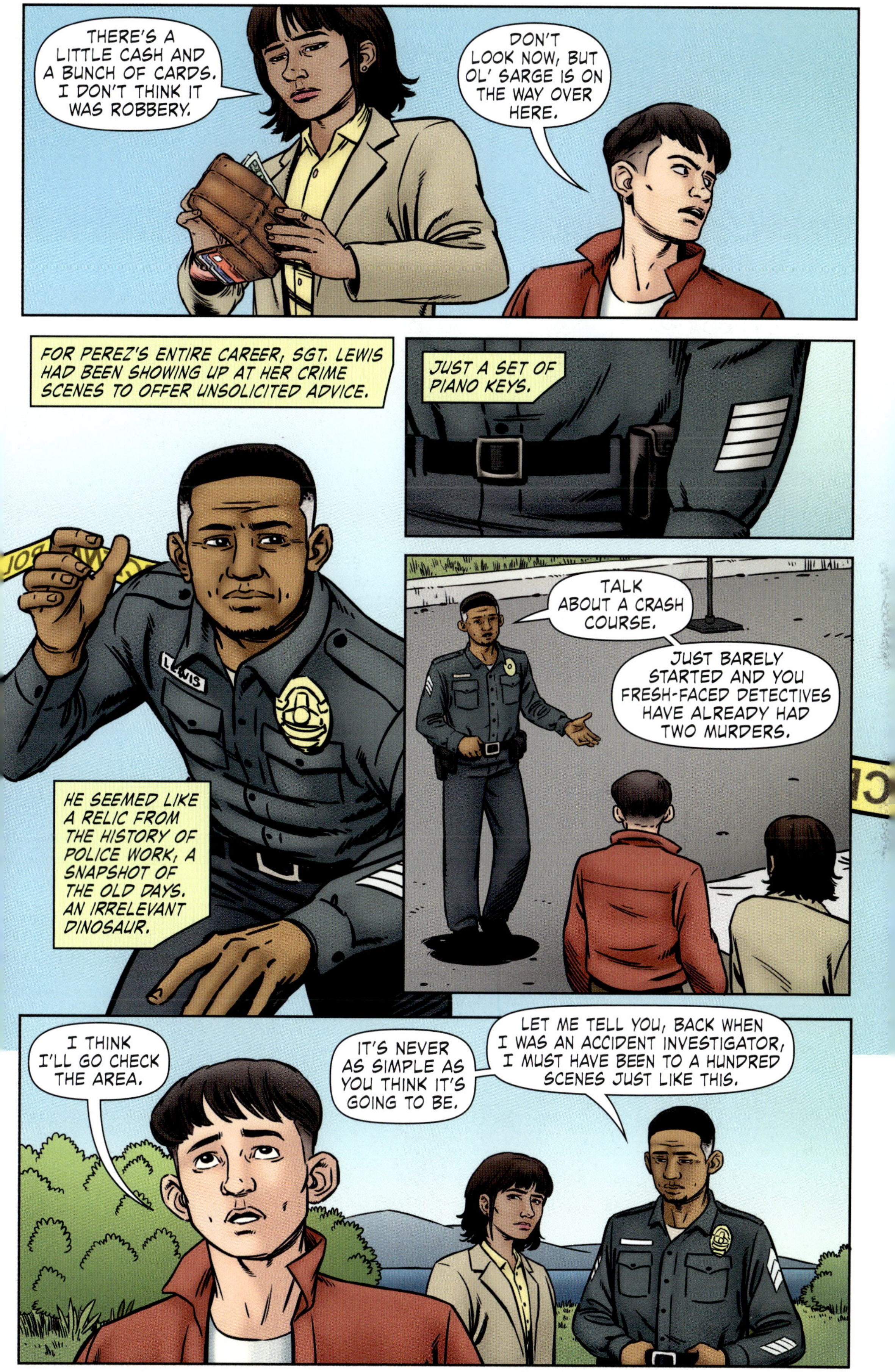
THERE'S A LITTLE CASH AND A BUNCH OF CARDS. I DON'T THINK IT WAS ROBBERY.
DON'T LOOK NOW, BUT OL' SARGE IS ON THE WAY OVER HERE.
FOR PEREZ'S ENTIRE CAREER, SGT. LEWIS HAD BEEN SHOWING UP AT HER CRIME SCENES TO OFFER UNSOLICITED ADVICE.
LEWIS
HE SEEMED LIKE A RELIC FROM THE HISTORY OF POLICE WORK, A SNAPSHOT OF THE OLD DAYS. AN IRRELEVANT DINOSAUR.
JUST A SET OF PIANO KEYS.
TALK ABOUT A CRASH COURSE.
JUST BARELY STARTED AND YOU FRESH-FACED DETECTIVES HAVE ALREADY HAD TWO MURDERS.
I THINK I'LL GO CHECK THE AREA.
LET ME TELL YOU, BACK WHEN I WAS AN ACCIDENT INVESTIGATOR, I MUST HAVE BEEN TO A HUNDRED SCENES JUST LIKE THIS.
IT'S NEVER AS SIMPLE AS YOU THINK IT'S GOING TO BE.

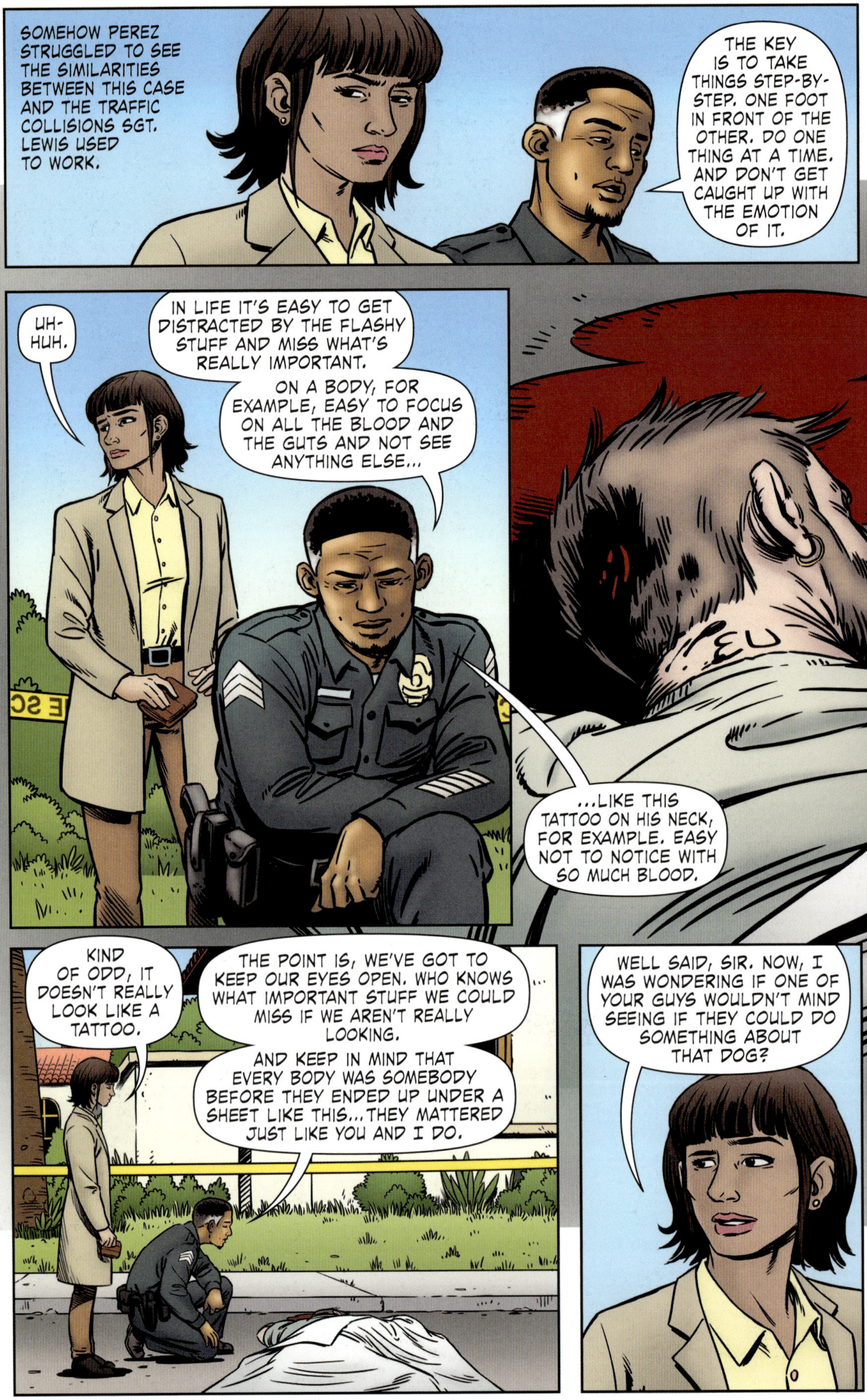
SOMEHOW PEREZ STRUGGLED TO SEE THE SIMILARITIES BETWEEN THIS CASE AND THE TRAFFIC COLLISIONS SGT. LEWIS USED TO WORK.
THE KEY IS TO TAKE THINGS STEP-BY-STEP. ONE FOOT IN FRONT OF THE OTHER. DO ONE THING AT A TIME. AND DON'T GET CAUGHT UP WITH THE EMOTION OF IT.
UH-HUH.
IN LIFE IT'S EASY TO GET DISTRACTED BY THE FLASHY STUFF AND MISS WHAT'S REALLY IMPORTANT.
ON A BODY, FOR EXAMPLE, EASY TO FOCUS ON ALL THE BLOOD AND THE GUTS AND NOT SEE ANYTHING ELSE...
...LIKE THIS TATTOO ON HIS NECK, FOR EXAMPLE. EASY NOT TO NOTICE WITH SO MUCH BLOOD.
KIND OF ODD, IT DOESN'T REALLY LOOK LIKE A TATTOO.
THE POINT IS, WE'VE GOT TO KEEP OUR EYES OPEN. WHO KNOWS WHAT IMPORTANT STUFF WE COULD MISS IF WE AREN'T REALLY LOOKING.
AND KEEP IN MIND THAT EVERY BODY WAS SOMEBODY BEFORE THEY ENDED UP UNDER A SHEET LIKE THIS...THEY MATTERED JUST LIKE YOU AND I DO.
WELL SAID, SIR. NOW, I WAS WONDERING IF ONE OF YOUR GUYS WOULDN'T MIND SEEING IF THEY COULD DO SOMETHING ABOUT THAT DOG?

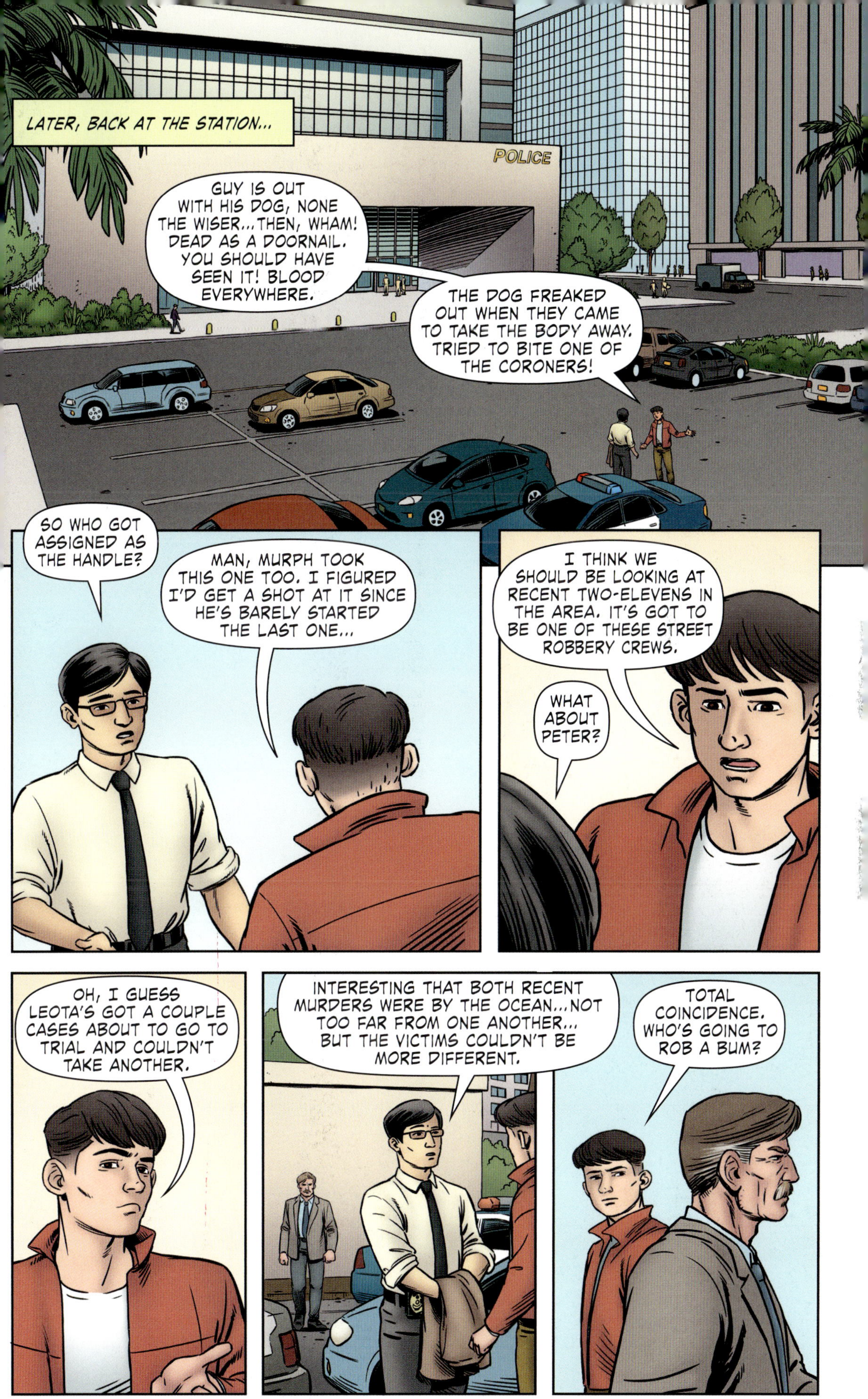
LATER, BACK AT THE STATION...
POLICE
GUY IS OUT WITH HIS DOG, NONE THE WISER...THEN, WHAM! DEAD AS A DOORNAIL. YOU SHOULD HAVE SEEN IT! BLOOD EVERYWHERE.
THE DOG FREAKED OUT WHEN THEY CAME TO TAKE THE BODY AWAY. TRIED TO BITE ONE OF THE CORONERS!
SO WHO GOT ASSIGNED AS THE HANDLE?
MAN, MURPH TOOK THIS ONE TOO. I FIGURED I'D GET A SHOT AT IT SINCE HE'S BARELY STARTED THE LAST ONE...
I THINK WE SHOULD BE LOOKING AT RECENT TWO-ELEVENS IN THE AREA. IT'S GOT TO BE ONE OF THESE STREET ROBBERY CREWS.
WHAT ABOUT PETER?
OH, I GUESS LEOTA'S GOT A COUPLE CASES ABOUT TO GO TO TRIAL AND COULDN'T TAKE ANOTHER.
INTERESTING THAT BOTH RECENT MURDERS WERE BY THE OCEAN...NOT TOO FAR FROM ONE ANOTHER... BUT THE VICTIMS COULDN'T BE MORE DIFFERENT.
TOTAL COINCIDENCE. WHO'S GOING TO ROB A BUM?

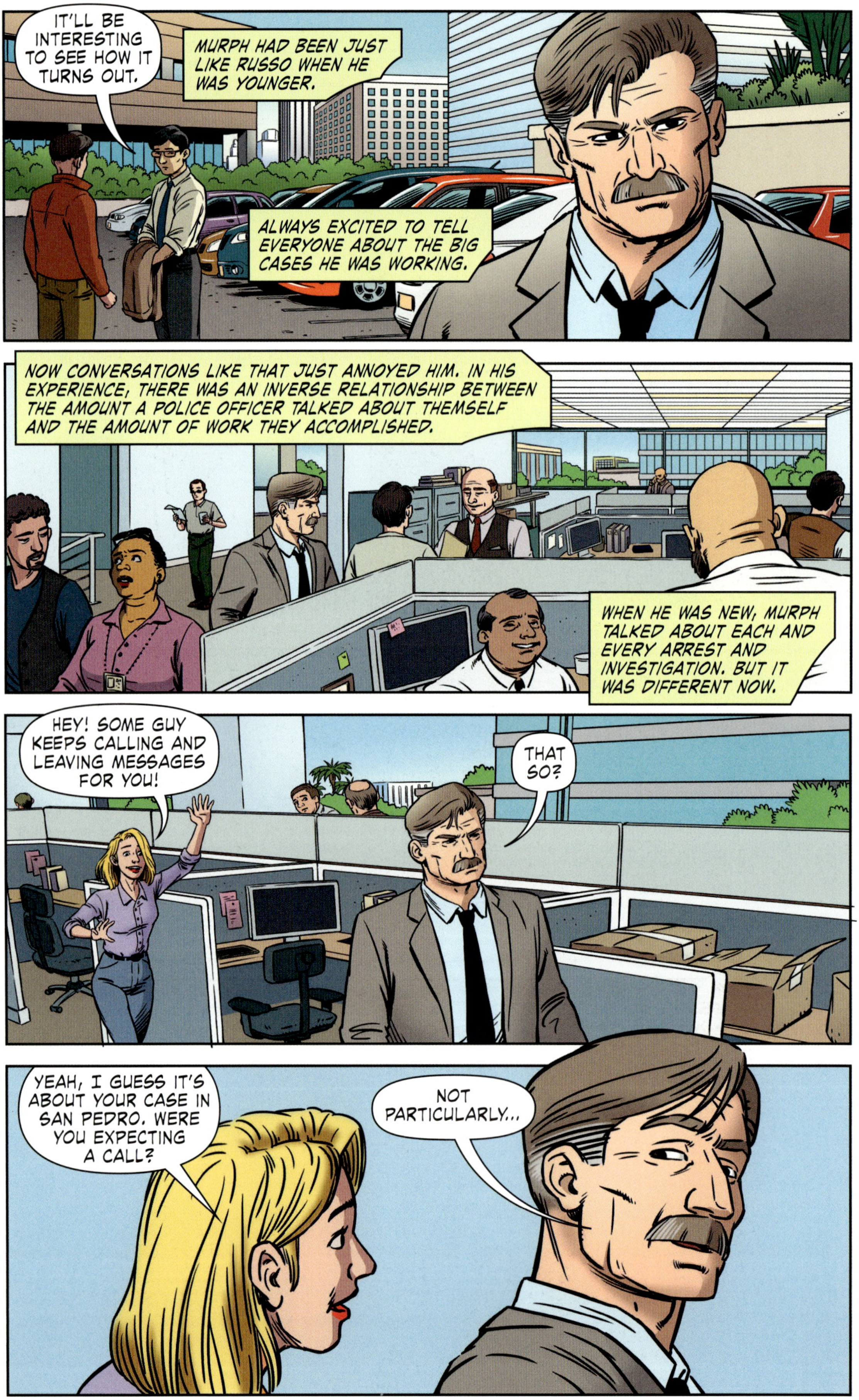
IT'LL BE INTERESTING TO SEE HOW IT TURNS OUT.
MURPH HAD BEEN JUST LIKE RUSSO WHEN HE WAS YOUNGER.
ALWAYS EXCITED TO TELL EVERYONE ABOUT THE BIG CASES HE WAS WORKING.
NOW CONVERSATIONS LIKE THAT JUST ANNOYED HIM. IN HIS EXPERIENCE, THERE WAS AN INVERSE RELATIONSHIP BETWEEN THE AMOUNT A POLICE OFFICER TALKED ABOUT THEMSELF AND THE AMOUNT OF WORK THEY ACCOMPLISHED.
WHEN HE WAS NEW, MURPH TALKED ABOUT EACH AND EVERY ARREST AND INVESTIGATION. BUT IT WAS DIFFERENT NOW.
HEY! SOME GUY KEEPS CALLING AND LEAVING MESSAGES FOR YOU!
THAT SO?
YEAH, I GUESS IT'S ABOUT YOUR CASE IN SAN PEDRO. WERE YOU EXPECTING A CALL?
NOT PARTICULARLY...

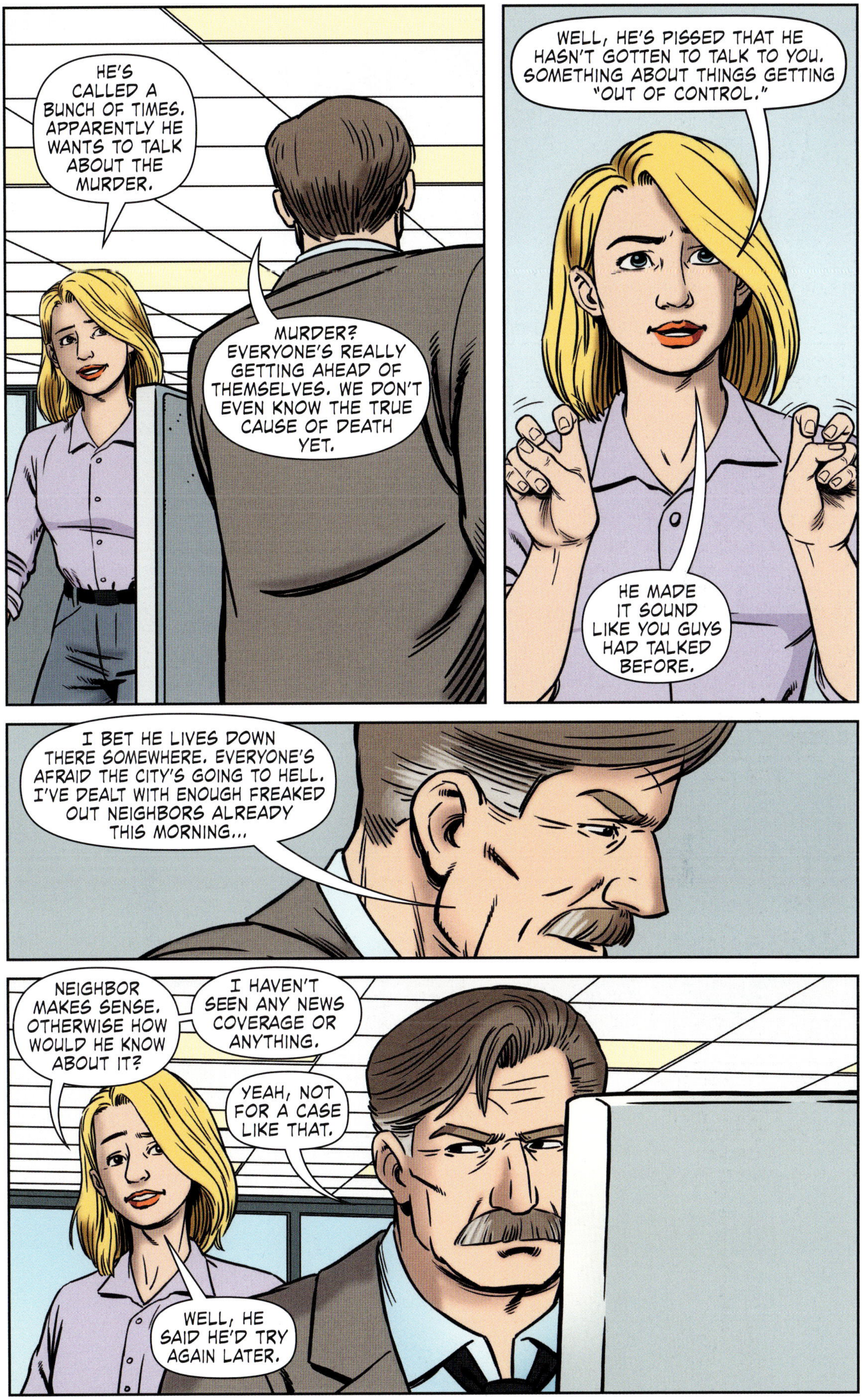
HE'S CALLED A BUNCH OF TIMES. APPARENTLY HE WANTS TO TALK ABOUT THE MURDER.
MURDER? EVERYONE'S REALLY GETTING AHEAD OF THEMSELVES. WE DON'T EVEN KNOW THE TRUE CAUSE OF DEATH YET.
WELL, HE'S PISSED THAT HE HASN'T GOTTEN TO TALK TO YOU. SOMETHING ABOUT THINGS GETTING "OUT OF CONTROL."
HE MADE IT SOUND LIKE YOU GUYS HAD TALKED BEFORE.
I BET HE LIVES DOWN THERE SOMEWHERE. EVERYONE'S AFRAID THE CITY'S GOING TO HELL. I'VE DEALT WITH ENOUGH FREAKED OUT NEIGHBORS ALREADY THIS MORNING...
NEIGHBOR MAKES SENSE. OTHERWISE HOW WOULD HE KNOW ABOUT IT?
I HAVEN'T SEEN ANY NEWS COVERAGE OR ANYTHING.
YEAH, NOT FOR A CASE LIKE THAT.
WELL, HE SAID HE'D TRY AGAIN LATER.

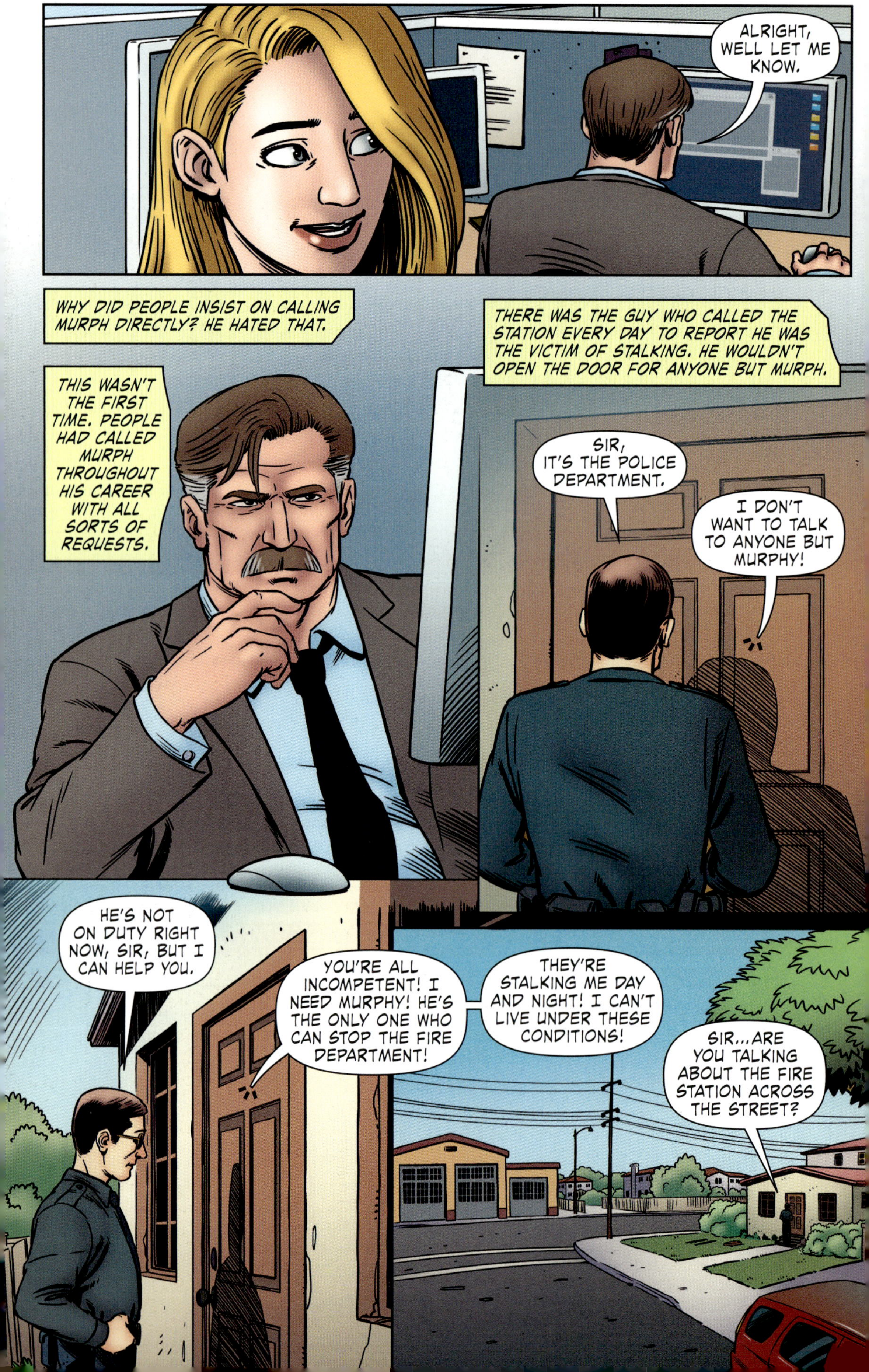
ALRIGHT, WELL LET ME KNOW.
WHY DID PEOPLE INSIST ON CALLING MURPH DIRECTLY? HE HATED THAT.
THIS WASN'T THE FIRST TIME. PEOPLE HAD CALLED MURPH THROUGHOUT HIS CAREER WITH ALL SORTS OF REQUESTS.
THERE WAS THE GUY WHO CALLED THE STATION EVERY DAY TO REPORT HE WAS THE VICTIM OF STALKING. HE WOULDN'T OPEN THE DOOR FOR ANYONE BUT MURPH.
SIR, IT'S THE POLICE DEPARTMENT.
I DON'T WANT TO TALK TO ANYONE BUT MURPHY!
HE'S NOT ON DUTY RIGHT NOW, SIR, BUT I CAN HELP YOU.
YOU'RE ALL INCOMPETENT! I NEED MURPHY! HE'S THE ONLY ONE WHO CAN STOP THE FIRE DEPARTMENT!
THEY'RE STALKING ME DAY AND NIGHT! I CAN'T LIVE UNDER THESE CONDITIONS!
SIR...ARE YOU TALKING ABOUT THE FIRE STATION ACROSS THE STREET?

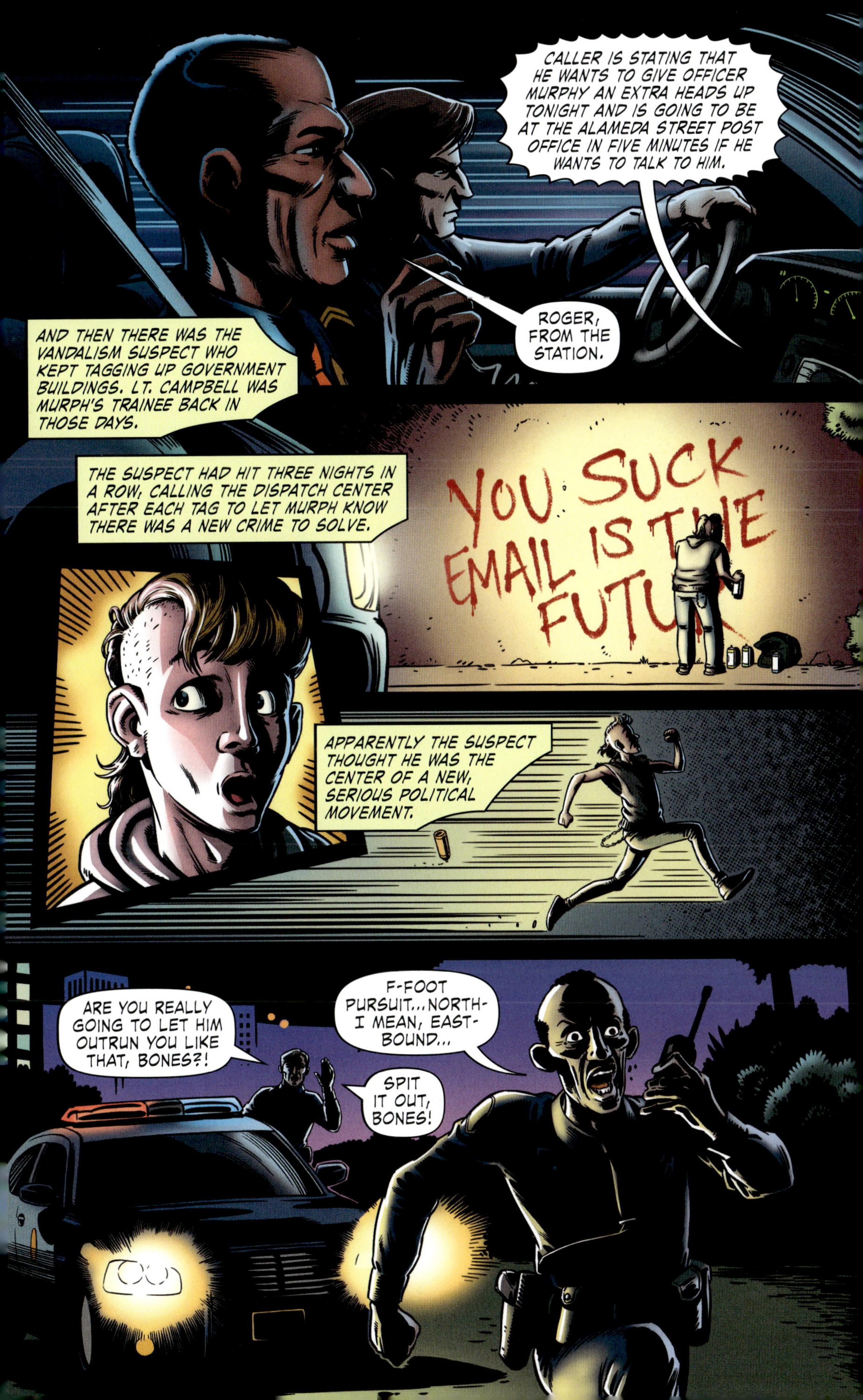
CALLER IS STATING THAT HE WANTS TO GIVE OFFICER MURPHY AN EXTRA HEADS UP TONIGHT AND IS GOING TO BE AT THE ALAMEDA STREET POST OFFICE IN FIVE MINUTES IF HE WANTS TO TALK TO HIM.
ROGER, FROM THE STATION.
AND THEN THERE WAS THE VANDALISM SUSPECT WHO KEPT TAGGING UP GOVERNMENT BUILDINGS. LT. CAMPBELL WAS MURPH'S TRAINEE BACK IN THOSE DAYS.
THE SUSPECT HAD HIT THREE NIGHTS IN A ROW, CALLING THE DISPATCH CENTER AFTER EACH TAG TO LET MURPH KNOW THERE WAS A NEW CRIME TO SOLVE.
YOU SUCK
EMAIL IS THE FUTU
APPARENTLY THE SUSPECT THOUGHT HE WAS THE CENTER OF A NEW, SERIOUS POLITICAL MOVEMENT.
ARE YOU REALLY GOING TO LET HIM OUTRUN YOU LIKE THAT, BONES?!
F-FOOT PURSUIT... NORTH- I MEAN, EAST-BOUND...
SPIT IT OUT, BONES!

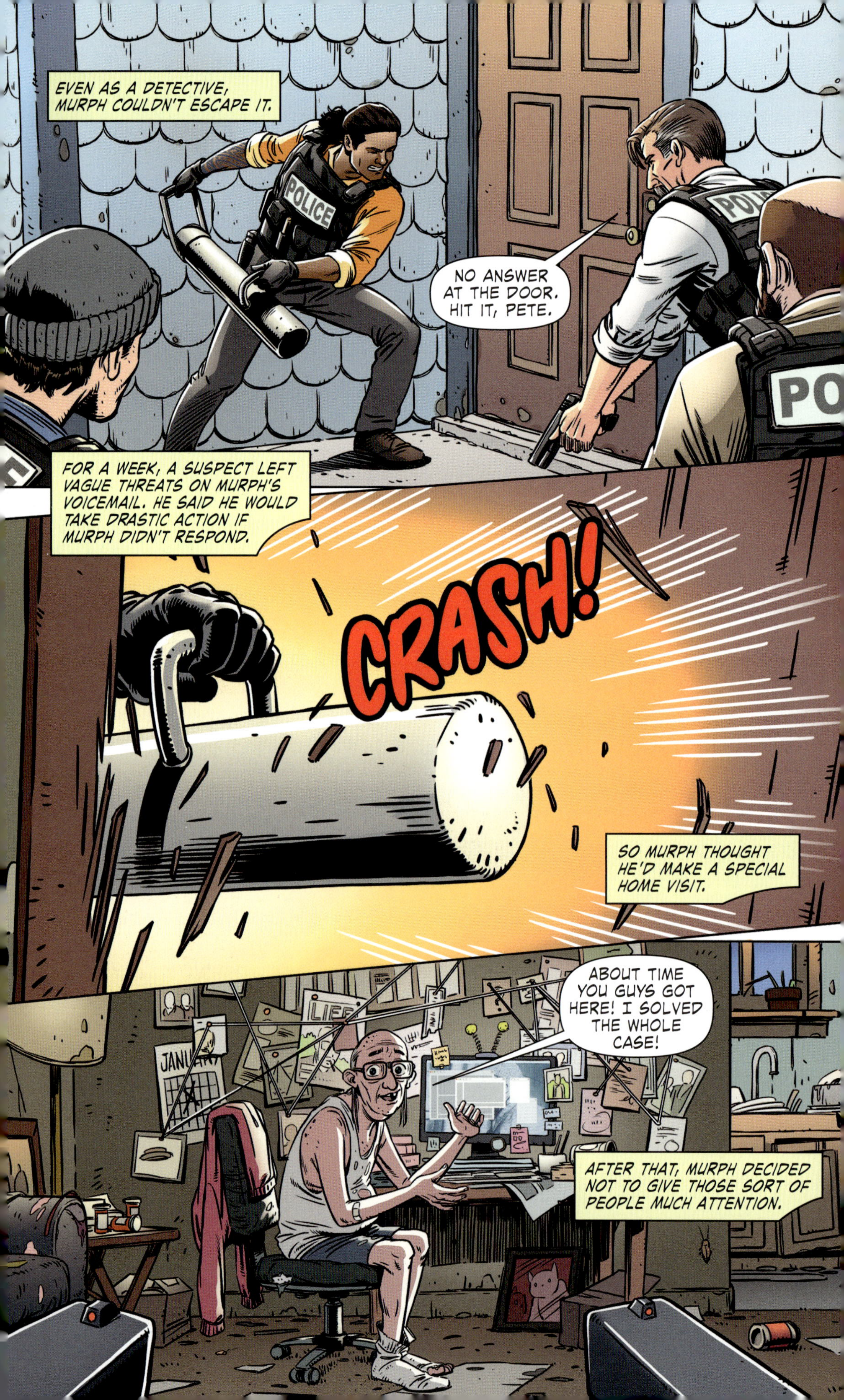
EVEN AS A DETECTIVE, MURPH COULDN'T ESCAPE IT.
POLICE
NO ANSWER AT THE DOOR. HIT IT, PETE.
FOR A WEEK, A SUSPECT LEFT VAGUE THREATS ON MURPH'S VOICEMAIL. HE SAID HE WOULD TAKE DRASTIC ACTION IF MURPH DIDN'T RESPOND.
CRASH!
SO MURPH THOUGHT HE'D MAKE A SPECIAL HOME VISIT.
ABOUT TIME YOU GUYS GOT HERE! I SOLVED THE WHOLE CASE!
AFTER THAT, MURPH DECIDED NOT TO GIVE THOSE SORT OF PEOPLE MUCH ATTENTION.

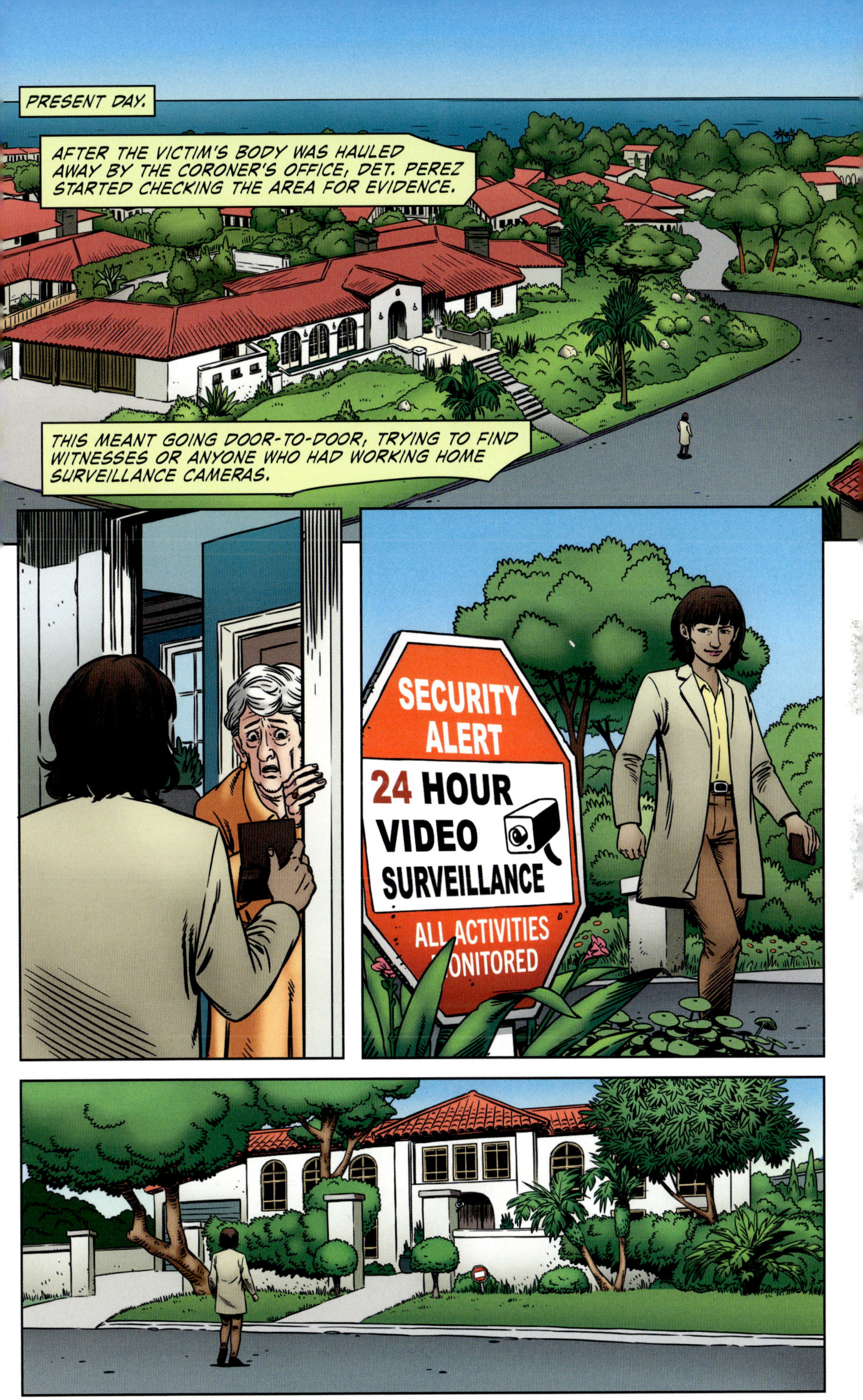
PRESENT DAY.
AFTER THE VICTIM'S BODY WAS HAULED AWAY BY THE CORONER'S OFFICE, DET. PEREZ STARTED CHECKING THE AREA FOR EVIDENCE.
THIS MEANT GOING DOOR-TO-DOOR, TRYING TO FIND WITNESSES OR ANYONE WHO HAD WORKING HOME SURVEILLANCE CAMERAS.
SECURITY ALERT
24 HOUR VIDEO SURVEILLANCE
ALL ACTIVITIES

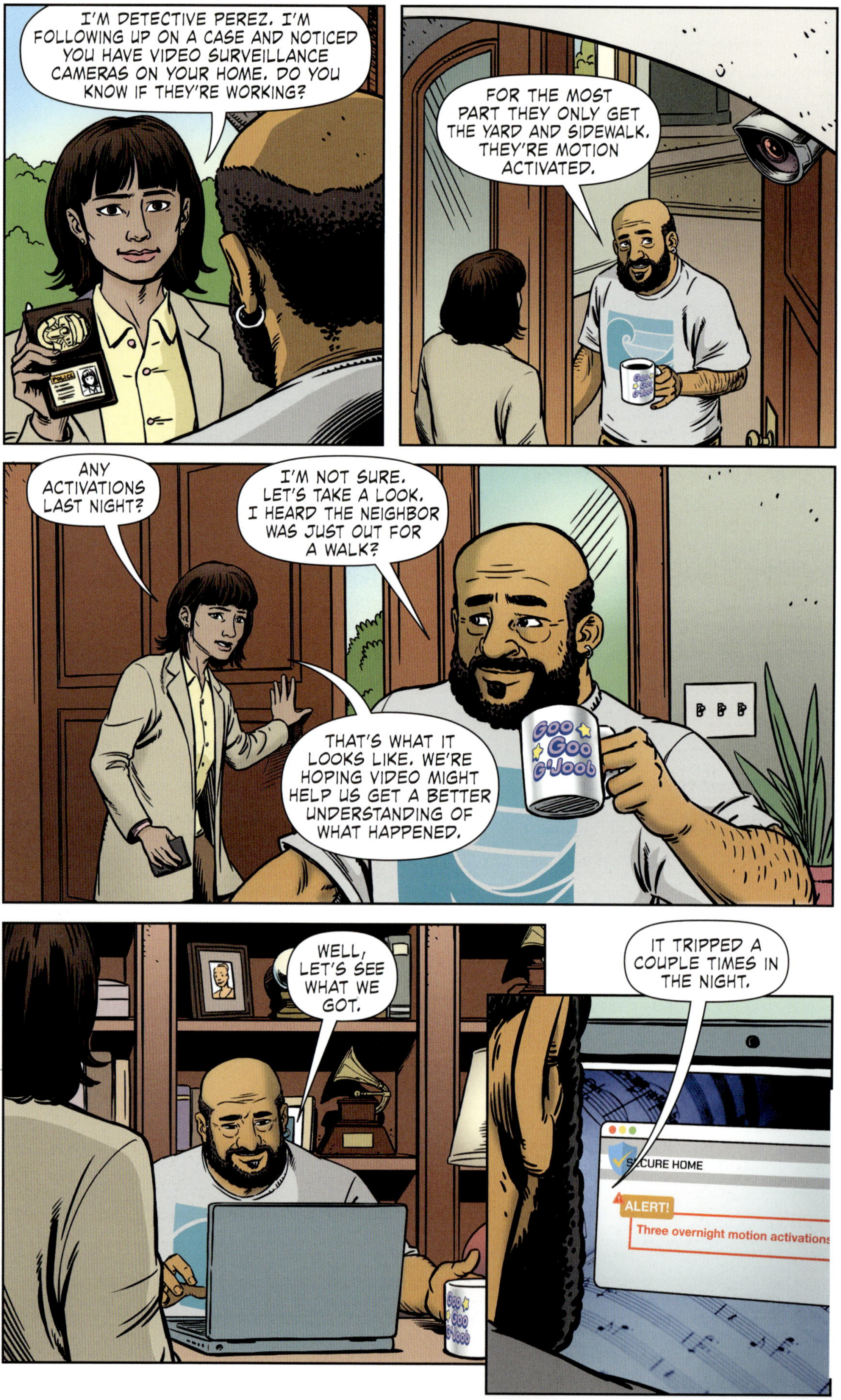
I'M DETECTIVE PEREZ. I'M FOLLOWING UP ON A CASE AND NOTICED YOU HAVE VIDEO SURVEILLANCE CAMERAS ON YOUR HOME. DO YOU KNOW IF THEY'RE WORKING?
POLICE
FOR THE MOST PART THEY ONLY GET THE YARD AND SIDEWALK. THEY'RE MOTION ACTIVATED.
ANY ACTIVATIONS LAST NIGHT?
I'M NOT SURE. LET'S TAKE A LOOK. I HEARD THE NEIGHBOR WAS JUST OUT FOR A WALK?
THAT'S WHAT IT LOOKS LIKE. WE'RE HOPING VIDEO MIGHT HELP US GET A BETTER UNDERSTANDING OF WHAT HAPPENED.
GOO GOO G'JOOB
WELL, LET'S SEE WHAT WE GOT.
IT TRIPPED A COUPLE TIMES IN THE NIGHT.
SECURE HOME
ALERT!
Three overnight motion activations

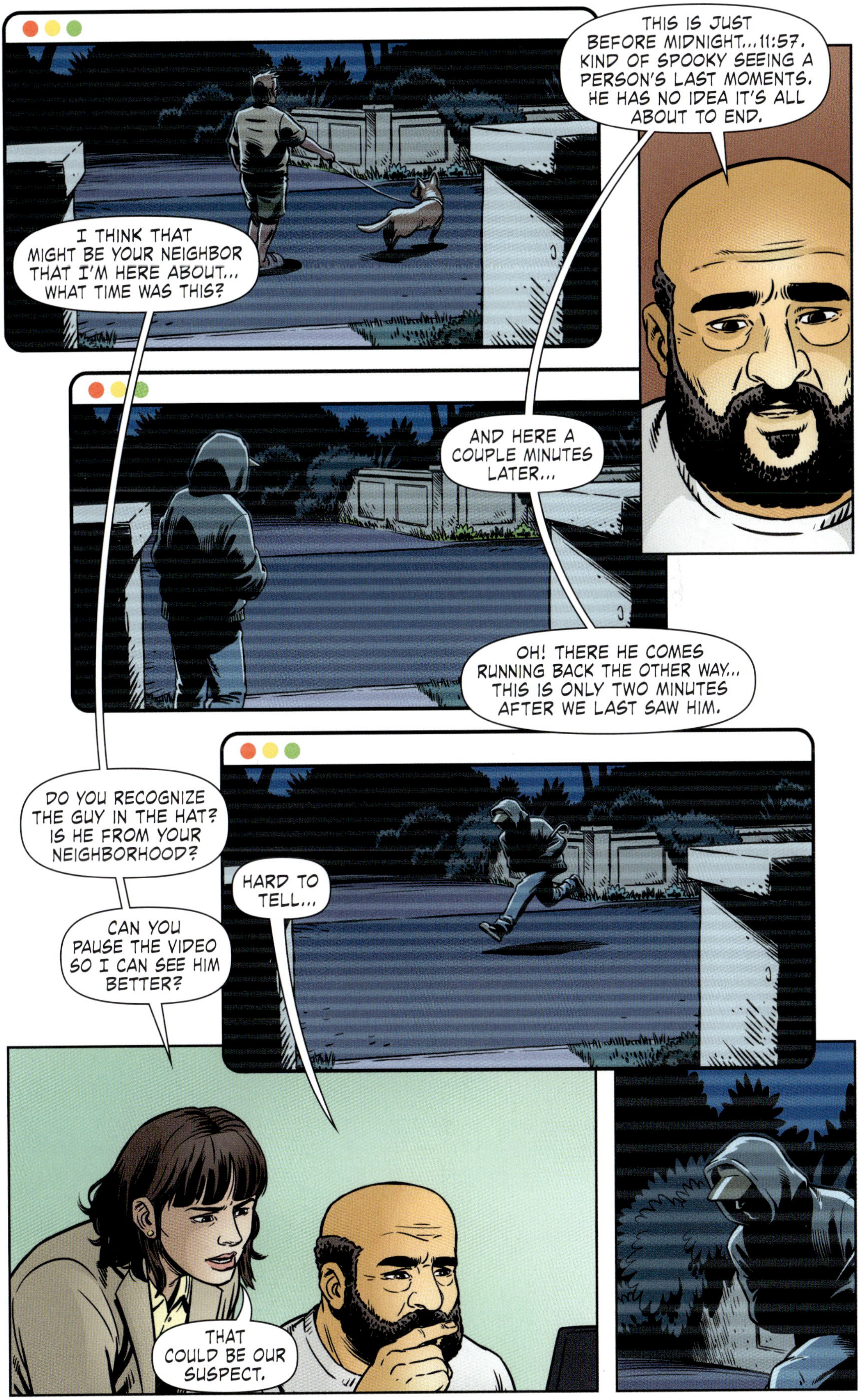

I THINK THAT MIGHT BE YOUR NEIGHBOR THAT I'M HERE ABOUT... WHAT TIME WAS THIS?
THIS IS JUST BEFORE MIDNIGHT...11:57. KIND OF SPOOKY SEEING A PERSON'S LAST MOMENTS. HE HAS NO IDEA IT'S ALL ABOUT TO END.
AND HERE A COUPLE MINUTES LATER...
OH! THERE HE COMES RUNNING BACK THE OTHER WAY... THIS IS ONLY TWO MINUTES AFTER WE LAST SAW HIM.
DO YOU RECOGNIZE THE GUY IN THE HAT? IS HE FROM YOUR NEIGHBORHOOD?
HARD TO TELL...
CAN YOU PAUSE THE VIDEO SO I CAN SEE HIM BETTER?
THAT COULD BE OUR SUSPECT.

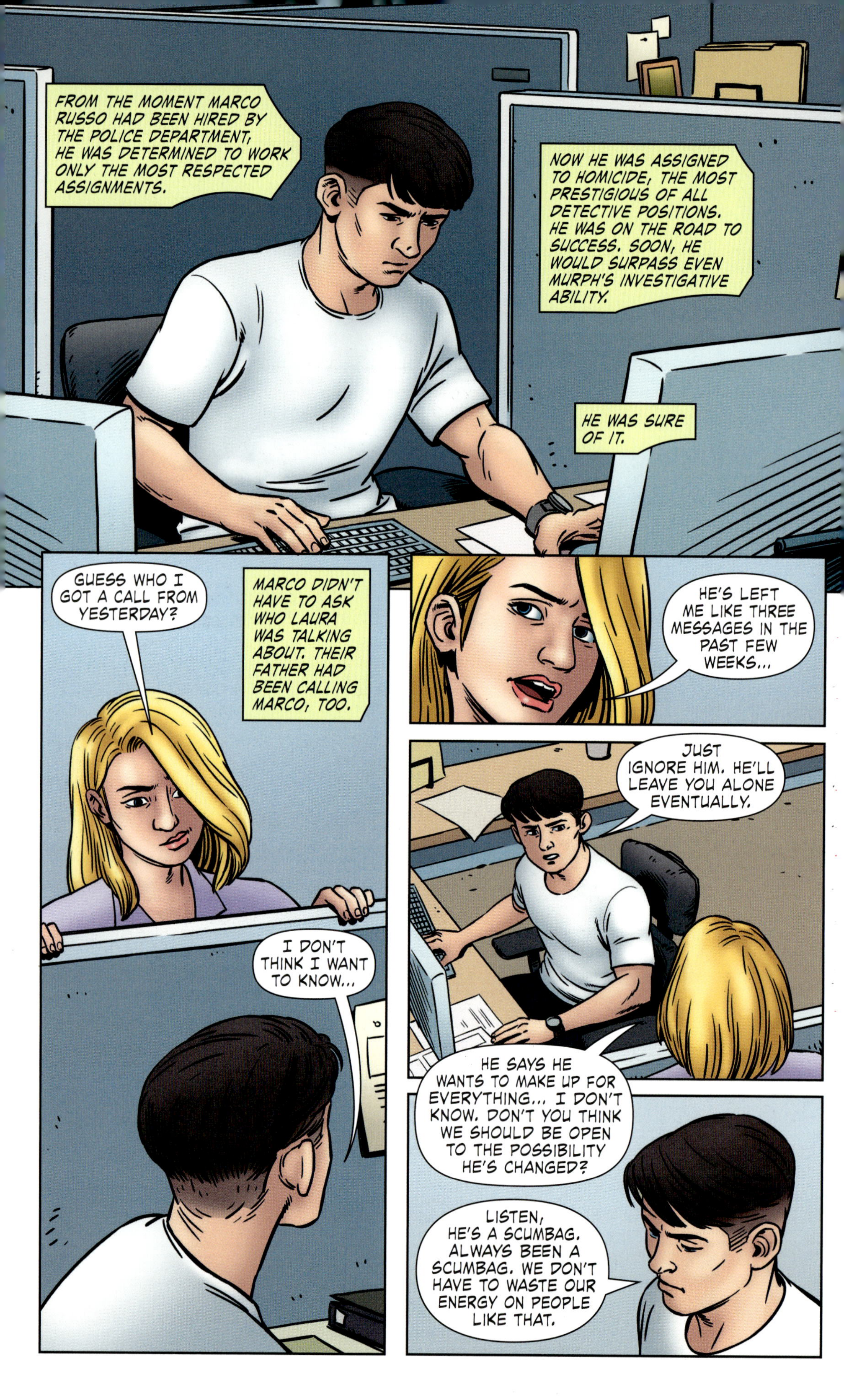
FROM THE MOMENT MARCO RUSSO HAD BEEN HIRED BY THE POLICE DEPARTMENT, HE WAS DETERMINED TO WORK ONLY THE MOST RESPECTED ASSIGNMENTS.
NOW HE WAS ASSIGNED TO HOMICIDE, THE MOST PRESTIGIOUS OF ALL DETECTIVE POSITIONS. HE WAS ON THE ROAD TO SUCCESS. SOON, HE WOULD SURPASS EVEN MURPH'S INVESTIGATIVE ABILITY.
HE WAS SURE OF IT.
GUESS WHO I GOT A CALL FROM YESTERDAY?
MARCO DIDN'T HAVE TO ASK WHO LAURA WAS TALKING ABOUT. THEIR FATHER HAD BEEN CALLING MARCO, TOO.
I DON'T THINK I WANT TO KNOW...
HE'S LEFT ME LIKE THREE MESSAGES IN THE PAST FEW WEEKS...
JUST IGNORE HIM. HE'LL LEAVE YOU ALONE EVENTUALLY.
HE SAYS HE WANTS TO MAKE UP FOR EVERYTHING... I DON'T KNOW. DON'T YOU THINK WE SHOULD BE OPEN TO THE POSSIBILITY HE'S CHANGED?
LISTEN, HE'S A SCUMBAG. ALWAYS BEEN A SCUMBAG. WE DON'T HAVE TO WASTE OUR ENERGY ON PEOPLE LIKE THAT.

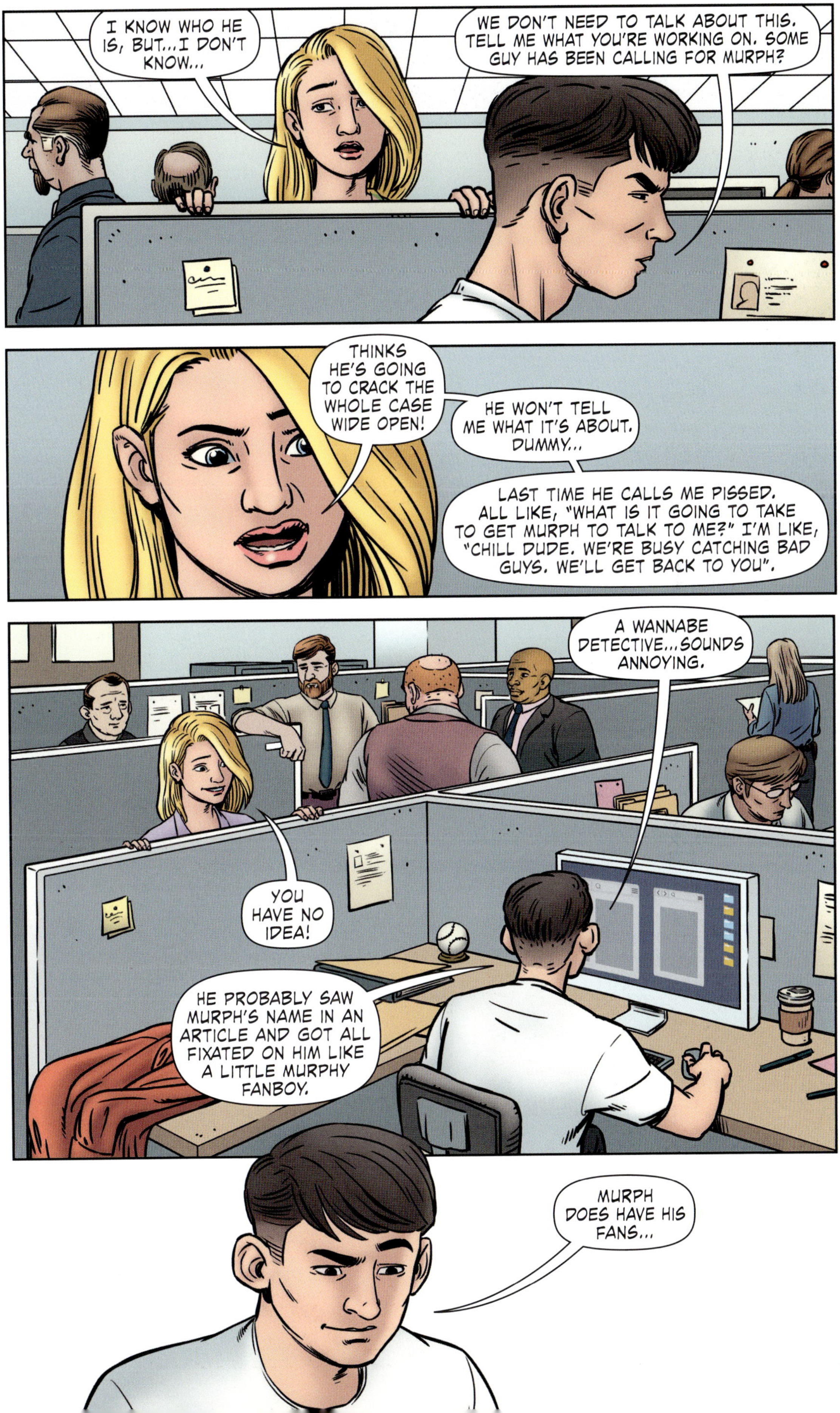
I KNOW WHO HE IS, BUT...I DON'T KNOW...
WE DON'T NEED TO TALK ABOUT THIS. TELL ME WHAT YOU'RE WORKING ON. SOME GUY HAS BEEN CALLING FOR MURPH?
THINKS HE'S GOING TO CRACK THE WHOLE CASE WIDE OPEN!
HE WON'T TELL ME WHAT IT'S ABOUT. DUMMY...
LAST TIME HE CALLS ME PISSED. ALL LIKE, "WHAT IS IT GOING TO TAKE TO GET MURPH TO TALK TO ME?" I'M LIKE, "CHILL DUDE. WE'RE BUSY CATCHING BAD GUYS. WE'LL GET BACK TO YOU".
A WANNABE DETECTIVE...SOUNDS ANNOYING.
YOU HAVE NO IDEA!
HE PROBABLY SAW MURPH'S NAME IN AN ARTICLE AND GOT ALL FIXATED ON HIM LIKE A LITTLE MURPHY FANBOY.
MURPH DOES HAVE HIS FANS...

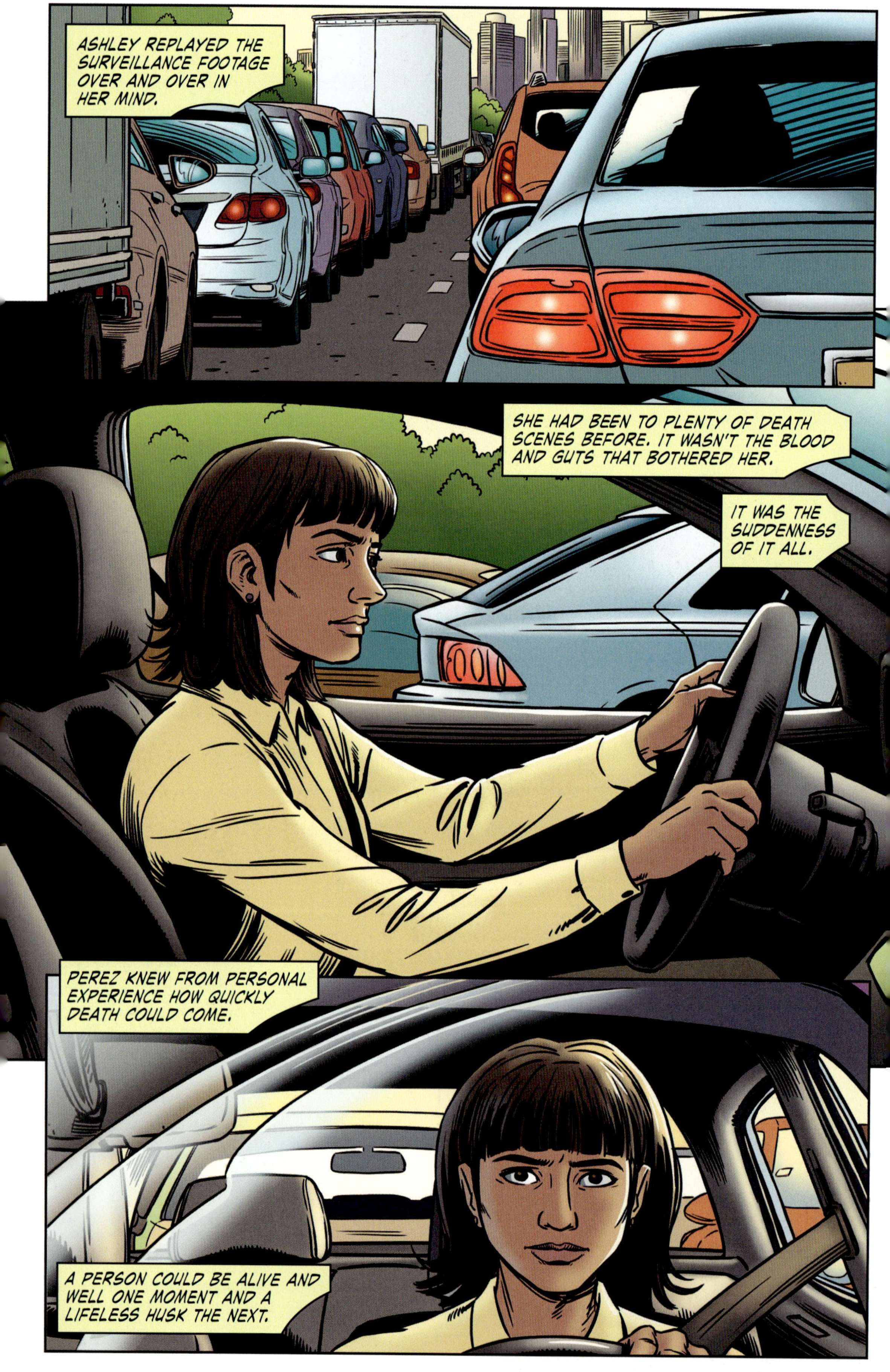
ASHLEY REPLAYED THE SURVEILLANCE FOOTAGE OVER AND OVER IN HER MIND.
SHE HAD BEEN TO PLENTY OF DEATH SCENES BEFORE. IT WASN'T THE BLOOD AND GUTS THAT BOTHERED HER.
IT WAS THE SUDDENNESS OF IT ALL.
PEREZ KNEW FROM PERSONAL EXPERIENCE HOW QUICKLY DEATH COULD COME.
A PERSON COULD BE ALIVE AND WELL ONE MOMENT AND A LIFELESS HUSK THE NEXT.

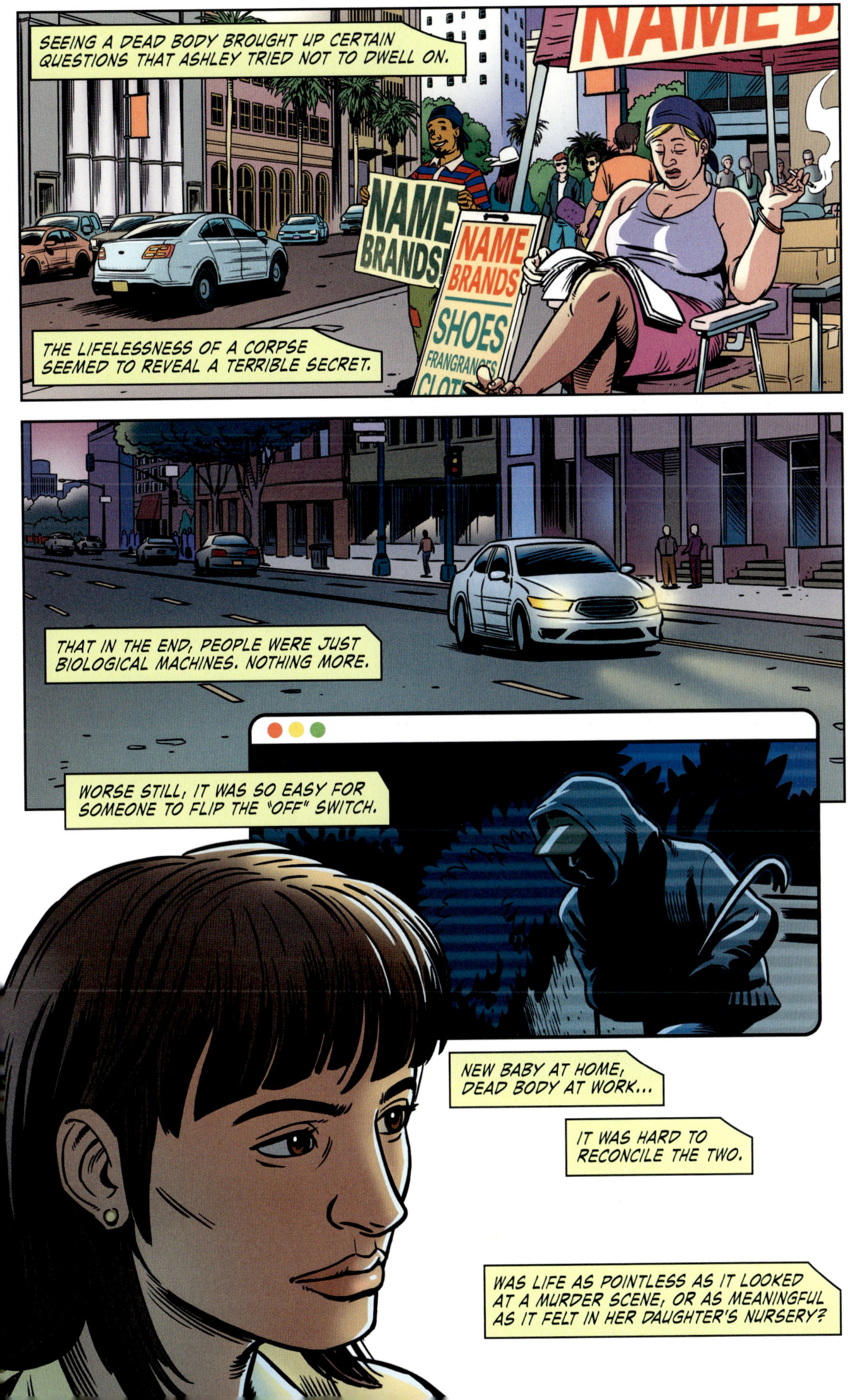
SEEING A DEAD BODY BROUGHT UP CERTAIN QUESTIONS THAT ASHLEY TRIED NOT TO DWELL ON.
NAME B
NAME BRANDS!
NAME BRANDS
SHOES
THE LIFELESSNESS OF A CORPSE SEEMED TO REVEAL A TERRIBLE SECRET.
THAT IN THE END, PEOPLE WERE JUST BIOLOGICAL MACHINES. NOTHING MORE.
WORSE STILL, IT WAS SO EASY FOR SOMEONE TO FLIP THE "OFF" SWITCH.
NEW BABY AT HOME, DEAD BODY AT WORK...
IT WAS HARD TO RECONCILE THE TWO.
WAS LIFE AS POINTLESS AS IT LOOKED AT A MURDER SCENE, OR AS MEANINGFUL AS IT FELT IN HER DAUGHTER'S NURSERY?

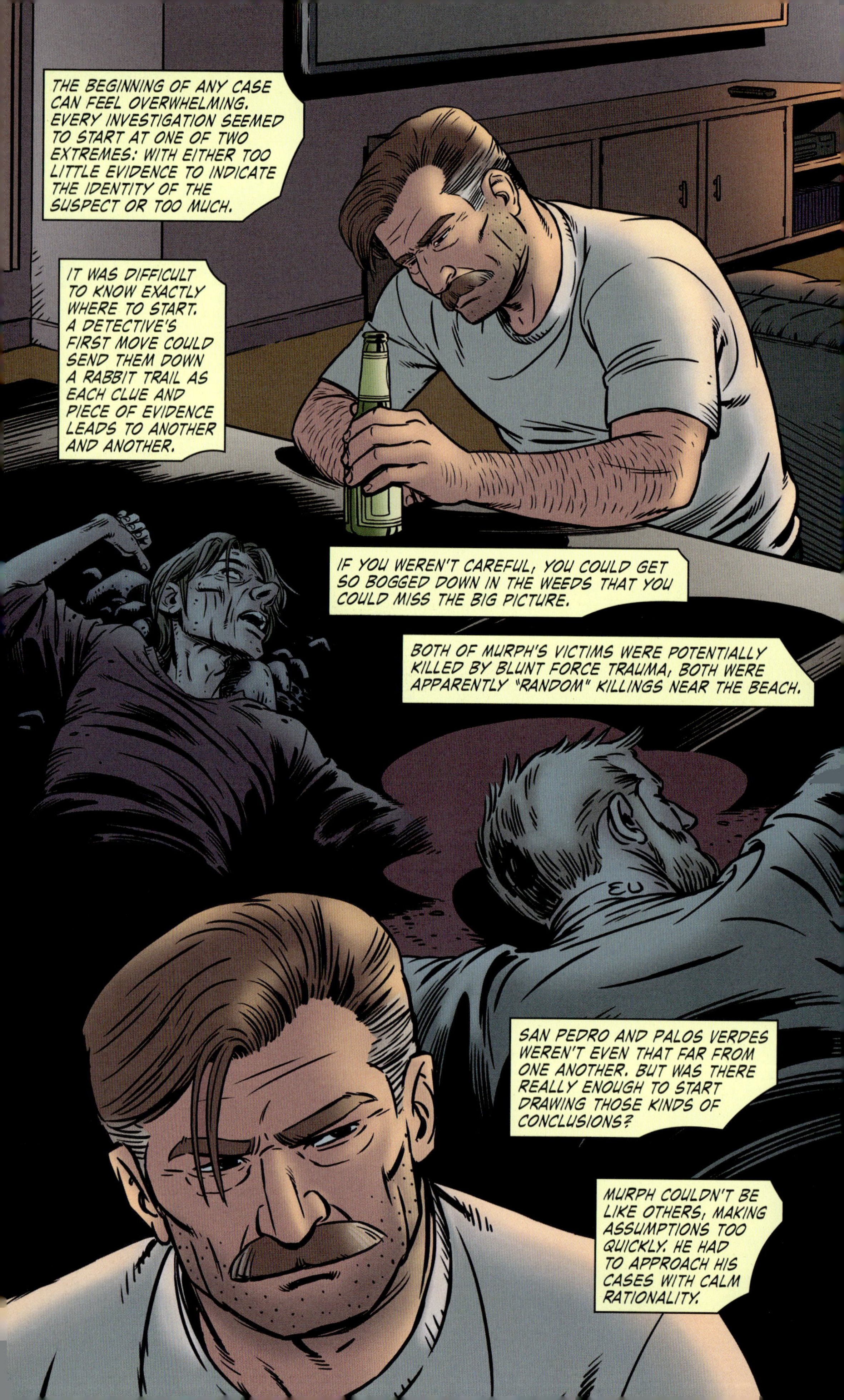
THE BEGINNING OF ANY CASE CAN FEEL OVERWHELMING. EVERY INVESTIGATION SEEMED TO START AT ONE OF TWO EXTREMES: WITH EITHER TOO LITTLE EVIDENCE TO INDICATE THE IDENTITY OF THE SUSPECT OR TOO MUCH.
IT WAS DIFFICULT TO KNOW EXACTLY WHERE TO START. A DETECTIVE'S FIRST MOVE COULD SEND THEM DOWN A RABBIT TRAIL AS EACH CLUE AND PIECE OF EVIDENCE LEADS TO ANOTHER AND ANOTHER.
IF YOU WEREN'T CAREFUL, YOU COULD GET SO BOGGED DOWN IN THE WEEDS THAT YOU COULD MISS THE BIG PICTURE.
BOTH OF MURPH'S VICTIMS WERE POTENTIALLY KILLED BY BLUNT FORCE TRAUMA, BOTH WERE APPARENTLY "RANDOM" KILLINGS NEAR THE BEACH.
EU
SAN PEDRO AND PALOS VERDES WEREN'T EVEN THAT FAR FROM ONE ANOTHER. BUT WAS THERE REALLY ENOUGH TO START DRAWING THOSE KINDS OF CONCLUSIONS?
MURPH COULDN'T BE LIKE OTHERS, MAKING ASSUMPTIONS TOO QUICKLY. HE HAD TO APPROACH HIS CASES WITH CALM RATIONALITY.

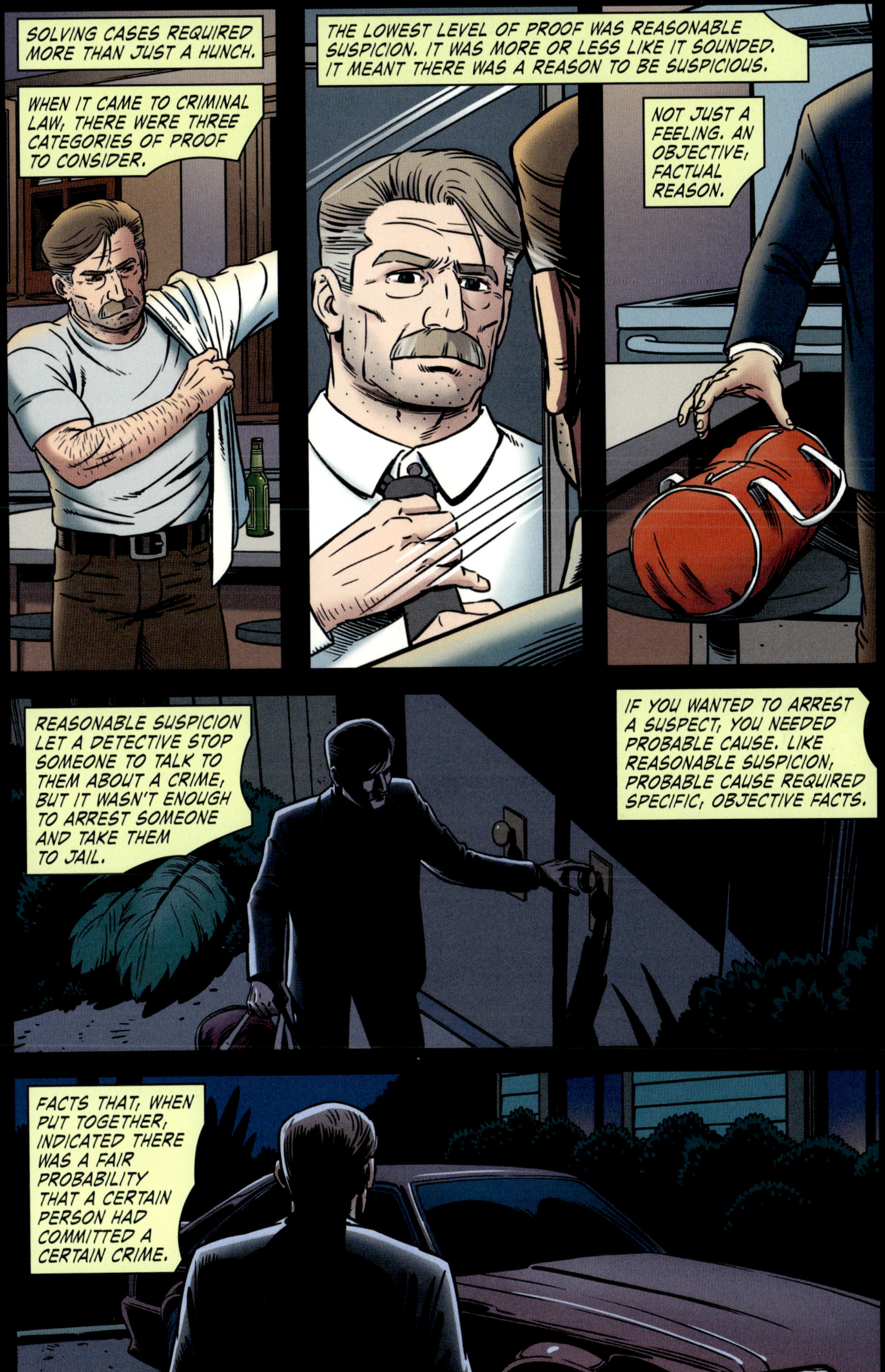
SOLVING CASES REQUIRED MORE THAN JUST A HUNCH.
WHEN IT CAME TO CRIMINAL LAW, THERE WERE THREE CATEGORIES OF PROOF TO CONSIDER.
THE LOWEST LEVEL OF PROOF WAS REASONABLE SUSPICION. IT WAS MORE OR LESS LIKE IT SOUNDED. IT MEANT THERE WAS A REASON TO BE SUSPICIOUS.
NOT JUST A FEELING. AN OBJECTIVE, FACTUAL REASON.
REASONABLE SUSPICION LET A DETECTIVE STOP SOMEONE TO TALK TO THEM ABOUT A CRIME, BUT IT WASN'T ENOUGH TO ARREST SOMEONE AND TAKE THEM TO JAIL.
IF YOU WANTED TO ARREST A SUSPECT, YOU NEEDED PROBABLE CAUSE. LIKE REASONABLE SUSPICION, PROBABLE CAUSE REQUIRED SPECIFIC, OBJECTIVE FACTS.
FACTS THAT, WHEN PUT TOGETHER, INDICATED THERE WAS A FAIR PROBABILITY THAT A CERTAIN PERSON HAD COMMITTED A CERTAIN CRIME.

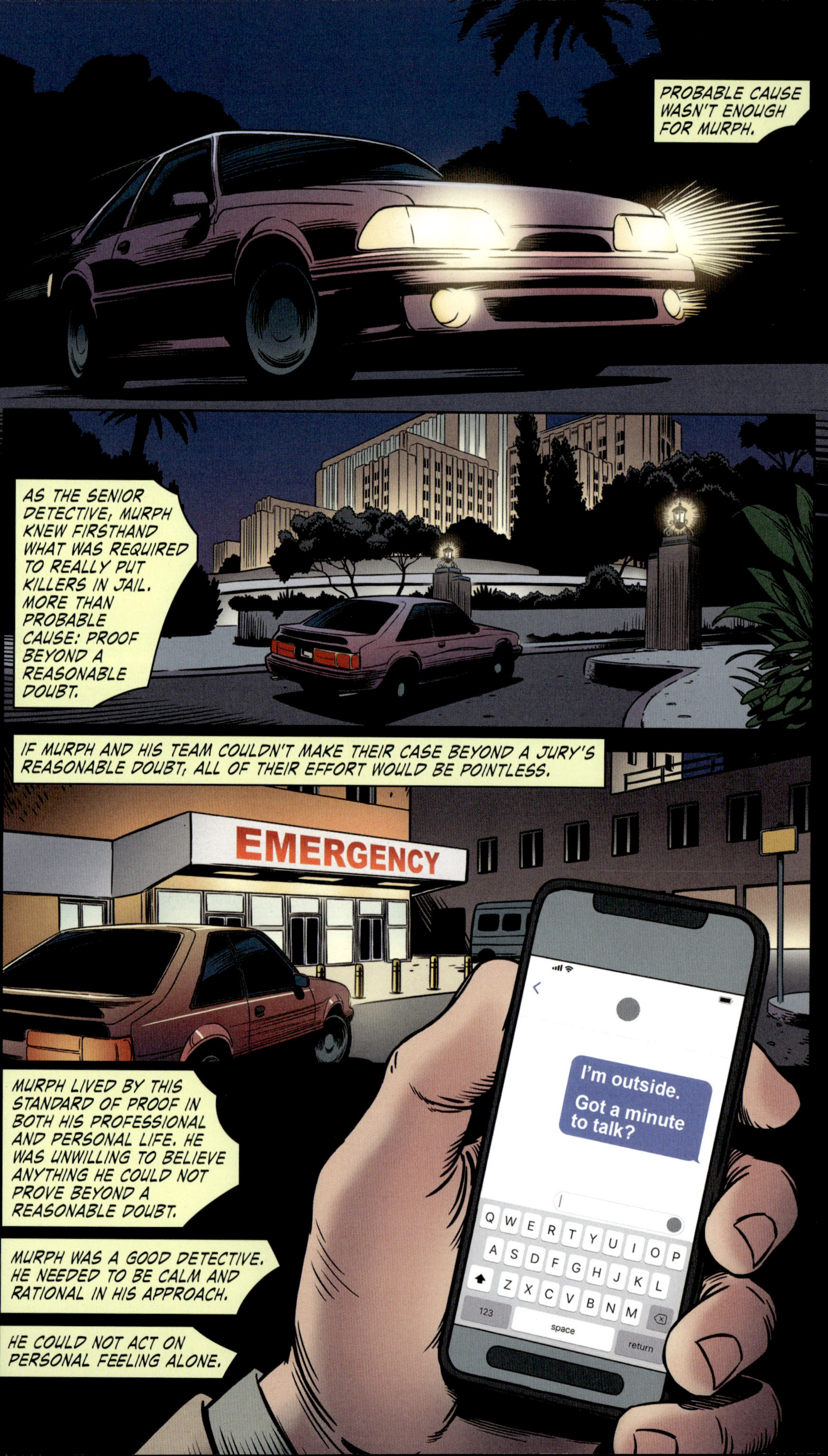
PROBABLE CAUSE WASN'T ENOUGH FOR MURPH.
AS THE SENIOR DETECTIVE, MURPH KNEW FIRSTHAND WHAT WAS REQUIRED TO REALLY PUT KILLERS IN JAIL. MORE THAN PROBABLE CAUSE: PROOF BEYOND A REASONABLE DOUBT.
IF MURPH AND HIS TEAM COULDN'T MAKE THEIR CASE BEYOND A JURY'S REASONABLE DOUBT, ALL OF THEIR EFFORT WOULD BE POINTLESS.
EMERGENCY
I'm outside.
Got a minute to talk?
MURPH LIVED BY THIS STANDARD OF PROOF IN BOTH HIS PROFESSIONAL AND PERSONAL LIFE. HE WAS UNWILLING TO BELIEVE ANYTHING HE COULD NOT PROVE BEYOND A REASONABLE DOUBT.
MURPH WAS A GOOD DETECTIVE. HE NEEDED TO BE CALM AND RATIONAL IN HIS APPROACH.
HE COULD NOT ACT ON PERSONAL FEELING ALONE.

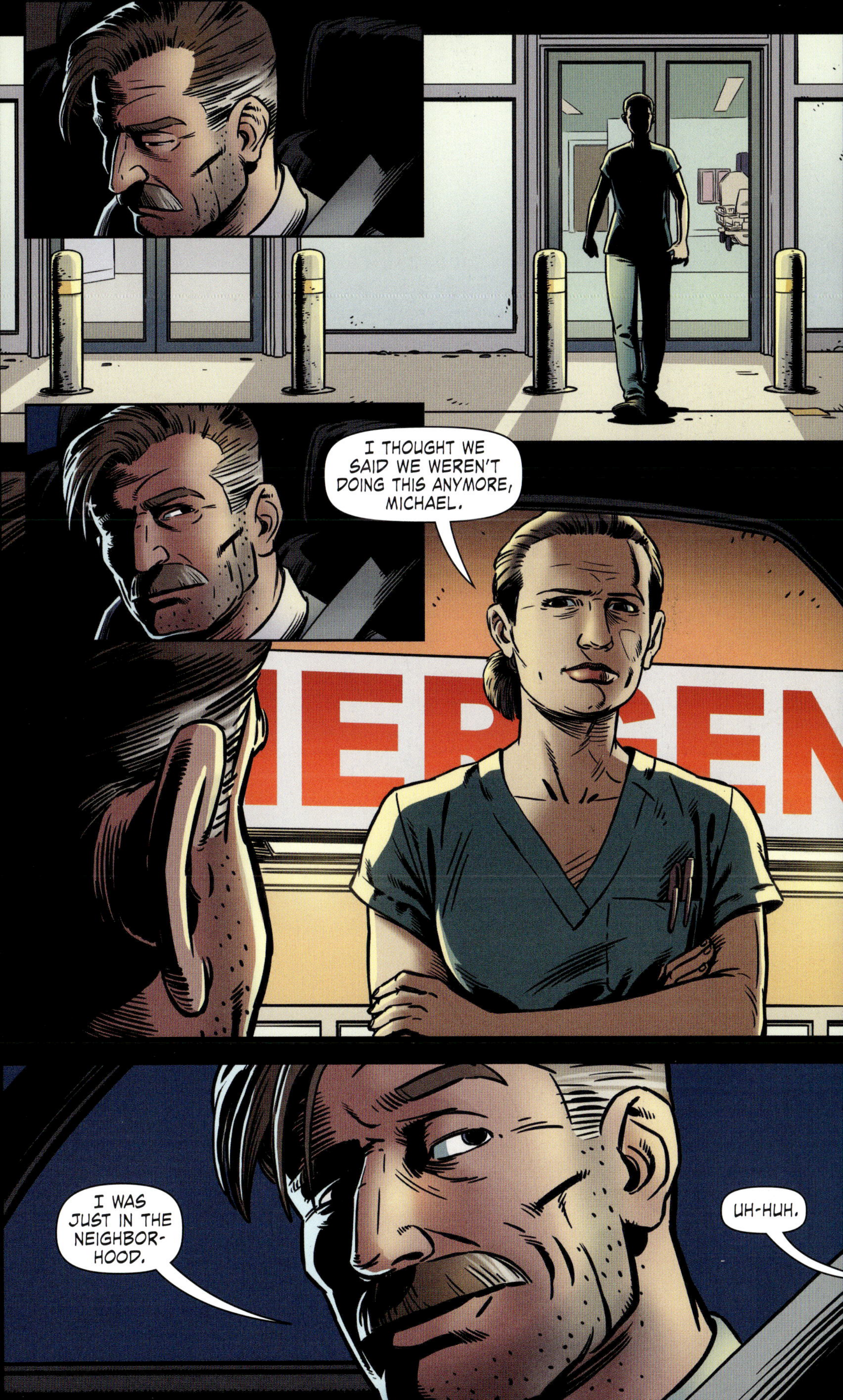
I THOUGHT WE SAID WE WEREN'T DOING THIS ANYMORE, MICHAEL.
I WAS JUST IN THE NEIGHBOR-HOOD.
UH-HUH.

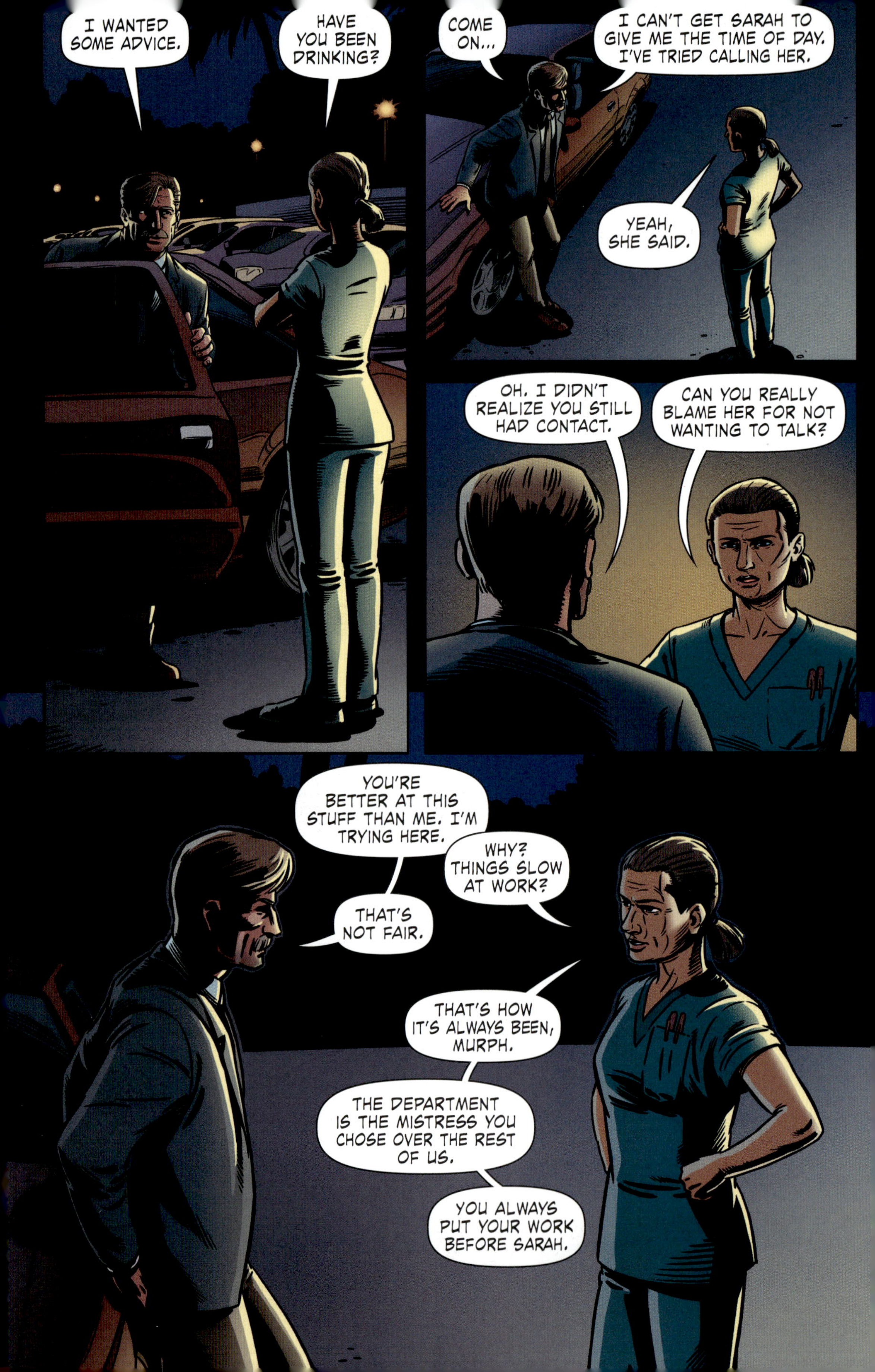
I WANTED SOME ADVICE.
HAVE YOU BEEN DRINKING?
COME ON...
I CAN'T GET SARAH TO GIVE ME THE TIME OF DAY. I'VE TRIED CALLING HER.
YEAH, SHE SAID.
OH. I DIDN'T REALIZE YOU STILL HAD CONTACT.
CAN YOU REALLY BLAME HER FOR NOT WANTING TO TALK?
YOU'RE BETTER AT THIS STUFF THAN ME. I'M TRYING HERE.
WHY? THINGS SLOW AT WORK?
THAT'S NOT FAIR.
THAT'S HOW IT'S ALWAYS BEEN, MURPH.
THE DEPARTMENT IS THE MISTRESS YOU CHOSE OVER THE REST OF US.
YOU ALWAYS PUT YOUR WORK BEFORE SARAH.

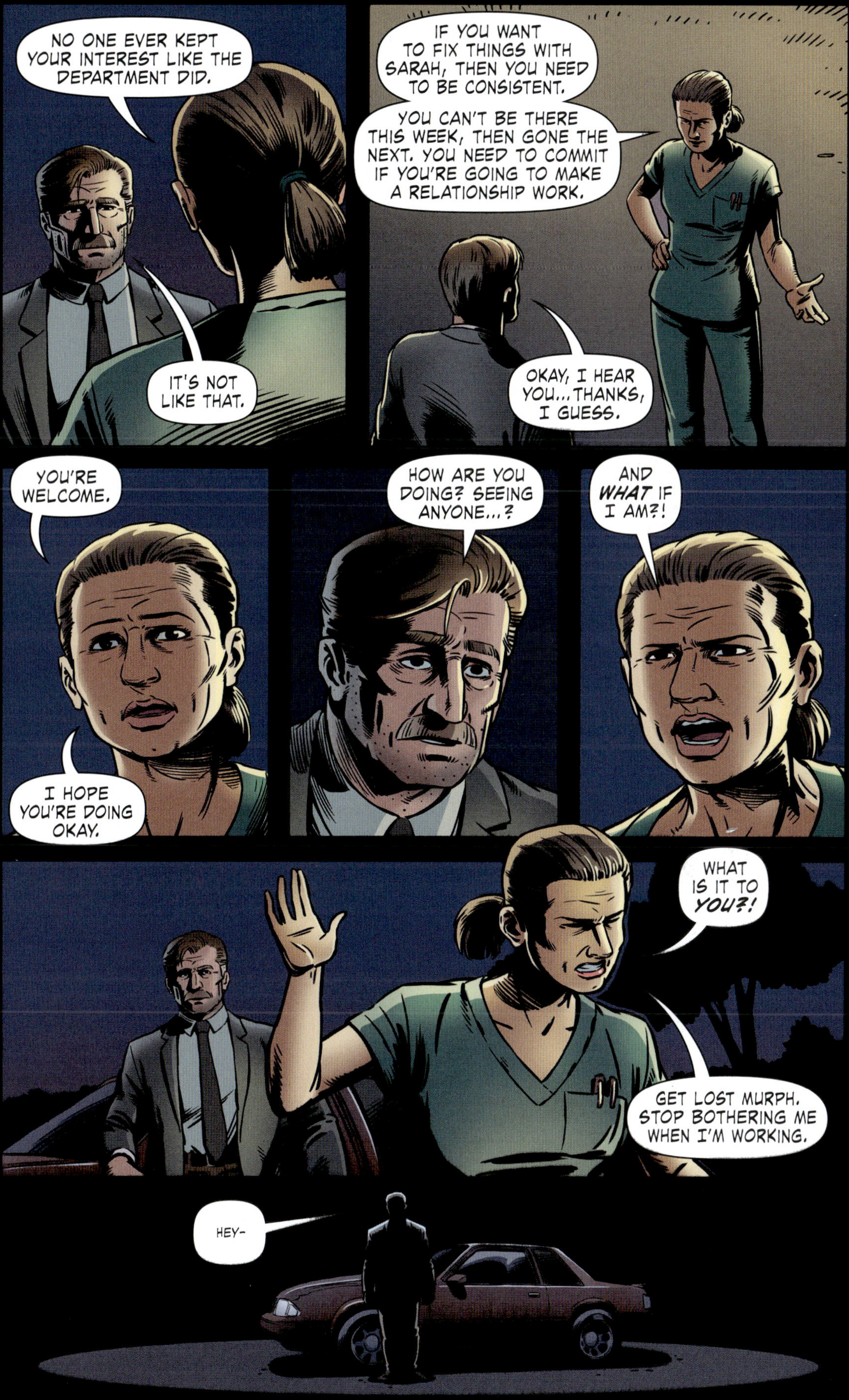
NO ONE EVER KEPT YOUR INTEREST LIKE THE DEPARTMENT DID.
IT'S NOT LIKE THAT.
IF YOU WANT TO FIX THINGS WITH SARAH, THEN YOU NEED TO BE CONSISTENT.
YOU CAN'T BE THERE THIS WEEK, THEN GONE THE NEXT. YOU NEED TO COMMIT IF YOU'RE GOING TO MAKE A RELATIONSHIP WORK.
OKAY, I HEAR YOU...THANKS, I GUESS.
YOU'RE WELCOME.
I HOPE YOU'RE DOING OKAY.
HOW ARE YOU DOING? SEEING ANYONE...?
AND *WHAT* IF I AM?!
WHAT IS IT TO *YOU?!*
GET LOST MURPH. STOP BOTHERING ME WHEN I'M WORKING.
HEY-

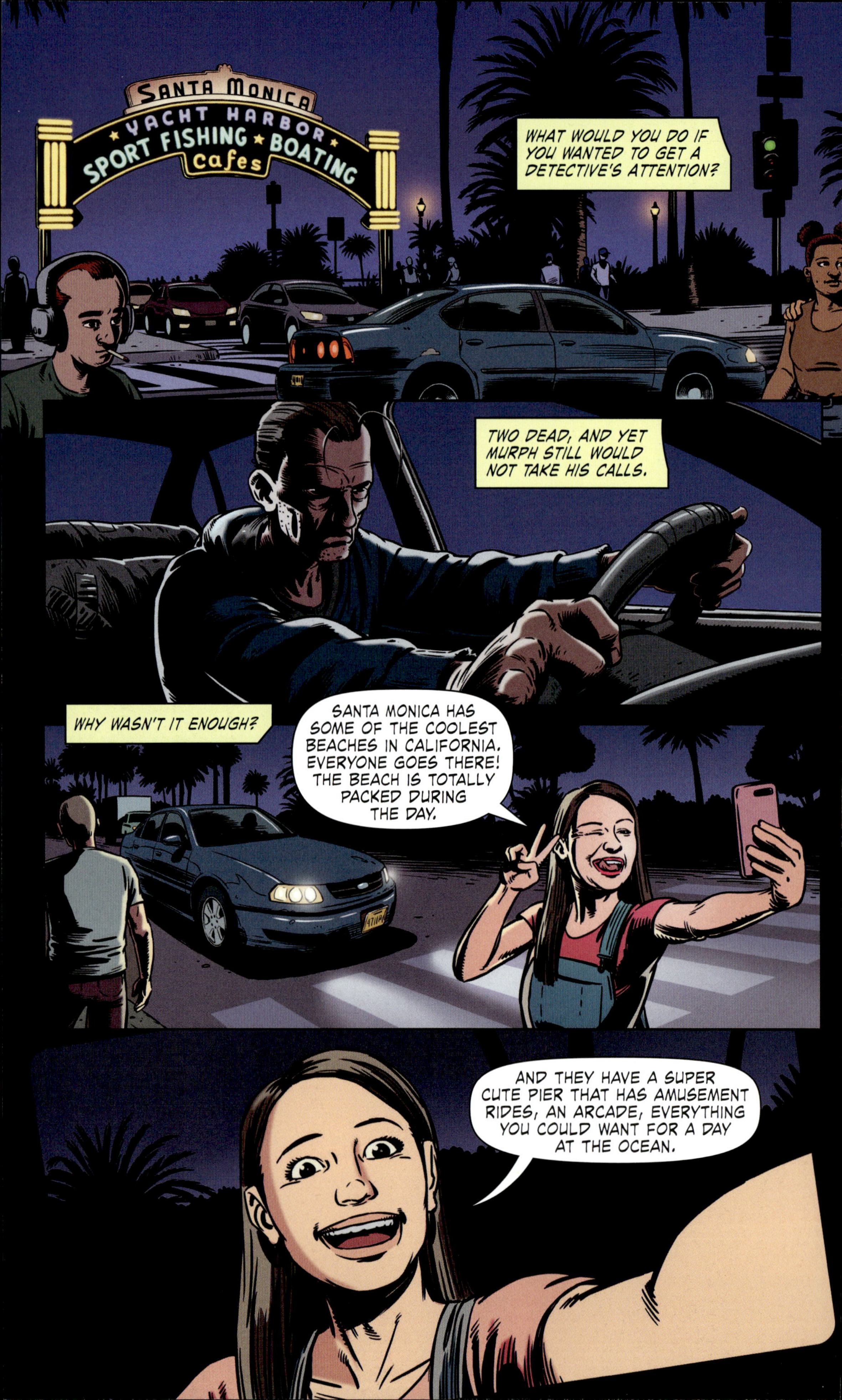
SANTA MONICA
YACHT HARBOR
SPORT FISHING BOATING
cafes
WHAT WOULD YOU DO IF YOU WANTED TO GET A DETECTIVE'S ATTENTION?
TWO DEAD, AND YET MURPH STILL WOULD NOT TAKE HIS CALLS.
WHY WASN'T IT ENOUGH?
SANTA MONICA HAS SOME OF THE COOLEST BEACHES IN CALIFORNIA. EVERYONE GOES THERE! THE BEACH IS TOTALLY PACKED DURING THE DAY.
AND THEY HAVE A SUPER CUTE PIER THAT HAS AMUSEMENT RIDES, AN ARCADE, EVERYTHING YOU COULD WANT FOR A DAY AT THE OCEAN.

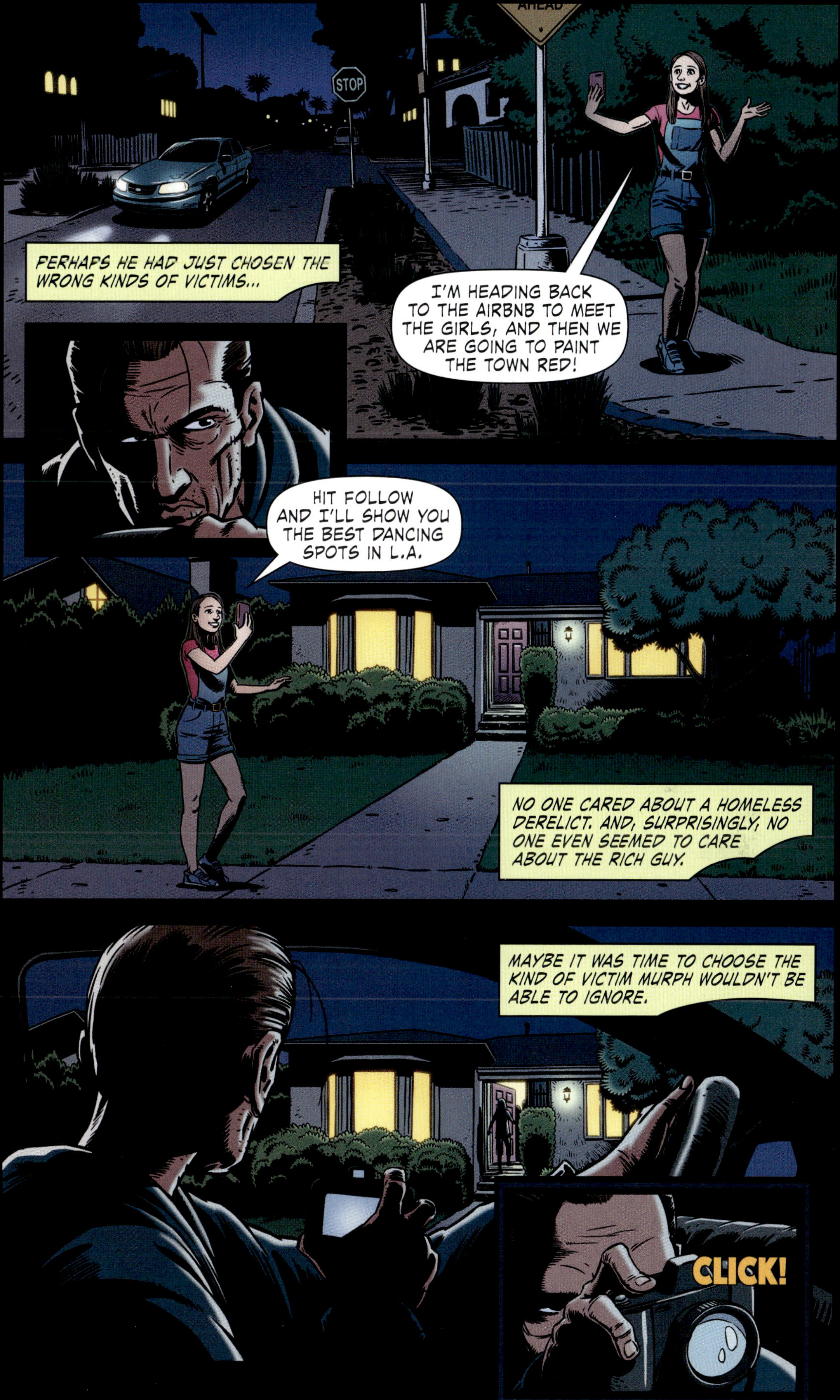
PERHAPS HE HAD JUST CHOSEN THE WRONG KINDS OF VICTIMS...
I'M HEADING BACK TO THE AIRBNB TO MEET THE GIRLS, AND THEN WE ARE GOING TO PAINT THE TOWN RED!
HIT FOLLOW AND I'LL SHOW YOU THE BEST DANCING SPOTS IN L.A.
NO ONE CARED ABOUT A HOMELESS DERELICT. AND, SURPRISINGLY, NO ONE EVEN SEEMED TO CARE ABOUT THE RICH GUY.
MAYBE IT WAS TIME TO CHOOSE THE KIND OF VICTIM MURPH WOULDN'T BE ABLE TO IGNORE.
CLICK!

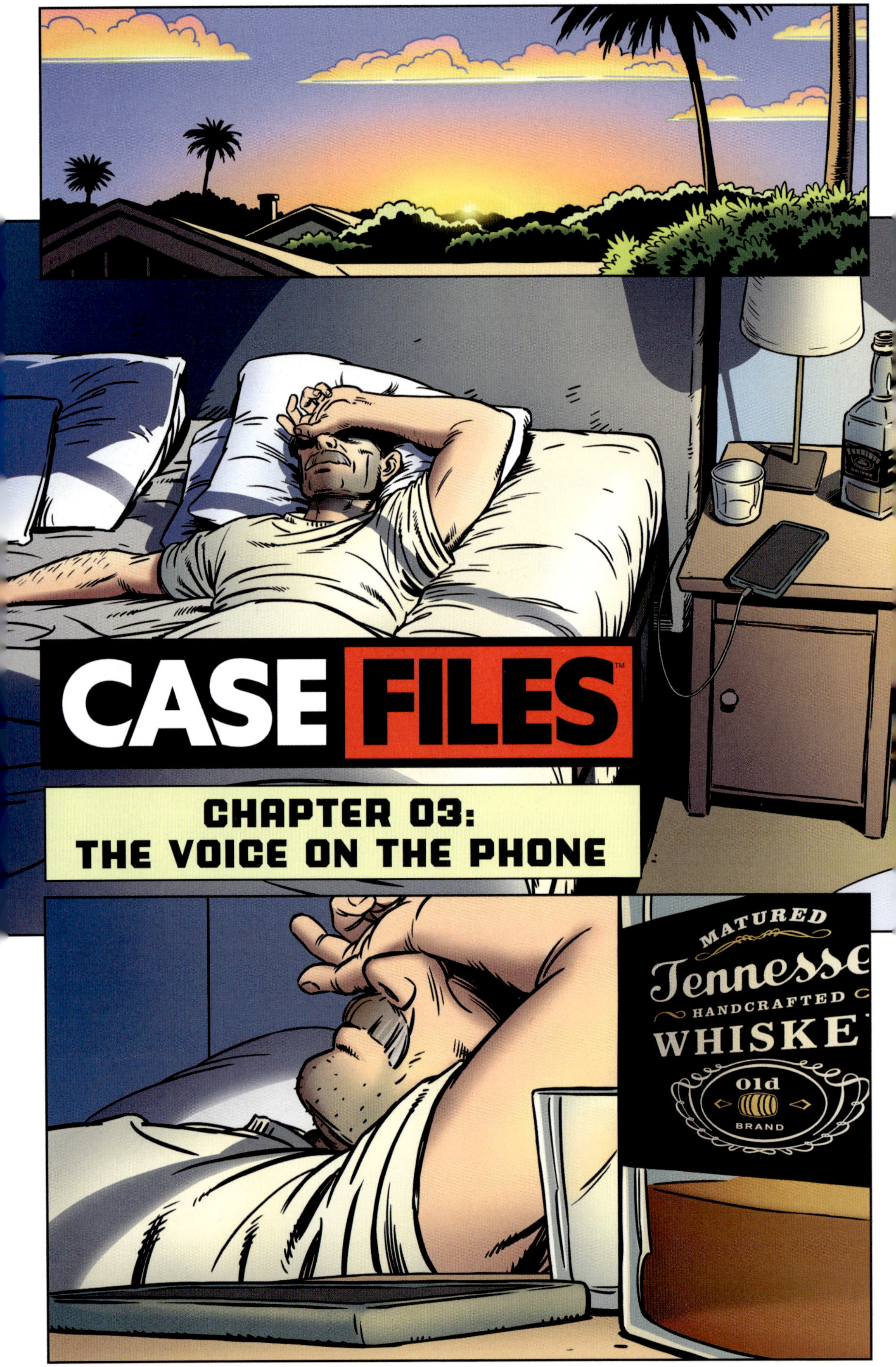
CASE FILES™
CHAPTER 03:
THE VOICE ON THE PHONE
MATURED
Tennesse
HANDCRAFTED
WHISKE
Old
BRAND

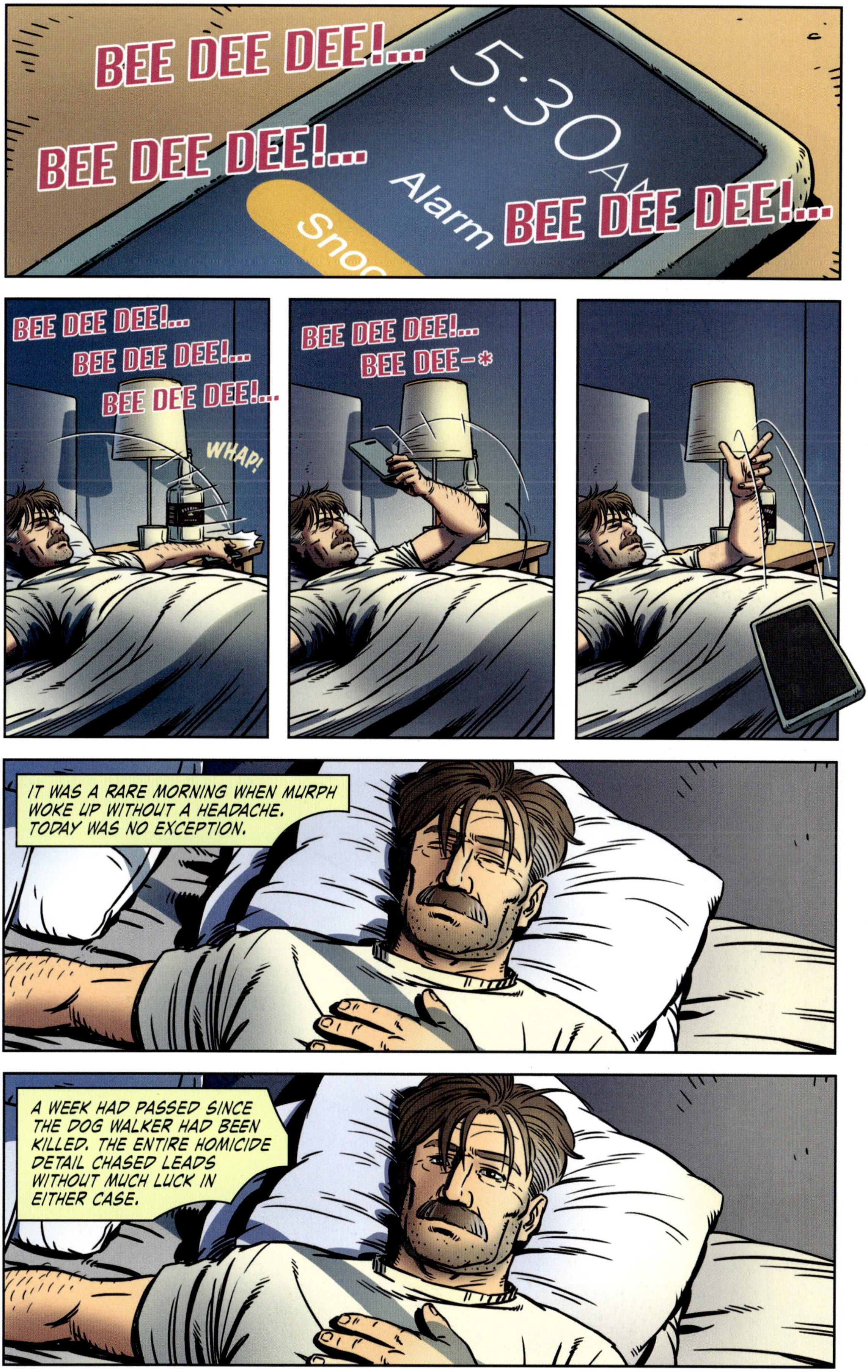
BEE DEE DEE!...
BEE DEE DEE!...
5:30 AM
Alarm
Snoo
BEE DEE DEE!...
BEE DEE DEE!...
BEE DEE DEE!...
BEE DEE DEE!...
WHAP!
BEE DEE DEE!...
BEE DEE-*
IT WAS A RARE MORNING WHEN MURPH WOKE UP WITHOUT A HEADACHE. TODAY WAS NO EXCEPTION.
A WEEK HAD PASSED SINCE THE DOG WALKER HAD BEEN KILLED. THE ENTIRE HOMICIDE DETAIL CHASED LEADS WITHOUT MUCH LUCK IN EITHER CASE.

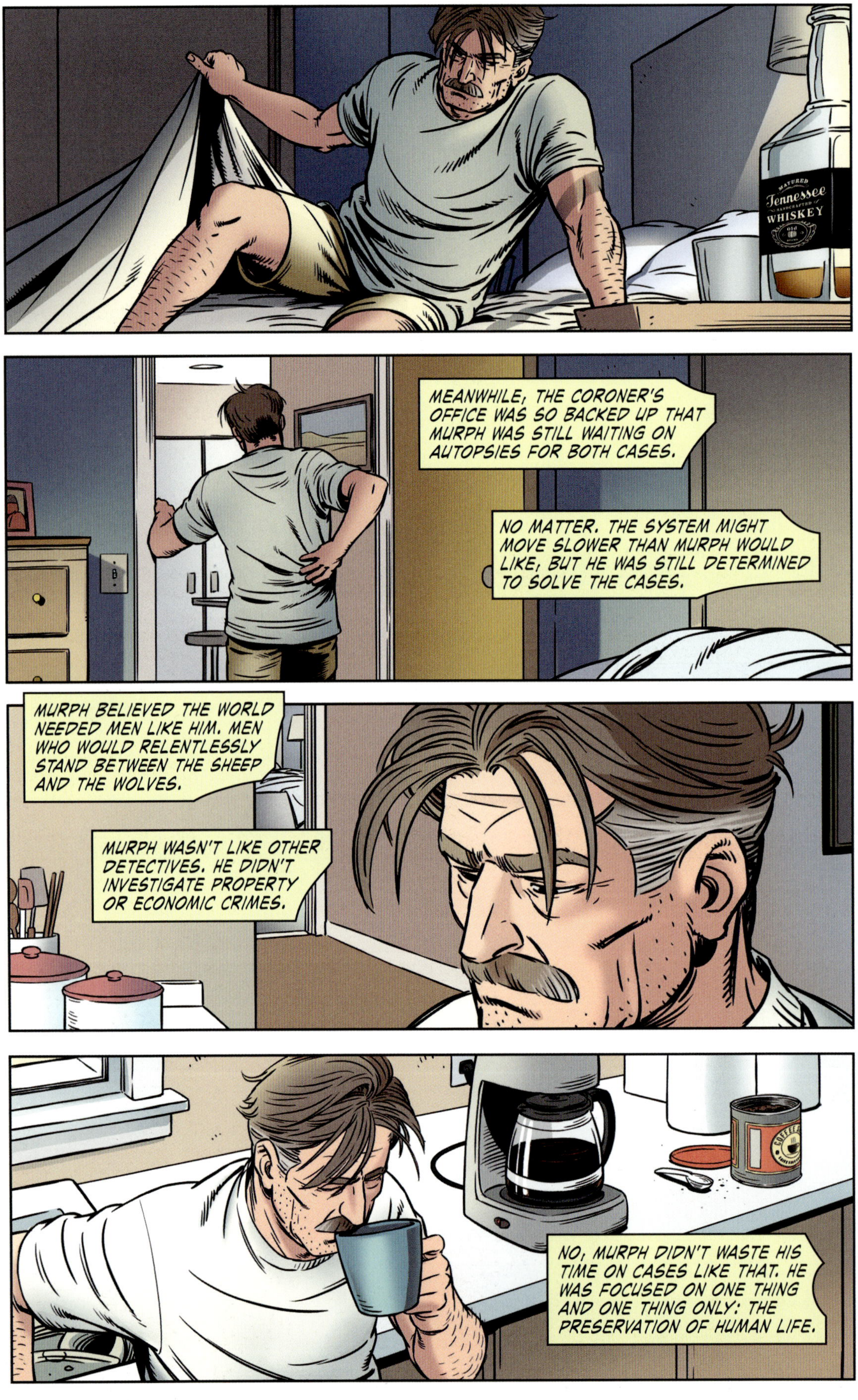
Tennessee
WHISKEY
MEANWHILE, THE CORONER'S OFFICE WAS SO BACKED UP THAT MURPH WAS STILL WAITING ON AUTOPSIES FOR BOTH CASES.
NO MATTER. THE SYSTEM MIGHT MOVE SLOWER THAN MURPH WOULD LIKE, BUT HE WAS STILL DETERMINED TO SOLVE THE CASES.
MURPH BELIEVED THE WORLD NEEDED MEN LIKE HIM. MEN WHO WOULD RELENTLESSLY STAND BETWEEN THE SHEEP AND THE WOLVES.
MURPH WASN'T LIKE OTHER DETECTIVES. HE DIDN'T INVESTIGATE PROPERTY OR ECONOMIC CRIMES.
NO, MURPH DIDN'T WASTE HIS TIME ON CASES LIKE THAT. HE WAS FOCUSED ON ONE THING AND ONE THING ONLY: THE PRESERVATION OF HUMAN LIFE.

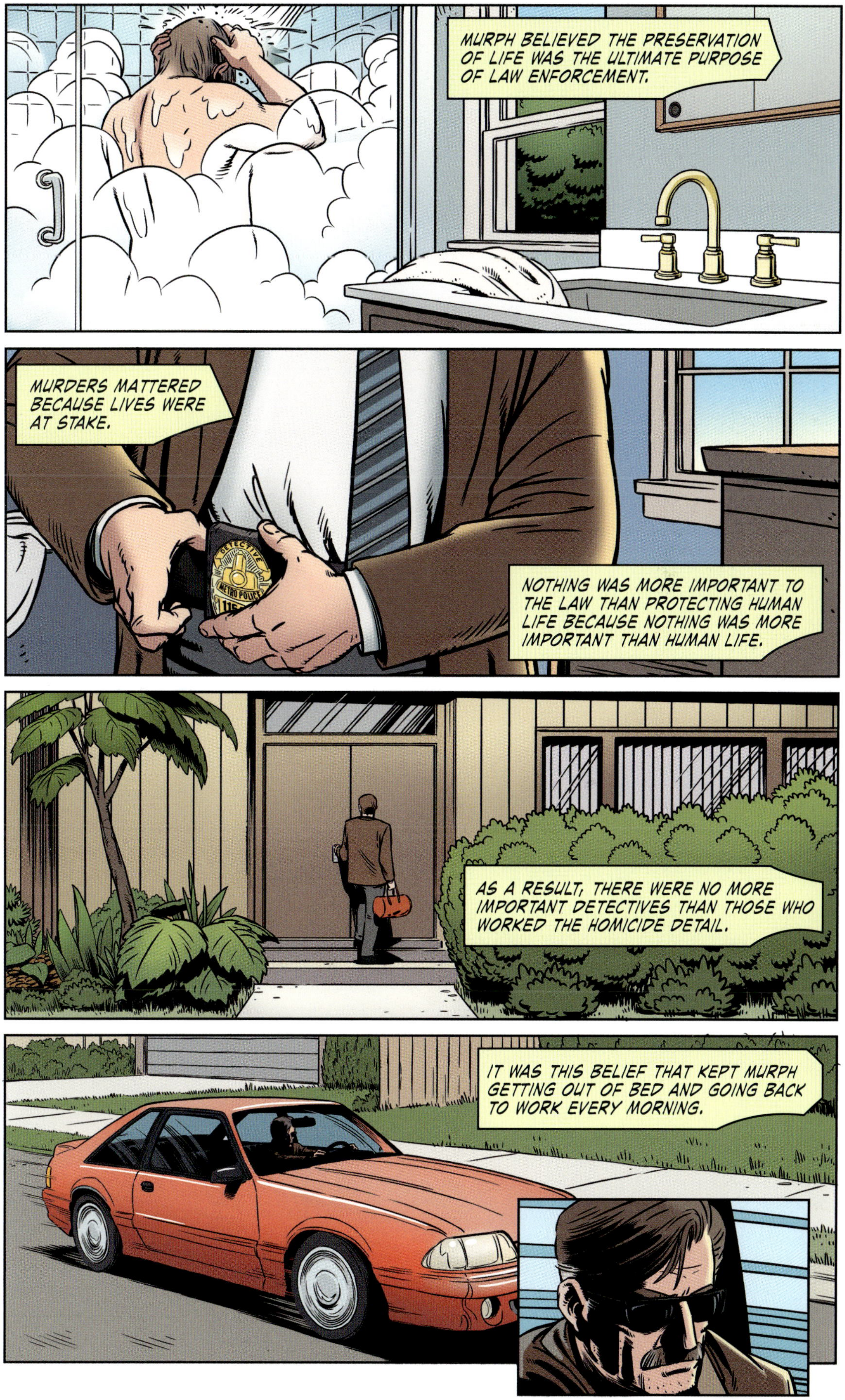
MURPH BELIEVED THE PRESERVATION OF LIFE WAS THE ULTIMATE PURPOSE OF LAW ENFORCEMENT.
MURDERS MATTERED BECAUSE LIVES WERE AT STAKE.
DETECTIVE
METRO POLICE
NOTHING WAS MORE IMPORTANT TO THE LAW THAN PROTECTING HUMAN LIFE BECAUSE NOTHING WAS MORE IMPORTANT THAN HUMAN LIFE.
AS A RESULT, THERE WERE NO MORE IMPORTANT DETECTIVES THAN THOSE WHO WORKED THE HOMICIDE DETAIL.
IT WAS THIS BELIEF THAT KEPT MURPH GETTING OUT OF BED AND GOING BACK TO WORK EVERY MORNING.

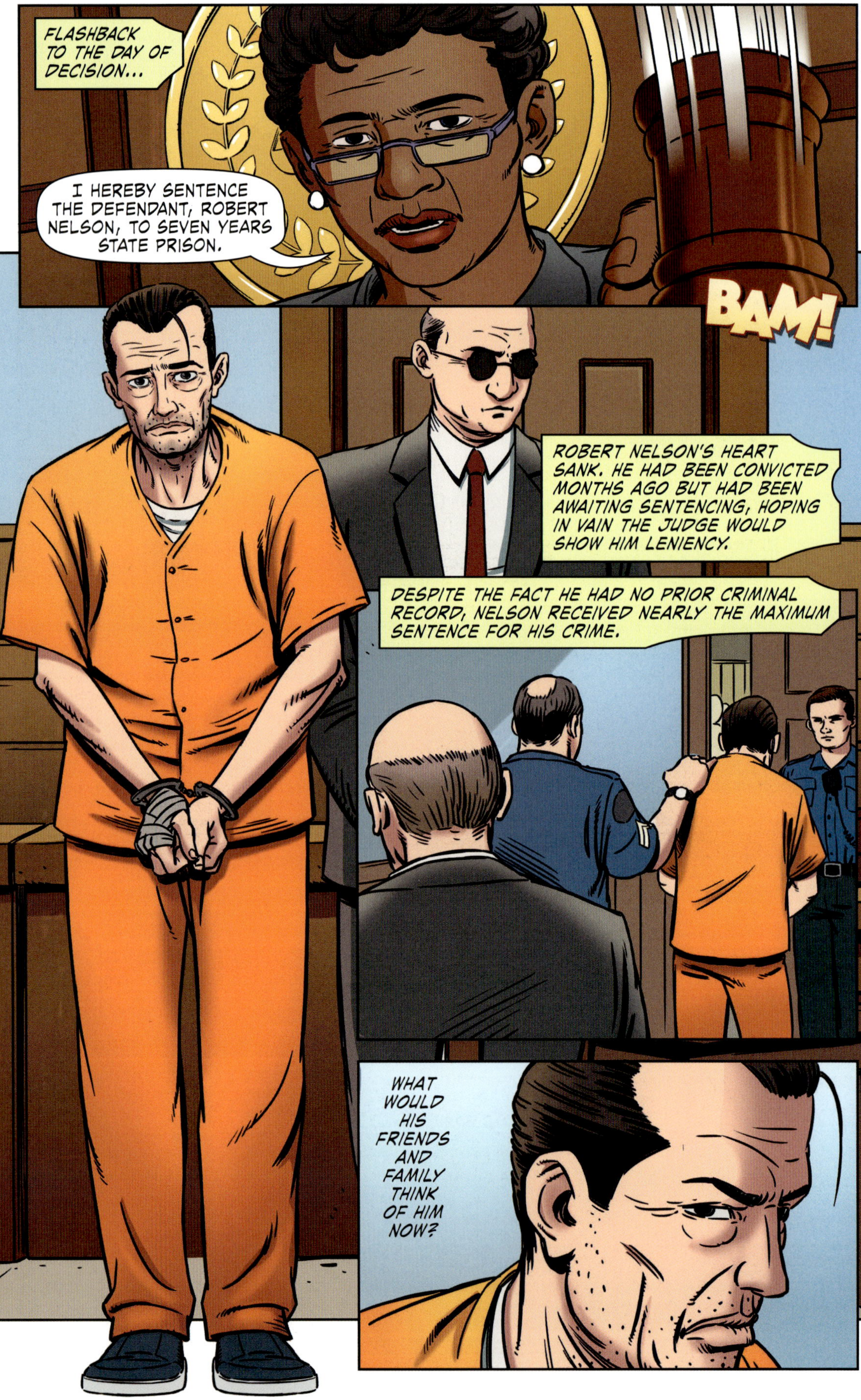
FLASHBACK TO THE DAY OF DECISION...
I HEREBY SENTENCE THE DEFENDANT, ROBERT NELSON, TO SEVEN YEARS STATE PRISON.
BAM!
ROBERT NELSON'S HEART SANK. HE HAD BEEN CONVICTED MONTHS AGO BUT HAD BEEN AWAITING SENTENCING, HOPING IN VAIN THE JUDGE WOULD SHOW HIM LENIENCY.
DESPITE THE FACT HE HAD NO PRIOR CRIMINAL RECORD, NELSON RECEIVED NEARLY THE MAXIMUM SENTENCE FOR HIS CRIME.
WHAT WOULD HIS FRIENDS AND FAMILY THINK OF HIM NOW?

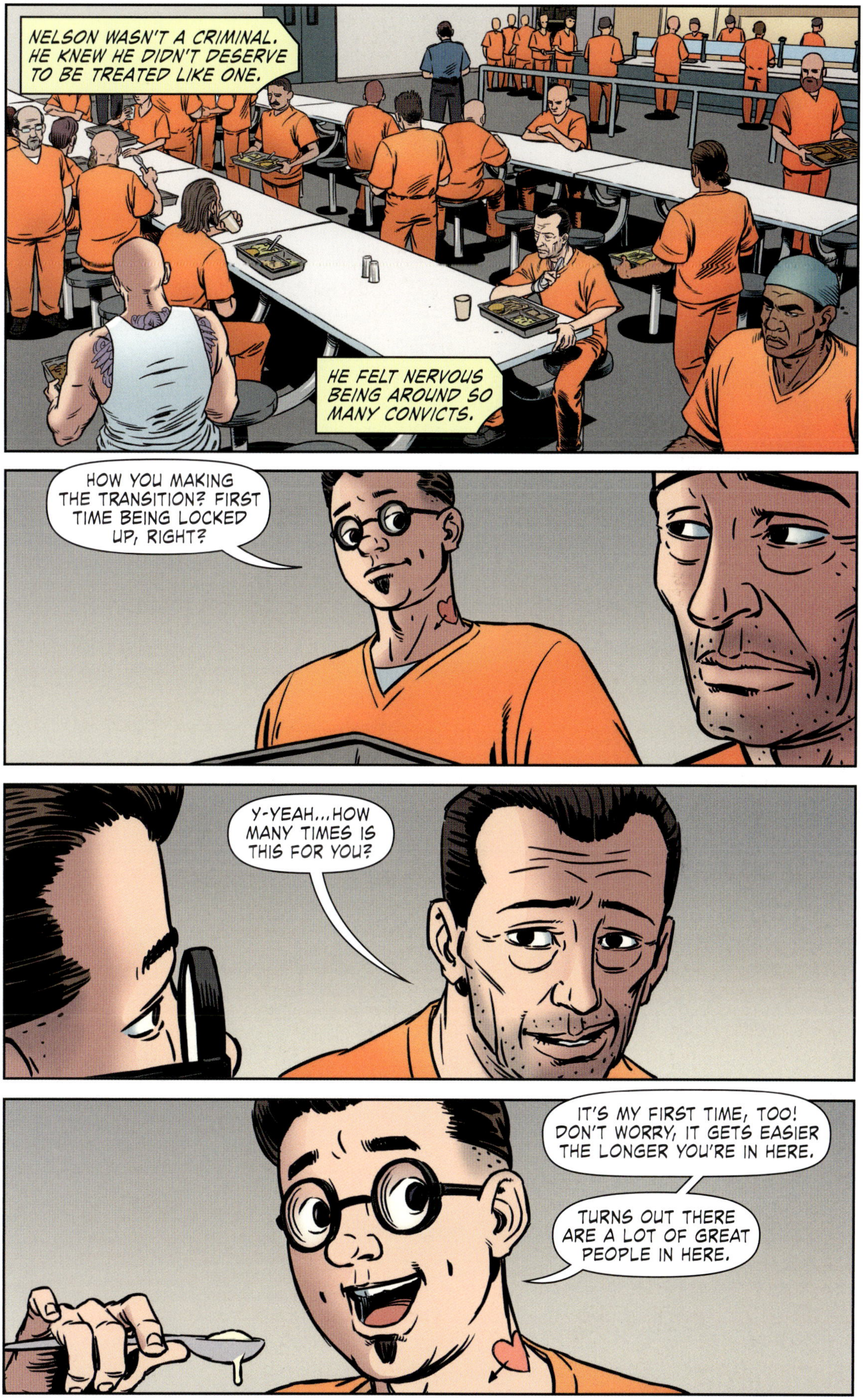
NELSON WASN'T A CRIMINAL. HE KNEW HE DIDN'T DESERVE TO BE TREATED LIKE ONE.
HE FELT NERVOUS BEING AROUND SO MANY CONVICTS.
HOW YOU MAKING THE TRANSITION? FIRST TIME BEING LOCKED UP, RIGHT?
Y-YEAH...HOW MANY TIMES IS THIS FOR YOU?
IT'S MY FIRST TIME, TOO! DON'T WORRY, IT GETS EASIER THE LONGER YOU'RE IN HERE.
TURNS OUT THERE ARE A LOT OF GREAT PEOPLE IN HERE.

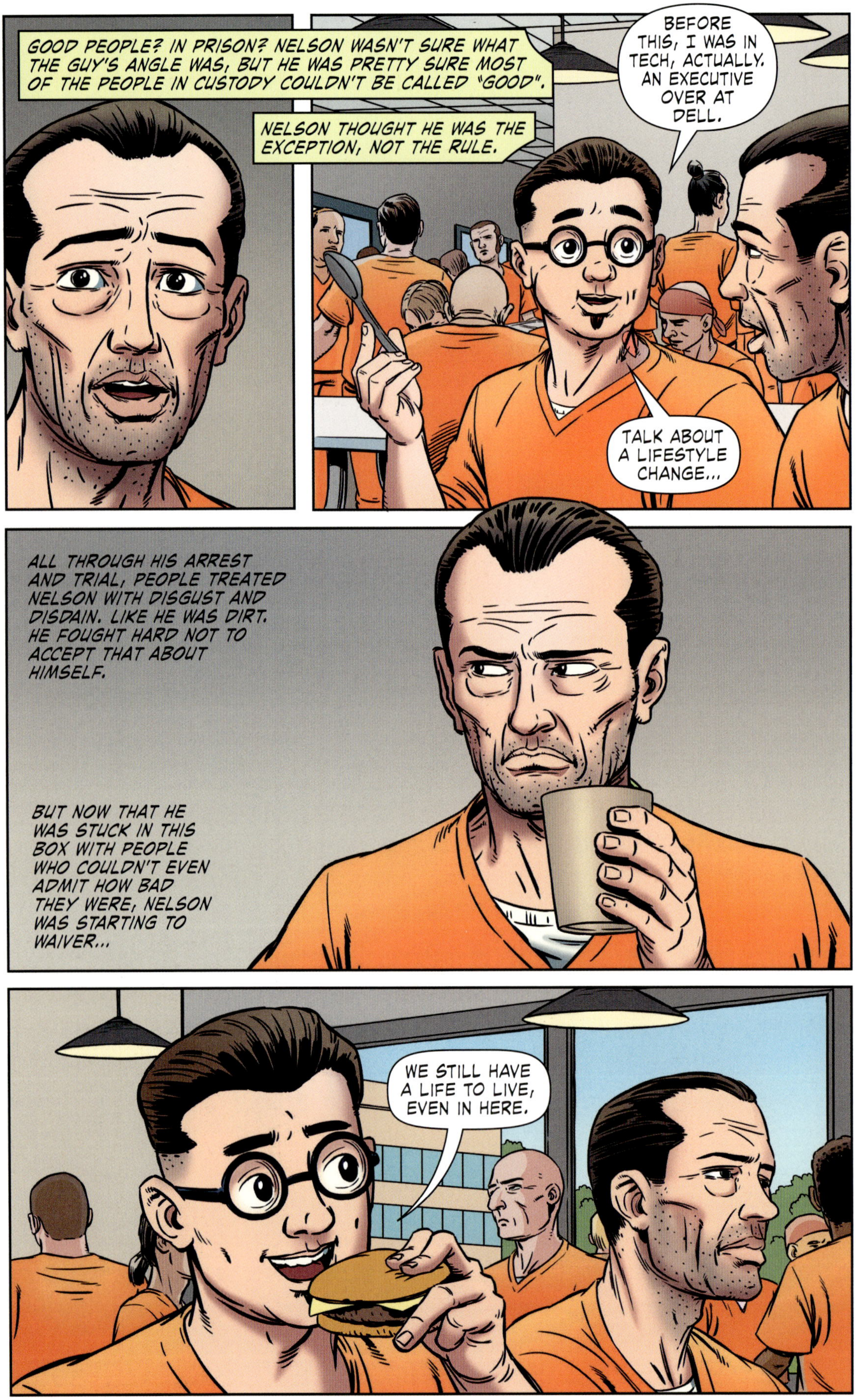
GOOD PEOPLE? IN PRISON? NELSON WASN'T SURE WHAT THE GUY'S ANGLE WAS, BUT HE WAS PRETTY SURE MOST OF THE PEOPLE IN CUSTODY COULDN'T BE CALLED "GOOD".
NELSON THOUGHT HE WAS THE EXCEPTION, NOT THE RULE.
BEFORE THIS, I WAS IN TECH, ACTUALLY. AN EXECUTIVE OVER AT DELL.
TALK ABOUT A LIFESTYLE CHANGE...
ALL THROUGH HIS ARREST AND TRIAL, PEOPLE TREATED NELSON WITH DISGUST AND DISDAIN. LIKE HE WAS DIRT. HE FOUGHT HARD NOT TO ACCEPT THAT ABOUT HIMSELF.
BUT NOW THAT HE WAS STUCK IN THIS BOX WITH PEOPLE WHO COULDN'T EVEN ADMIT HOW BAD THEY WERE, NELSON WAS STARTING TO WAIVER...
WE STILL HAVE A LIFE TO LIVE, EVEN IN HERE.

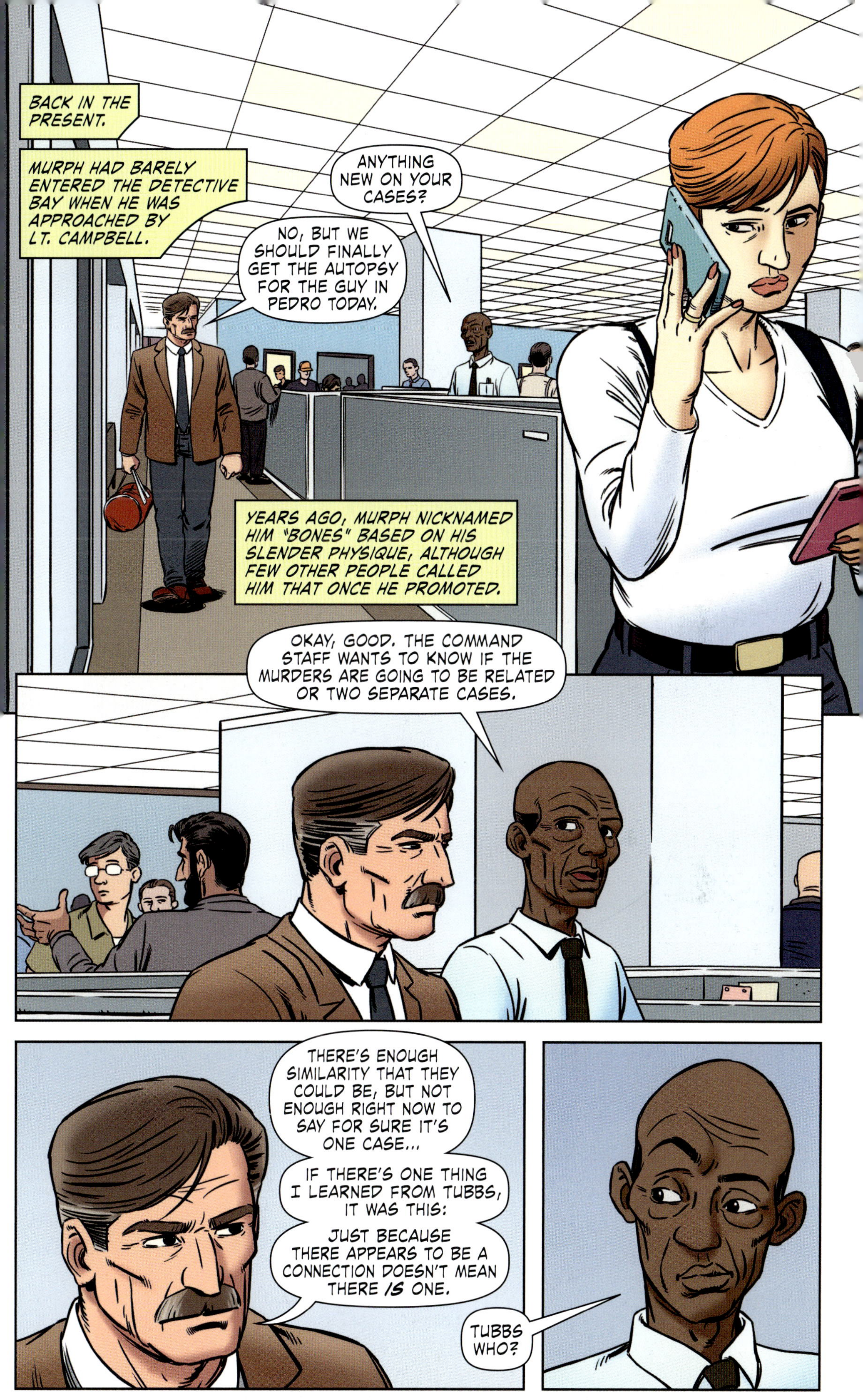
BACK IN THE PRESENT.
MURPH HAD BARELY ENTERED THE DETECTIVE BAY WHEN HE WAS APPROACHED BY LT. CAMPBELL.
ANYTHING NEW ON YOUR CASES?
NO, BUT WE SHOULD FINALLY GET THE AUTOPSY FOR THE GUY IN PEDRO TODAY.
YEARS AGO, MURPH NICKNAMED HIM "BONES" BASED ON HIS SLENDER PHYSIQUE, ALTHOUGH FEW OTHER PEOPLE CALLED HIM THAT ONCE HE PROMOTED.
OKAY, GOOD. THE COMMAND STAFF WANTS TO KNOW IF THE MURDERS ARE GOING TO BE RELATED OR TWO SEPARATE CASES.
THERE'S ENOUGH SIMILARITY THAT THEY COULD BE, BUT NOT ENOUGH RIGHT NOW TO SAY FOR SURE IT'S ONE CASE...
IF THERE'S ONE THING I LEARNED FROM TUBBS, IT WAS THIS:
JUST BECAUSE THERE APPEARS TO BE A CONNECTION DOESN'T MEAN THERE IS ONE.
TUBBS WHO?

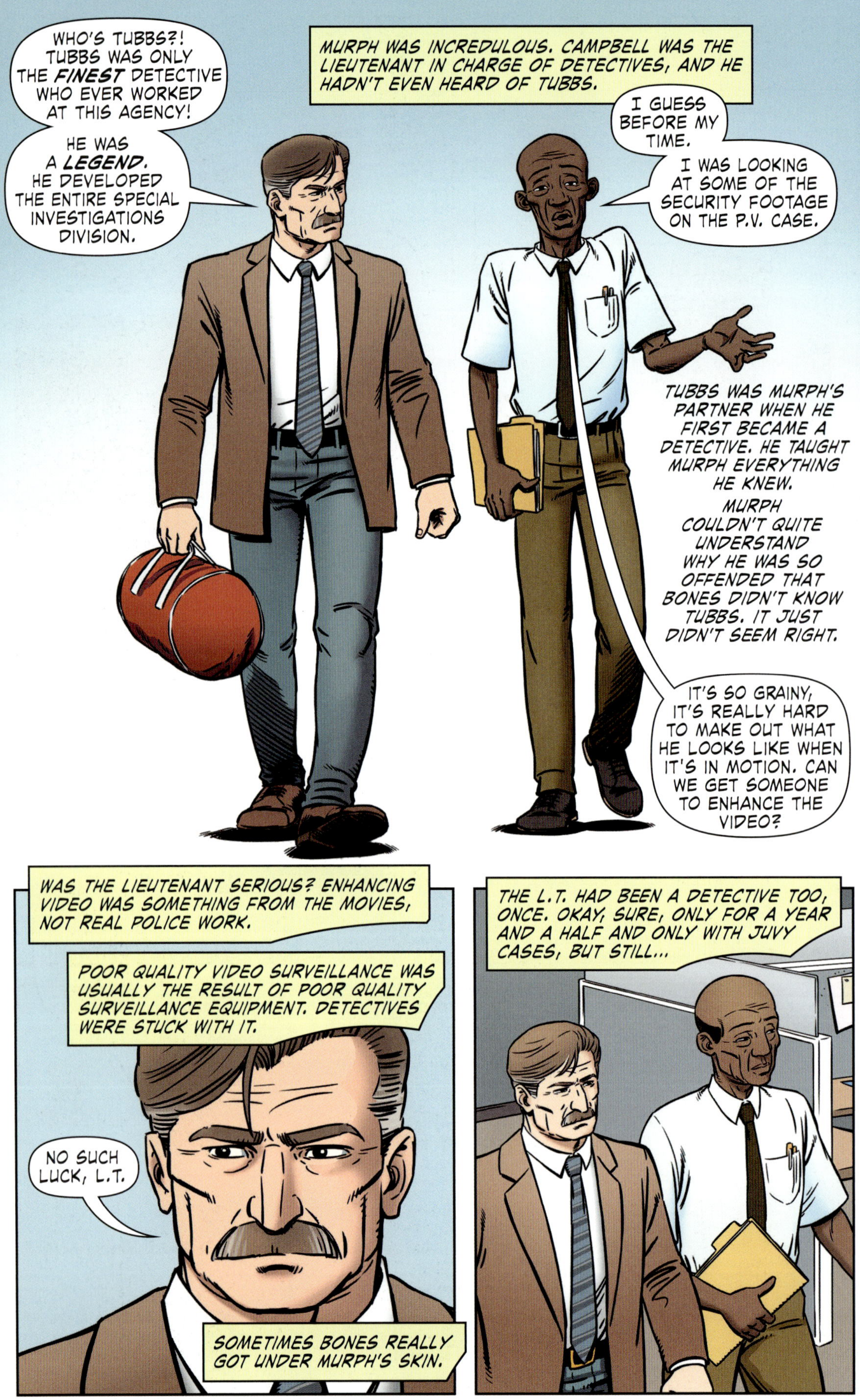
WHO'S TUBBS?! TUBBS WAS ONLY THE FINEST DETECTIVE WHO EVER WORKED AT THIS AGENCY!
HE WAS A LEGEND. HE DEVELOPED THE ENTIRE SPECIAL INVESTIGATIONS DIVISION.
MURPH WAS INCREDULOUS. CAMPBELL WAS THE LIEUTENANT IN CHARGE OF DETECTIVES, AND HE HADN'T EVEN HEARD OF TUBBS.
I GUESS BEFORE MY TIME.
I WAS LOOKING AT SOME OF THE SECURITY FOOTAGE ON THE P.V. CASE.
TUBBS WAS MURPH'S PARTNER WHEN HE FIRST BECAME A DETECTIVE. HE TAUGHT MURPH EVERYTHING HE KNEW.
MURPH COULDN'T QUITE UNDERSTAND WHY HE WAS SO OFFENDED THAT BONES DIDN'T KNOW TUBBS. IT JUST DIDN'T SEEM RIGHT.
IT'S SO GRAINY, IT'S REALLY HARD TO MAKE OUT WHAT HE LOOKS LIKE WHEN IT'S IN MOTION. CAN WE GET SOMEONE TO ENHANCE THE VIDEO?
WAS THE LIEUTENANT SERIOUS? ENHANCING VIDEO WAS SOMETHING FROM THE MOVIES, NOT REAL POLICE WORK.
POOR QUALITY VIDEO SURVEILLANCE WAS USUALLY THE RESULT OF POOR QUALITY SURVEILLANCE EQUIPMENT. DETECTIVES WERE STUCK WITH IT.
NO SUCH LUCK, L.T.
SOMETIMES BONES REALLY GOT UNDER MURPH'S SKIN.
THE L.T. HAD BEEN A DETECTIVE TOO, ONCE. OKAY, SURE, ONLY FOR A YEAR AND A HALF AND ONLY WITH JUVY CASES, BUT STILL...

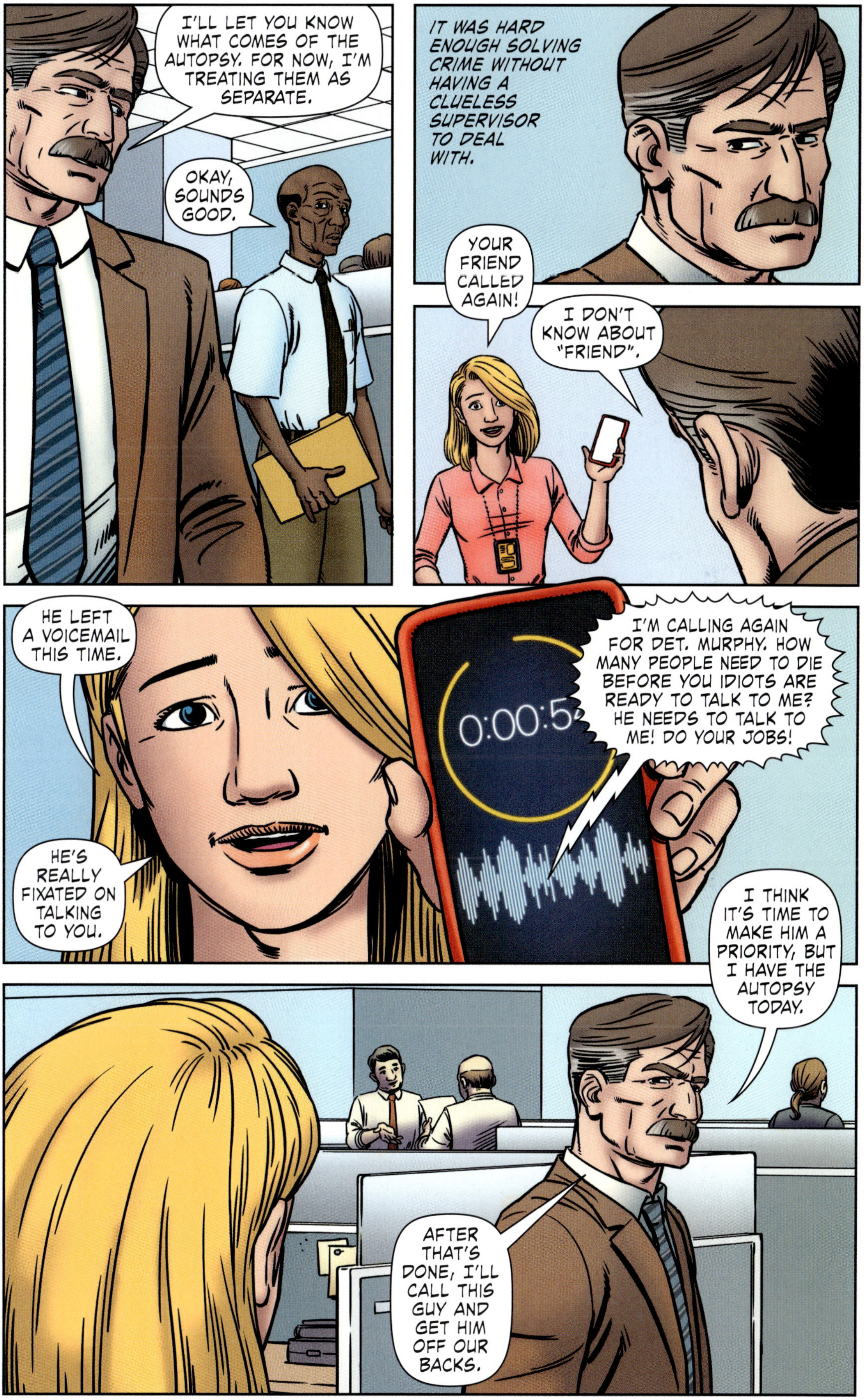
I'LL LET YOU KNOW WHAT COMES OF THE AUTOPSY. FOR NOW, I'M TREATING THEM AS SEPARATE.
OKAY, SOUNDS GOOD.
IT WAS HARD ENOUGH SOLVING CRIME WITHOUT HAVING A CLUELESS SUPERVISOR TO DEAL WITH.
YOUR FRIEND CALLED AGAIN!
I DON'T KNOW ABOUT "FRIEND".
HE LEFT A VOICEMAIL THIS TIME.
I'M CALLING AGAIN FOR DET. MURPHY. HOW MANY PEOPLE NEED TO DIE BEFORE YOU IDIOTS ARE READY TO TALK TO ME? HE NEEDS TO TALK TO ME! DO YOUR JOBS!
HE'S REALLY FIXATED ON TALKING TO YOU.
I THINK IT'S TIME TO MAKE HIM A PRIORITY, BUT I HAVE THE AUTOPSY TODAY.
AFTER THAT'S DONE, I'LL CALL THIS GUY AND GET HIM OFF OUR BACKS.

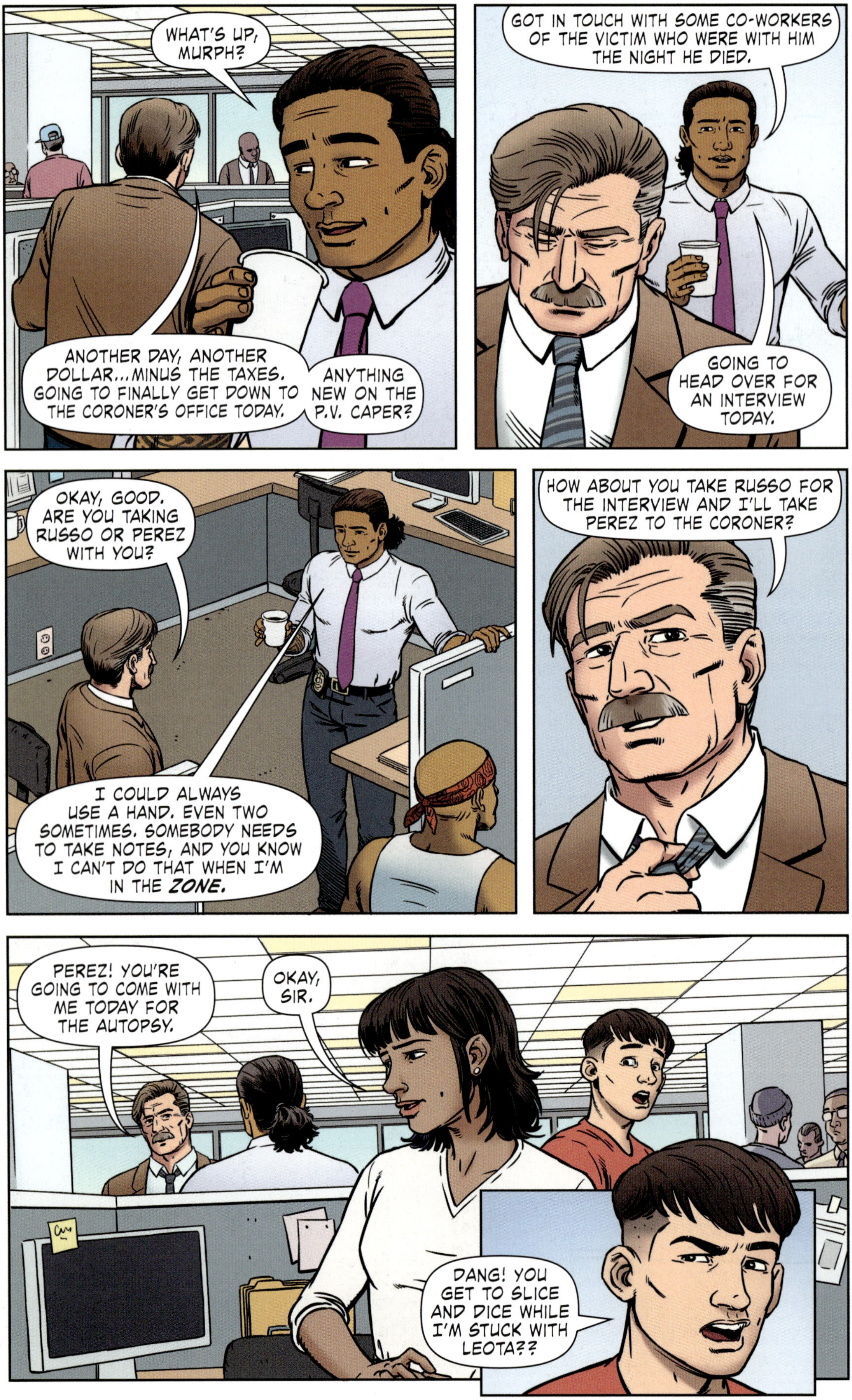
WHAT'S UP, MURPH?
ANOTHER DAY, ANOTHER DOLLAR...MINUS THE TAXES. GOING TO FINALLY GET DOWN TO THE CORONER'S OFFICE TODAY.
ANYTHING NEW ON THE P.V. CAPER?
GOT IN TOUCH WITH SOME CO-WORKERS OF THE VICTIM WHO WERE WITH HIM THE NIGHT HE DIED.
GOING TO HEAD OVER FOR AN INTERVIEW TODAY.
OKAY, GOOD. ARE YOU TAKING RUSSO OR PEREZ WITH YOU?
I COULD ALWAYS USE A HAND. EVEN TWO SOMETIMES. SOMEBODY NEEDS TO TAKE NOTES, AND YOU KNOW I CAN'T DO THAT WHEN I'M IN THE *ZONE.*
HOW ABOUT YOU TAKE RUSSO FOR THE INTERVIEW AND I'LL TAKE PEREZ TO THE CORONER?
PEREZ! YOU'RE GOING TO COME WITH ME TODAY FOR THE AUTOPSY.
OKAY, SIR.
DANG! YOU GET TO SLICE AND DICE WHILE I'M STUCK WITH LEOTA??

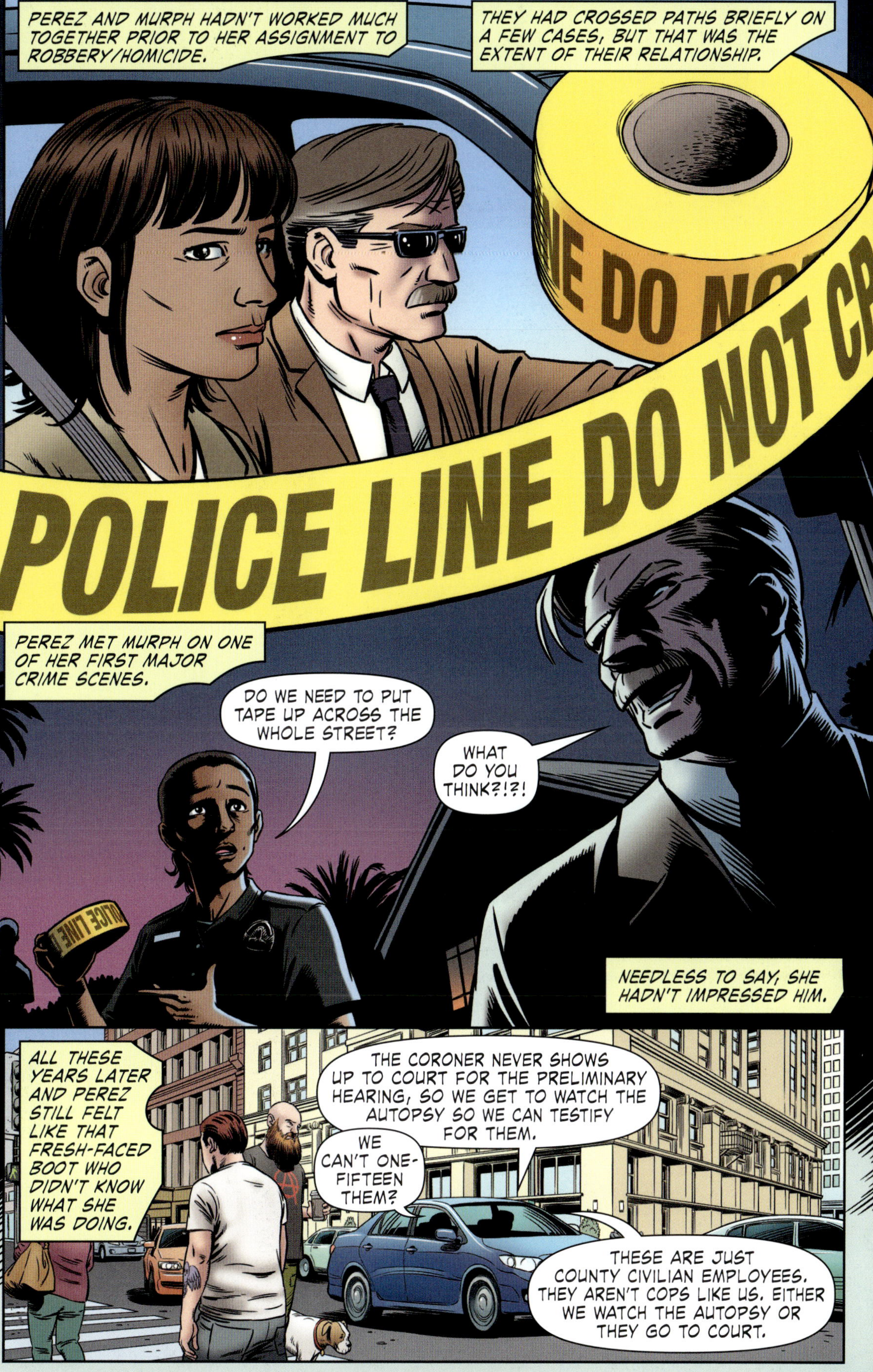
PEREZ AND MURPH HADN'T WORKED MUCH TOGETHER PRIOR TO HER ASSIGNMENT TO ROBBERY/HOMICIDE.
THEY HAD CROSSED PATHS BRIEFLY ON A FEW CASES, BUT THAT WAS THE EXTENT OF THEIR RELATIONSHIP.
POLICE LINE DO NOT CR
PEREZ MET MURPH ON ONE OF HER FIRST MAJOR CRIME SCENES.
DO WE NEED TO PUT TAPE UP ACROSS THE WHOLE STREET?
WHAT DO YOU THINK?!?!
NEEDLESS TO SAY, SHE HADN'T IMPRESSED HIM.
ALL THESE YEARS LATER AND PEREZ STILL FELT LIKE THAT FRESH-FACED BOOT WHO DIDN'T KNOW WHAT SHE WAS DOING.
THE CORONER NEVER SHOWS UP TO COURT FOR THE PRELIMINARY HEARING, SO WE GET TO WATCH THE AUTOPSY SO WE CAN TESTIFY FOR THEM.
WE CAN'T ONE-FIFTEEN THEM?
THESE ARE JUST COUNTY CIVILIAN EMPLOYEES. THEY AREN'T COPS LIKE US. EITHER WE WATCH THE AUTOPSY OR THEY GO TO COURT.

"THE CASELOAD IS DEFINITELY AN ADJUSTMENT. I USED TO HAVE MAYBE TWO, THREE CASES AT A TIME, AND I COULD PICK AND CHOOSE WHAT NEW CASES TO WORK..."

"IT SEEMS LIKE YOU GUYS ALL HAVE DOZENS OF CASES PENDING AT ONCE."

"CASE MANAGEMENT IS A BIG PART OF THE JOB. GOT TO KNOW WHAT CASES ARE WORTH YOUR TIME AND WHICH ONES TO LET GO. YOU CAN'T PUT ONE HUNDRED PERCENT INTO EACH AND EVERY CASE."

"IT'S NICE TO HAVE A REGULAR SCHEDULE AGAIN AT LEAST. I DON'T KNOW HOW ANYONE WORKS SURVEILLANCE WITH KIDS."

"TELL ME ABOUT IT. HARD ENOUGH BEING UP ALL NIGHT WITH AN INFANT WITHOUT HAVING TO DEAL WITH MIDDLE OF THE NIGHT CALLOUTS. ALTHOUGH WE'LL HAVE A FEW OF THOSE WORKING HOMICIDE TOO."

"FOR THE MOST PART, WE'RE JUST GOING TO LET THE CORONER DO THEIR THING. BUT TAKE NOTES ON ANYTHING YOU THINK YOU'LL NEED TO REMEMBER."

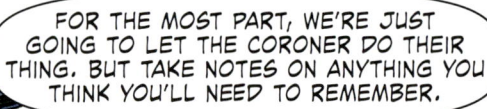

"I GUARANTEE YOU'VE NEVER SMELLED ANYTHING LIKE THE UNIQUE MIXTURE OF DEATH AND CLEANING CHEMICALS THAT YOU ARE ABOUT TO EXPERIENCE."

"WONDERFUL..."

"YOU MAY NOTICE CORONERS CAN BE A LITTLE... DIFFERENT."

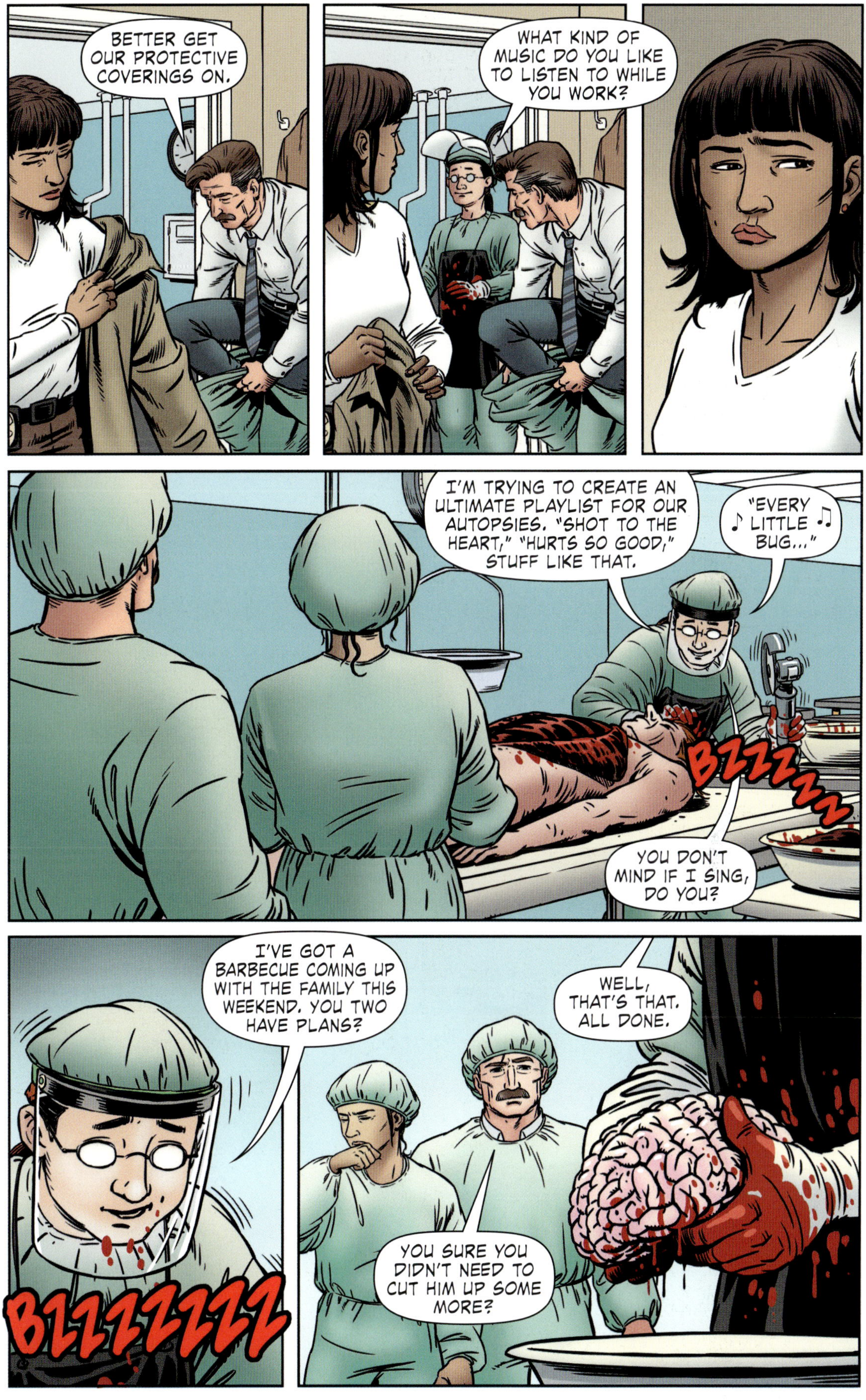
BETTER GET OUR PROTECTIVE COVERINGS ON.
WHAT KIND OF MUSIC DO YOU LIKE TO LISTEN TO WHILE YOU WORK?
I'M TRYING TO CREATE AN ULTIMATE PLAYLIST FOR OUR AUTOPSIES. "SHOT TO THE HEART," "HURTS SO GOOD," STUFF LIKE THAT.
"EVERY LITTLE BUG..."
BZZZZZ
YOU DON'T MIND IF I SING, DO YOU?
I'VE GOT A BARBECUE COMING UP WITH THE FAMILY THIS WEEKEND. YOU TWO HAVE PLANS?
BZZZZZZZ
WELL, THAT'S THAT. ALL DONE.
YOU SURE YOU DIDN'T NEED TO CUT HIM UP SOME MORE?

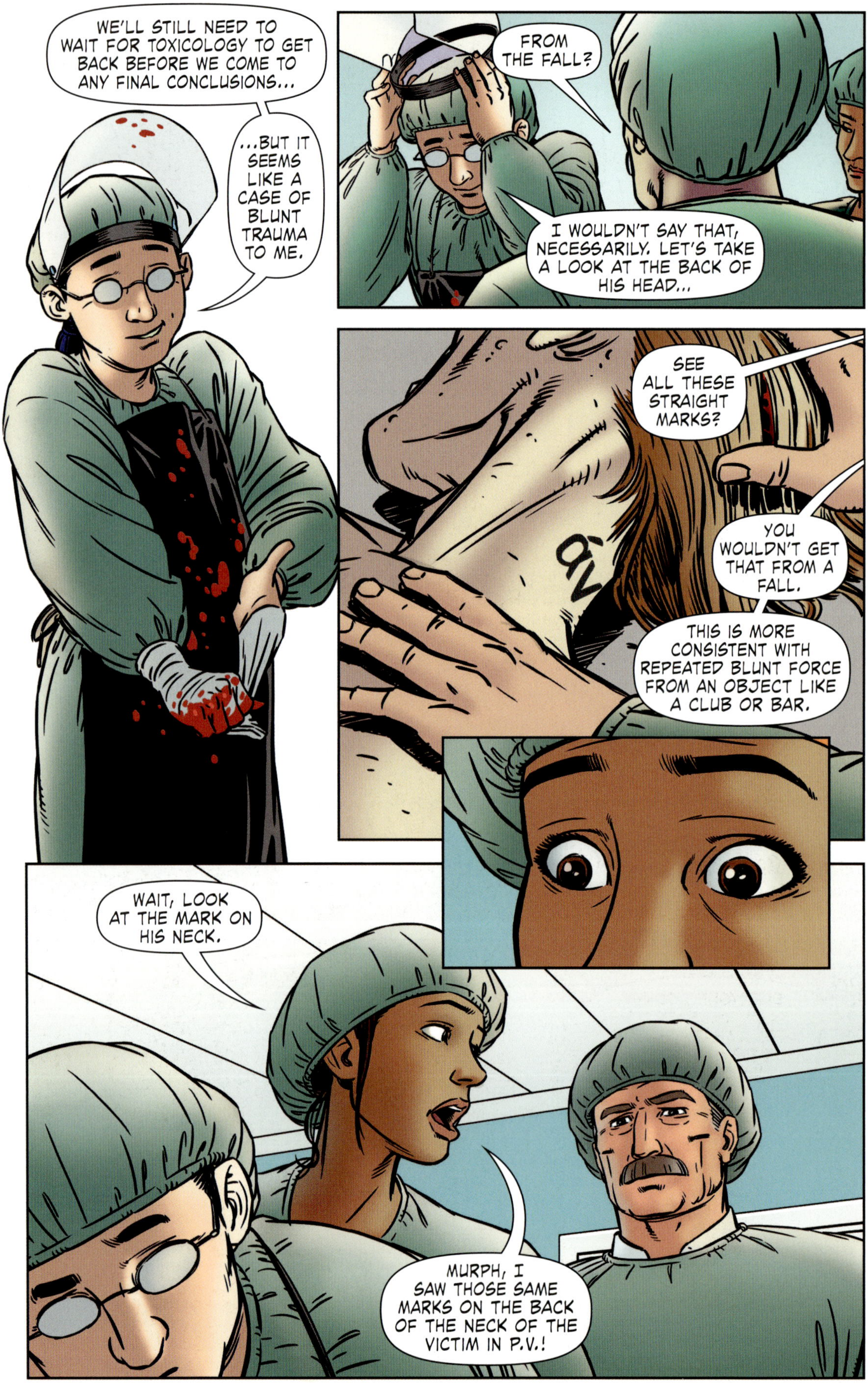
WE'LL STILL NEED TO WAIT FOR TOXICOLOGY TO GET BACK BEFORE WE COME TO ANY FINAL CONCLUSIONS...
...BUT IT SEEMS LIKE A CASE OF BLUNT TRAUMA TO ME.
FROM THE FALL?
I WOULDN'T SAY THAT, NECESSARILY. LET'S TAKE A LOOK AT THE BACK OF HIS HEAD...
SEE ALL THESE STRAIGHT MARKS?
YOU WOULDN'T GET THAT FROM A FALL.
THIS IS MORE CONSISTENT WITH REPEATED BLUNT FORCE FROM AN OBJECT LIKE A CLUB OR BAR.
WAIT, LOOK AT THE MARK ON HIS NECK.
MURPH, I SAW THOSE SAME MARKS ON THE BACK OF THE NECK OF THE VICTIM IN P.V.!

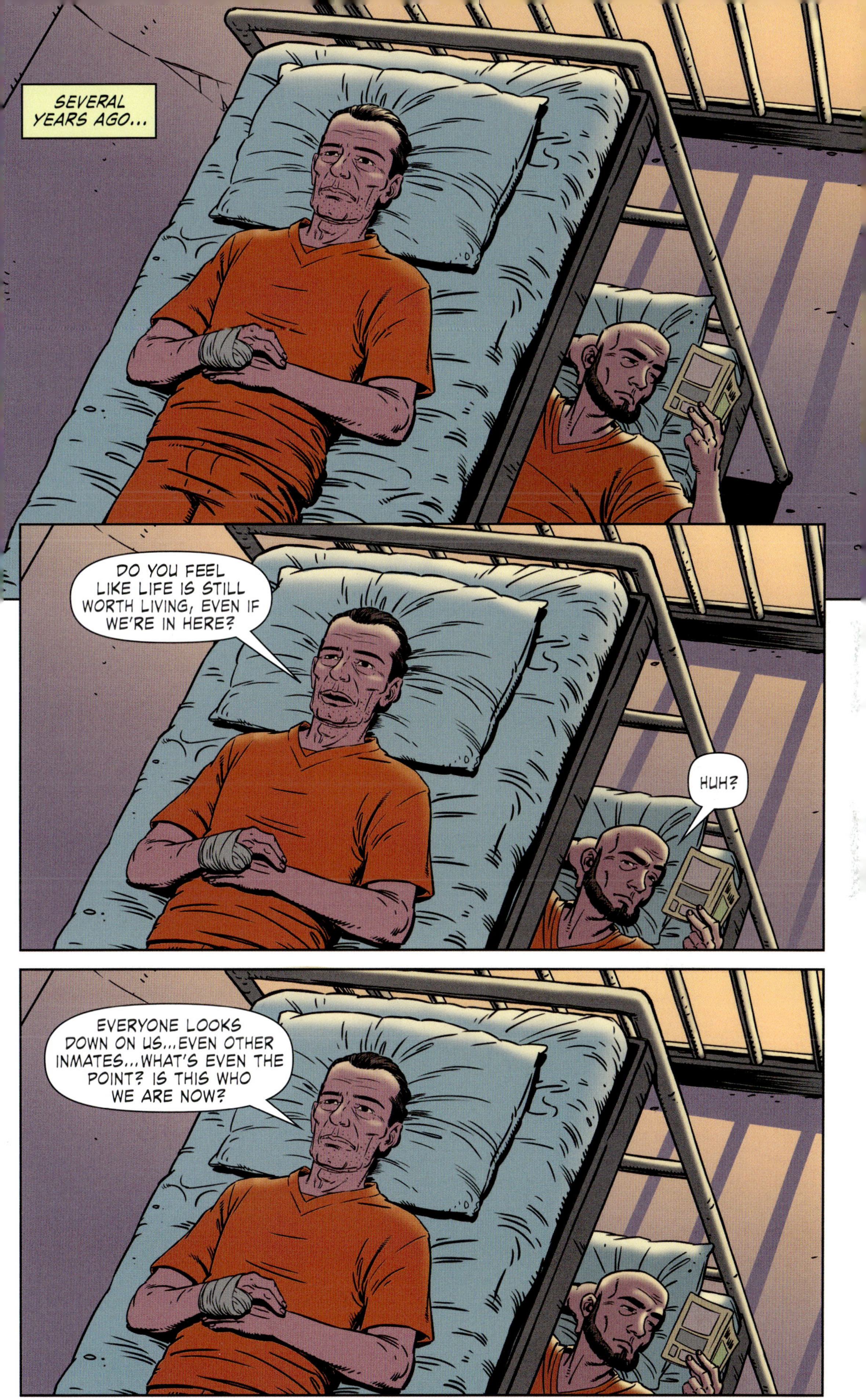
SEVERAL YEARS AGO...
DO YOU FEEL LIKE LIFE IS STILL WORTH LIVING, EVEN IF WE'RE IN HERE?
HUH?
EVERYONE LOOKS DOWN ON US...EVEN OTHER INMATES...WHAT'S EVEN THE POINT? IS THIS WHO WE ARE NOW?

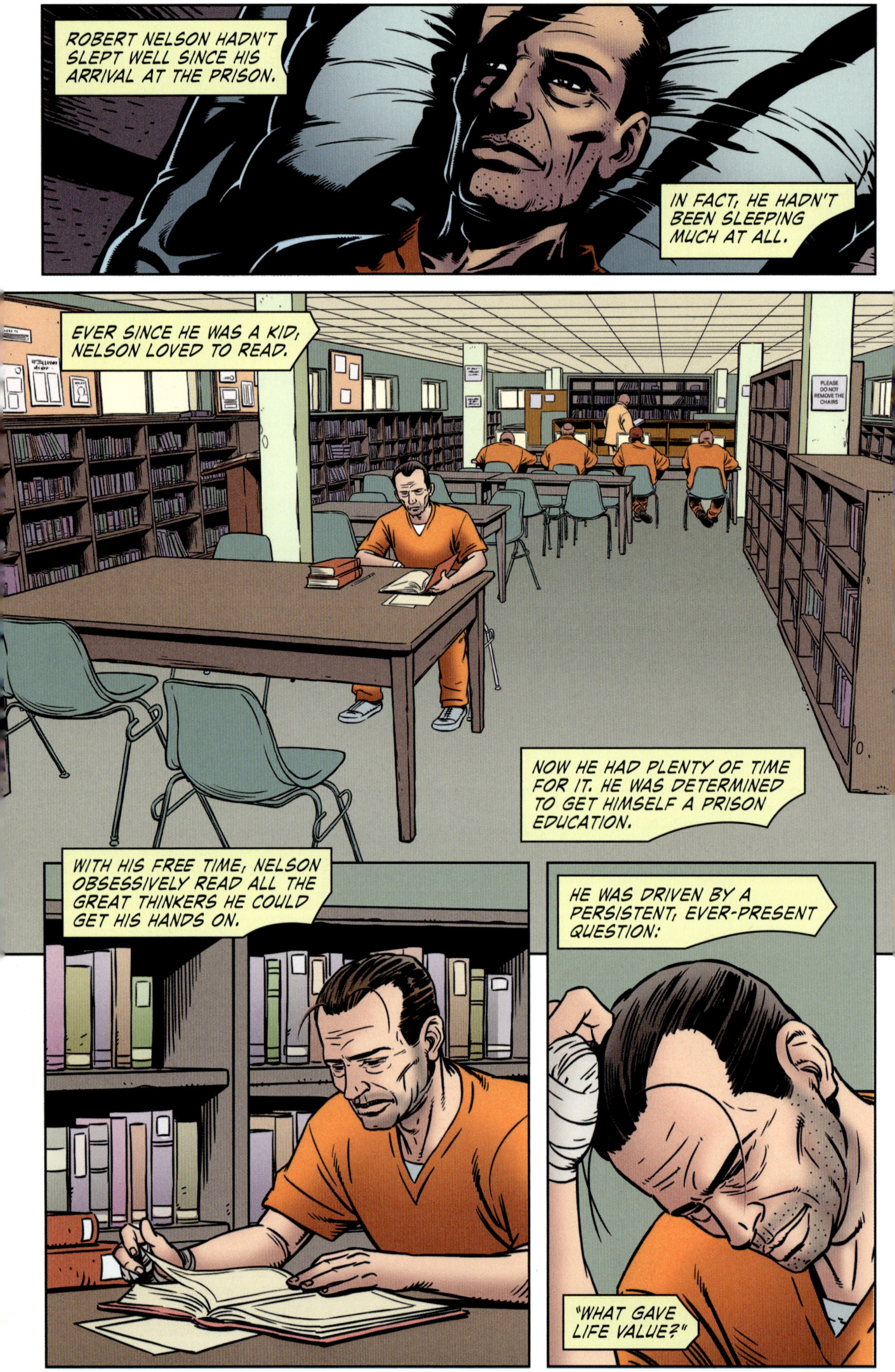
ROBERT NELSON HADN'T SLEPT WELL SINCE HIS ARRIVAL AT THE PRISON.
IN FACT, HE HADN'T BEEN SLEEPING MUCH AT ALL.
EVER SINCE HE WAS A KID, NELSON LOVED TO READ.
PLEASE DO NOT REMOVE THE CHAIRS
NOW HE HAD PLENTY OF TIME FOR IT. HE WAS DETERMINED TO GET HIMSELF A PRISON EDUCATION.
WITH HIS FREE TIME, NELSON OBSESSIVELY READ ALL THE GREAT THINKERS HE COULD GET HIS HANDS ON.
HE WAS DRIVEN BY A PERSISTENT, EVER-PRESENT QUESTION:
"WHAT GAVE LIFE VALUE?"

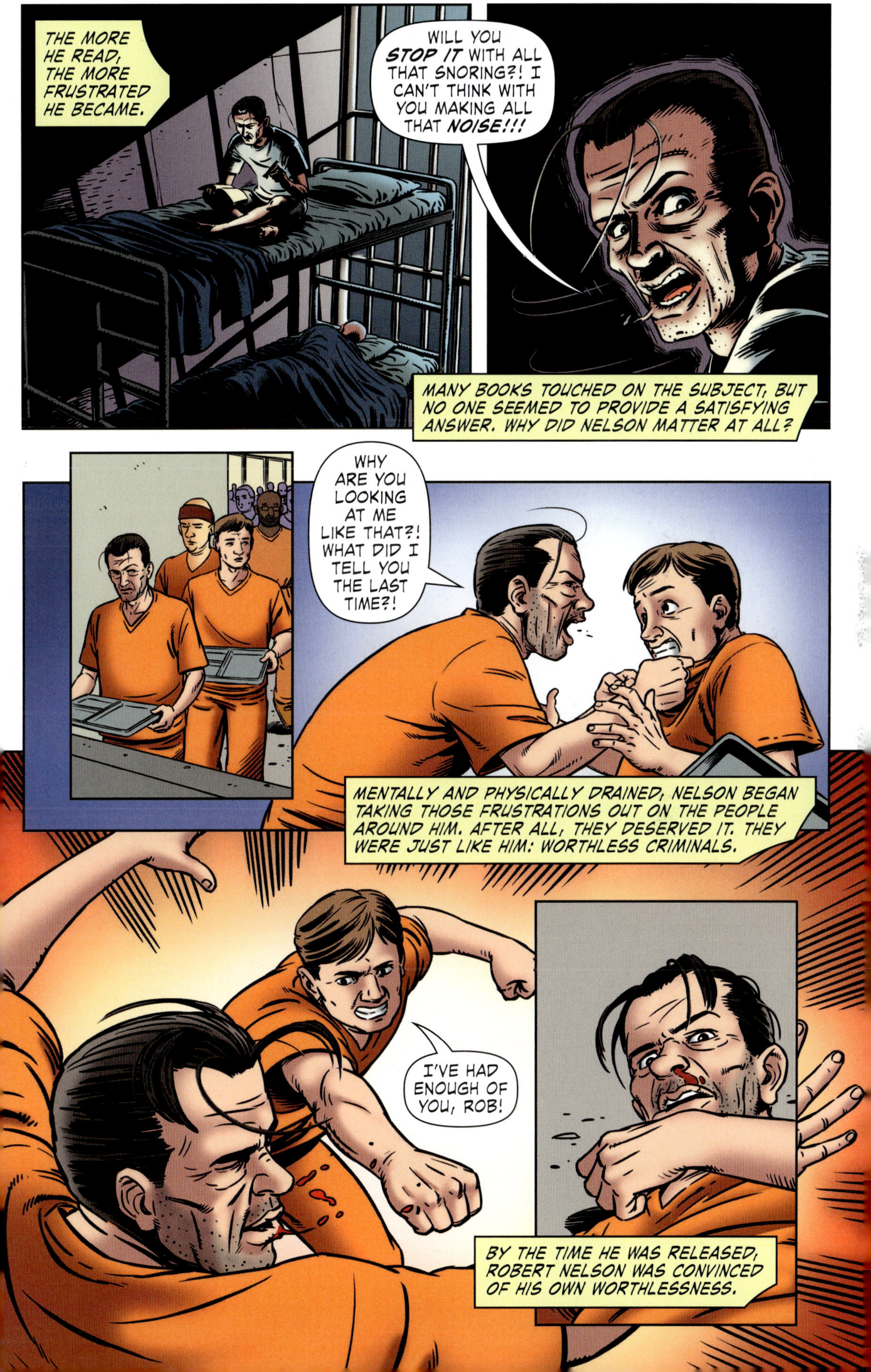
THE MORE HE READ, THE MORE FRUSTRATED HE BECAME.
WILL YOU STOP IT WITH ALL THAT SNORING?! I CAN'T THINK WITH YOU MAKING ALL THAT NOISE!!!
MANY BOOKS TOUCHED ON THE SUBJECT, BUT NO ONE SEEMED TO PROVIDE A SATISFYING ANSWER. WHY DID NELSON MATTER AT ALL?
WHY ARE YOU LOOKING AT ME LIKE THAT?! WHAT DID I TELL YOU THE LAST TIME?!
MENTALLY AND PHYSICALLY DRAINED, NELSON BEGAN TAKING THOSE FRUSTRATIONS OUT ON THE PEOPLE AROUND HIM. AFTER ALL, THEY DESERVED IT. THEY WERE JUST LIKE HIM: WORTHLESS CRIMINALS.
I'VE HAD ENOUGH OF YOU, ROB!
BY THE TIME HE WAS RELEASED, ROBERT NELSON WAS CONVINCED OF HIS OWN WORTHLESSNESS.

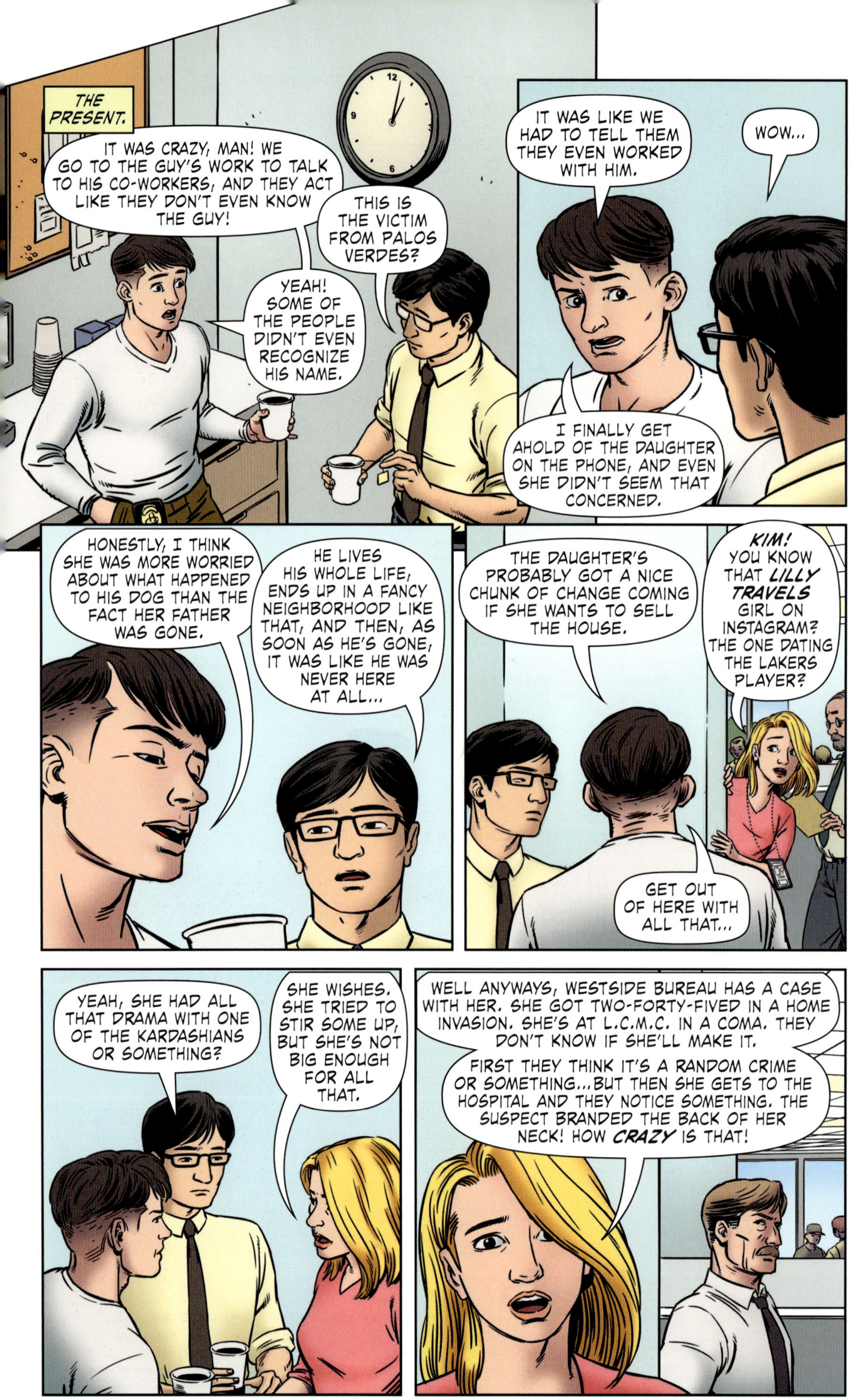
THE PRESENT.
IT WAS CRAZY, MAN! WE GO TO THE GUY'S WORK TO TALK TO HIS CO-WORKERS, AND THEY ACT LIKE THEY DON'T EVEN KNOW THE GUY!
THIS IS THE VICTIM FROM PALOS VERDES?
YEAH! SOME OF THE PEOPLE DIDN'T EVEN RECOGNIZE HIS NAME.
IT WAS LIKE WE HAD TO TELL THEM THEY EVEN WORKED WITH HIM.
WOW...
I FINALLY GET AHOLD OF THE DAUGHTER ON THE PHONE, AND EVEN SHE DIDN'T SEEM THAT CONCERNED.
HONESTLY, I THINK SHE WAS MORE WORRIED ABOUT WHAT HAPPENED TO HIS DOG THAN THE FACT HER FATHER WAS GONE.
HE LIVES HIS WHOLE LIFE, ENDS UP IN A FANCY NEIGHBORHOOD LIKE THAT, AND THEN, AS SOON AS HE'S GONE, IT WAS LIKE HE WAS NEVER HERE AT ALL...
THE DAUGHTER'S PROBABLY GOT A NICE CHUNK OF CHANGE COMING IF SHE WANTS TO SELL THE HOUSE.
KIM! YOU KNOW THAT LILLY TRAVELS GIRL ON INSTAGRAM? THE ONE DATING THE LAKERS PLAYER?
GET OUT OF HERE WITH ALL THAT...
YEAH, SHE HAD ALL THAT DRAMA WITH ONE OF THE KARDASHIANS OR SOMETHING?
SHE WISHES. SHE TRIED TO STIR SOME UP, BUT SHE'S NOT BIG ENOUGH FOR ALL THAT.
WELL ANYWAYS, WESTSIDE BUREAU HAS A CASE WITH HER. SHE GOT TWO-FORTY-FIVED IN A HOME INVASION. SHE'S AT L.C.M.C. IN A COMA. THEY DON'T KNOW IF SHE'LL MAKE IT.
FIRST THEY THINK IT'S A RANDOM CRIME OR SOMETHING...BUT THEN SHE GETS TO THE HOSPITAL AND THEY NOTICE SOMETHING. THE SUSPECT BRANDED THE BACK OF HER NECK! HOW CRAZY IS THAT!

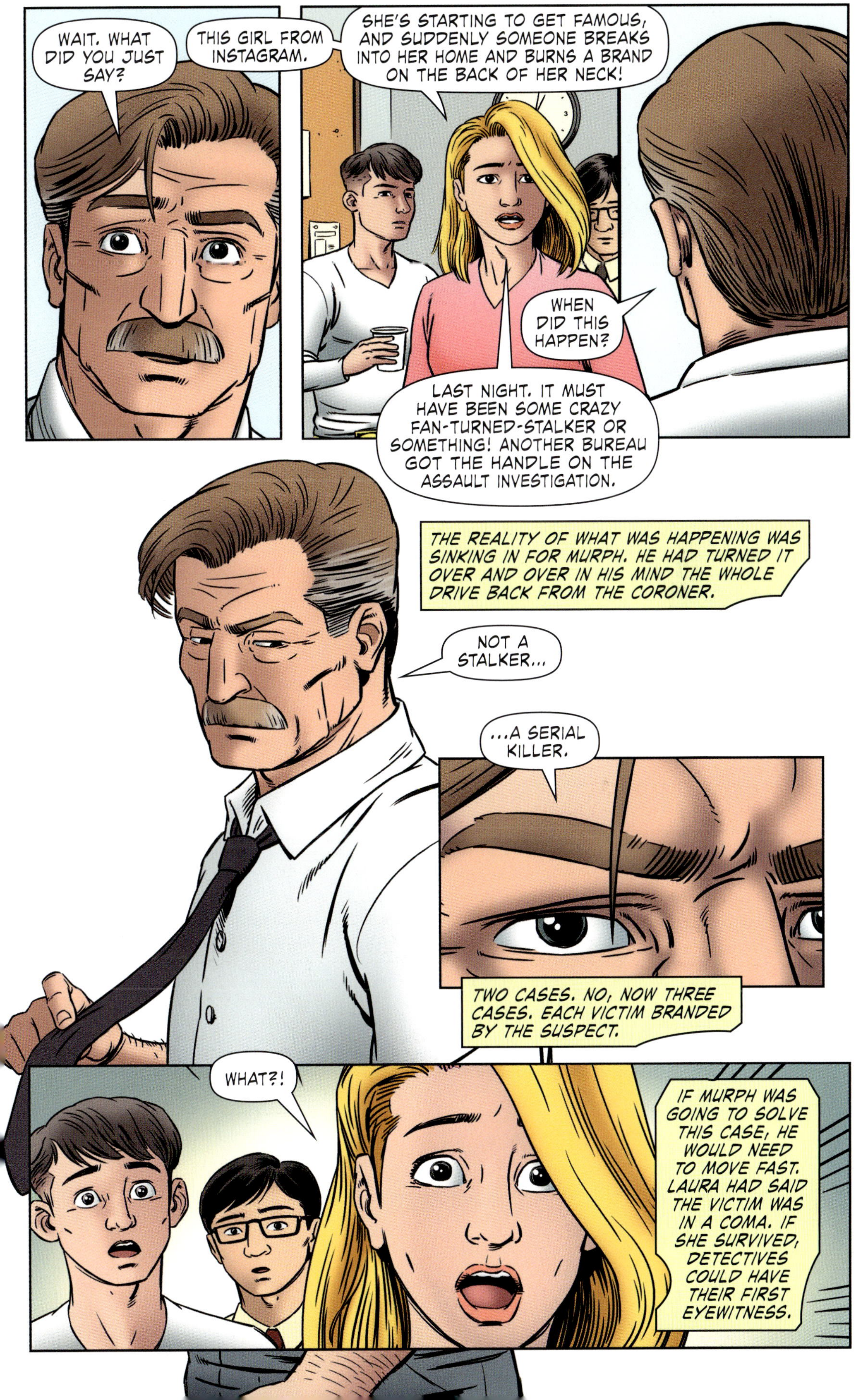
WAIT. WHAT DID YOU JUST SAY?
THIS GIRL FROM INSTAGRAM.
SHE'S STARTING TO GET FAMOUS, AND SUDDENLY SOMEONE BREAKS INTO HER HOME AND BURNS A BRAND ON THE BACK OF HER NECK!
WHEN DID THIS HAPPEN?
LAST NIGHT. IT MUST HAVE BEEN SOME CRAZY FAN-TURNED-STALKER OR SOMETHING! ANOTHER BUREAU GOT THE HANDLE ON THE ASSAULT INVESTIGATION.
THE REALITY OF WHAT WAS HAPPENING WAS SINKING IN FOR MURPH. HE HAD TURNED IT OVER AND OVER IN HIS MIND THE WHOLE DRIVE BACK FROM THE CORONER.
NOT A STALKER...
...A SERIAL KILLER.
TWO CASES. NO, NOW THREE CASES. EACH VICTIM BRANDED BY THE SUSPECT.
WHAT?!
IF MURPH WAS GOING TO SOLVE THIS CASE, HE WOULD NEED TO MOVE FAST. LAURA HAD SAID THE VICTIM WAS IN A COMA. IF SHE SURVIVED, DETECTIVES COULD HAVE THEIR FIRST EYEWITNESS.

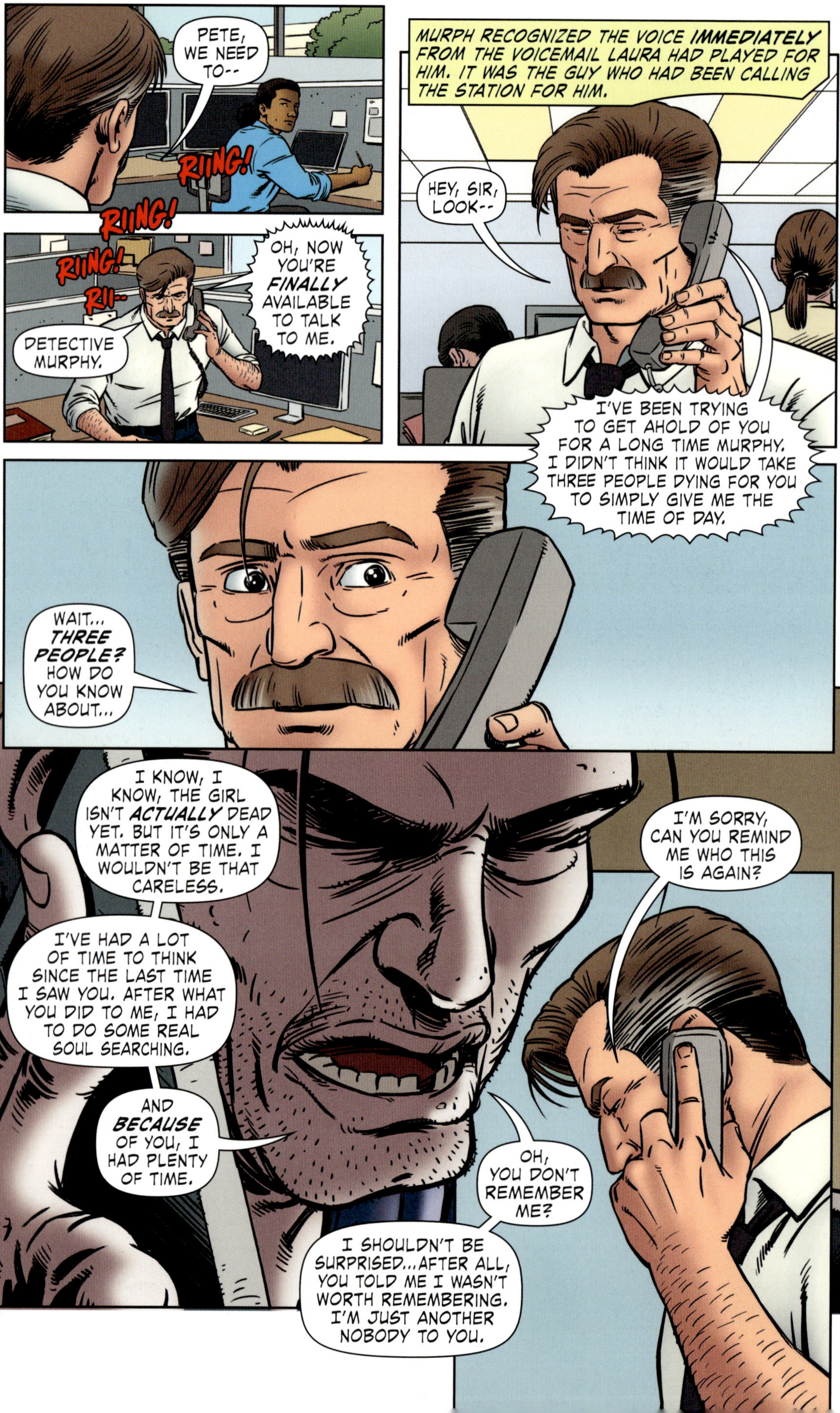
PETE, WE NEED TO--
RIING!
RIING!
RIING!
RII--
DETECTIVE MURPHY.
OH, NOW YOU'RE FINALLY AVAILABLE TO TALK TO ME.
MURPH RECOGNIZED THE VOICE IMMEDIATELY FROM THE VOICEMAIL LAURA HAD PLAYED FOR HIM. IT WAS THE GUY WHO HAD BEEN CALLING THE STATION FOR HIM.
HEY, SIR, LOOK--
I'VE BEEN TRYING TO GET AHOLD OF YOU FOR A LONG TIME MURPHY. I DIDN'T THINK IT WOULD TAKE THREE PEOPLE DYING FOR YOU TO SIMPLY GIVE ME THE TIME OF DAY.
WAIT... THREE PEOPLE? HOW DO YOU KNOW ABOUT...
I KNOW, I KNOW, THE GIRL ISN'T ACTUALLY DEAD YET. BUT IT'S ONLY A MATTER OF TIME. I WOULDN'T BE THAT CARELESS.
I'VE HAD A LOT OF TIME TO THINK SINCE THE LAST TIME I SAW YOU. AFTER WHAT YOU DID TO ME, I HAD TO DO SOME REAL SOUL SEARCHING.
AND BECAUSE OF YOU, I HAD PLENTY OF TIME.
I'M SORRY, CAN YOU REMIND ME WHO THIS IS AGAIN?
OH, YOU DON'T REMEMBER ME?
I SHOULDN'T BE SURPRISED...AFTER ALL, YOU TOLD ME I WASN'T WORTH REMEMBERING. I'M JUST ANOTHER NOBODY TO YOU.

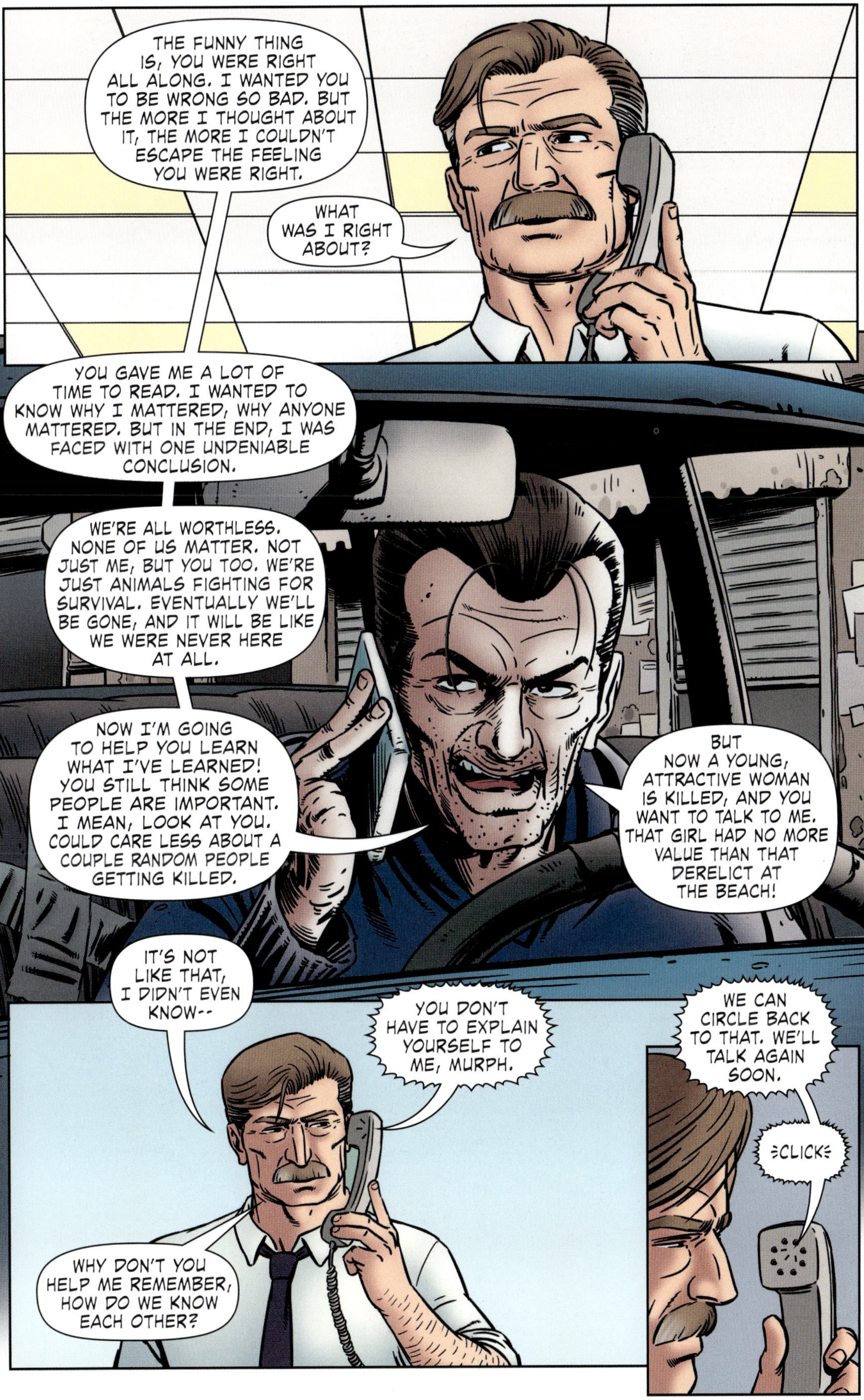
THE FUNNY THING IS, YOU WERE RIGHT ALL ALONG. I WANTED YOU TO BE WRONG SO BAD. BUT THE MORE I THOUGHT ABOUT IT, THE MORE I COULDN'T ESCAPE THE FEELING YOU WERE RIGHT.
WHAT WAS I RIGHT ABOUT?
YOU GAVE ME A LOT OF TIME TO READ. I WANTED TO KNOW WHY I MATTERED, WHY ANYONE MATTERED. BUT IN THE END, I WAS FACED WITH ONE UNDENIABLE CONCLUSION.
WE'RE ALL WORTHLESS. NONE OF US MATTER. NOT JUST ME, BUT YOU TOO. WE'RE JUST ANIMALS FIGHTING FOR SURVIVAL. EVENTUALLY WE'LL BE GONE, AND IT WILL BE LIKE WE WERE NEVER HERE AT ALL.
NOW I'M GOING TO HELP YOU LEARN WHAT I'VE LEARNED! YOU STILL THINK SOME PEOPLE ARE IMPORTANT. I MEAN, LOOK AT YOU. COULD CARE LESS ABOUT A COUPLE RANDOM PEOPLE GETTING KILLED.
BUT NOW A YOUNG, ATTRACTIVE WOMAN IS KILLED, AND YOU WANT TO TALK TO ME. THAT GIRL HAD NO MORE VALUE THAN THAT DERELICT AT THE BEACH!
IT'S NOT LIKE THAT, I DIDN'T EVEN KNOW--
YOU DON'T HAVE TO EXPLAIN YOURSELF TO ME, MURPH.
WHY DON'T YOU HELP ME REMEMBER, HOW DO WE KNOW EACH OTHER?
WE CAN CIRCLE BACK TO THAT. WE'LL TALK AGAIN SOON.
CLICK

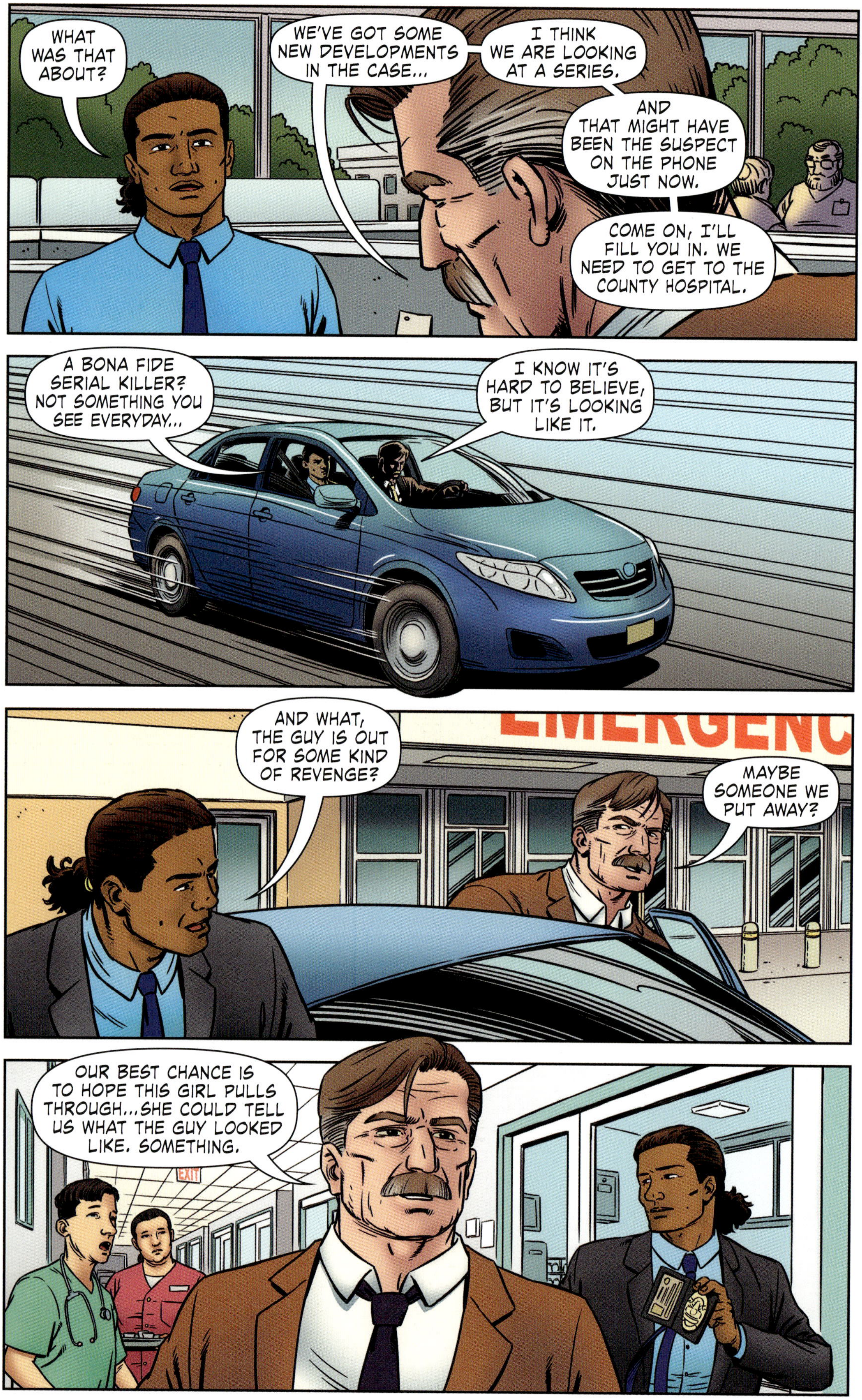
WHAT WAS THAT ABOUT?
WE'VE GOT SOME NEW DEVELOPMENTS IN THE CASE...
I THINK WE ARE LOOKING AT A SERIES.
AND THAT MIGHT HAVE BEEN THE SUSPECT ON THE PHONE JUST NOW.
COME ON, I'LL FILL YOU IN. WE NEED TO GET TO THE COUNTY HOSPITAL.
A BONA FIDE SERIAL KILLER? NOT SOMETHING YOU SEE EVERYDAY...
I KNOW IT'S HARD TO BELIEVE, BUT IT'S LOOKING LIKE IT.
EMERGENC
AND WHAT, THE GUY IS OUT FOR SOME KIND OF REVENGE?
MAYBE SOMEONE WE PUT AWAY?
OUR BEST CHANCE IS TO HOPE THIS GIRL PULLS THROUGH...SHE COULD TELL US WHAT THE GUY LOOKED LIKE. SOMETHING.
EXIT

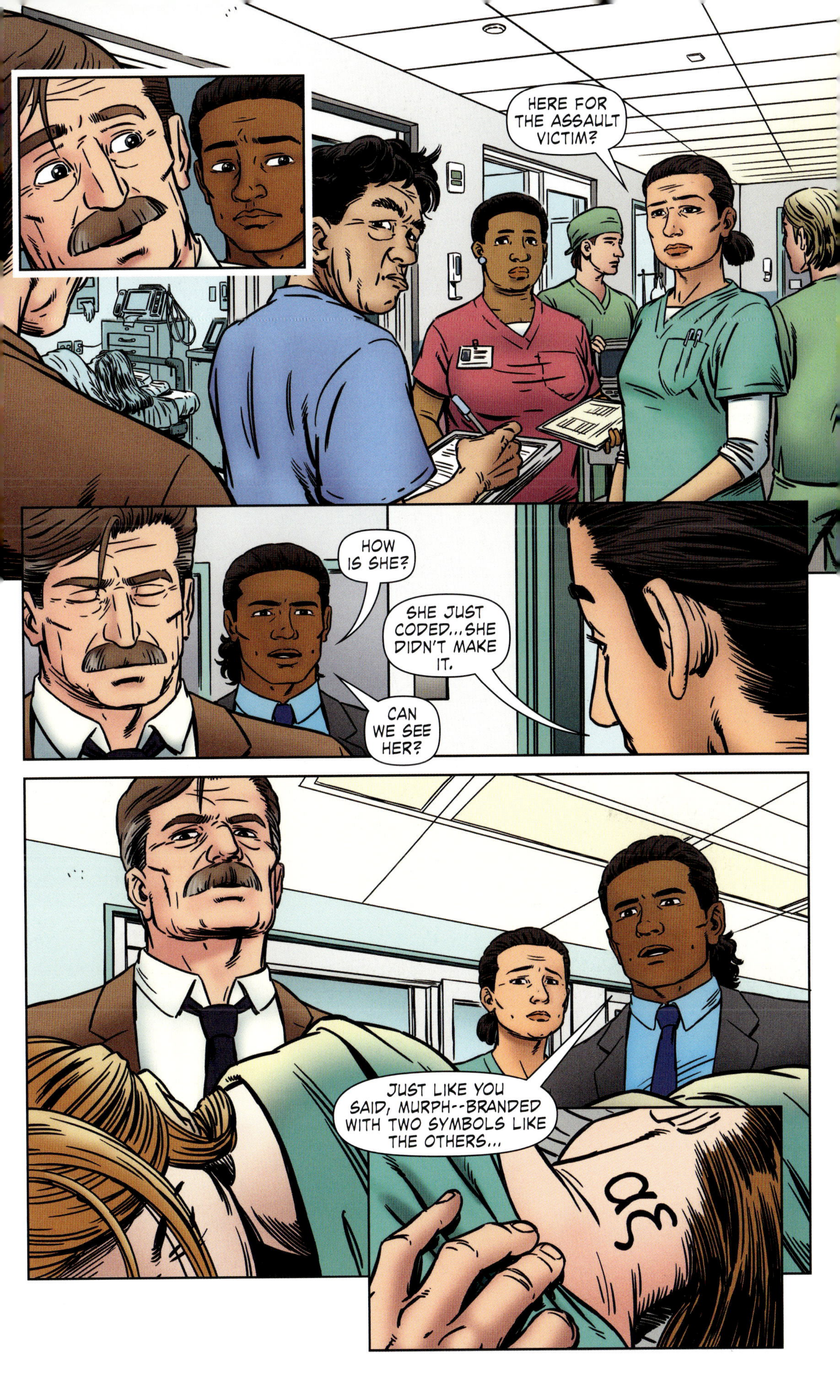
HERE FOR THE ASSAULT VICTIM?
HOW IS SHE?
SHE JUST CODED...SHE DIDN'T MAKE IT.
CAN WE SEE HER?
JUST LIKE YOU SAID, MURPH--BRANDED WITH TWO SYMBOLS LIKE THE OTHERS...

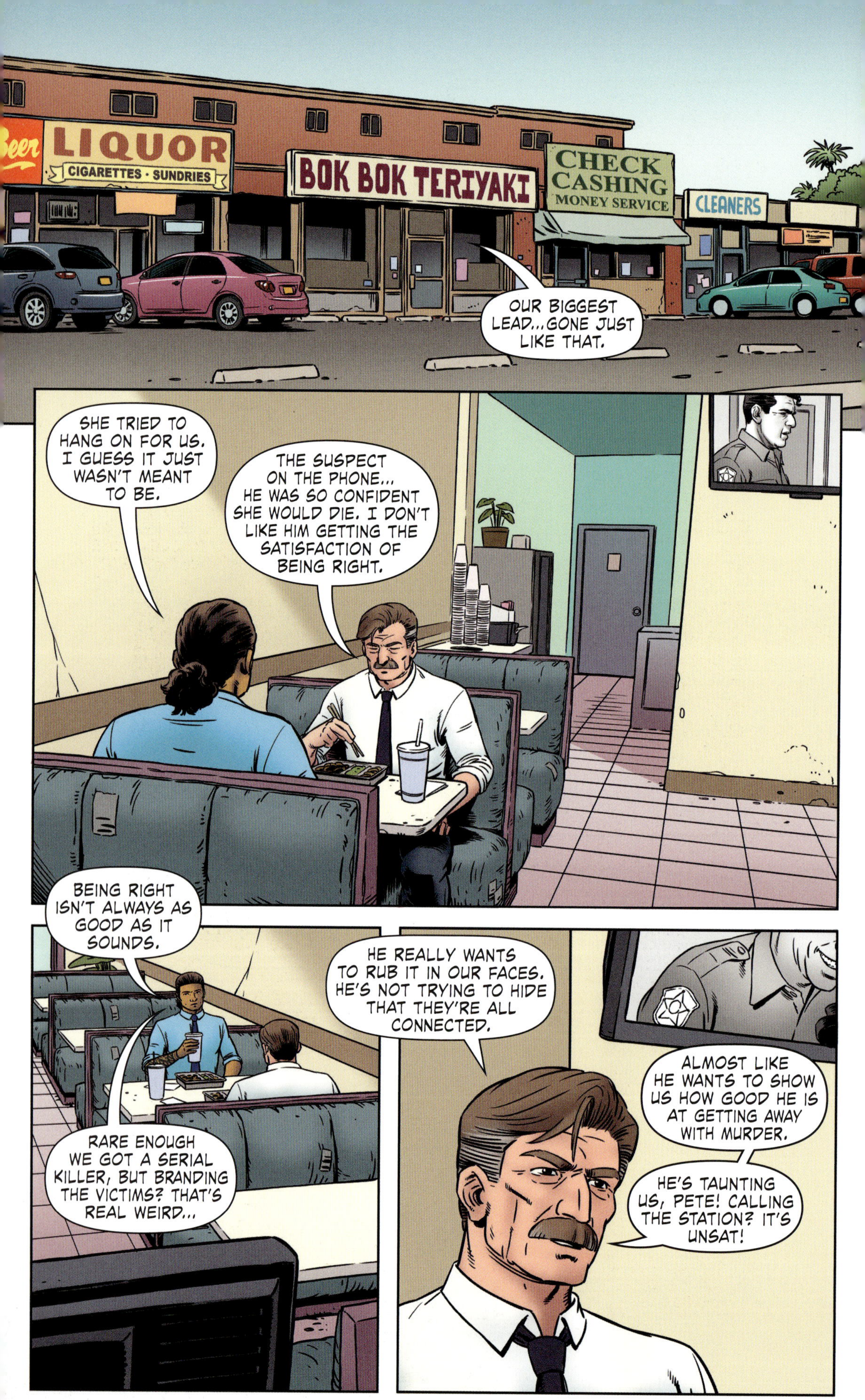
Beer
LIQUOR
CIGARETTES · SUNDRIES
BOK BOK TERIYAKI
CHECK CASHING
MONEY SERVICE
CLEANERS
OUR BIGGEST LEAD...GONE JUST LIKE THAT.
SHE TRIED TO HANG ON FOR US. I GUESS IT JUST WASN'T MEANT TO BE.
THE SUSPECT ON THE PHONE... HE WAS SO CONFIDENT SHE WOULD DIE. I DON'T LIKE HIM GETTING THE SATISFACTION OF BEING RIGHT.
BEING RIGHT ISN'T ALWAYS AS GOOD AS IT SOUNDS.
RARE ENOUGH WE GOT A SERIAL KILLER, BUT BRANDING THE VICTIMS? THAT'S REAL WEIRD...
HE REALLY WANTS TO RUB IT IN OUR FACES. HE'S NOT TRYING TO HIDE THAT THEY'RE ALL CONNECTED.
ALMOST LIKE HE WANTS TO SHOW US HOW GOOD HE IS AT GETTING AWAY WITH MURDER.
HE'S TAUNTING US, PETE! CALLING THE STATION? IT'S UNSAT!

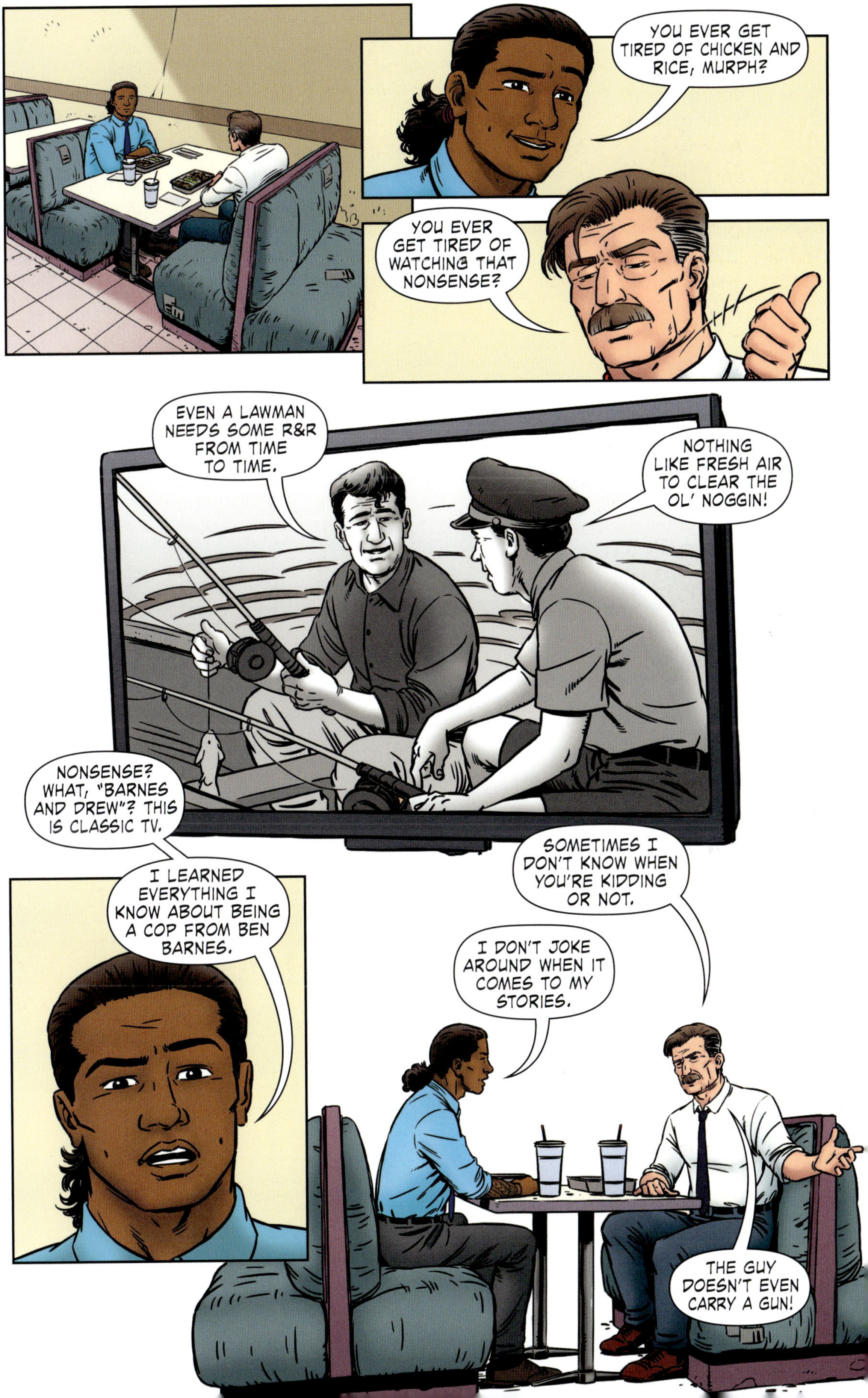

YOU EVER GET TIRED OF CHICKEN AND RICE, MURPH?
YOU EVER GET TIRED OF WATCHING THAT NONSENSE?
EVEN A LAWMAN NEEDS SOME R&R FROM TIME TO TIME.
NOTHING LIKE FRESH AIR TO CLEAR THE OL' NOGGIN!
NONSENSE? WHAT, "BARNES AND DREW"? THIS IS CLASSIC TV.
I LEARNED EVERYTHING I KNOW ABOUT BEING A COP FROM BEN BARNES.
SOMETIMES I DON'T KNOW WHEN YOU'RE KIDDING OR NOT.
I DON'T JOKE AROUND WHEN IT COMES TO MY STORIES.
THE GUY DOESN'T EVEN CARRY A GUN!

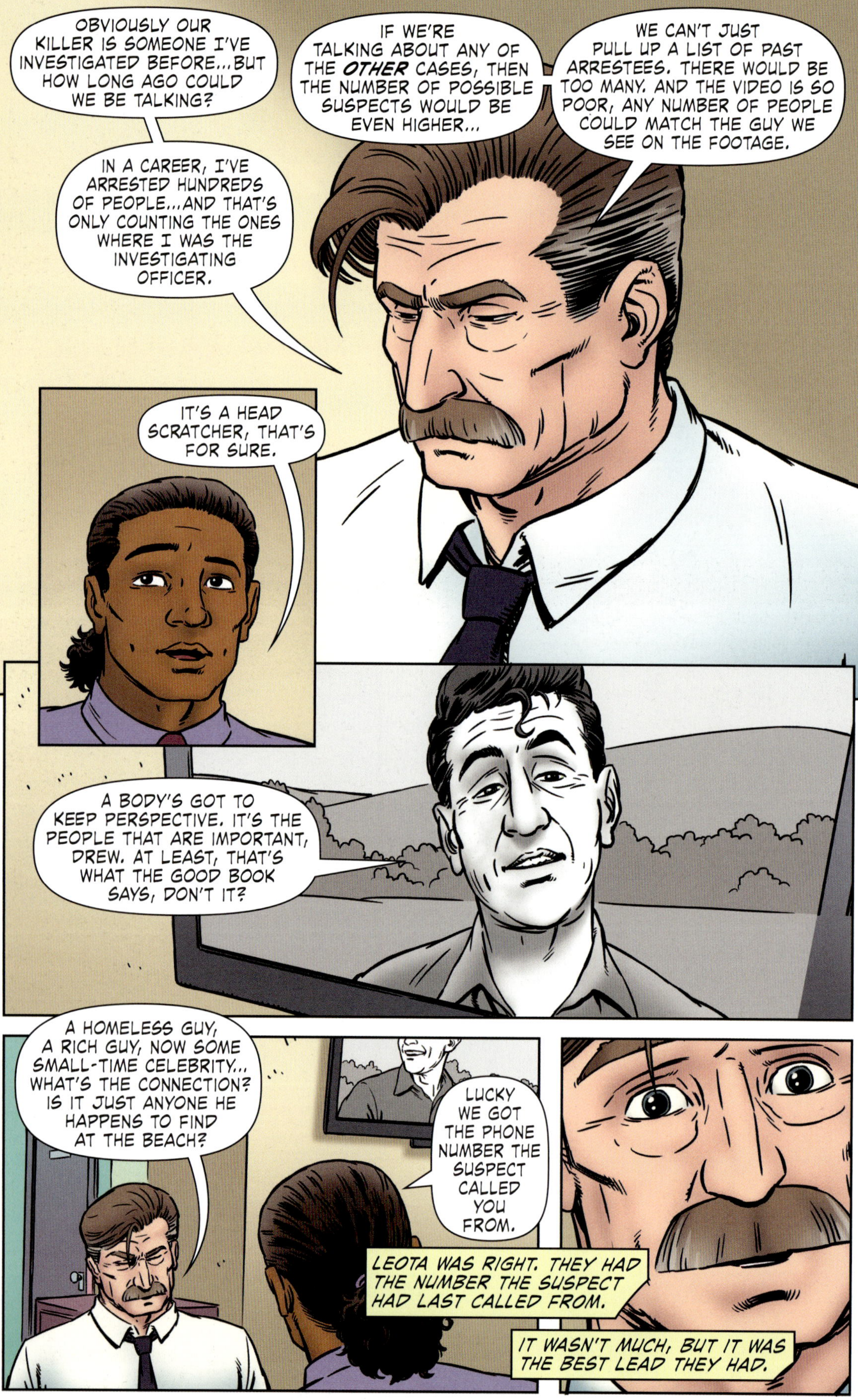
OBVIOUSLY OUR KILLER IS SOMEONE I'VE INVESTIGATED BEFORE...BUT HOW LONG AGO COULD WE BE TALKING?
IN A CAREER, I'VE ARRESTED HUNDREDS OF PEOPLE...AND THAT'S ONLY COUNTING THE ONES WHERE I WAS THE INVESTIGATING OFFICER.
IF WE'RE TALKING ABOUT ANY OF THE *OTHER* CASES, THEN THE NUMBER OF POSSIBLE SUSPECTS WOULD BE EVEN HIGHER...
WE CAN'T JUST PULL UP A LIST OF PAST ARRESTEES. THERE WOULD BE TOO MANY. AND THE VIDEO IS SO POOR, ANY NUMBER OF PEOPLE COULD MATCH THE GUY WE SEE ON THE FOOTAGE.
IT'S A HEAD SCRATCHER, THAT'S FOR SURE.
A BODY'S GOT TO KEEP PERSPECTIVE. IT'S THE PEOPLE THAT ARE IMPORTANT, DREW. AT LEAST, THAT'S WHAT THE GOOD BOOK SAYS, DON'T IT?
A HOMELESS GUY, A RICH GUY, NOW SOME SMALL-TIME CELEBRITY... WHAT'S THE CONNECTION? IS IT JUST ANYONE HE HAPPENS TO FIND AT THE BEACH?
LUCKY WE GOT THE PHONE NUMBER THE SUSPECT CALLED YOU FROM.
LEOTA WAS RIGHT. THEY HAD THE NUMBER THE SUSPECT HAD LAST CALLED FROM.
IT WASN'T MUCH, BUT IT WAS THE BEST LEAD THEY HAD.

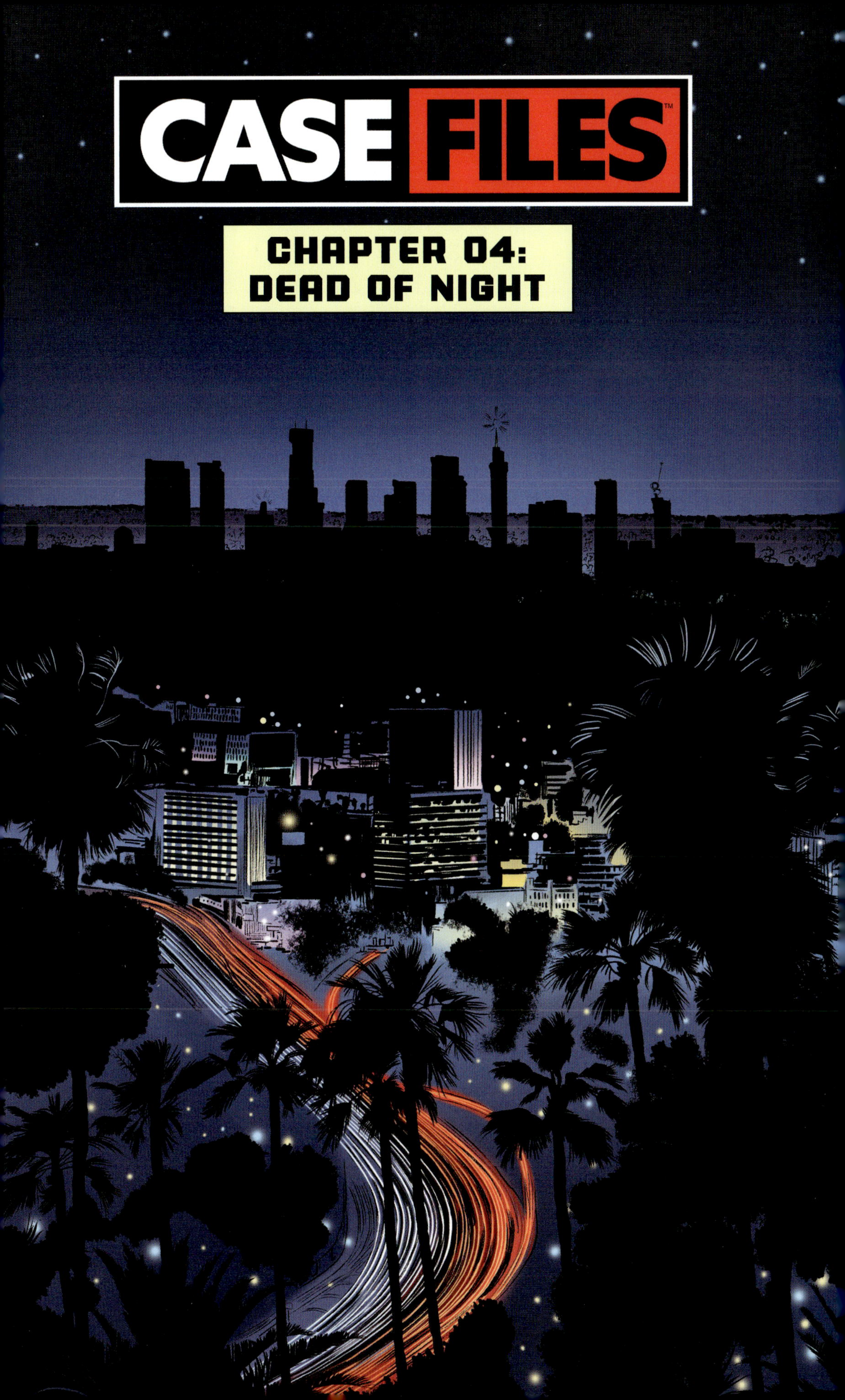
CASE FILES™
CHAPTER 04:
DEAD OF NIGHT

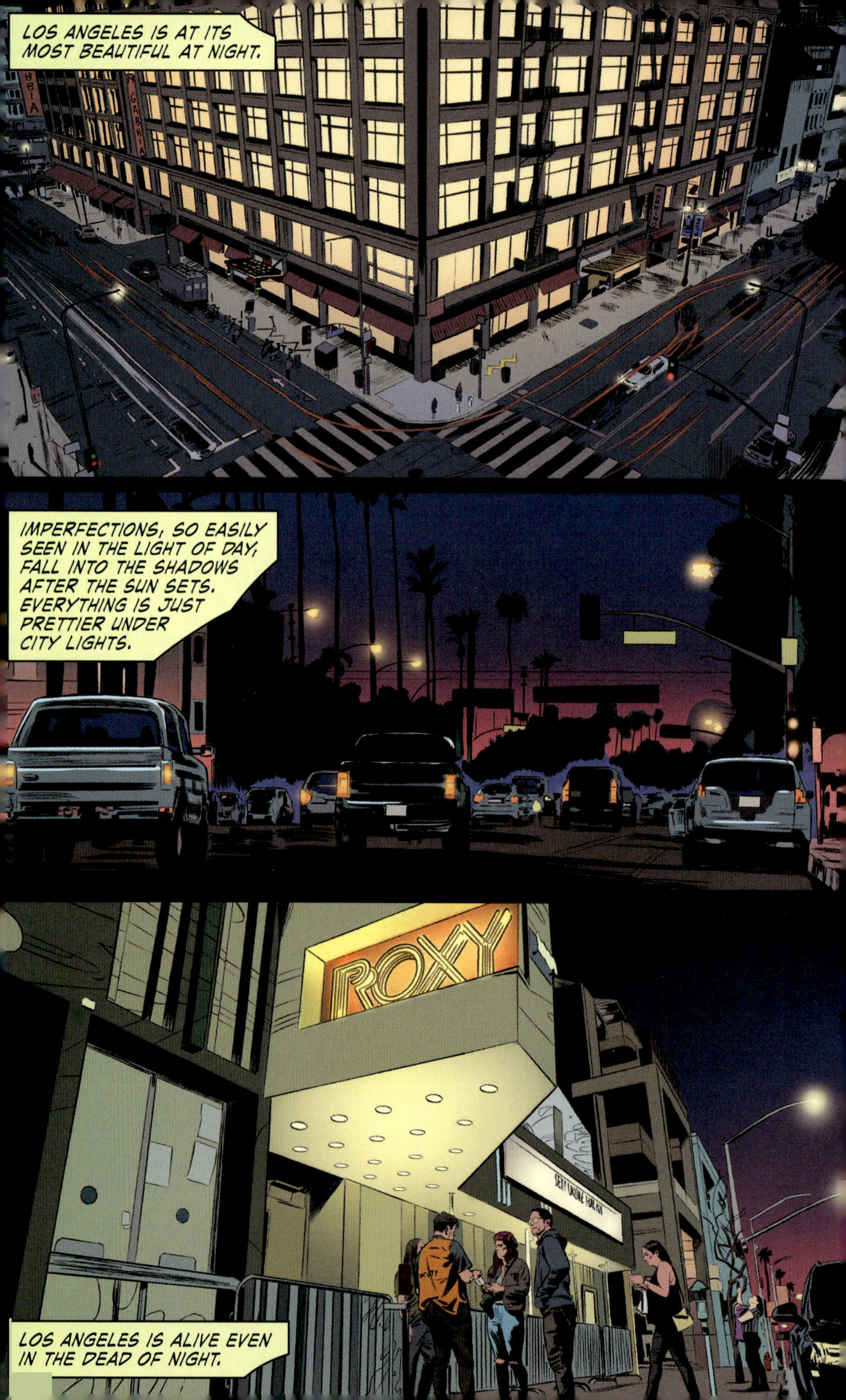
LOS ANGELES IS AT ITS MOST BEAUTIFUL AT NIGHT.
IMPERFECTIONS, SO EASILY SEEN IN THE LIGHT OF DAY, FALL INTO THE SHADOWS AFTER THE SUN SETS. EVERYTHING IS JUST PRETTIER UNDER CITY LIGHTS.
ROXY
LOS ANGELES IS ALIVE EVEN IN THE DEAD OF NIGHT.

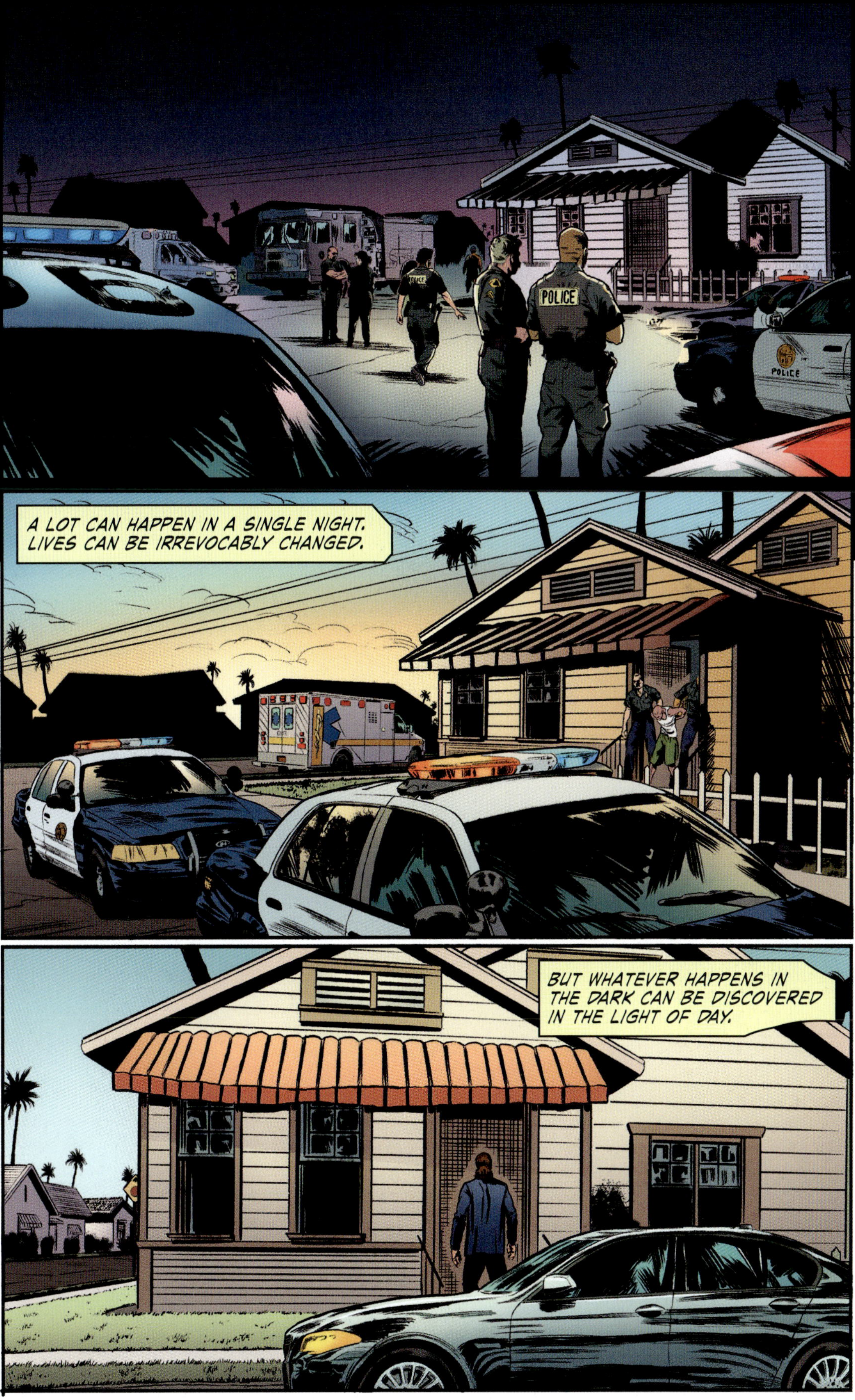
POLICE
POLICE
A LOT CAN HAPPEN IN A SINGLE NIGHT. LIVES CAN BE IRREVOCABLY CHANGED.
BUT WHATEVER HAPPENS IN THE DARK CAN BE DISCOVERED IN THE LIGHT OF DAY.

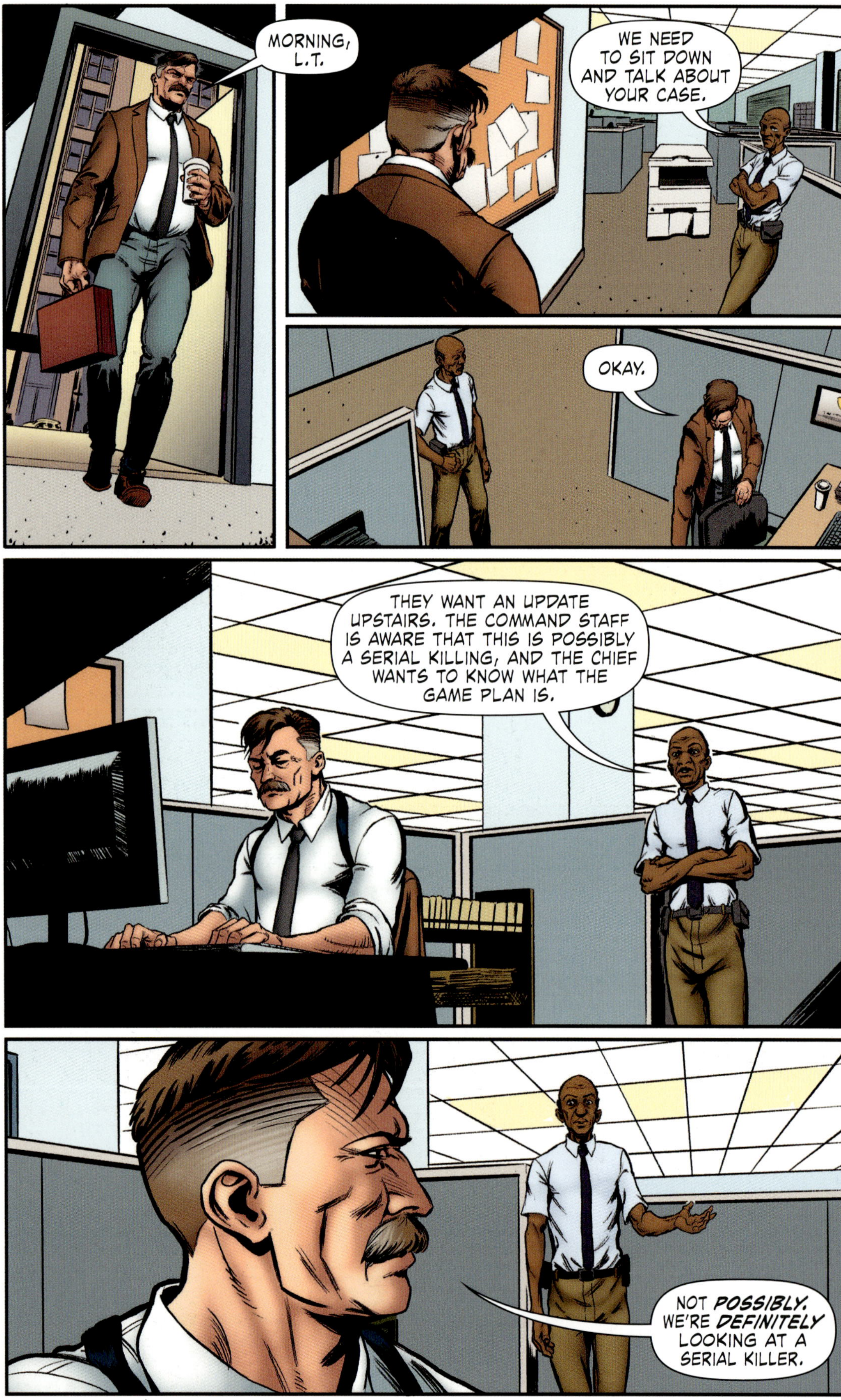
MORNING, L.T.
WE NEED TO SIT DOWN AND TALK ABOUT YOUR CASE.
OKAY.
THEY WANT AN UPDATE UPSTAIRS. THE COMMAND STAFF IS AWARE THAT THIS IS POSSIBLY A SERIAL KILLING, AND THE CHIEF WANTS TO KNOW WHAT THE GAME PLAN IS.
NOT *POSSIBLY.* WE'RE *DEFINITELY* LOOKING AT A SERIAL KILLER.

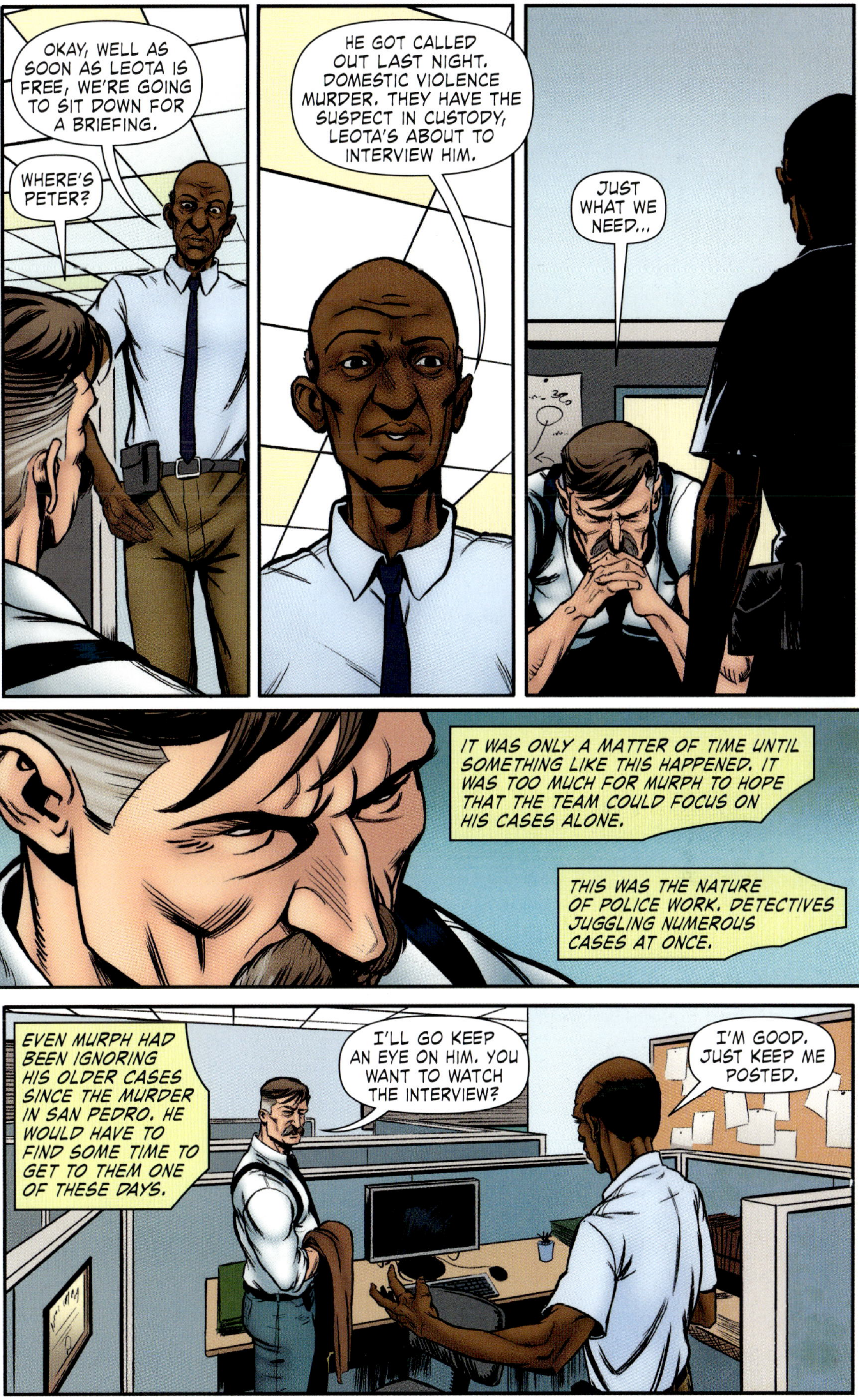
OKAY, WELL AS SOON AS LEOTA IS FREE, WE'RE GOING TO SIT DOWN FOR A BRIEFING.
WHERE'S PETER?
HE GOT CALLED OUT LAST NIGHT. DOMESTIC VIOLENCE MURDER. THEY HAVE THE SUSPECT IN CUSTODY, LEOTA'S ABOUT TO INTERVIEW HIM.
JUST WHAT WE NEED...
IT WAS ONLY A MATTER OF TIME UNTIL SOMETHING LIKE THIS HAPPENED. IT WAS TOO MUCH FOR MURPH TO HOPE THAT THE TEAM COULD FOCUS ON HIS CASES ALONE.
THIS WAS THE NATURE OF POLICE WORK. DETECTIVES JUGGLING NUMEROUS CASES AT ONCE.
EVEN MURPH HAD BEEN IGNORING HIS OLDER CASES SINCE THE MURDER IN SAN PEDRO. HE WOULD HAVE TO FIND SOME TIME TO GET TO THEM ONE OF THESE DAYS.
I'LL GO KEEP AN EYE ON HIM. YOU WANT TO WATCH THE INTERVIEW?
I'M GOOD. JUST KEEP ME POSTED.

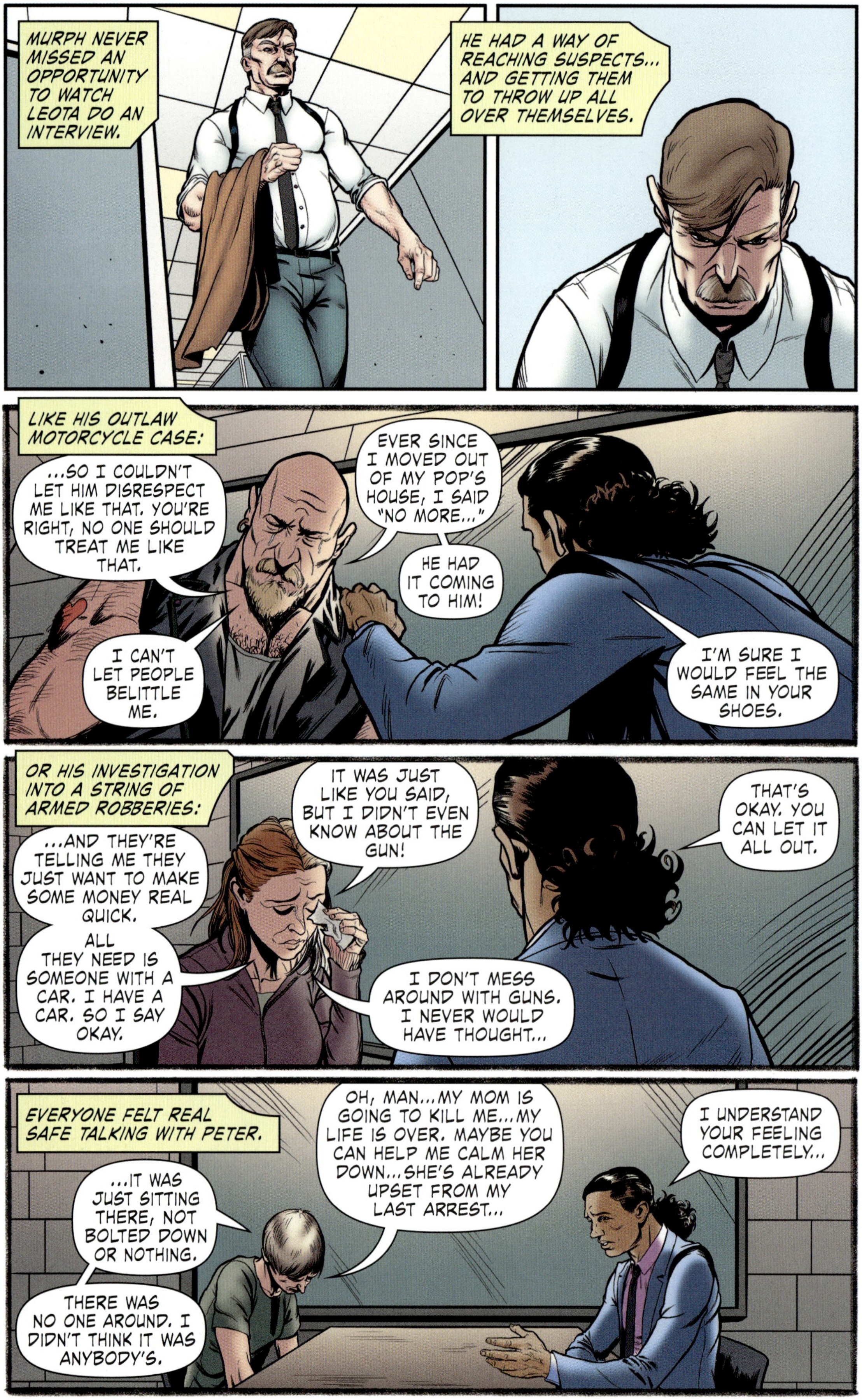
MURPH NEVER MISSED AN OPPORTUNITY TO WATCH LEOTA DO AN INTERVIEW.
HE HAD A WAY OF REACHING SUSPECTS... AND GETTING THEM TO THROW UP ALL OVER THEMSELVES.
LIKE HIS OUTLAW MOTORCYCLE CASE:
...SO I COULDN'T LET HIM DISRESPECT ME LIKE THAT. YOU'RE RIGHT, NO ONE SHOULD TREAT ME LIKE THAT.
I CAN'T LET PEOPLE BELITTLE ME.
EVER SINCE I MOVED OUT OF MY POP'S HOUSE, I SAID "NO MORE..."
HE HAD IT COMING TO HIM!
I'M SURE I WOULD FEEL THE SAME IN YOUR SHOES.
OR HIS INVESTIGATION INTO A STRING OF ARMED ROBBERIES:
...AND THEY'RE TELLING ME THEY JUST WANT TO MAKE SOME MONEY REAL QUICK.
ALL THEY NEED IS SOMEONE WITH A CAR. I HAVE A CAR. SO I SAY OKAY.
IT WAS JUST LIKE YOU SAID, BUT I DIDN'T EVEN KNOW ABOUT THE GUN!
I DON'T MESS AROUND WITH GUNS. I NEVER WOULD HAVE THOUGHT...
THAT'S OKAY. YOU CAN LET IT ALL OUT.
EVERYONE FELT REAL SAFE TALKING WITH PETER.
...IT WAS JUST SITTING THERE, NOT BOLTED DOWN OR NOTHING.
THERE WAS NO ONE AROUND. I DIDN'T THINK IT WAS ANYBODY'S.
OH, MAN...MY MOM IS GOING TO KILL ME...MY LIFE IS OVER. MAYBE YOU CAN HELP ME CALM HER DOWN...SHE'S ALREADY UPSET FROM MY LAST ARREST...
I UNDERSTAND YOUR FEELING COMPLETELY...

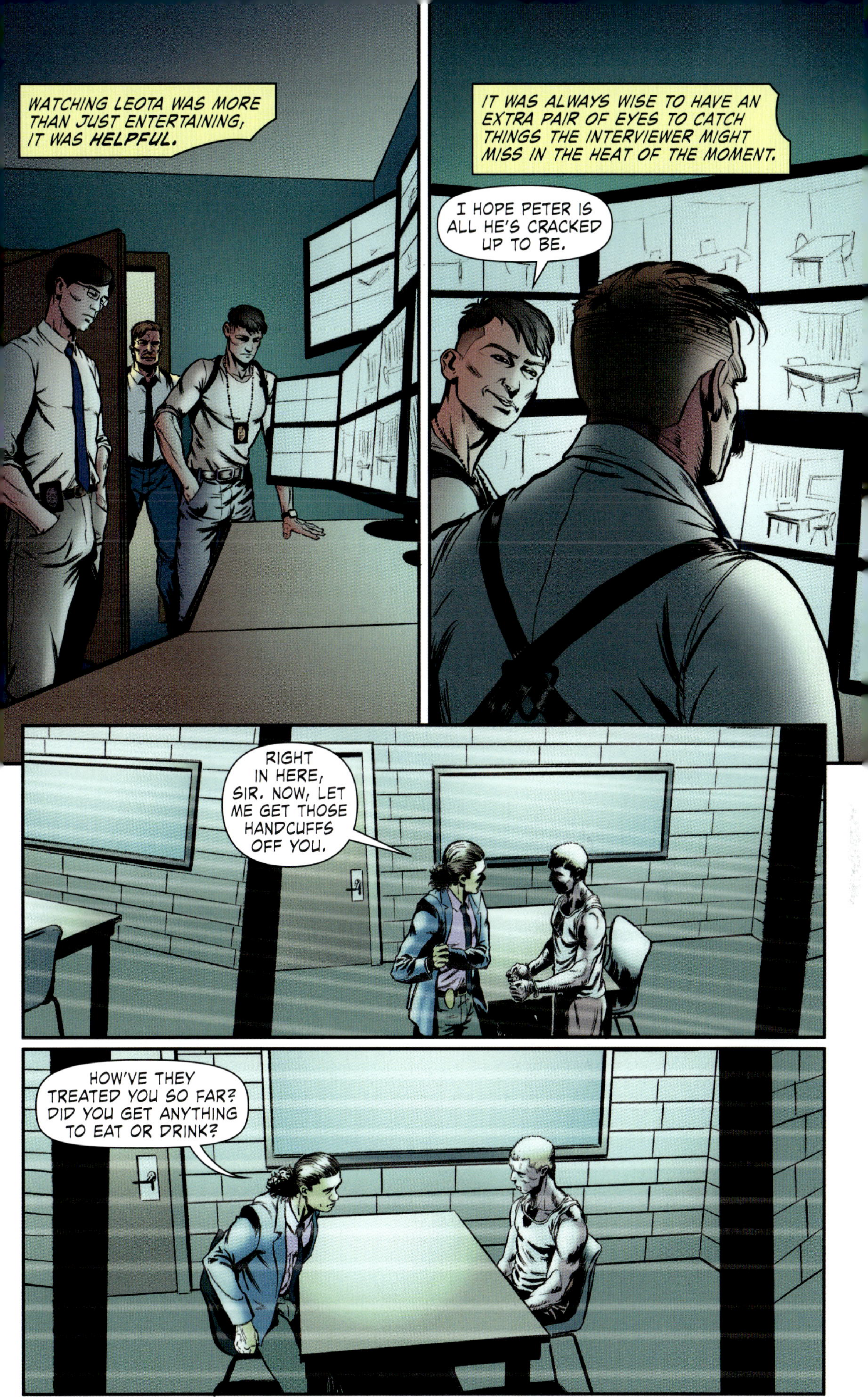

WATCHING LEOTA WAS MORE THAN JUST ENTERTAINING, IT WAS **HELPFUL.**
IT WAS ALWAYS WISE TO HAVE AN EXTRA PAIR OF EYES TO CATCH THINGS THE INTERVIEWER MIGHT MISS IN THE HEAT OF THE MOMENT.
I HOPE PETER IS ALL HE'S CRACKED UP TO BE.
RIGHT IN HERE, SIR. NOW, LET ME GET THOSE HANDCUFFS OFF YOU.
HOW'VE THEY TREATED YOU SO FAR? DID YOU GET ANYTHING TO EAT OR DRINK?

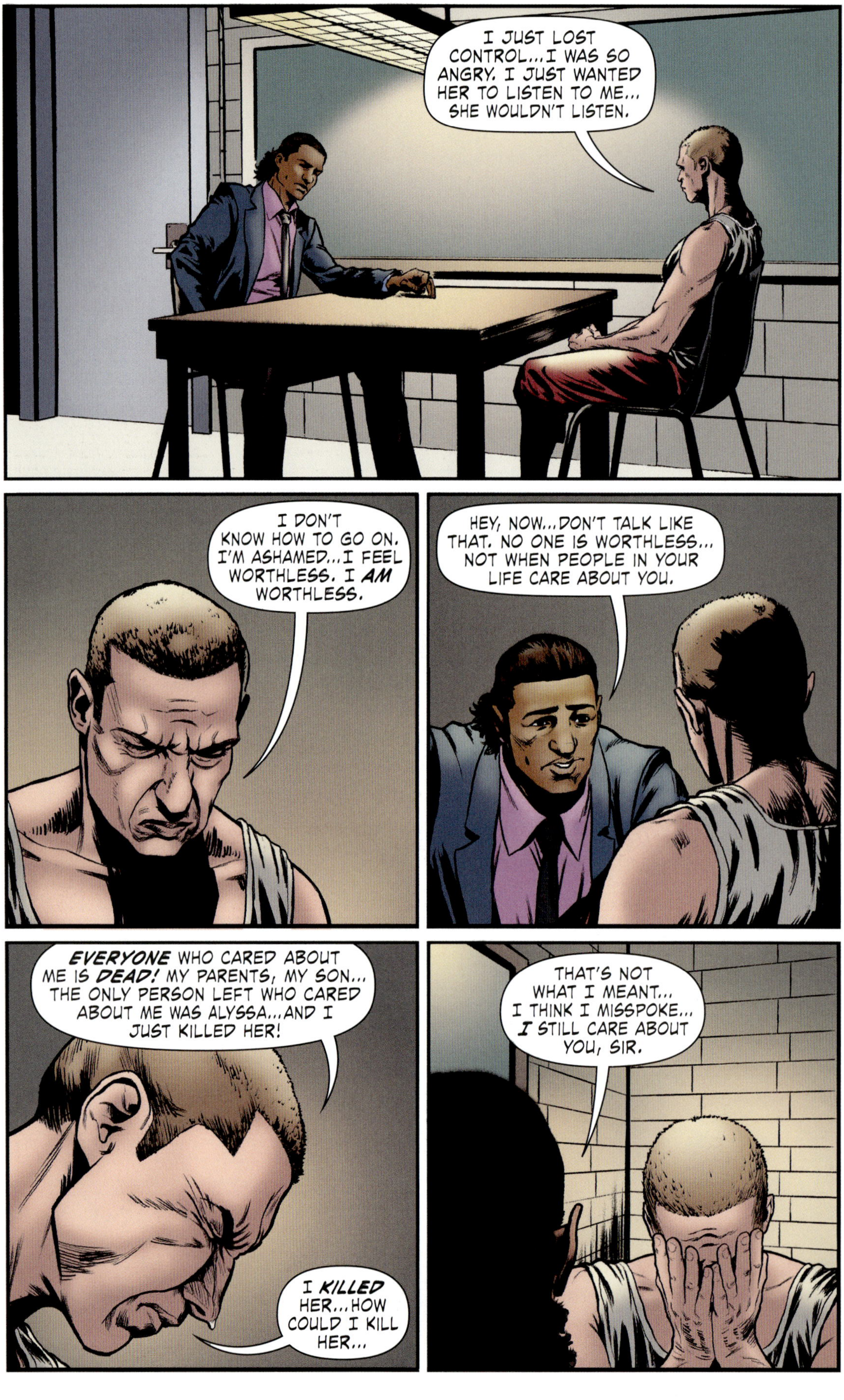
I JUST LOST CONTROL...I WAS SO ANGRY. I JUST WANTED HER TO LISTEN TO ME... SHE WOULDN'T LISTEN.
I DON'T KNOW HOW TO GO ON. I'M ASHAMED...I FEEL WORTHLESS. I ***AM*** WORTHLESS.
HEY, NOW...DON'T TALK LIKE THAT. NO ONE IS WORTHLESS... NOT WHEN PEOPLE IN YOUR LIFE CARE ABOUT YOU.
EVERYONE WHO CARED ABOUT ME IS ***DEAD!*** MY PARENTS, MY SON... THE ONLY PERSON LEFT WHO CARED ABOUT ME WAS ALYSSA...AND I JUST KILLED HER!
I ***KILLED*** HER...HOW COULD I KILL HER...
THAT'S NOT WHAT I MEANT... I THINK I MISSPOKE... ***I*** STILL CARE ABOUT YOU, SIR.

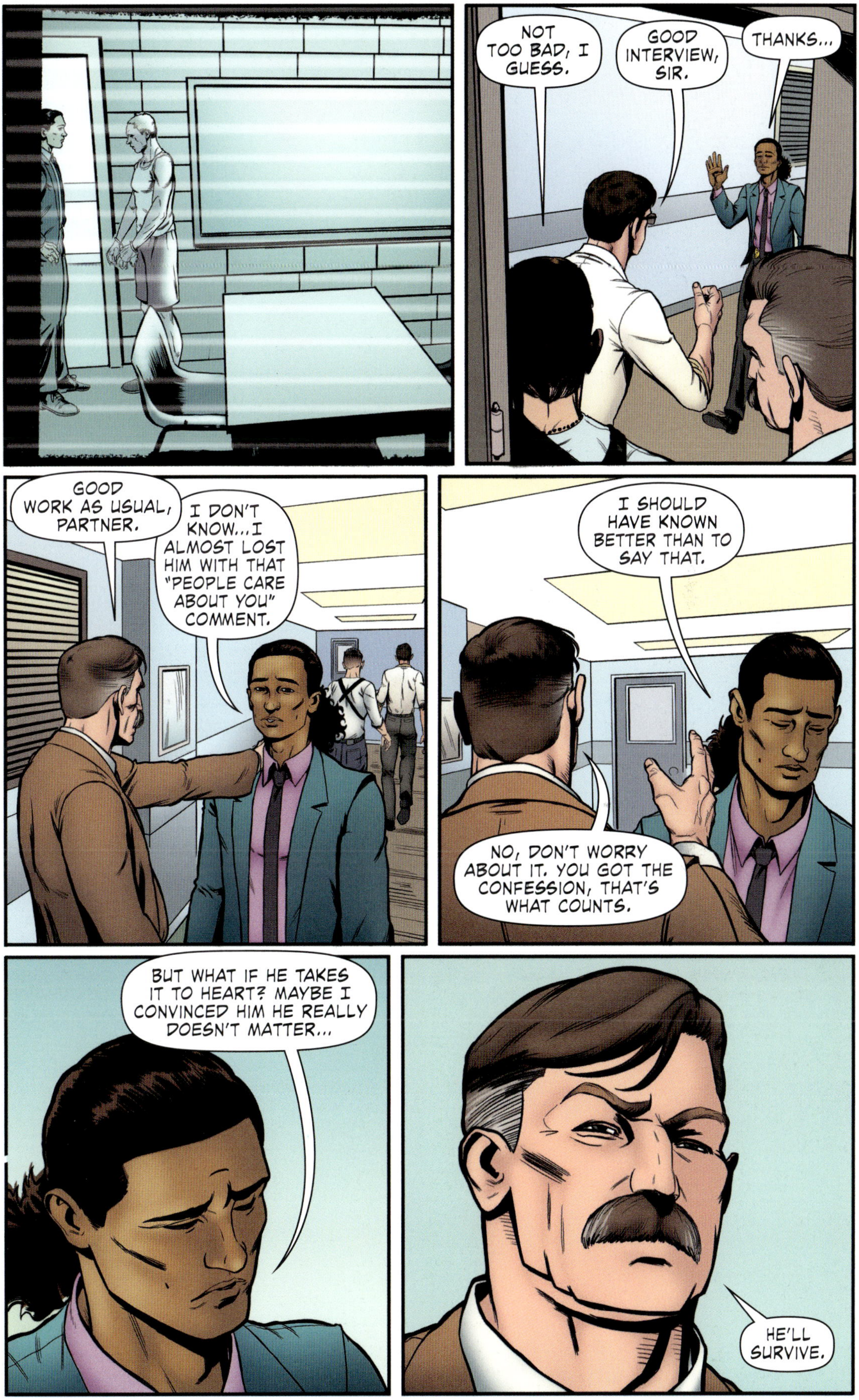
NOT TOO BAD, I GUESS.
GOOD INTERVIEW, SIR.
THANKS...
GOOD WORK AS USUAL, PARTNER.
I DON'T KNOW...I ALMOST LOST HIM WITH THAT "PEOPLE CARE ABOUT YOU" COMMENT.
I SHOULD HAVE KNOWN BETTER THAN TO SAY THAT.
NO, DON'T WORRY ABOUT IT. YOU GOT THE CONFESSION, THAT'S WHAT COUNTS.
BUT WHAT IF HE TAKES IT TO HEART? MAYBE I CONVINCED HIM HE REALLY DOESN'T MATTER...
HE'LL SURVIVE.

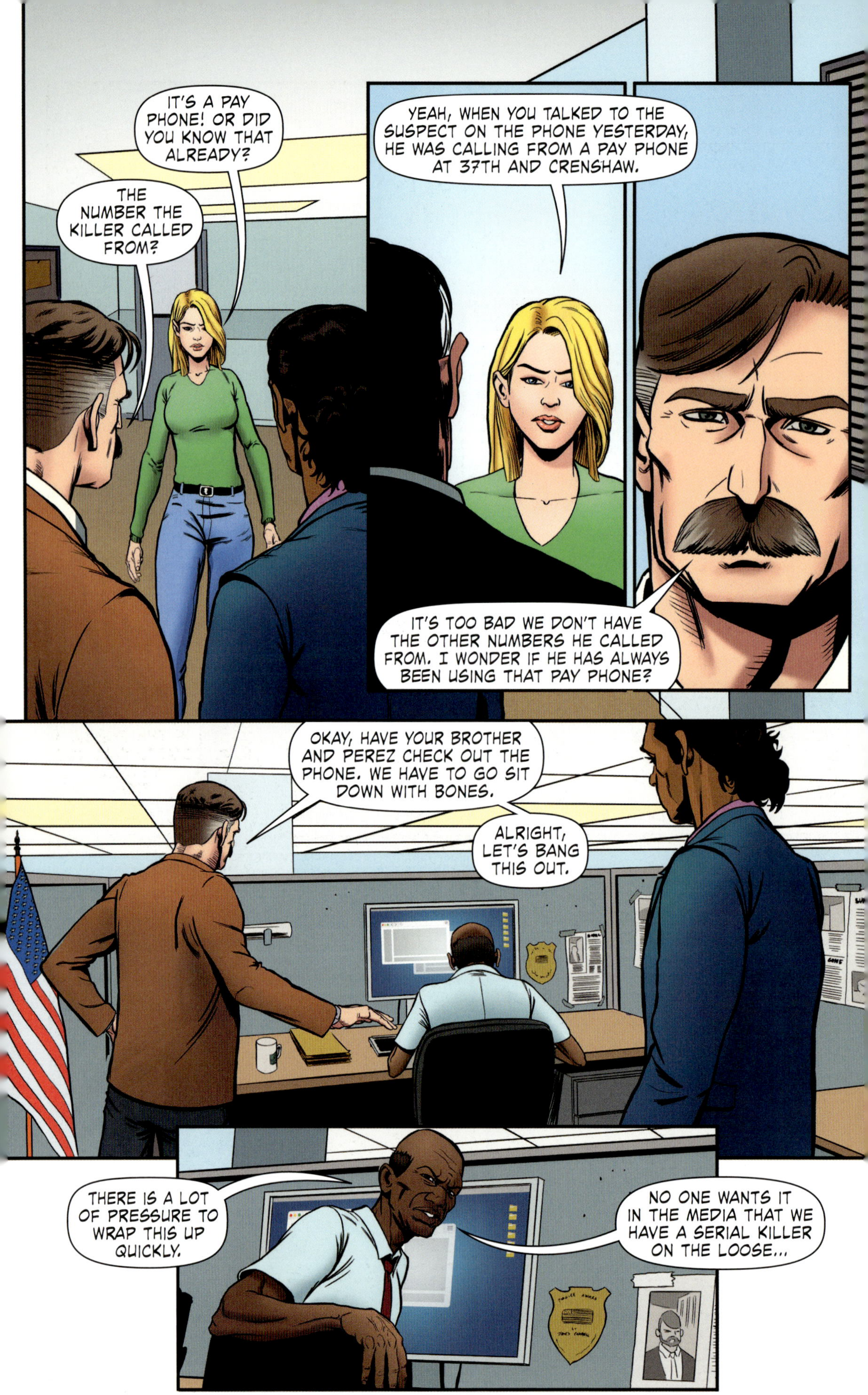
THE NUMBER THE KILLER CALLED FROM?
IT'S A PAY PHONE! OR DID YOU KNOW THAT ALREADY?
YEAH, WHEN YOU TALKED TO THE SUSPECT ON THE PHONE YESTERDAY, HE WAS CALLING FROM A PAY PHONE AT 37TH AND CRENSHAW.
IT'S TOO BAD WE DON'T HAVE THE OTHER NUMBERS HE CALLED FROM. I WONDER IF HE HAS ALWAYS BEEN USING THAT PAY PHONE?
OKAY, HAVE YOUR BROTHER AND PEREZ CHECK OUT THE PHONE. WE HAVE TO GO SIT DOWN WITH BONES.
ALRIGHT, LET'S BANG THIS OUT.
THERE IS A LOT OF PRESSURE TO WRAP THIS UP QUICKLY.
NO ONE WANTS IT IN THE MEDIA THAT WE HAVE A SERIAL KILLER ON THE LOOSE...

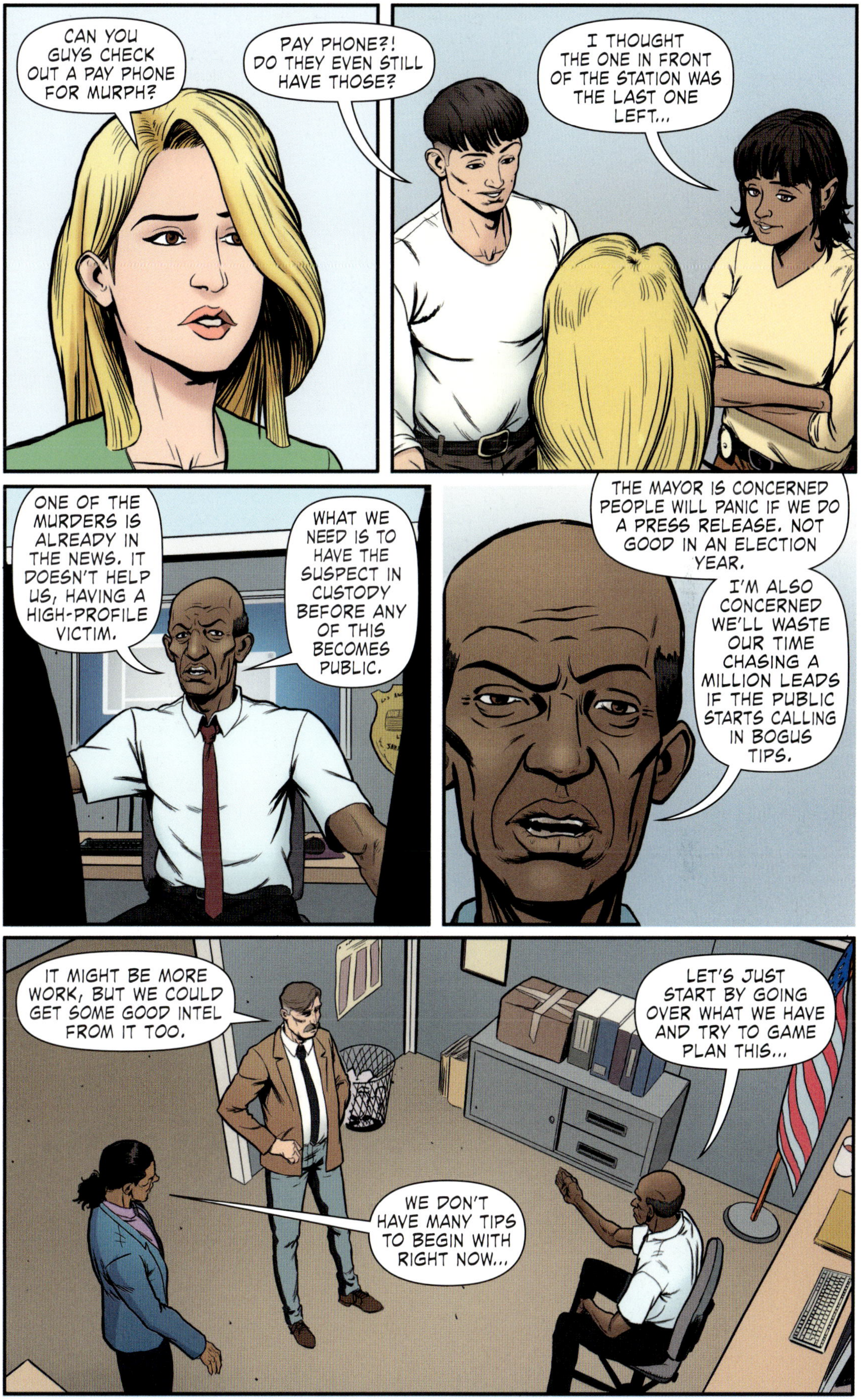
CAN YOU GUYS CHECK OUT A PAY PHONE FOR MURPH?
PAY PHONE?! DO THEY EVEN STILL HAVE THOSE?
I THOUGHT THE ONE IN FRONT OF THE STATION WAS THE LAST ONE LEFT...
ONE OF THE MURDERS IS ALREADY IN THE NEWS. IT DOESN'T HELP US, HAVING A HIGH-PROFILE VICTIM.
WHAT WE NEED IS TO HAVE THE SUSPECT IN CUSTODY BEFORE ANY OF THIS BECOMES PUBLIC.
THE MAYOR IS CONCERNED PEOPLE WILL PANIC IF WE DO A PRESS RELEASE. NOT GOOD IN AN ELECTION YEAR.
I'M ALSO CONCERNED WE'LL WASTE OUR TIME CHASING A MILLION LEADS IF THE PUBLIC STARTS CALLING IN BOGUS TIPS.
IT MIGHT BE MORE WORK, BUT WE COULD GET SOME GOOD INTEL FROM IT TOO.
LET'S JUST START BY GOING OVER WHAT WE HAVE AND TRY TO GAME PLAN THIS...
WE DON'T HAVE MANY TIPS TO BEGIN WITH RIGHT NOW...

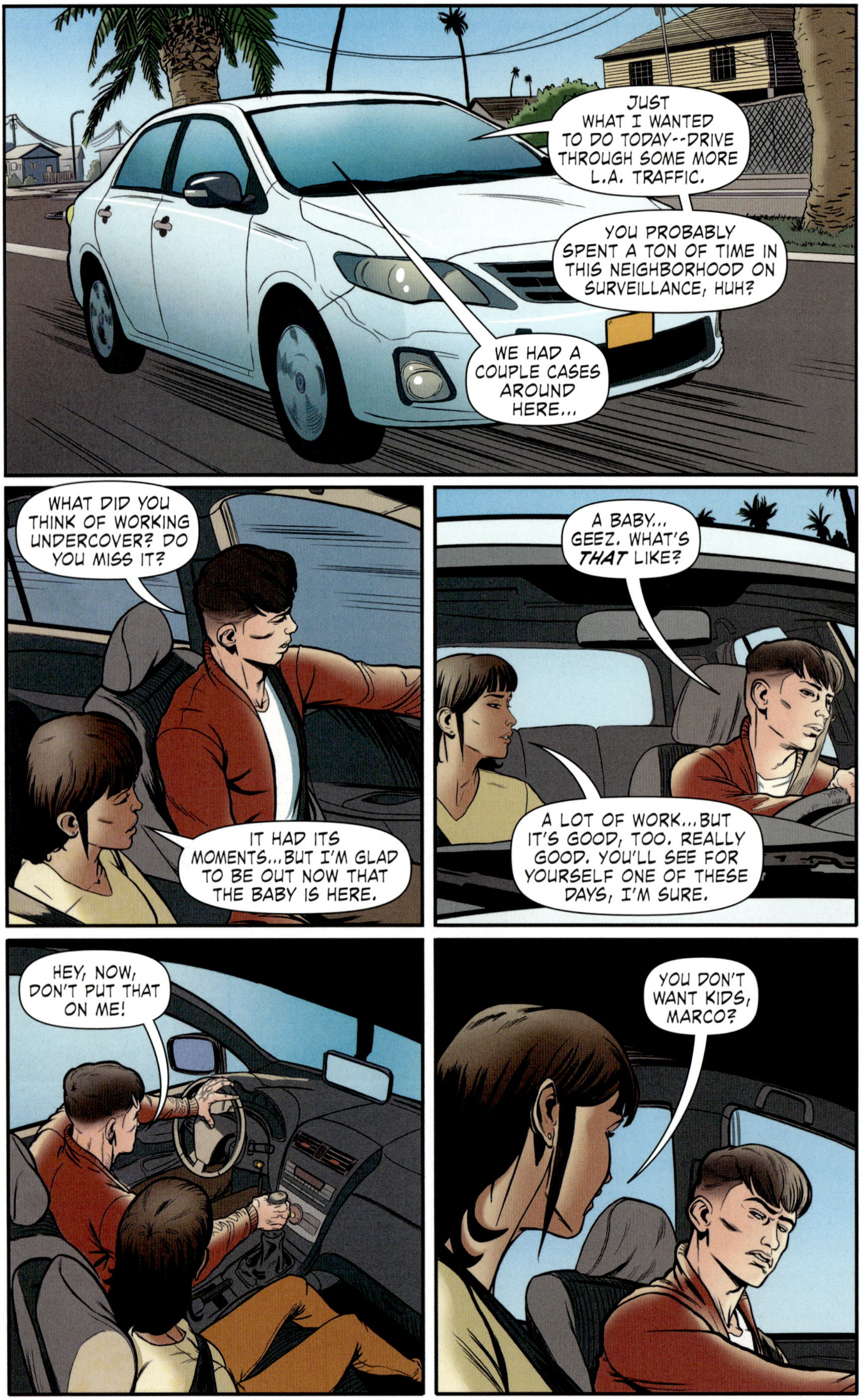
JUST WHAT I WANTED TO DO TODAY--DRIVE THROUGH SOME MORE L.A. TRAFFIC.
YOU PROBABLY SPENT A TON OF TIME IN THIS NEIGHBORHOOD ON SURVEILLANCE, HUH?
WE HAD A COUPLE CASES AROUND HERE...
WHAT DID YOU THINK OF WORKING UNDERCOVER? DO YOU MISS IT?
IT HAD ITS MOMENTS...BUT I'M GLAD TO BE OUT NOW THAT THE BABY IS HERE.
A BABY... GEEZ. WHAT'S *THAT* LIKE?
A LOT OF WORK...BUT IT'S GOOD, TOO. REALLY GOOD. YOU'LL SEE FOR YOURSELF ONE OF THESE DAYS, I'M SURE.
HEY, NOW, DON'T PUT THAT ON ME!
YOU DON'T WANT KIDS, MARCO?

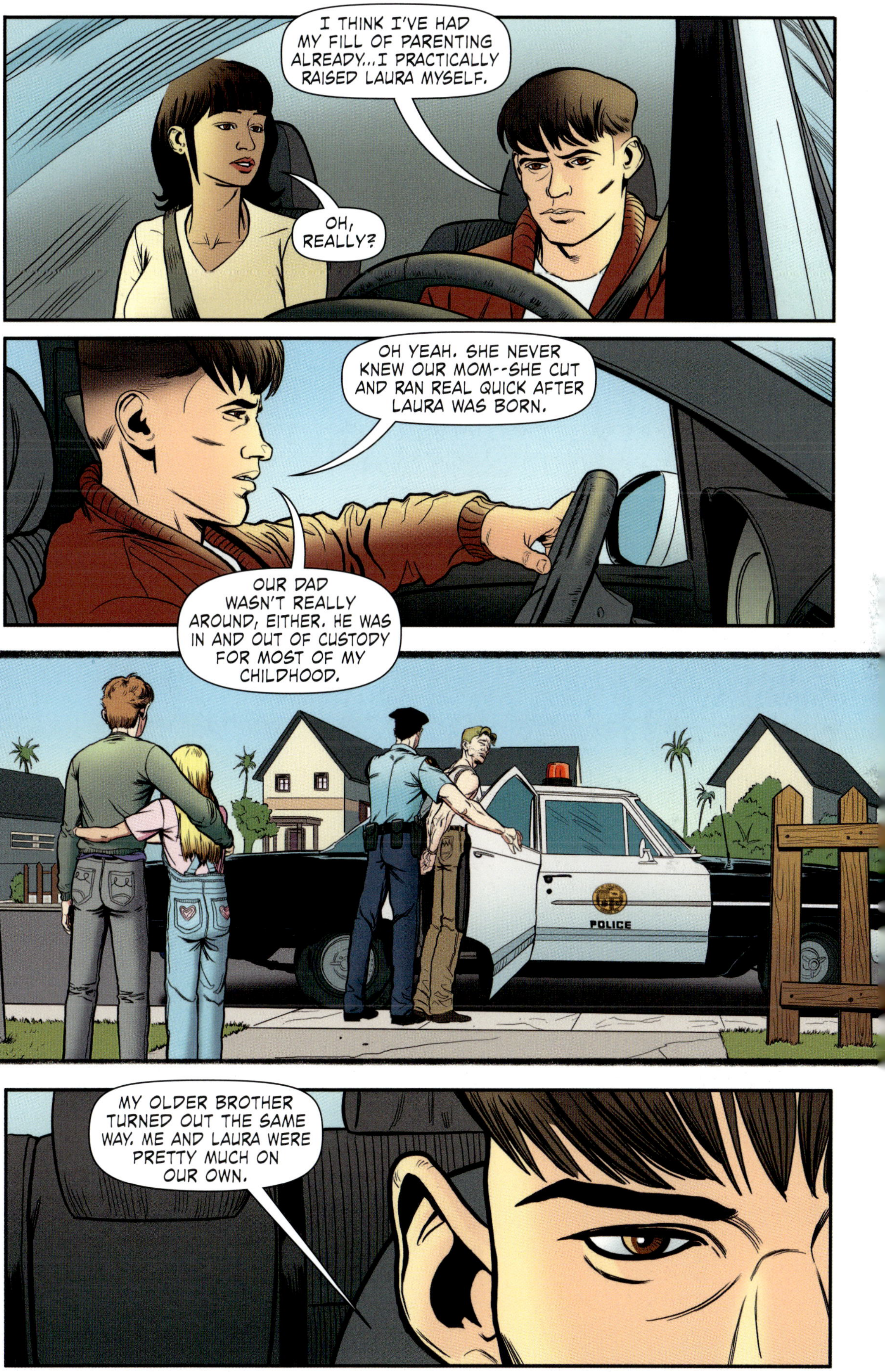
I THINK I'VE HAD MY FILL OF PARENTING ALREADY...I PRACTICALLY RAISED LAURA MYSELF.
OH, REALLY?
OH YEAH. SHE NEVER KNEW OUR MOM--SHE CUT AND RAN REAL QUICK AFTER LAURA WAS BORN.
OUR DAD WASN'T REALLY AROUND, EITHER. HE WAS IN AND OUT OF CUSTODY FOR MOST OF MY CHILDHOOD.
POLICE
MY OLDER BROTHER TURNED OUT THE SAME WAY. ME AND LAURA WERE PRETTY MUCH ON OUR OWN.

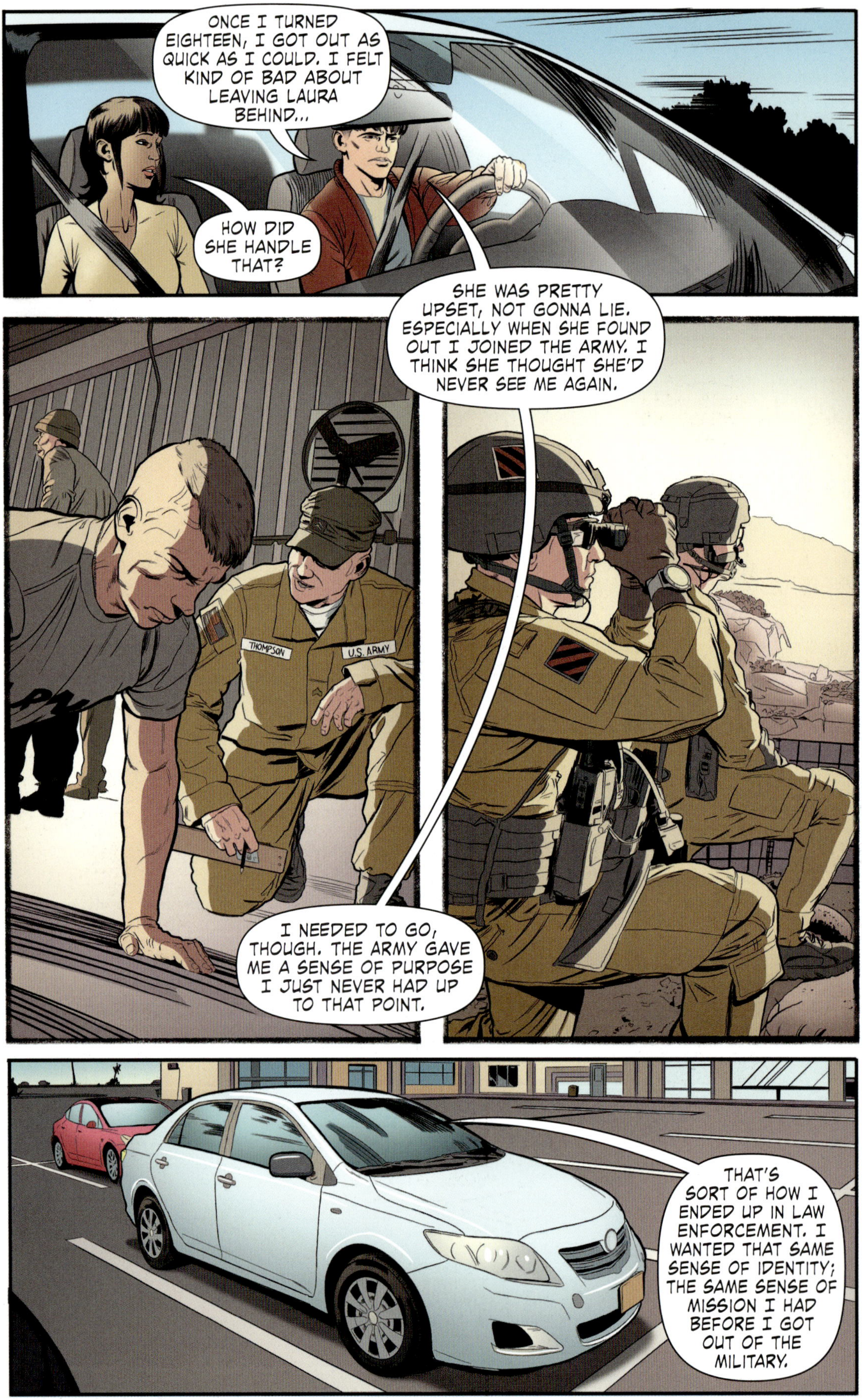
ONCE I TURNED EIGHTEEN, I GOT OUT AS QUICK AS I COULD. I FELT KIND OF BAD ABOUT LEAVING LAURA BEHIND...
HOW DID SHE HANDLE THAT?
SHE WAS PRETTY UPSET, NOT GONNA LIE. ESPECIALLY WHEN SHE FOUND OUT I JOINED THE ARMY. I THINK SHE THOUGHT SHE'D NEVER SEE ME AGAIN.
THOMPSON
U.S. ARMY
I NEEDED TO GO, THOUGH. THE ARMY GAVE ME A SENSE OF PURPOSE I JUST NEVER HAD UP TO THAT POINT.
THAT'S SORT OF HOW I ENDED UP IN LAW ENFORCEMENT. I WANTED THAT SAME SENSE OF IDENTITY; THE SAME SENSE OF MISSION I HAD BEFORE I GOT OUT OF THE MILITARY.

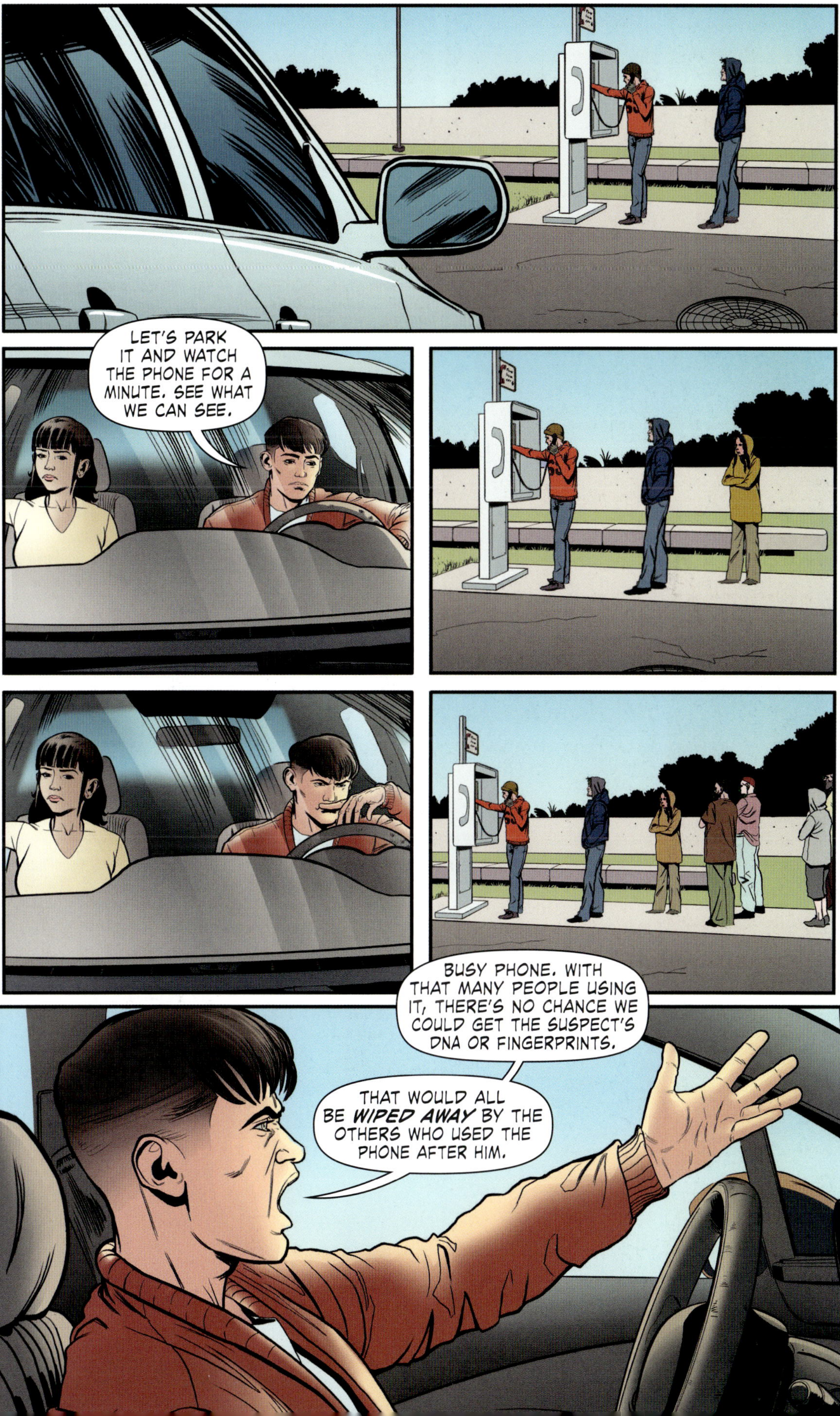

LET'S PARK IT AND WATCH THE PHONE FOR A MINUTE. SEE WHAT WE CAN SEE.
BUSY PHONE. WITH THAT MANY PEOPLE USING IT, THERE'S NO CHANCE WE COULD GET THE SUSPECT'S DNA OR FINGERPRINTS.
THAT WOULD ALL BE *WIPED AWAY* BY THE OTHERS WHO USED THE PHONE AFTER HIM.

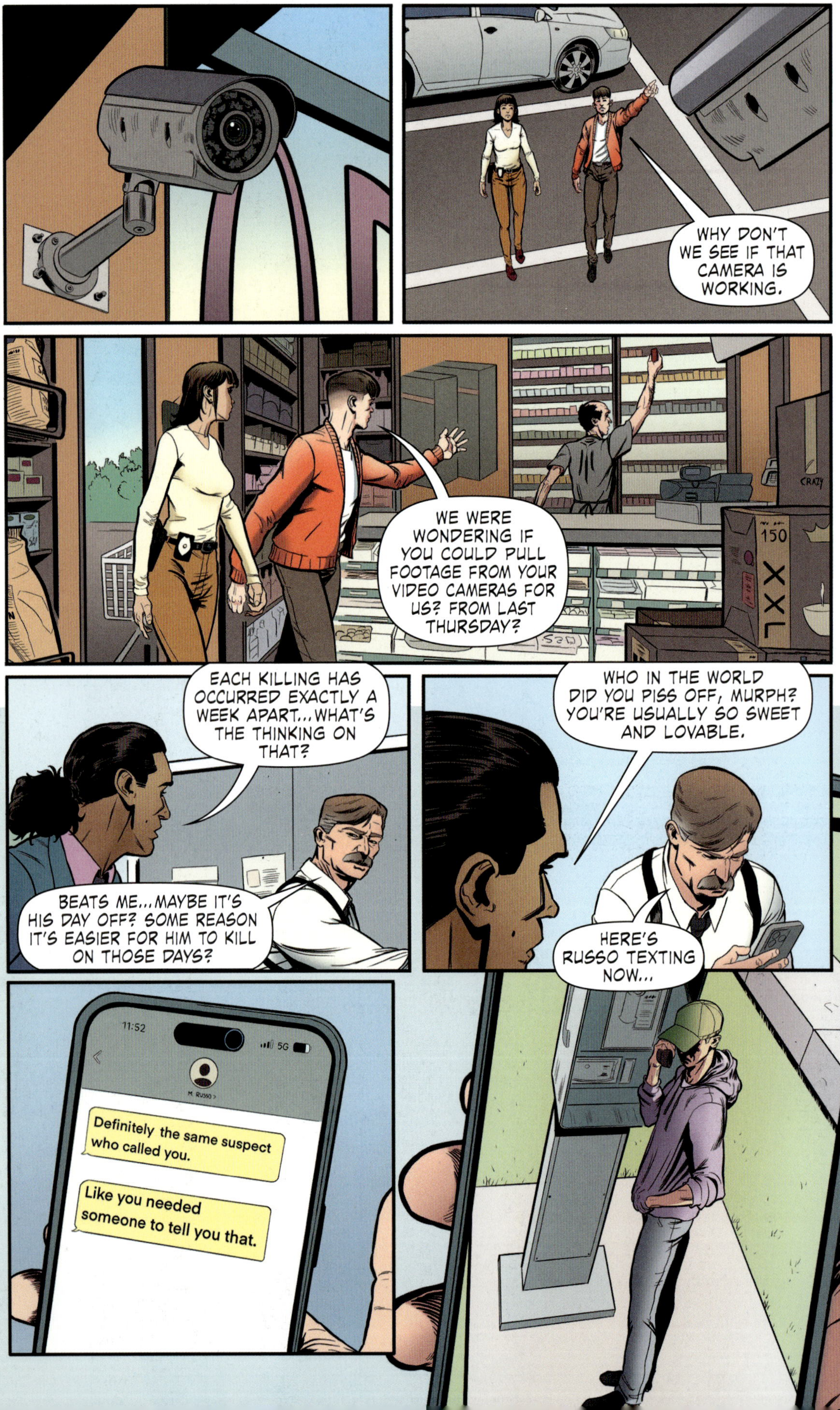
WHY DON'T WE SEE IF THAT CAMERA IS WORKING.
WE WERE WONDERING IF YOU COULD PULL FOOTAGE FROM YOUR VIDEO CAMERAS FOR US? FROM LAST THURSDAY?
150
XXL
EACH KILLING HAS OCCURRED EXACTLY A WEEK APART...WHAT'S THE THINKING ON THAT?
BEATS ME...MAYBE IT'S HIS DAY OFF? SOME REASON IT'S EASIER FOR HIM TO KILL ON THOSE DAYS?
WHO IN THE WORLD DID YOU PISS OFF, MURPH? YOU'RE USUALLY SO SWEET AND LOVABLE.
HERE'S RUSSO TEXTING NOW...
11:52
5G
Definitely the same suspect who called you.
Like you needed someone to tell you that.

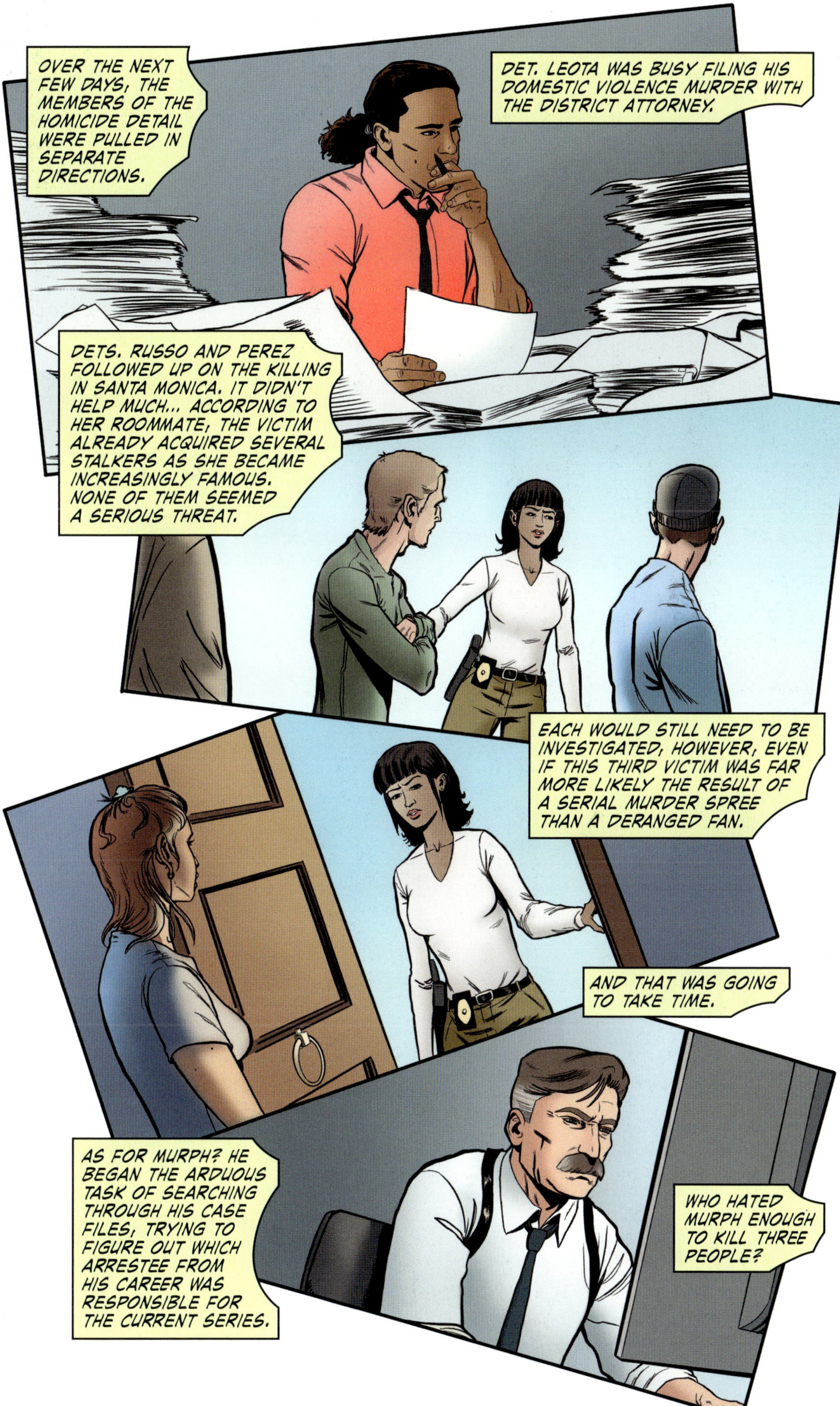
OVER THE NEXT FEW DAYS, THE MEMBERS OF THE HOMICIDE DETAIL WERE PULLED IN SEPARATE DIRECTIONS.
DET. LEOTA WAS BUSY FILING HIS DOMESTIC VIOLENCE MURDER WITH THE DISTRICT ATTORNEY.
DETS. RUSSO AND PEREZ FOLLOWED UP ON THE KILLING IN SANTA MONICA. IT DIDN'T HELP MUCH... ACCORDING TO HER ROOMMATE, THE VICTIM ALREADY ACQUIRED SEVERAL STALKERS AS SHE BECAME INCREASINGLY FAMOUS. NONE OF THEM SEEMED A SERIOUS THREAT.
EACH WOULD STILL NEED TO BE INVESTIGATED, HOWEVER, EVEN IF THIS THIRD VICTIM WAS FAR MORE LIKELY THE RESULT OF A SERIAL MURDER SPREE THAN A DERANGED FAN.
AND THAT WAS GOING TO TAKE TIME.
AS FOR MURPH? HE BEGAN THE ARDUOUS TASK OF SEARCHING THROUGH HIS CASE FILES, TRYING TO FIGURE OUT WHICH ARRESTEE FROM HIS CAREER WAS RESPONSIBLE FOR THE CURRENT SERIES.
WHO HATED MURPH ENOUGH TO KILL THREE PEOPLE?

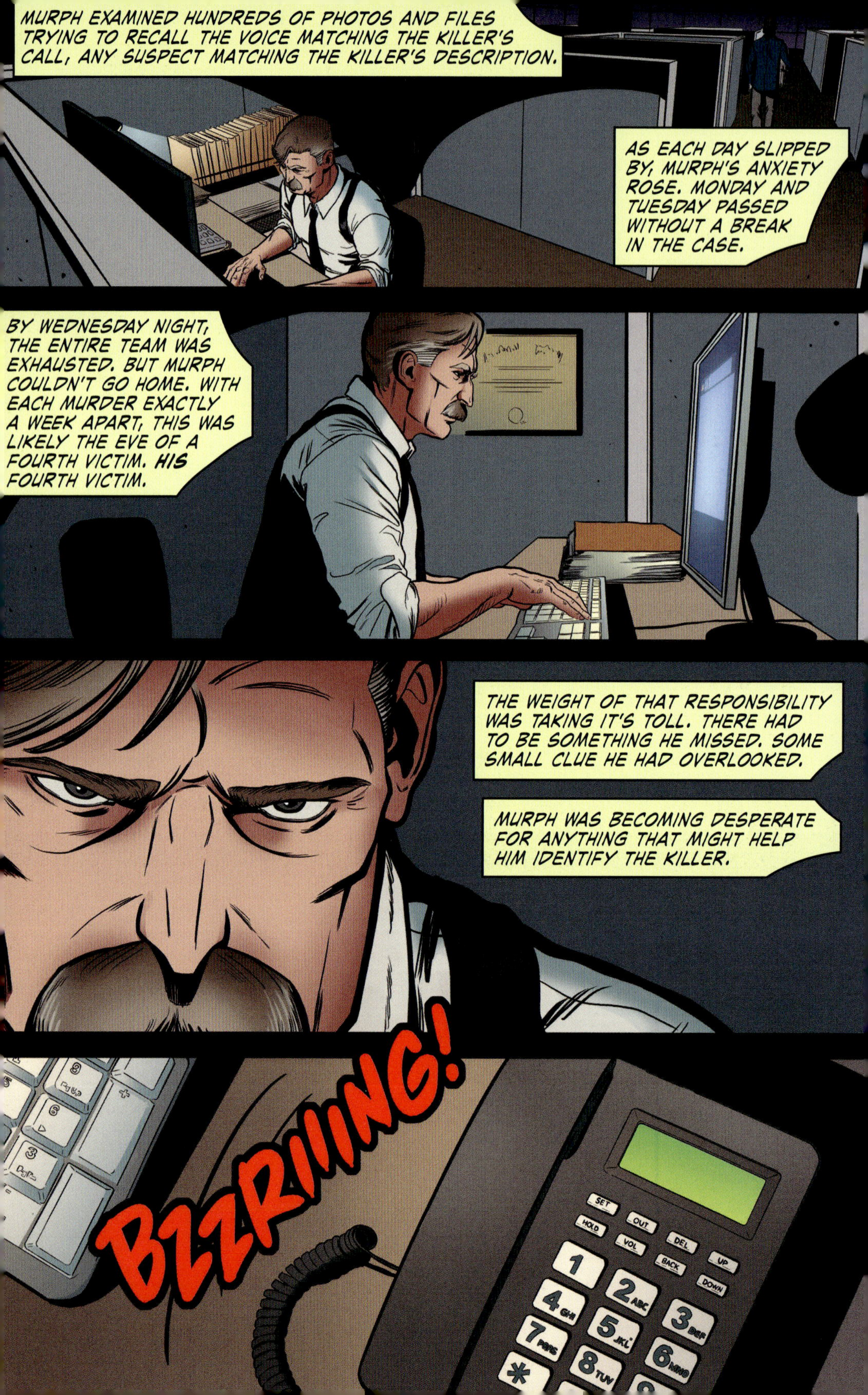
MURPH EXAMINED HUNDREDS OF PHOTOS AND FILES TRYING TO RECALL THE VOICE MATCHING THE KILLER'S CALL, ANY SUSPECT MATCHING THE KILLER'S DESCRIPTION.
AS EACH DAY SLIPPED BY, MURPH'S ANXIETY ROSE. MONDAY AND TUESDAY PASSED WITHOUT A BREAK IN THE CASE.
BY WEDNESDAY NIGHT, THE ENTIRE TEAM WAS EXHAUSTED. BUT MURPH COULDN'T GO HOME. WITH EACH MURDER EXACTLY A WEEK APART, THIS WAS LIKELY THE EVE OF A FOURTH VICTIM. **HIS** FOURTH VICTIM.
THE WEIGHT OF THAT RESPONSIBILITY WAS TAKING IT'S TOLL. THERE HAD TO BE SOMETHING HE MISSED. SOME SMALL CLUE HE HAD OVERLOOKED.
MURPH WAS BECOMING DESPERATE FOR ANYTHING THAT MIGHT HELP HIM IDENTIFY THE KILLER.
BZZRIIING!

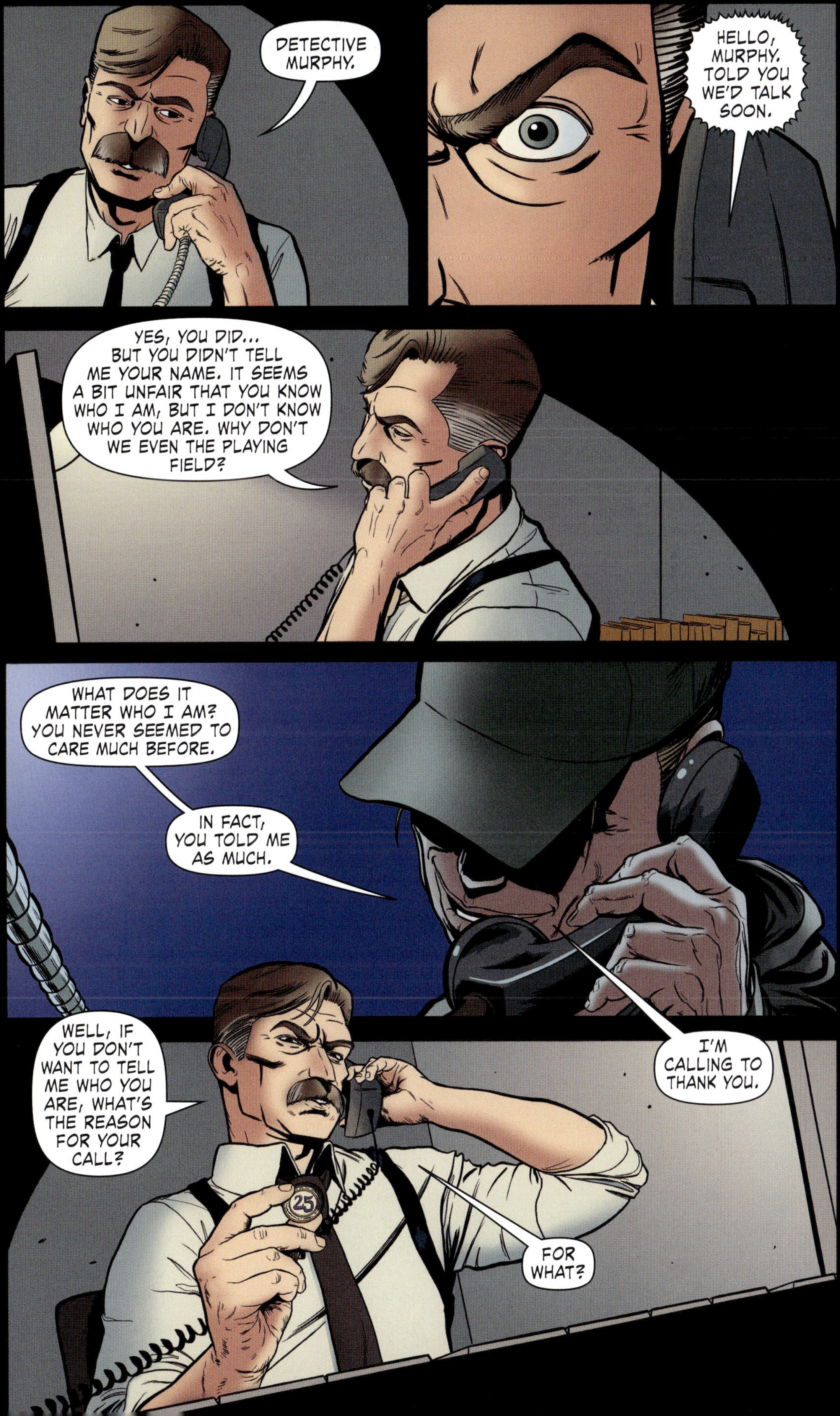
DETECTIVE MURPHY.
HELLO, MURPHY. TOLD YOU WE'D TALK SOON.
YES, YOU DID... BUT YOU DIDN'T TELL ME YOUR NAME. IT SEEMS A BIT UNFAIR THAT YOU KNOW WHO I AM, BUT I DON'T KNOW WHO YOU ARE. WHY DON'T WE EVEN THE PLAYING FIELD?
WHAT DOES IT MATTER WHO I AM? YOU NEVER SEEMED TO CARE MUCH BEFORE.
IN FACT, YOU TOLD ME AS MUCH.
WELL, IF YOU DON'T WANT TO TELL ME WHO YOU ARE, WHAT'S THE REASON FOR YOUR CALL?
I'M CALLING TO THANK YOU.
FOR WHAT?
25

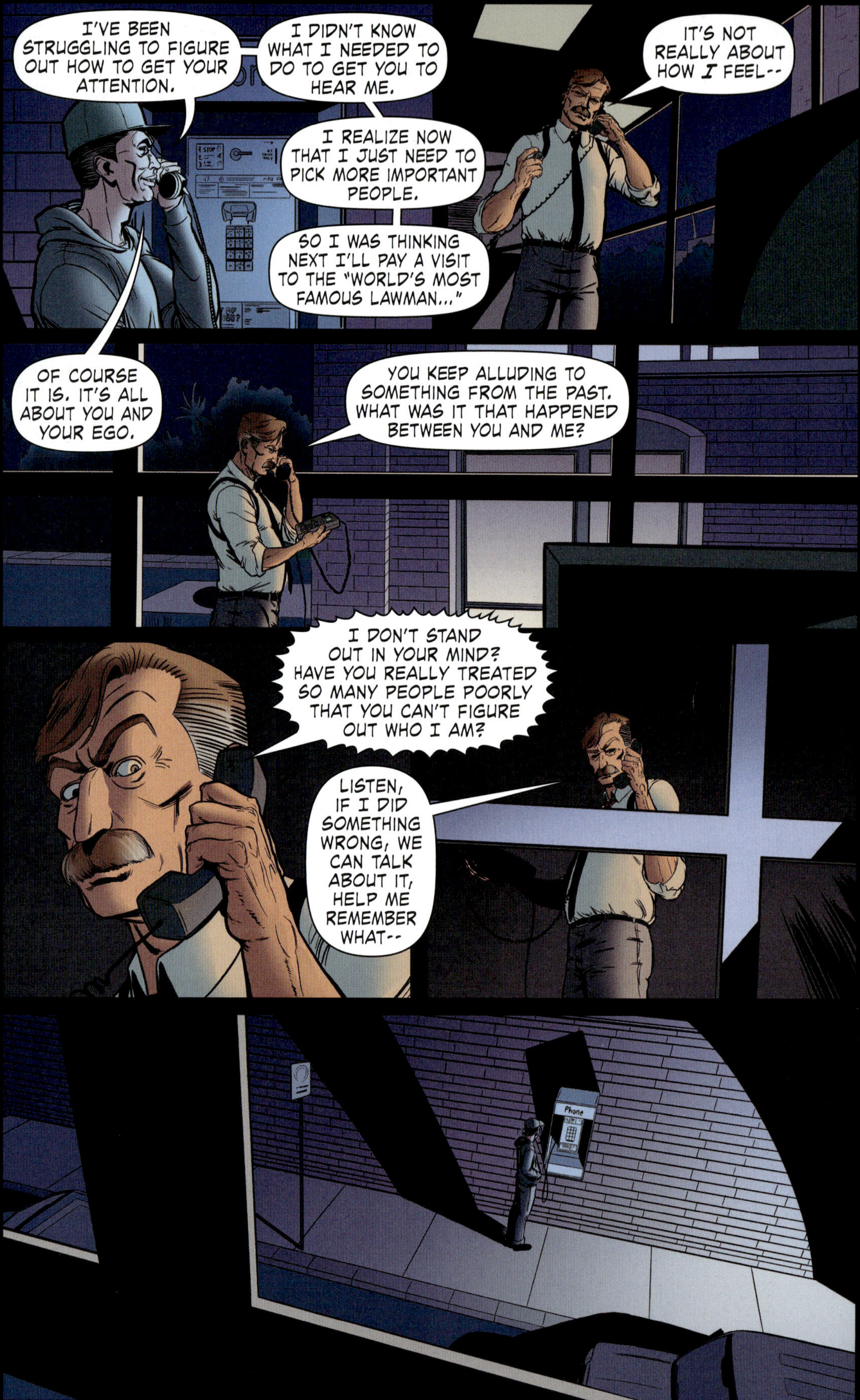
I'VE BEEN STRUGGLING TO FIGURE OUT HOW TO GET YOUR ATTENTION.
I DIDN'T KNOW WHAT I NEEDED TO DO TO GET YOU TO HEAR ME.
I REALIZE NOW THAT I JUST NEED TO PICK MORE IMPORTANT PEOPLE.
SO I WAS THINKING NEXT I'LL PAY A VISIT TO THE "WORLD'S MOST FAMOUS LAWMAN..."
IT'S NOT REALLY ABOUT HOW *I* FEEL--
OF COURSE IT IS. IT'S ALL ABOUT YOU AND YOUR EGO.
YOU KEEP ALLUDING TO SOMETHING FROM THE PAST. WHAT WAS IT THAT HAPPENED BETWEEN YOU AND ME?
I DON'T STAND OUT IN YOUR MIND? HAVE YOU REALLY TREATED SO MANY PEOPLE POORLY THAT YOU CAN'T FIGURE OUT WHO I AM?
LISTEN, IF I DID SOMETHING WRONG, WE CAN TALK ABOUT IT, HELP ME REMEMBER WHAT--
Phone

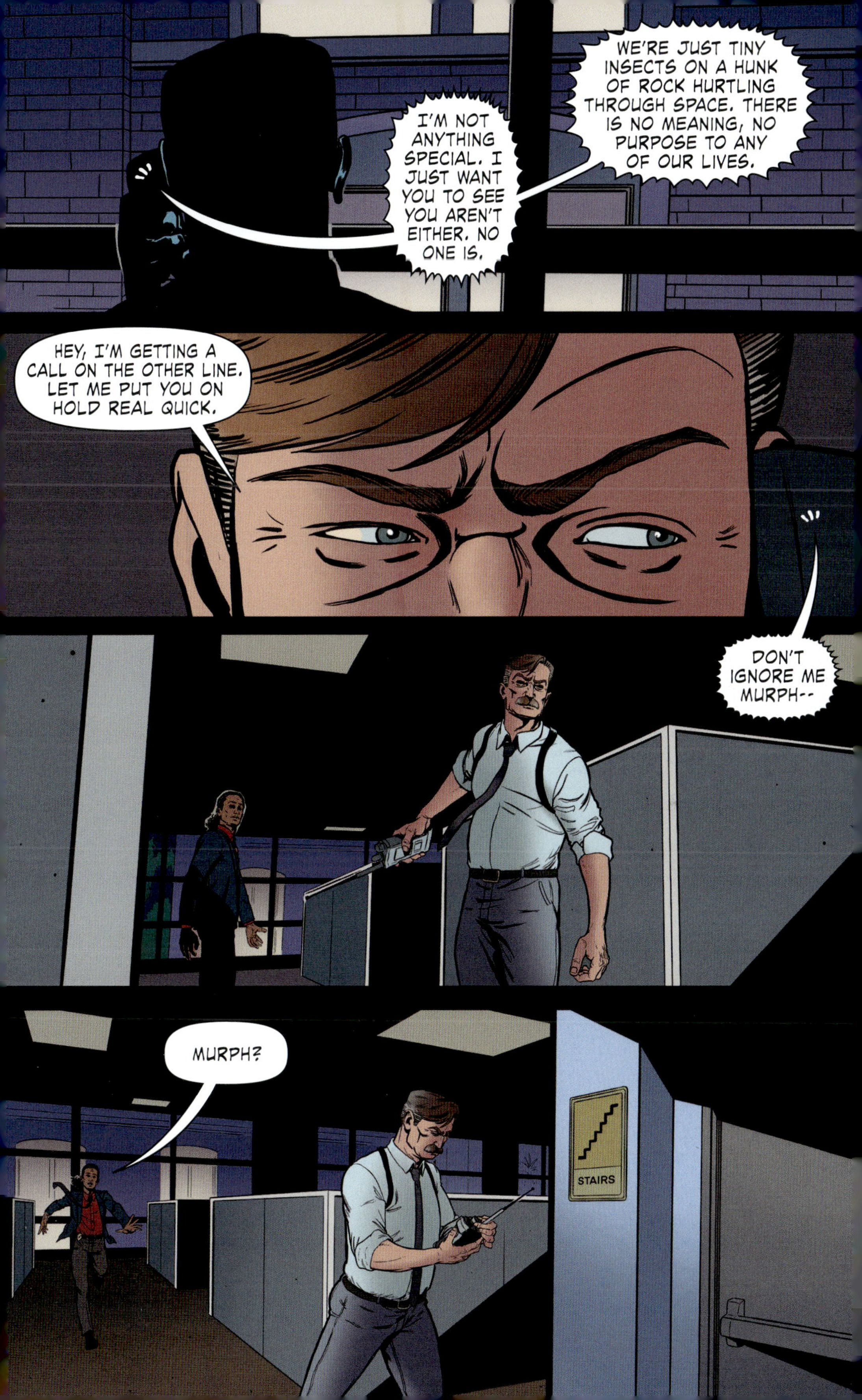

I'M NOT ANYTHING SPECIAL. I JUST WANT YOU TO SEE YOU AREN'T EITHER. NO ONE IS.
WE'RE JUST TINY INSECTS ON A HUNK OF ROCK HURTLING THROUGH SPACE. THERE IS NO MEANING, NO PURPOSE TO ANY OF OUR LIVES.
HEY, I'M GETTING A CALL ON THE OTHER LINE. LET ME PUT YOU ON HOLD REAL QUICK.
DON'T IGNORE ME MURPH--
MURPH?
STAIRS

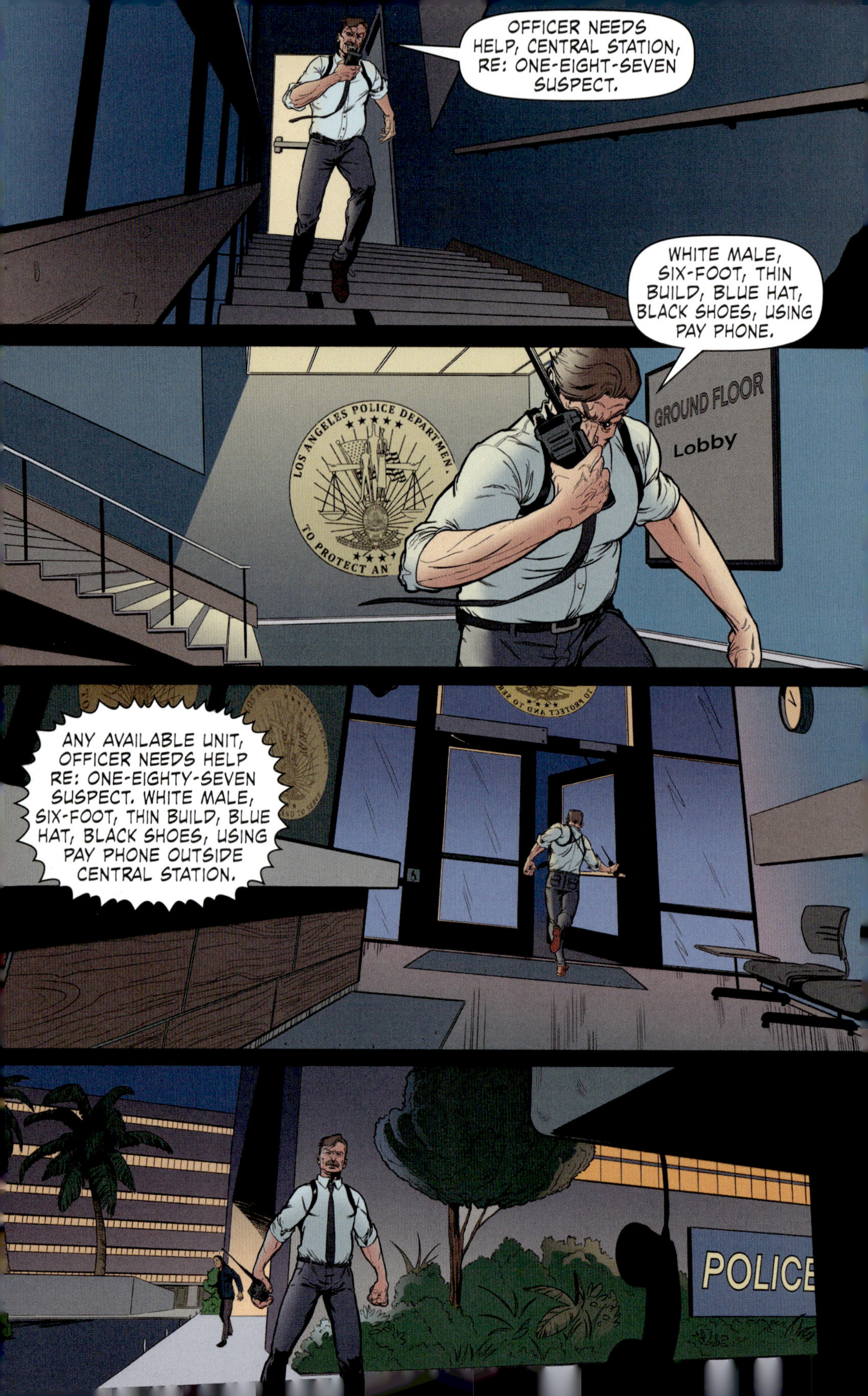
OFFICER NEEDS HELP, CENTRAL STATION, RE: ONE-EIGHT-SEVEN SUSPECT.
WHITE MALE, SIX-FOOT, THIN BUILD, BLUE HAT, BLACK SHOES, USING PAY PHONE.
LOS ANGELES POLICE DEPARTMENT
TO PROTECT AN
GROUND FLOOR
Lobby
ANY AVAILABLE UNIT, OFFICER NEEDS HELP RE: ONE-EIGHTY-SEVEN SUSPECT. WHITE MALE, SIX-FOOT, THIN BUILD, BLUE HAT, BLACK SHOES, USING PAY PHONE OUTSIDE CENTRAL STATION.
POLICE

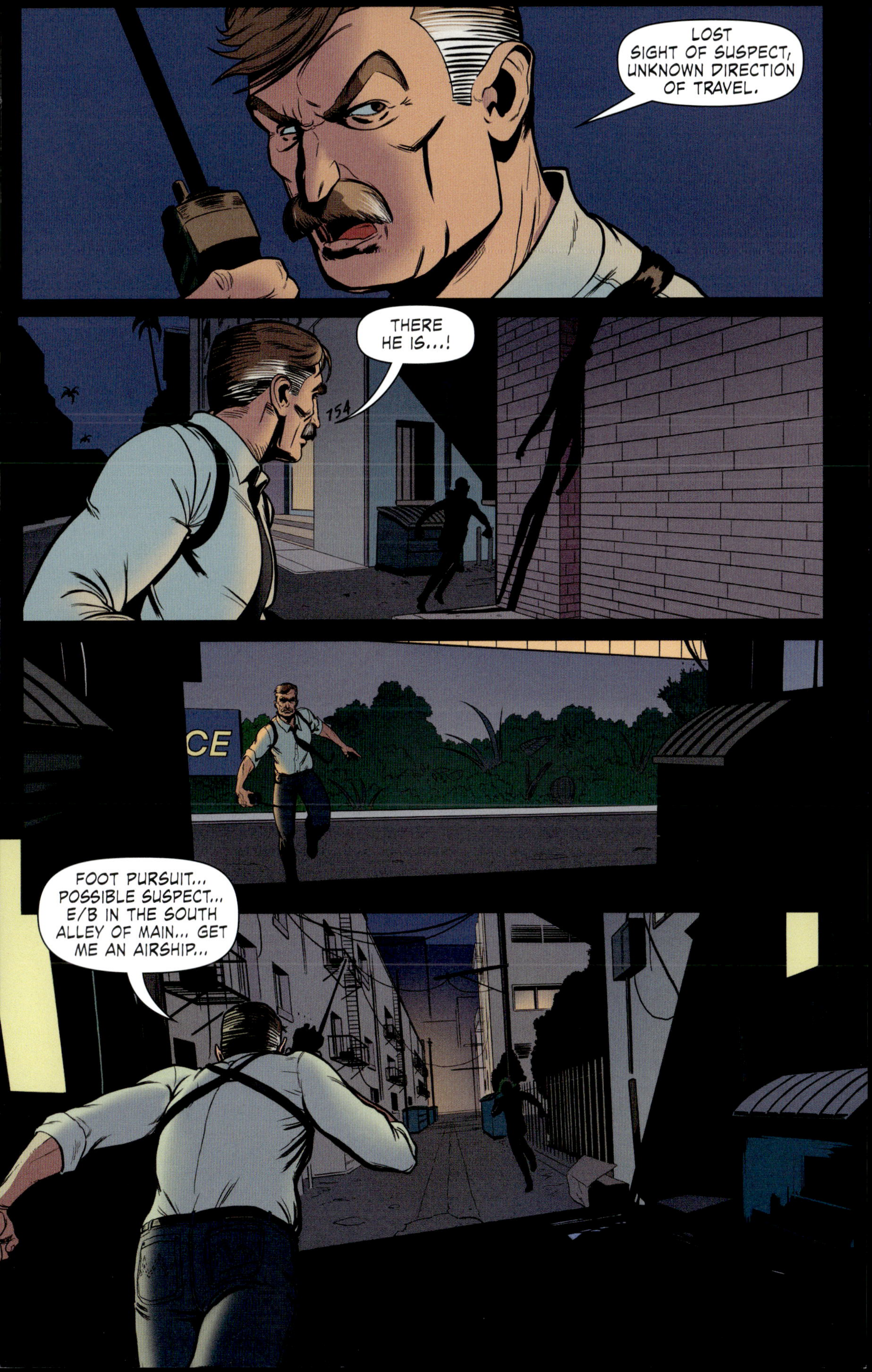
LOST SIGHT OF SUSPECT, UNKNOWN DIRECTION OF TRAVEL.
THERE HE IS...!
754
CE
FOOT PURSUIT... POSSIBLE SUSPECT... E/B IN THE SOUTH ALLEY OF MAIN... GET ME AN AIRSHIP...

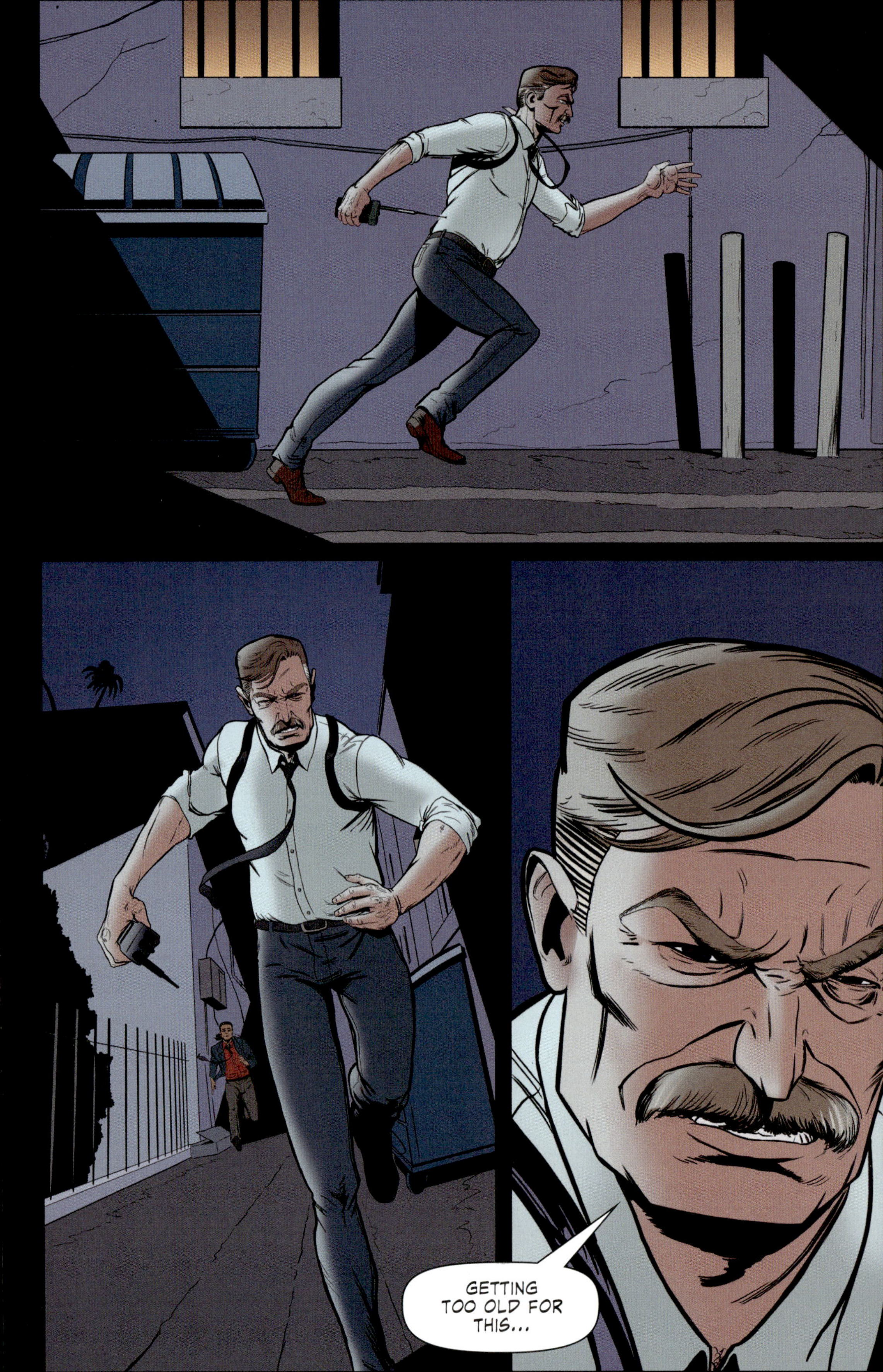
GETTING TOO OLD FOR THIS...

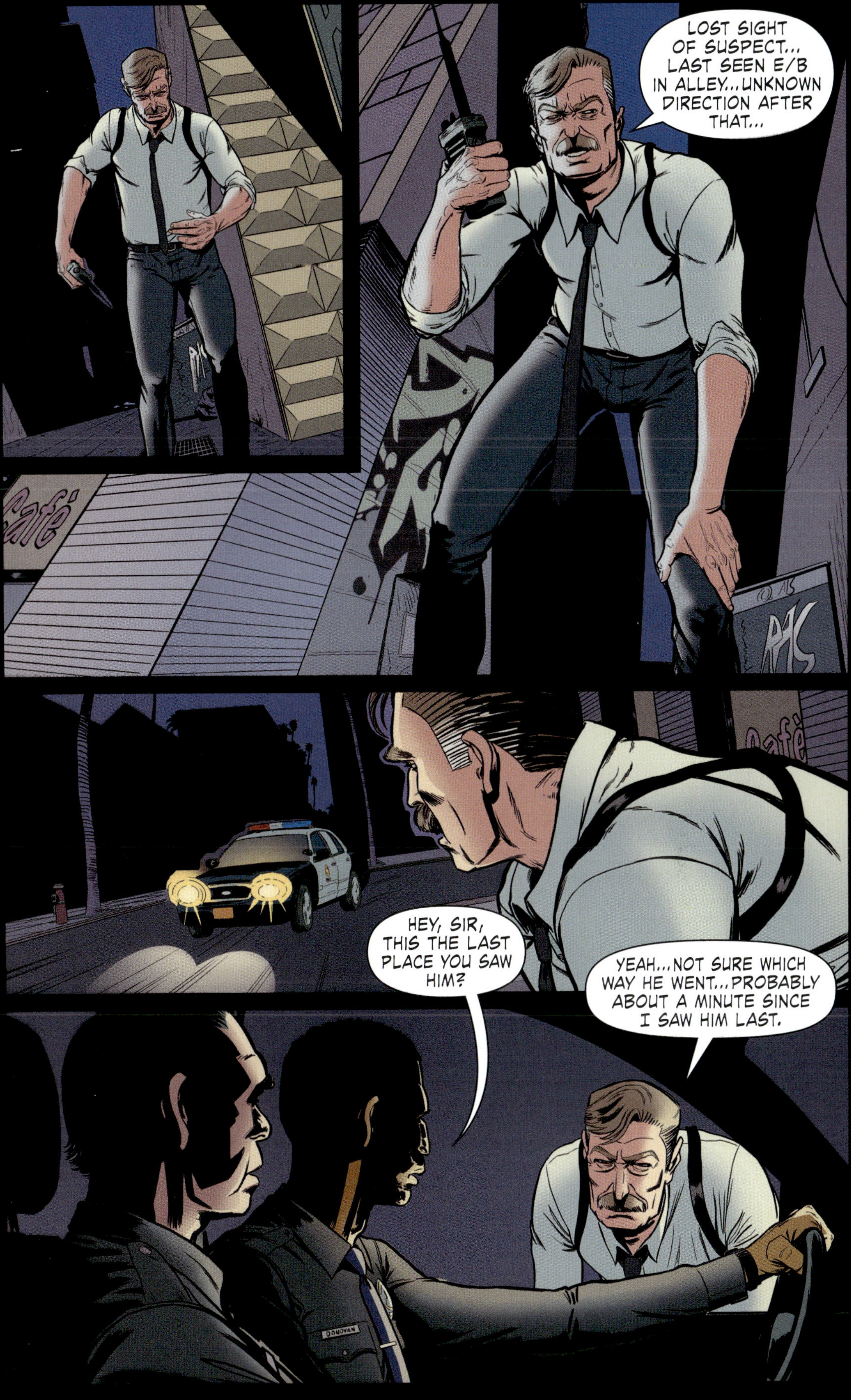

LOST SIGHT OF SUSPECT... LAST SEEN E/B IN ALLEY...UNKNOWN DIRECTION AFTER THAT...
Café
HEY, SIR, THIS THE LAST PLACE YOU SAW HIM?
YEAH...NOT SURE WHICH WAY HE WENT...PROBABLY ABOUT A MINUTE SINCE I SAW HIM LAST.
DONOVAN

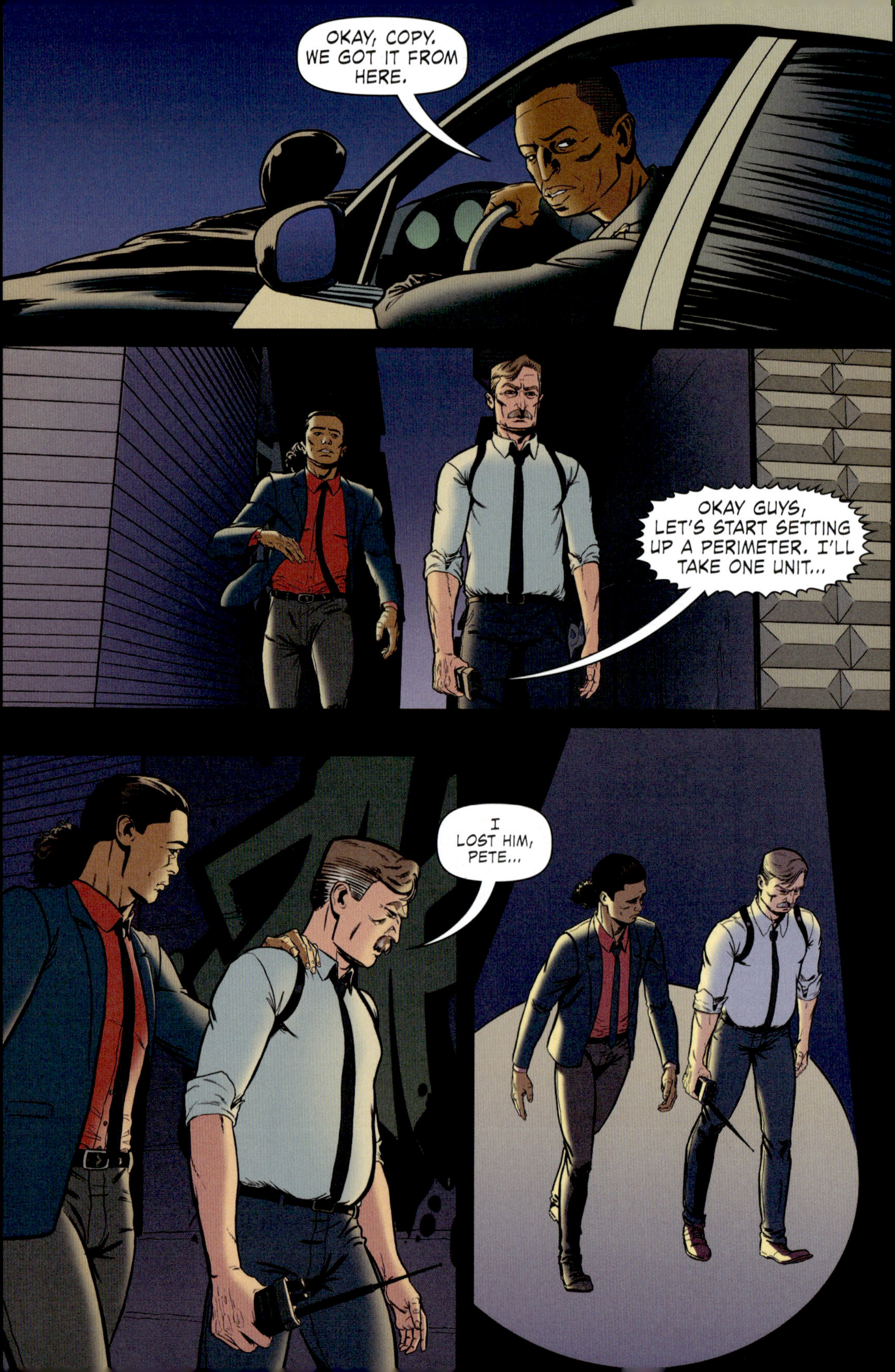
OKAY, COPY. WE GOT IT FROM HERE.
OKAY GUYS, LET'S START SETTING UP A PERIMETER. I'LL TAKE ONE UNIT...
I LOST HIM, PETE...

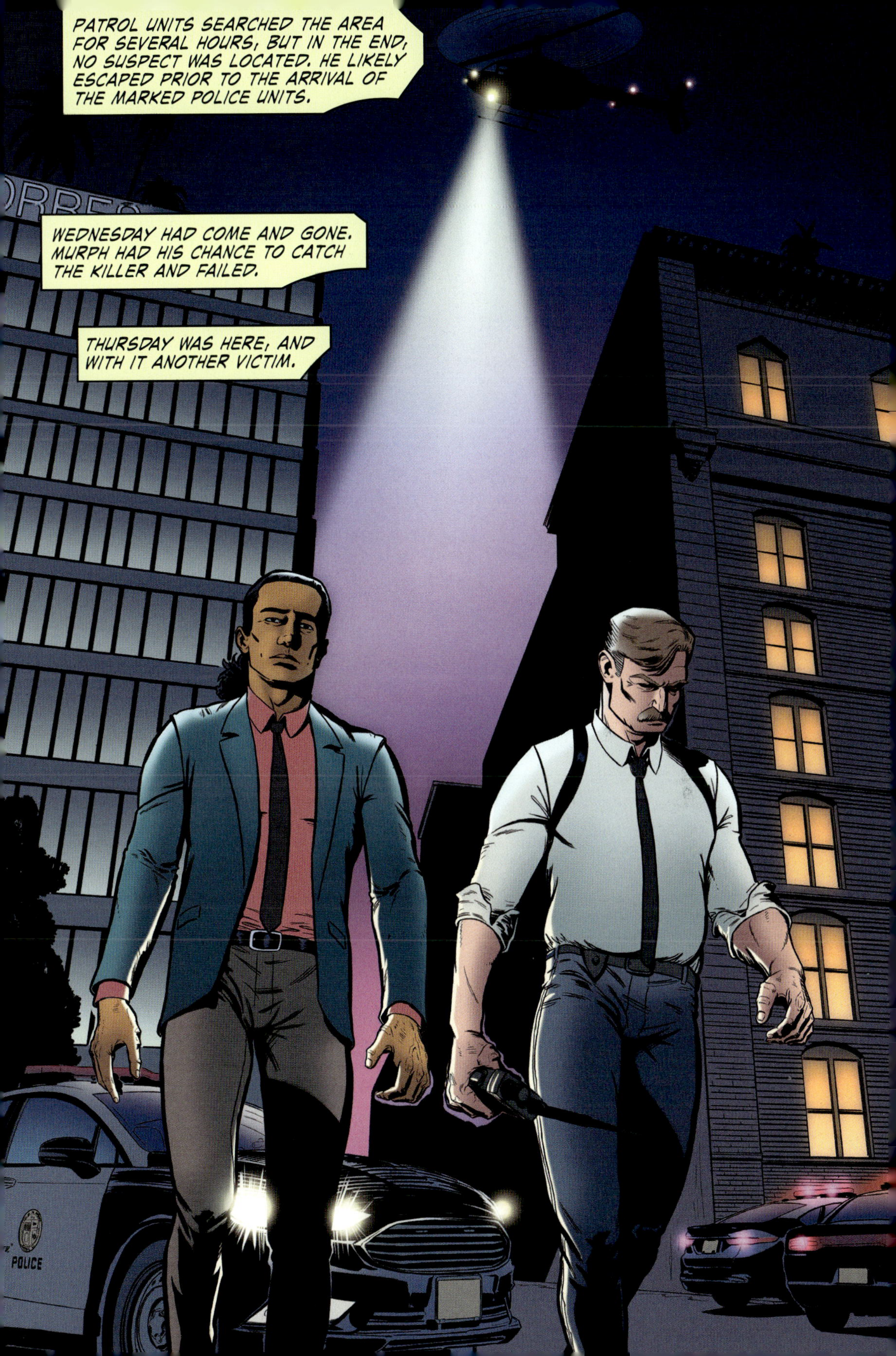
PATROL UNITS SEARCHED THE AREA FOR SEVERAL HOURS, BUT IN THE END, NO SUSPECT WAS LOCATED. HE LIKELY ESCAPED PRIOR TO THE ARRIVAL OF THE MARKED POLICE UNITS.
WEDNESDAY HAD COME AND GONE. MURPH HAD HIS CHANCE TO CATCH THE KILLER AND FAILED.
THURSDAY WAS HERE, AND WITH IT ANOTHER VICTIM.
POLICE

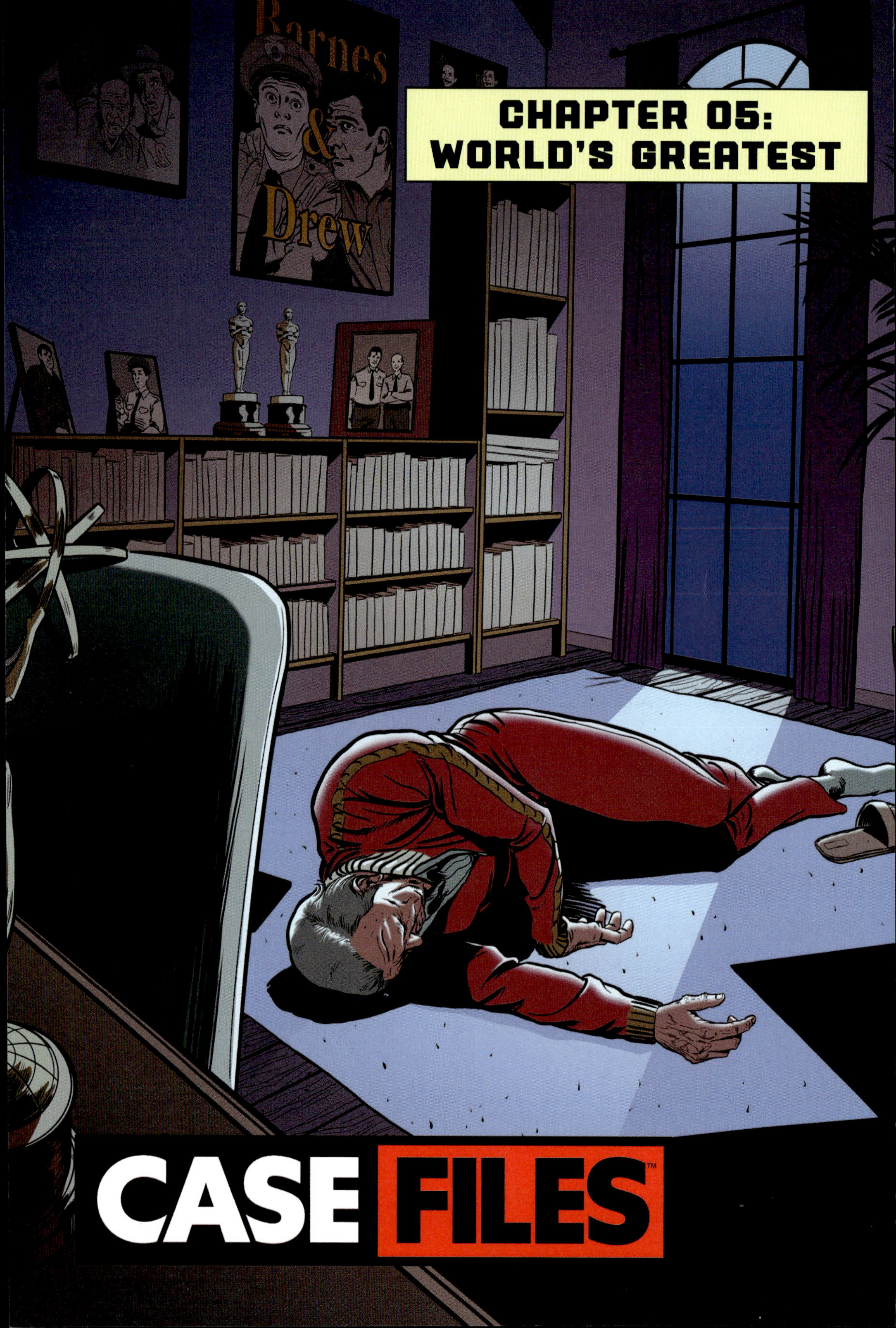
Barnes & Drew
CHAPTER 05:
WORLD'S GREATEST
CASE FILES™

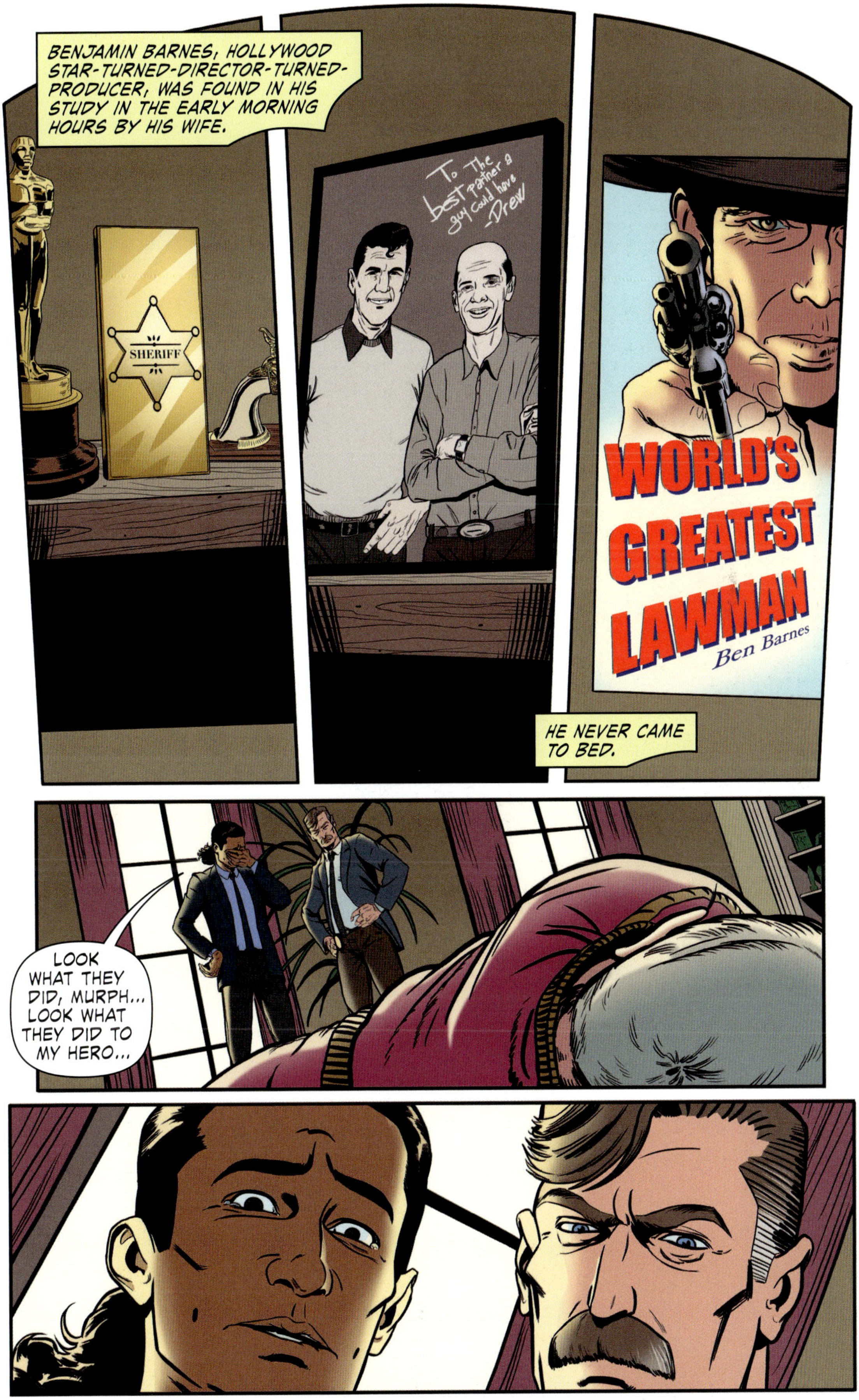

BENJAMIN BARNES, HOLLYWOOD STAR-TURNED-DIRECTOR-TURNED-PRODUCER, WAS FOUND IN HIS STUDY IN THE EARLY MORNING HOURS BY HIS WIFE.
SHERIFF
To the best partner a guy could have -Drew
WORLD'S GREATEST LAWMAN
Ben Barnes
HE NEVER CAME TO BED.
LOOK WHAT THEY DID, MURPH... LOOK WHAT THEY DID TO MY HERO...

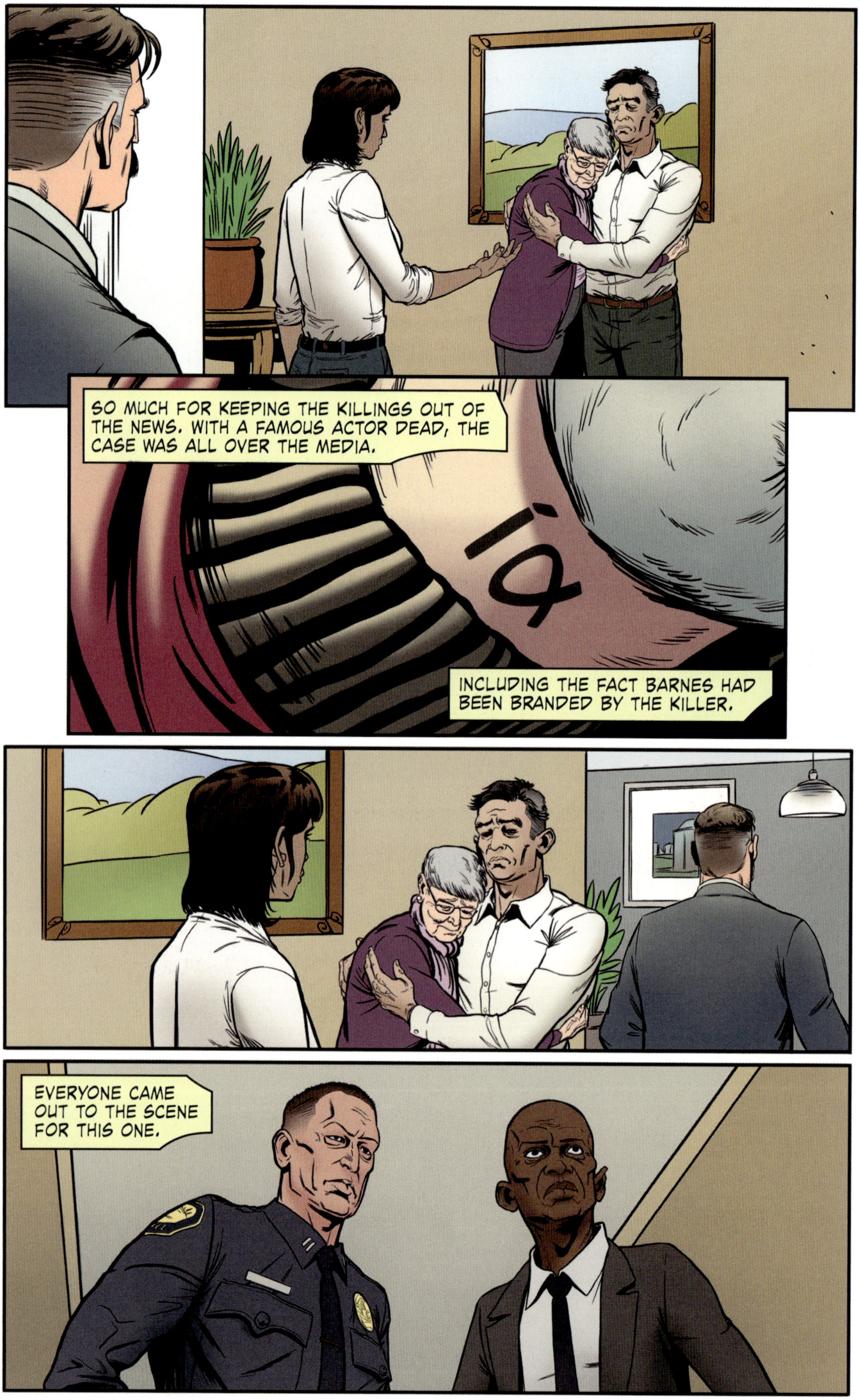
SO MUCH FOR KEEPING THE KILLINGS OUT OF THE NEWS. WITH A FAMOUS ACTOR DEAD, THE CASE WAS ALL OVER THE MEDIA.
INCLUDING THE FACT BARNES HAD BEEN BRANDED BY THE KILLER.
EVERYONE CAME OUT TO THE SCENE FOR THIS ONE.

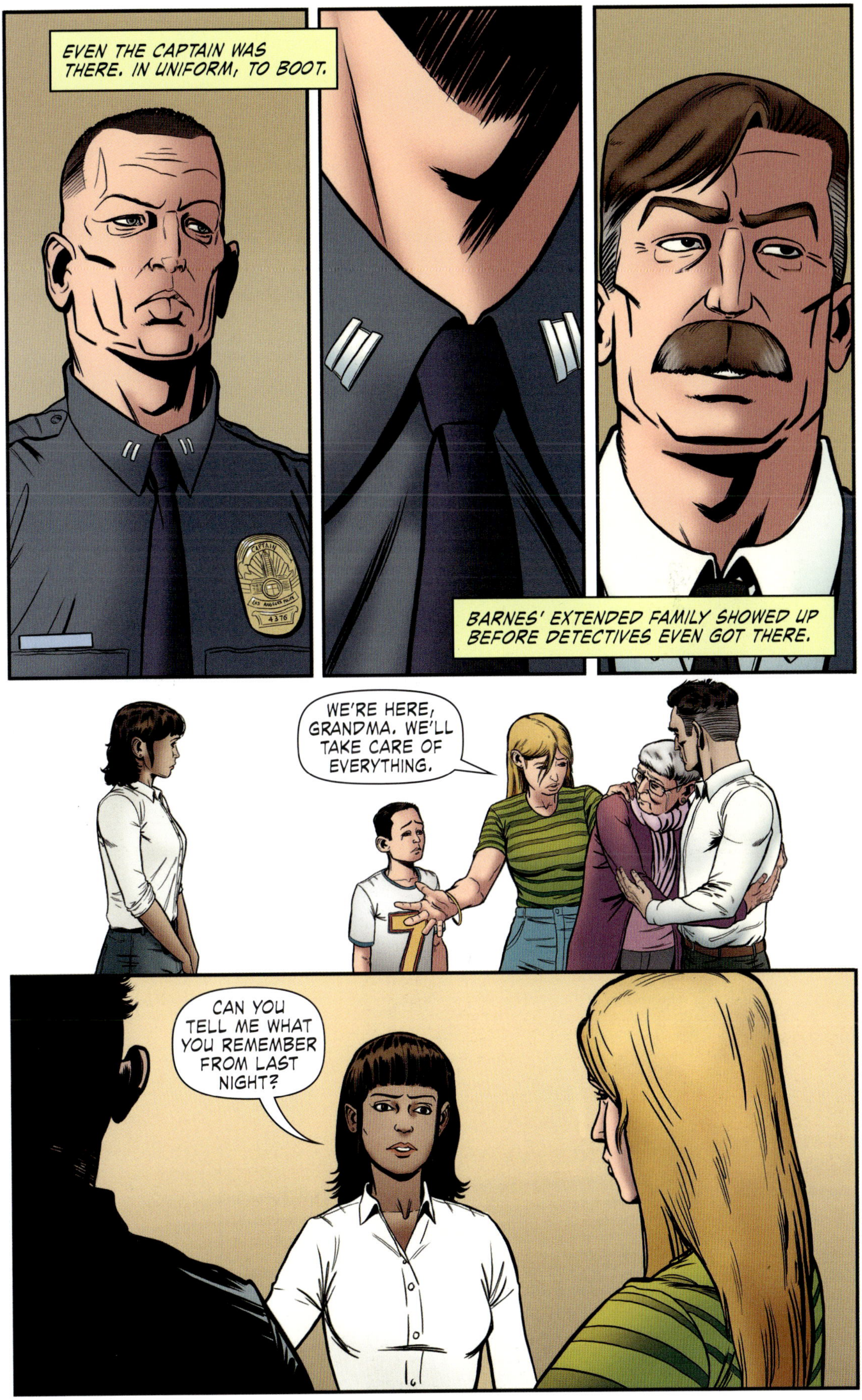
EVEN THE CAPTAIN WAS THERE. IN UNIFORM, TO BOOT.
BARNES' EXTENDED FAMILY SHOWED UP BEFORE DETECTIVES EVEN GOT THERE.
WE'RE HERE, GRANDMA. WE'LL TAKE CARE OF EVERYTHING.
CAN YOU TELL ME WHAT YOU REMEMBER FROM LAST NIGHT?

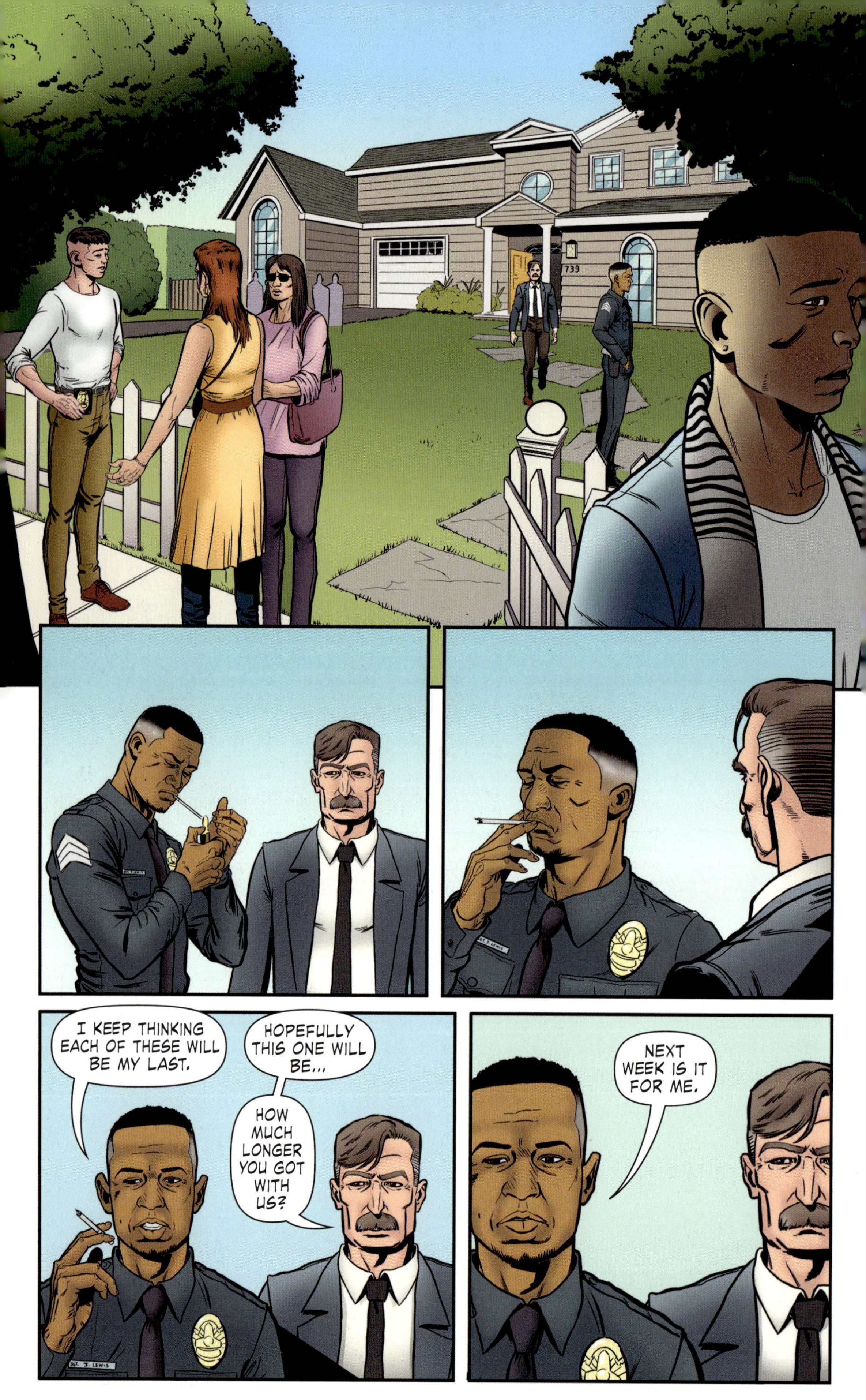
739
I KEEP THINKING EACH OF THESE WILL BE MY LAST.
HOPEFULLY THIS ONE WILL BE...
HOW MUCH LONGER YOU GOT WITH US?
NEXT WEEK IS IT FOR ME.

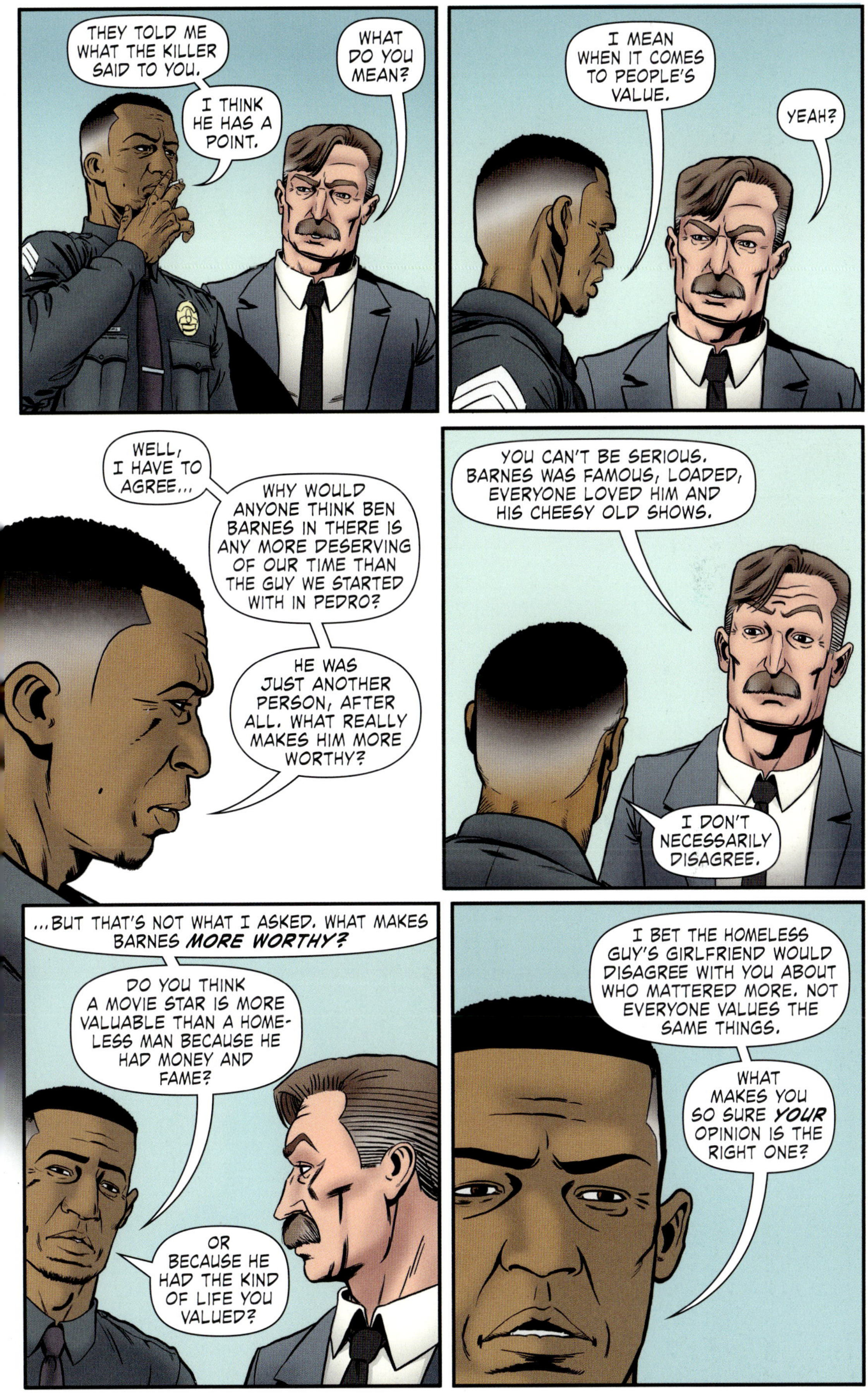
THEY TOLD ME WHAT THE KILLER SAID TO YOU.
I THINK HE HAS A POINT.
WHAT DO YOU MEAN?
I MEAN WHEN IT COMES TO PEOPLE'S VALUE.
YEAH?
WELL, I HAVE TO AGREE...
WHY WOULD ANYONE THINK BEN BARNES IN THERE IS ANY MORE DESERVING OF OUR TIME THAN THE GUY WE STARTED WITH IN PEDRO?
HE WAS JUST ANOTHER PERSON, AFTER ALL. WHAT REALLY MAKES HIM MORE WORTHY?
YOU CAN'T BE SERIOUS. BARNES WAS FAMOUS, LOADED, EVERYONE LOVED HIM AND HIS CHEESY OLD SHOWS.
I DON'T NECESSARILY DISAGREE.
...BUT THAT'S NOT WHAT I ASKED. WHAT MAKES BARNES *MORE WORTHY?*
DO YOU THINK A MOVIE STAR IS MORE VALUABLE THAN A HOME-LESS MAN BECAUSE HE HAD MONEY AND FAME?
OR BECAUSE HE HAD THE KIND OF LIFE YOU VALUED?
I BET THE HOMELESS GUY'S GIRLFRIEND WOULD DISAGREE WITH YOU ABOUT WHO MATTERED MORE. NOT EVERYONE VALUES THE SAME THINGS.
WHAT MAKES YOU SO SURE *YOUR* OPINION IS THE RIGHT ONE?

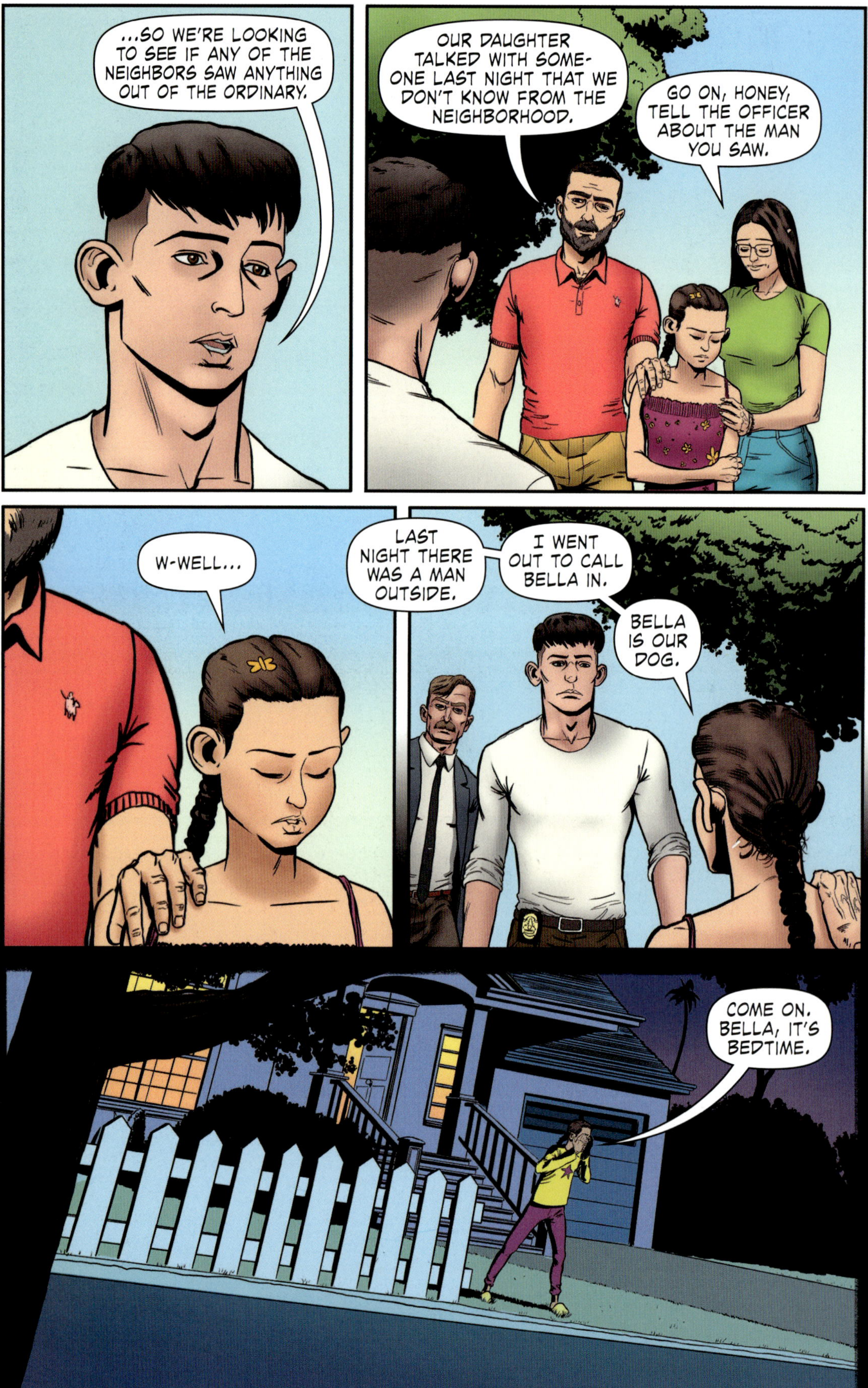
...SO WE'RE LOOKING TO SEE IF ANY OF THE NEIGHBORS SAW ANYTHING OUT OF THE ORDINARY.
OUR DAUGHTER TALKED WITH SOME-ONE LAST NIGHT THAT WE DON'T KNOW FROM THE NEIGHBORHOOD.
GO ON, HONEY, TELL THE OFFICER ABOUT THE MAN YOU SAW.
W-WELL...
LAST NIGHT THERE WAS A MAN OUTSIDE.
I WENT OUT TO CALL BELLA IN.
BELLA IS OUR DOG.
COME ON, BELLA, IT'S BEDTIME.

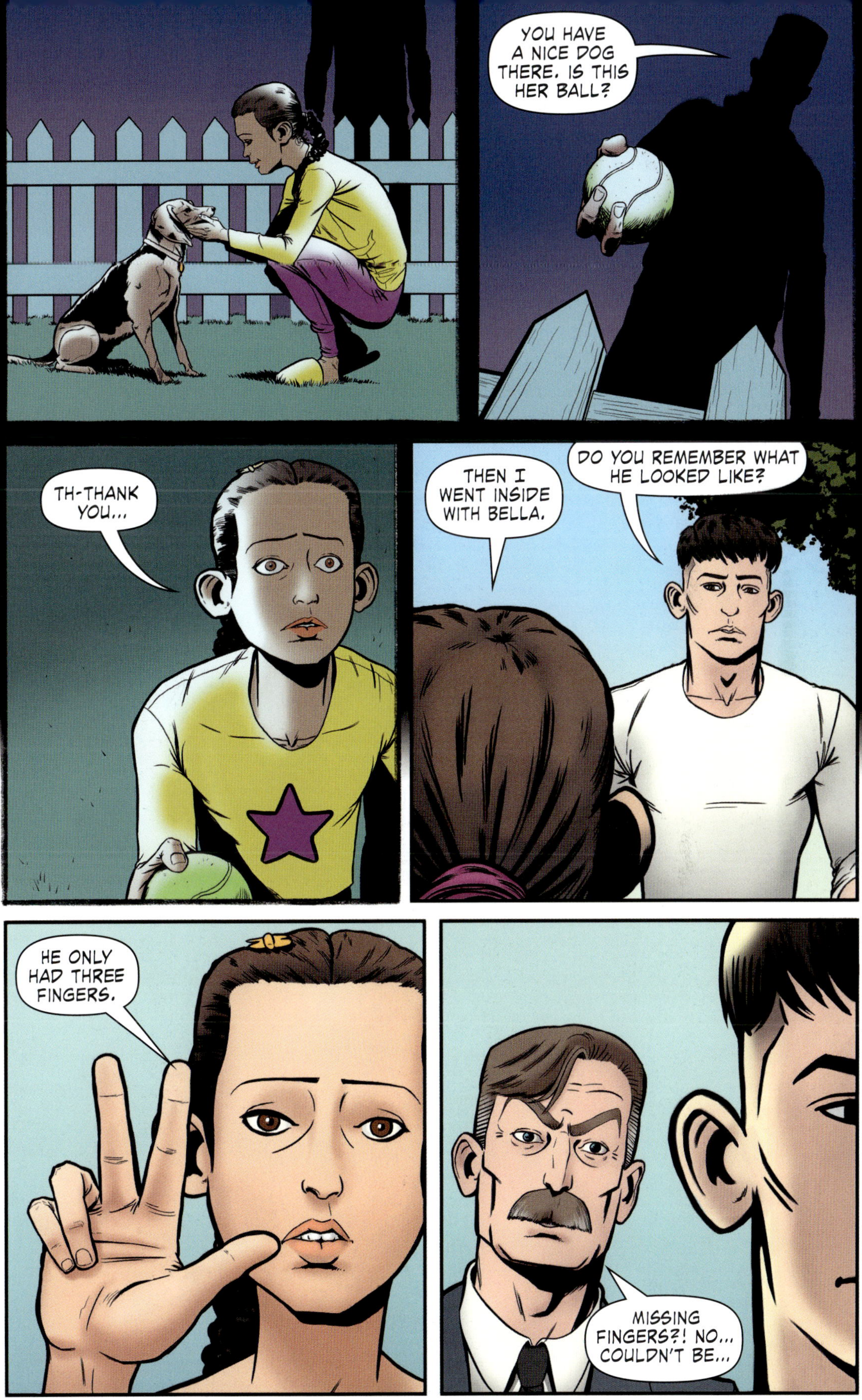
YOU HAVE A NICE DOG THERE. IS THIS HER BALL?
TH-THANK YOU...
THEN I WENT INSIDE WITH BELLA.
DO YOU REMEMBER WHAT HE LOOKED LIKE?
HE ONLY HAD THREE FINGERS.
MISSING FINGERS?! NO... COULDN'T BE...

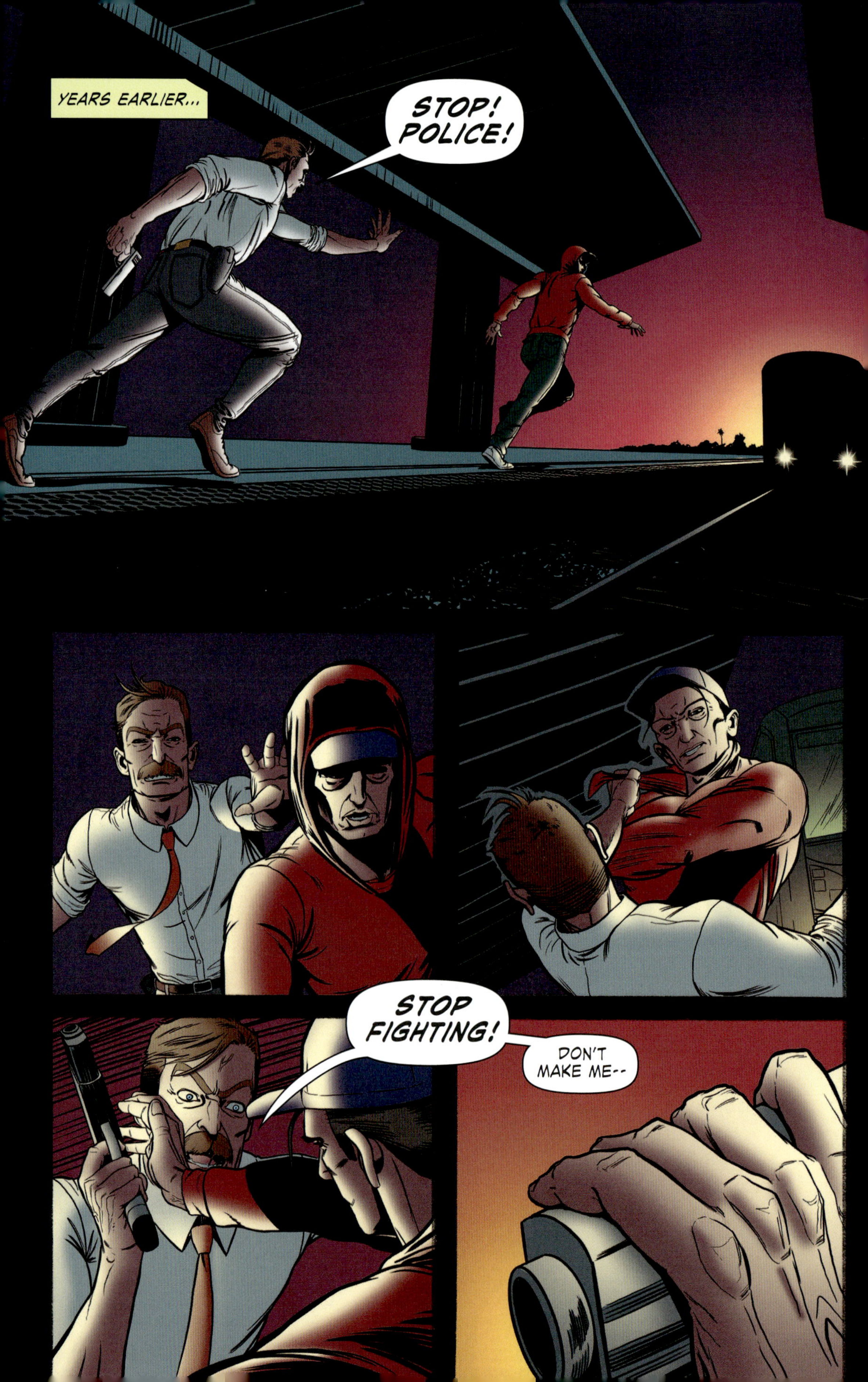
YEARS EARLIER...
STOP! POLICE!
STOP FIGHTING!
DON'T MAKE ME--

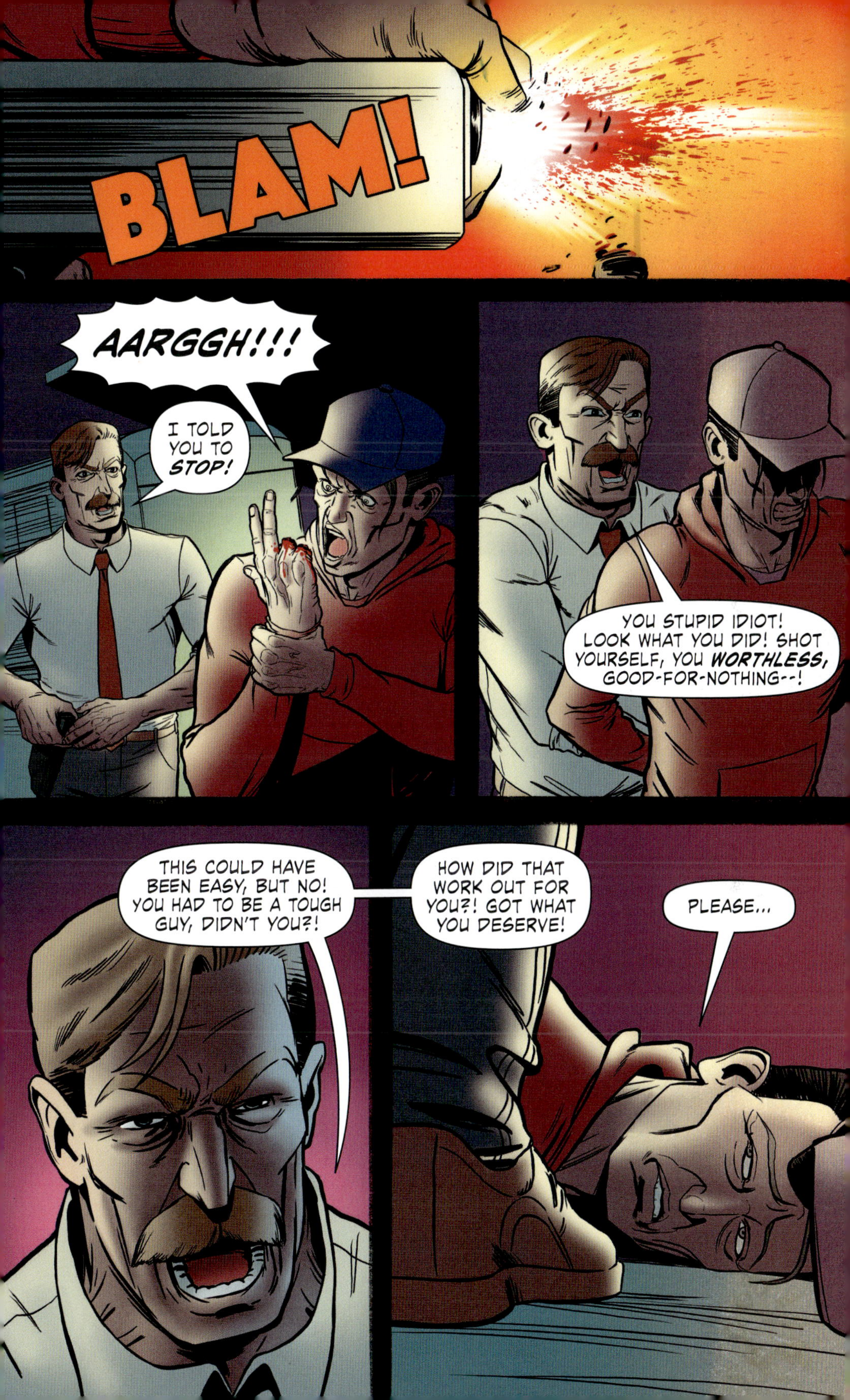
BLAM!
AARGGH!!!
I TOLD YOU TO *STOP!*
YOU STUPID IDIOT! LOOK WHAT YOU DID! SHOT YOURSELF, YOU ***WORTHLESS,*** GOOD-FOR-NOTHING--!
THIS COULD HAVE BEEN EASY, BUT NO! YOU HAD TO BE A TOUGH GUY, DIDN'T YOU?!
HOW DID THAT WORK OUT FOR YOU?! GOT WHAT YOU DESERVE!
PLEASE...

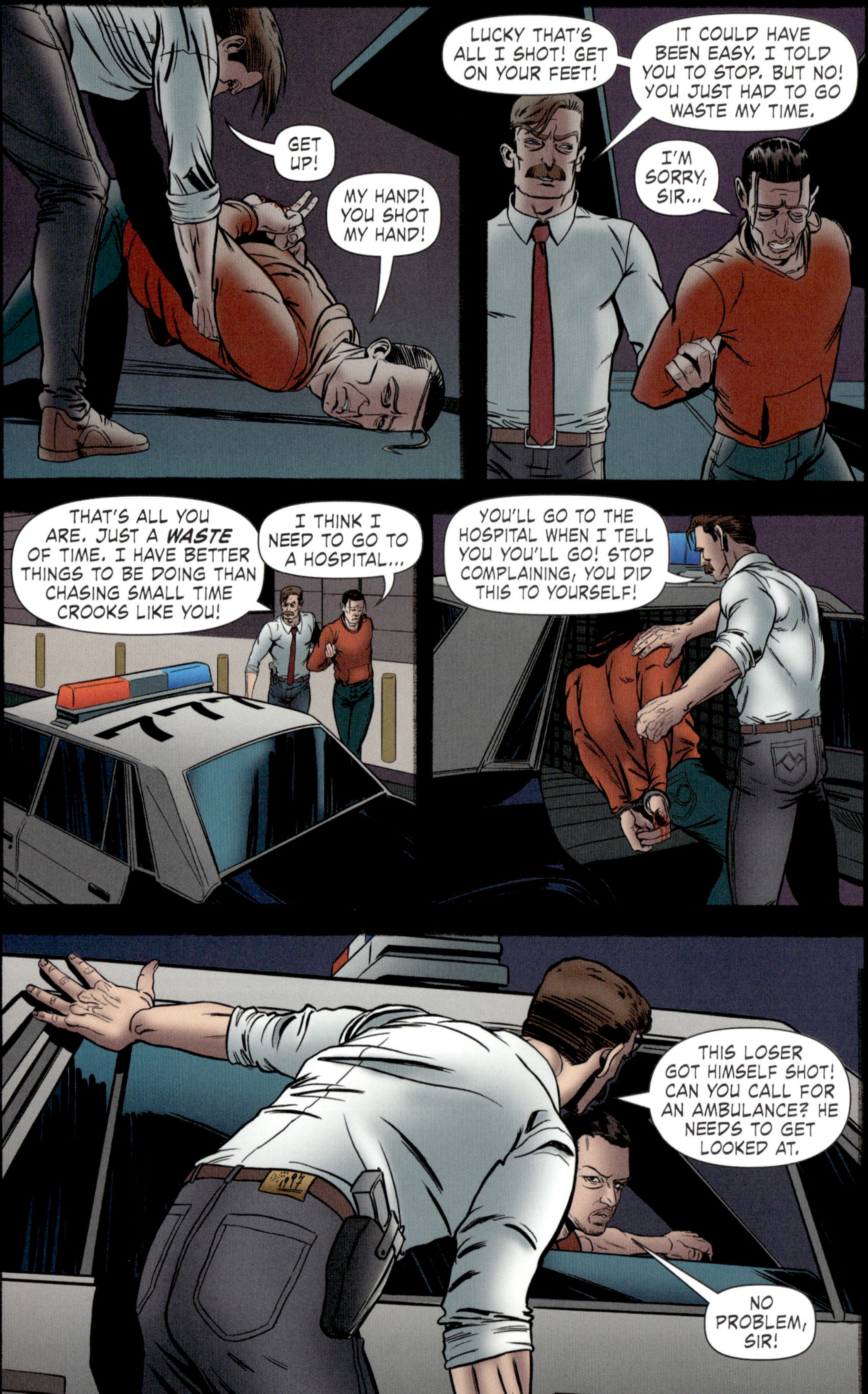
GET UP!
MY HAND! YOU SHOT MY HAND!
LUCKY THAT'S ALL I SHOT! GET ON YOUR FEET!
IT COULD HAVE BEEN EASY. I TOLD YOU TO STOP. BUT NO! YOU JUST HAD TO GO WASTE MY TIME.
I'M SORRY, SIR...
THAT'S ALL YOU ARE. JUST A ***WASTE*** OF TIME. I HAVE BETTER THINGS TO BE DOING THAN CHASING SMALL TIME CROOKS LIKE YOU!
I THINK I NEED TO GO TO A HOSPITAL...
777
YOU'LL GO TO THE HOSPITAL WHEN I TELL YOU YOU'LL GO! STOP COMPLAINING, YOU DID THIS TO YOURSELF!
THIS LOSER GOT HIMSELF SHOT! CAN YOU CALL FOR AN AMBULANCE? HE NEEDS TO GET LOOKED AT.
NO PROBLEM, SIR!

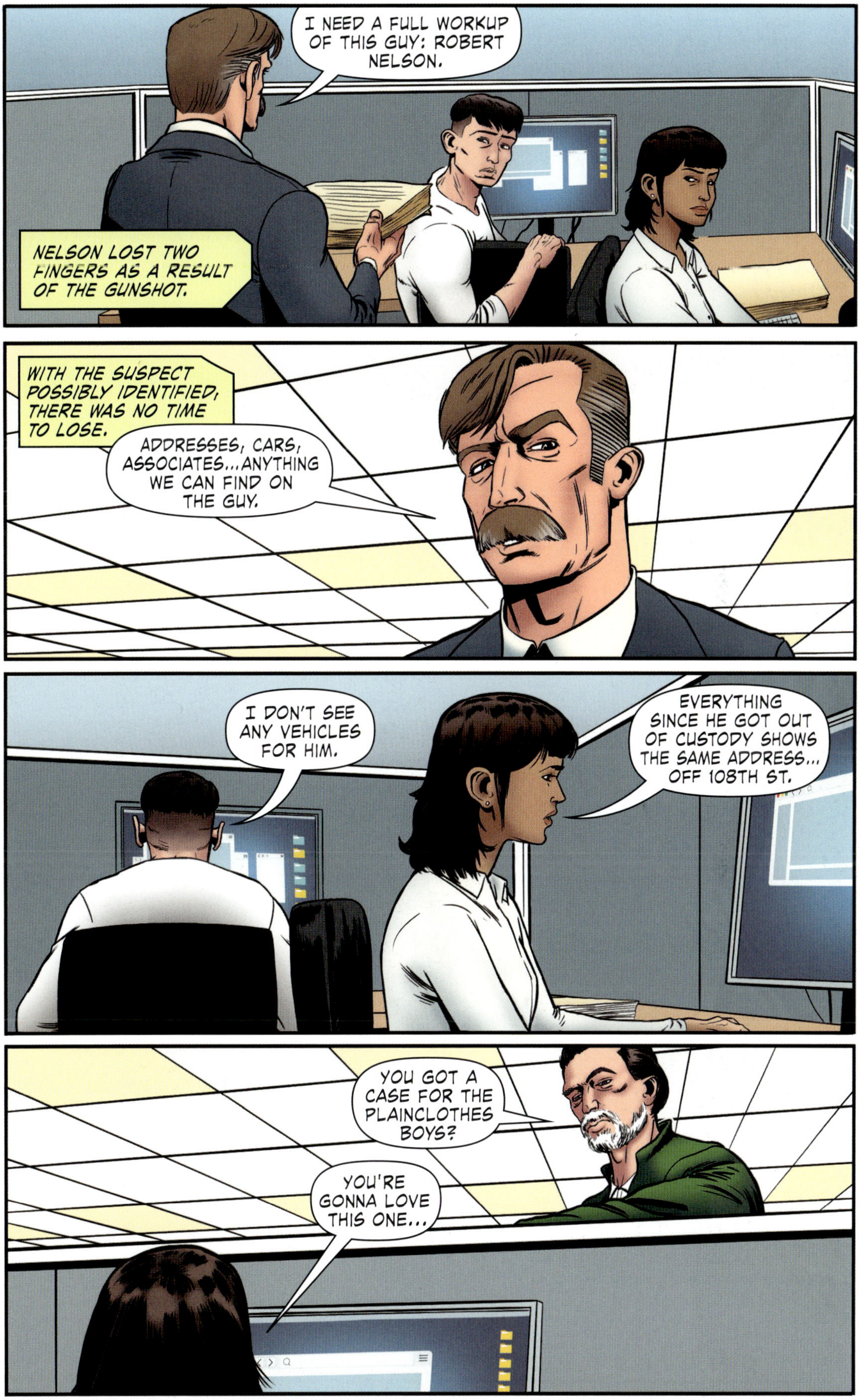
I NEED A FULL WORKUP OF THIS GUY: ROBERT NELSON.
NELSON LOST TWO FINGERS AS A RESULT OF THE GUNSHOT.
WITH THE SUSPECT POSSIBLY IDENTIFIED, THERE WAS NO TIME TO LOSE.
ADDRESSES, CARS, ASSOCIATES...ANYTHING WE CAN FIND ON THE GUY.
I DON'T SEE ANY VEHICLES FOR HIM.
EVERYTHING SINCE HE GOT OUT OF CUSTODY SHOWS THE SAME ADDRESS... OFF 108TH ST.
YOU GOT A CASE FOR THE PLAINCLOTHES BOYS?
YOU'RE GONNA LOVE THIS ONE...

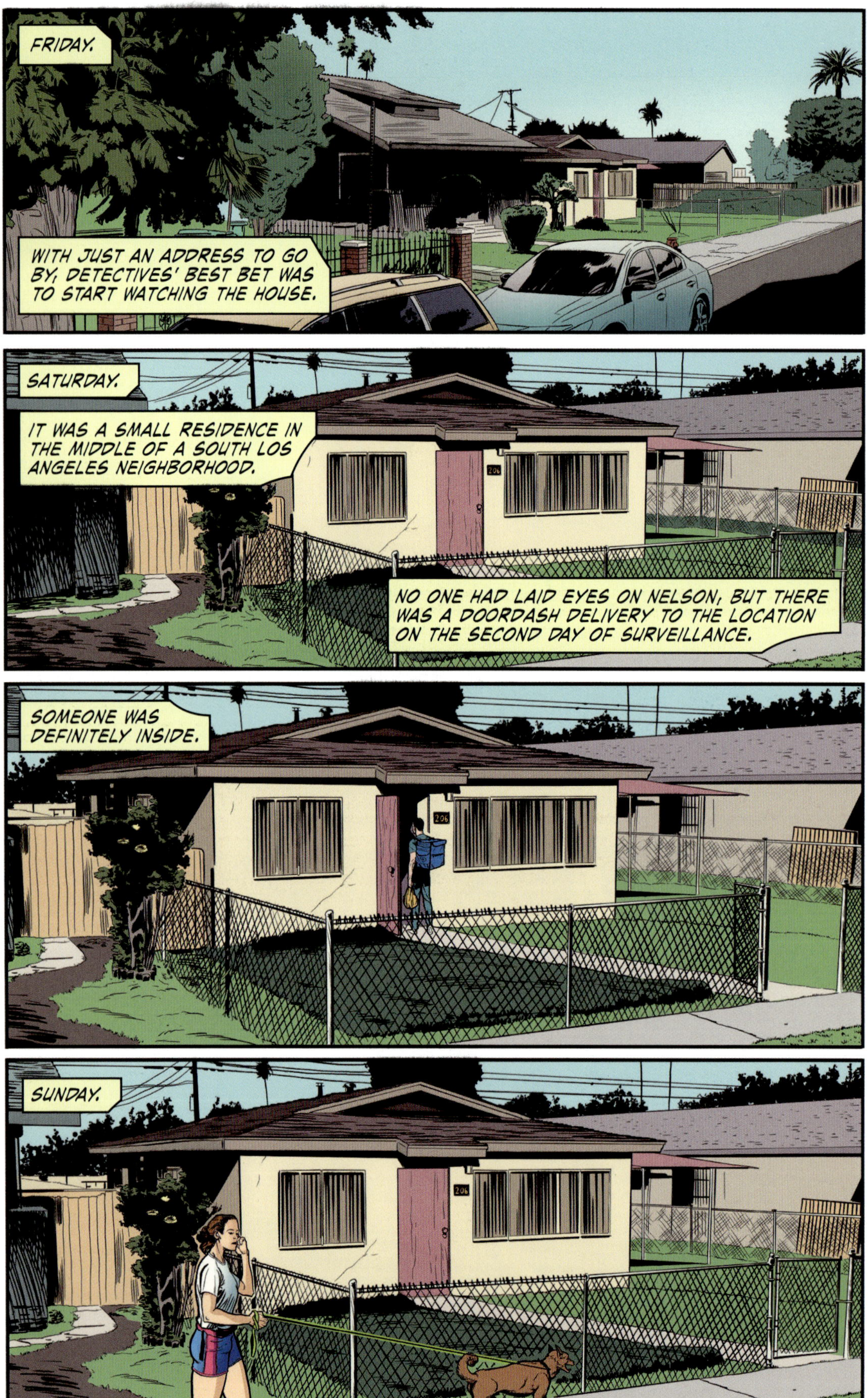
FRIDAY.
WITH JUST AN ADDRESS TO GO BY, DETECTIVES' BEST BET WAS TO START WATCHING THE HOUSE.
SATURDAY.
IT WAS A SMALL RESIDENCE IN THE MIDDLE OF A SOUTH LOS ANGELES NEIGHBORHOOD.
206
NO ONE HAD LAID EYES ON NELSON, BUT THERE WAS A DOORDASH DELIVERY TO THE LOCATION ON THE SECOND DAY OF SURVEILLANCE.
SOMEONE WAS DEFINITELY INSIDE.
206
SUNDAY.
206

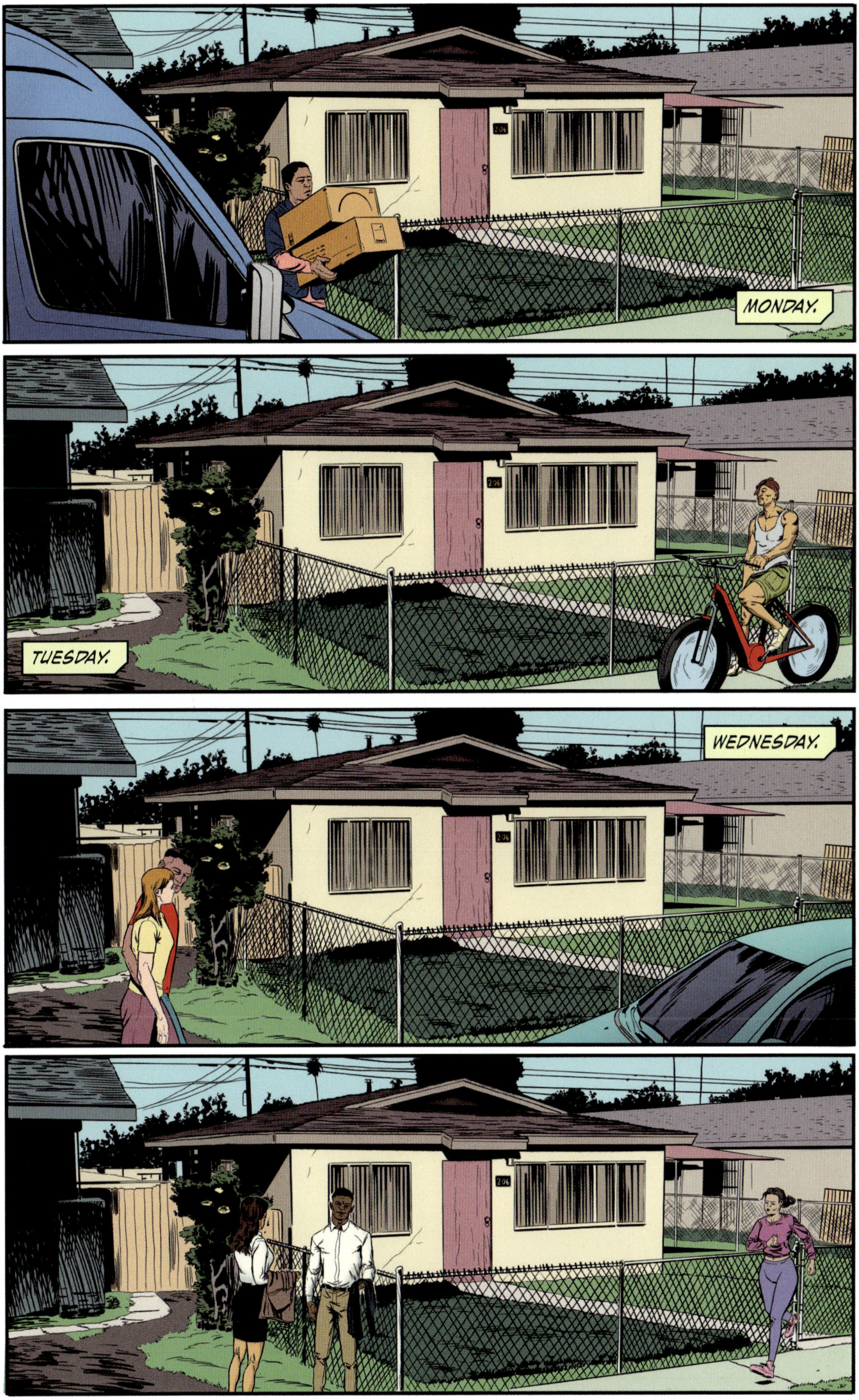
MONDAY.
TUESDAY.
WEDNESDAY.

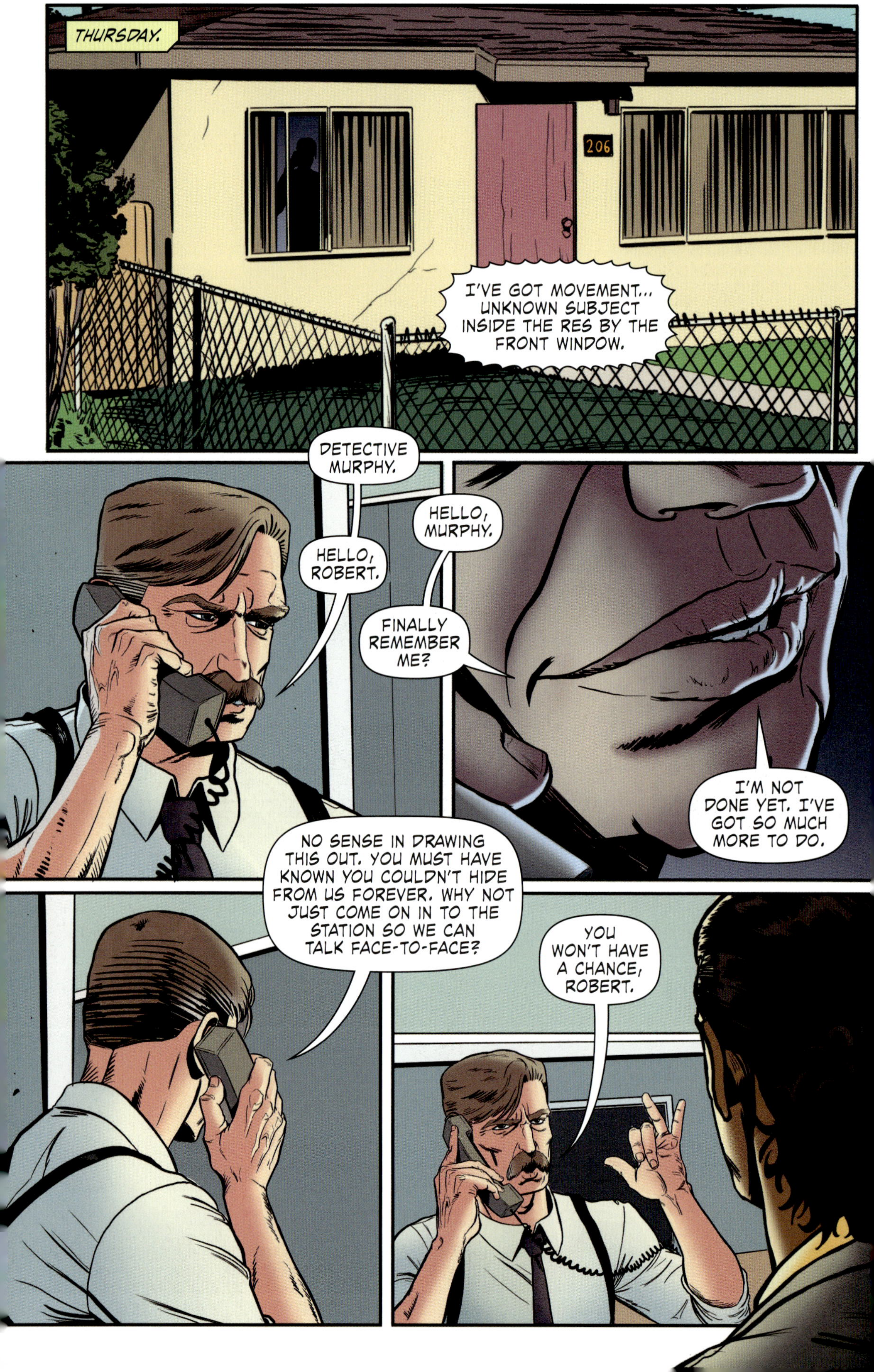
THURSDAY.
206
I'VE GOT MOVEMENT... UNKNOWN SUBJECT INSIDE THE RES BY THE FRONT WINDOW.
DETECTIVE MURPHY.
HELLO, MURPHY.
HELLO, ROBERT.
FINALLY REMEMBER ME?
I'M NOT DONE YET. I'VE GOT SO MUCH MORE TO DO.
NO SENSE IN DRAWING THIS OUT. YOU MUST HAVE KNOWN YOU COULDN'T HIDE FROM US FOREVER. WHY NOT JUST COME ON IN TO THE STATION SO WE CAN TALK FACE-TO-FACE?
YOU WON'T HAVE A CHANCE, ROBERT.

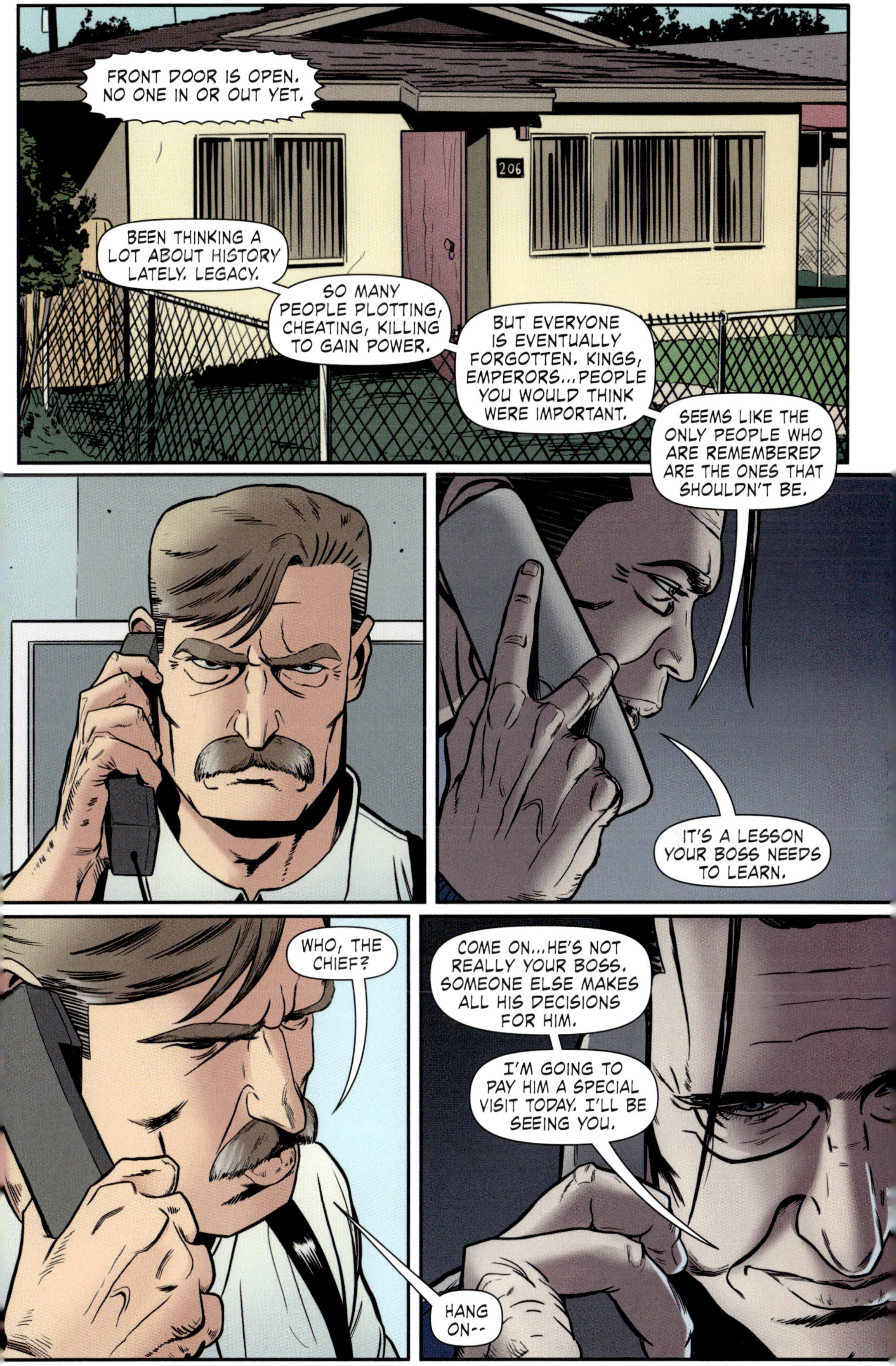
FRONT DOOR IS OPEN. NO ONE IN OR OUT YET.
206
BEEN THINKING A LOT ABOUT HISTORY LATELY. LEGACY.
SO MANY PEOPLE PLOTTING, CHEATING, KILLING TO GAIN POWER.
BUT EVERYONE IS EVENTUALLY FORGOTTEN. KINGS, EMPERORS...PEOPLE YOU WOULD THINK WERE IMPORTANT.
SEEMS LIKE THE ONLY PEOPLE WHO ARE REMEMBERED ARE THE ONES THAT SHOULDN'T BE.
IT'S A LESSON YOUR BOSS NEEDS TO LEARN.
WHO, THE CHIEF?
HANG ON--
COME ON...HE'S NOT REALLY YOUR BOSS. SOMEONE ELSE MAKES ALL HIS DECISIONS FOR HIM.
I'M GOING TO PAY HIM A SPECIAL VISIT TODAY. I'LL BE SEEING YOU.

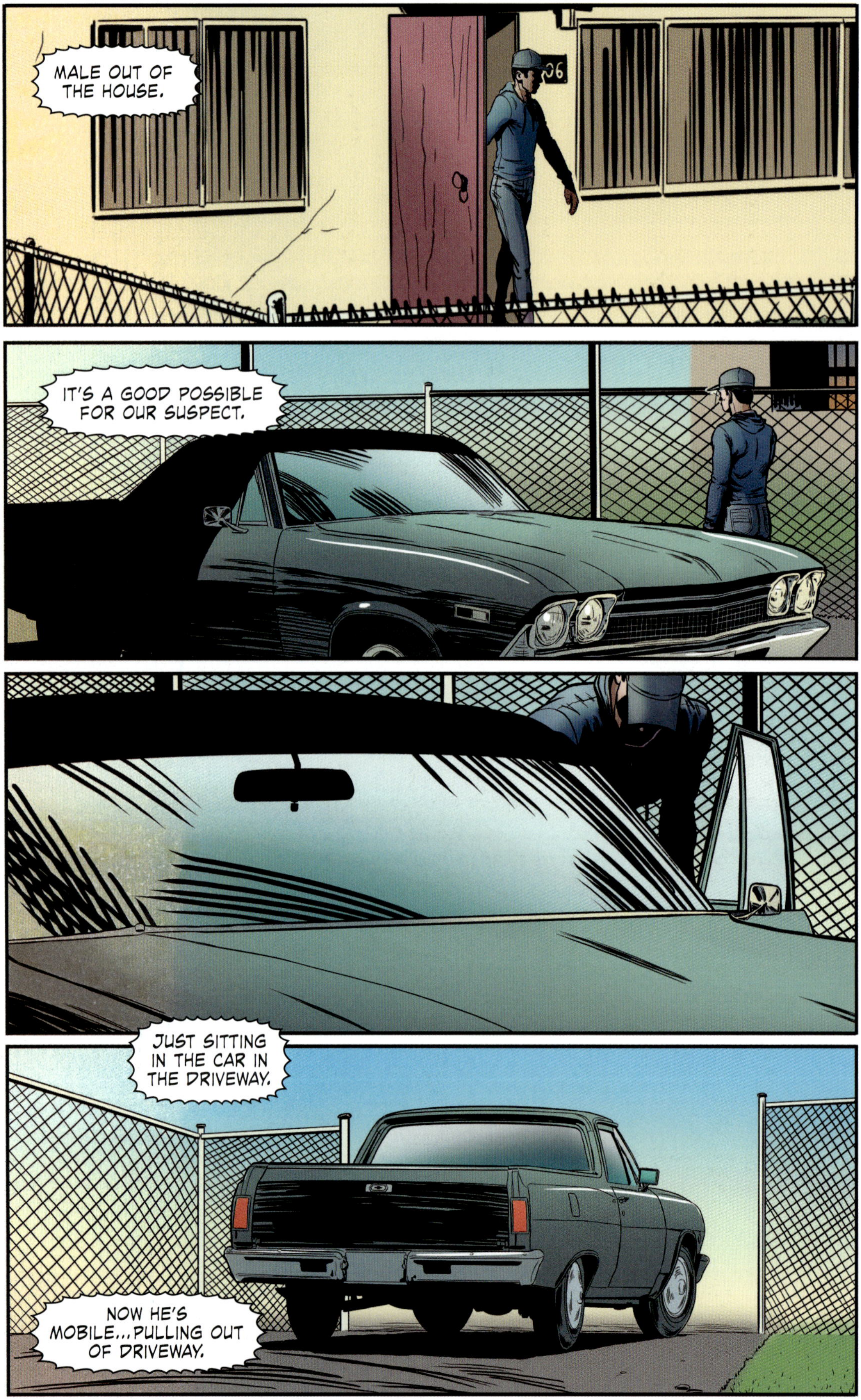
MALE OUT OF THE HOUSE.
IT'S A GOOD POSSIBLE FOR OUR SUSPECT.
JUST SITTING IN THE CAR IN THE DRIVEWAY.
NOW HE'S MOBILE...PULLING OUT OF DRIVEWAY.

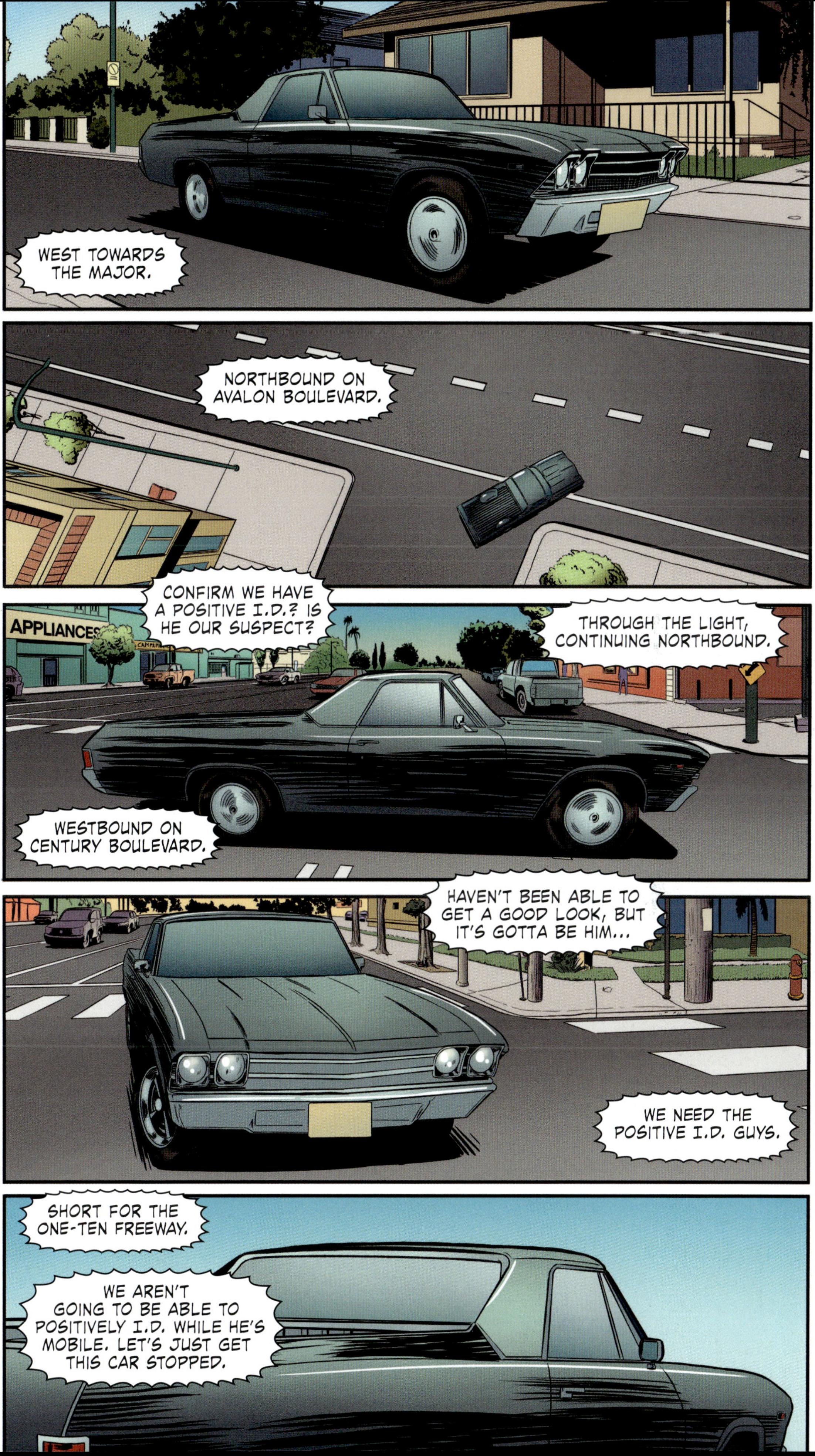
WEST TOWARDS THE MAJOR.
NORTHBOUND ON AVALON BOULEVARD.
CONFIRM WE HAVE A POSITIVE I.D.? IS HE OUR SUSPECT?
THROUGH THE LIGHT, CONTINUING NORTHBOUND.
APPLIANCES
WESTBOUND ON CENTURY BOULEVARD.
HAVEN'T BEEN ABLE TO GET A GOOD LOOK, BUT IT'S GOTTA BE HIM...
WE NEED THE POSITIVE I.D. GUYS.
SHORT FOR THE ONE-TEN FREEWAY.
WE AREN'T GOING TO BE ABLE TO POSITIVELY I.D. WHILE HE'S MOBILE. LET'S JUST GET THIS CAR STOPPED.

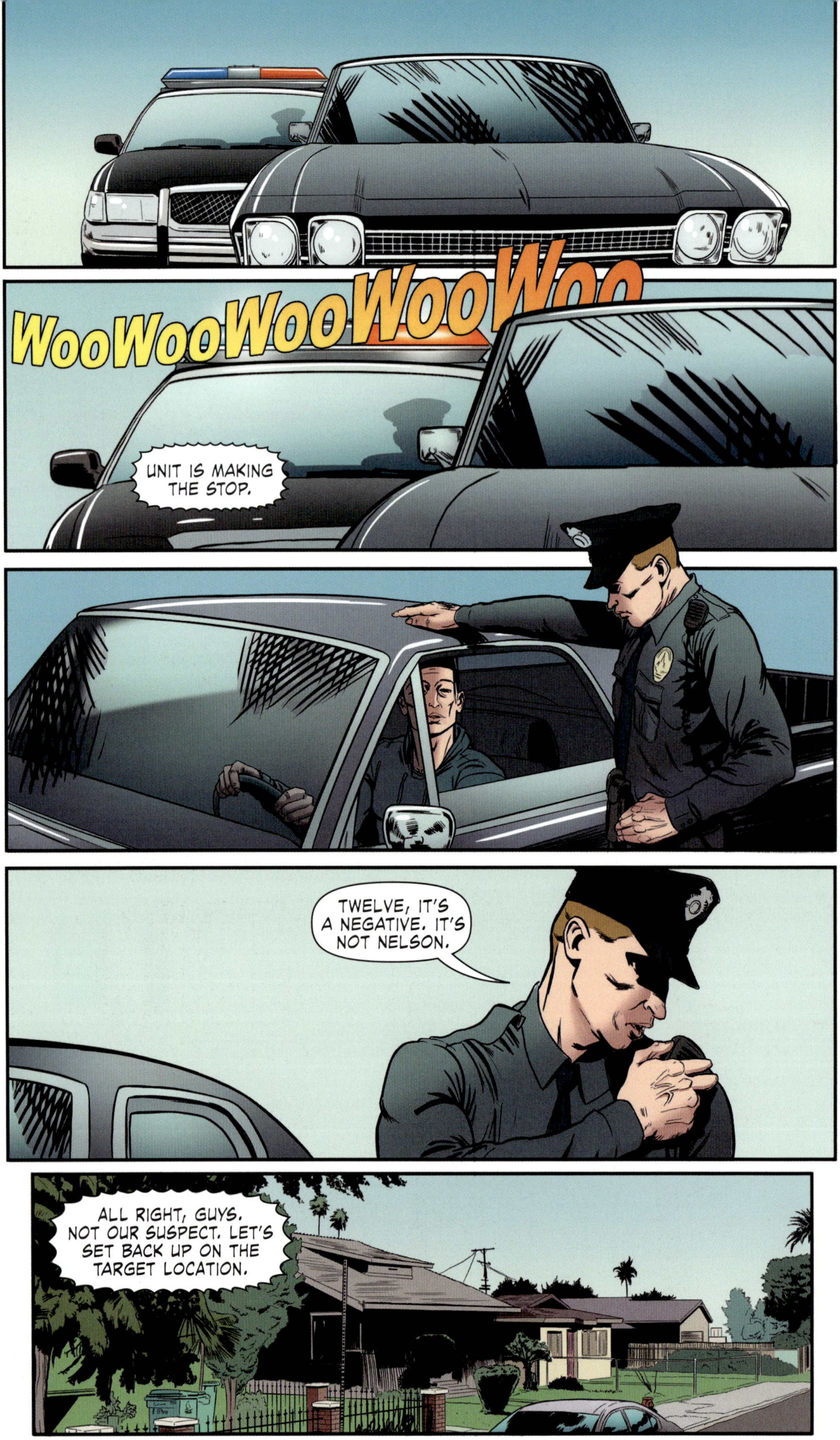
WooWooWooWooWoo
UNIT IS MAKING THE STOP.
TWELVE, IT'S A NEGATIVE. IT'S NOT NELSON.
ALL RIGHT, GUYS. NOT OUR SUSPECT. LET'S SET BACK UP ON THE TARGET LOCATION.

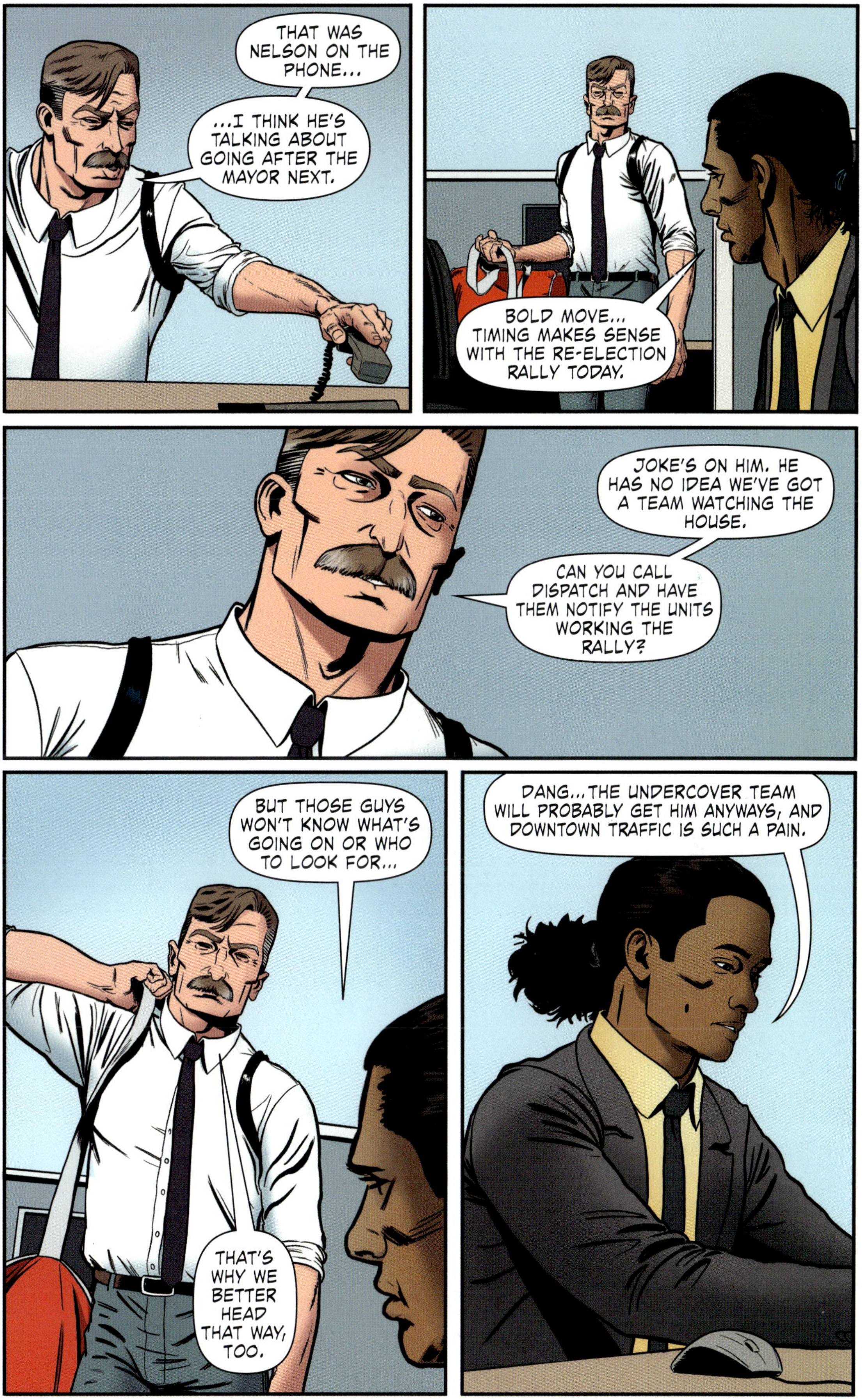
THAT WAS NELSON ON THE PHONE...
...I THINK HE'S TALKING ABOUT GOING AFTER THE MAYOR NEXT.
BOLD MOVE... TIMING MAKES SENSE WITH THE RE-ELECTION RALLY TODAY.
JOKE'S ON HIM. HE HAS NO IDEA WE'VE GOT A TEAM WATCHING THE HOUSE.
CAN YOU CALL DISPATCH AND HAVE THEM NOTIFY THE UNITS WORKING THE RALLY?
BUT THOSE GUYS WON'T KNOW WHAT'S GOING ON OR WHO TO LOOK FOR...
THAT'S WHY WE BETTER HEAD THAT WAY, TOO.
DANG...THE UNDERCOVER TEAM WILL PROBABLY GET HIM ANYWAYS, AND DOWNTOWN TRAFFIC IS SUCH A PAIN.

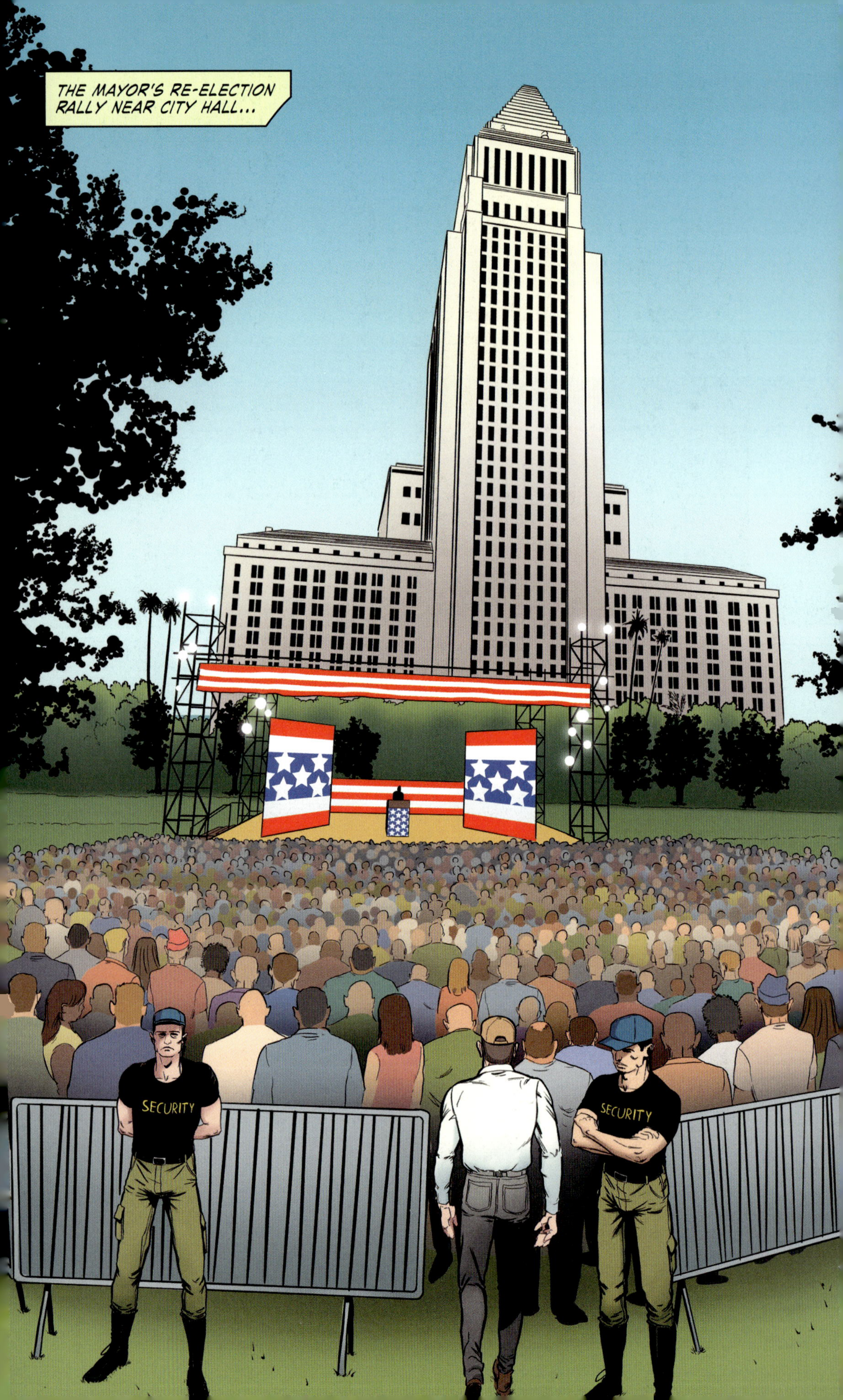
THE MAYOR'S RE-ELECTION RALLY NEAR CITY HALL...
SECURITY
SECURITY

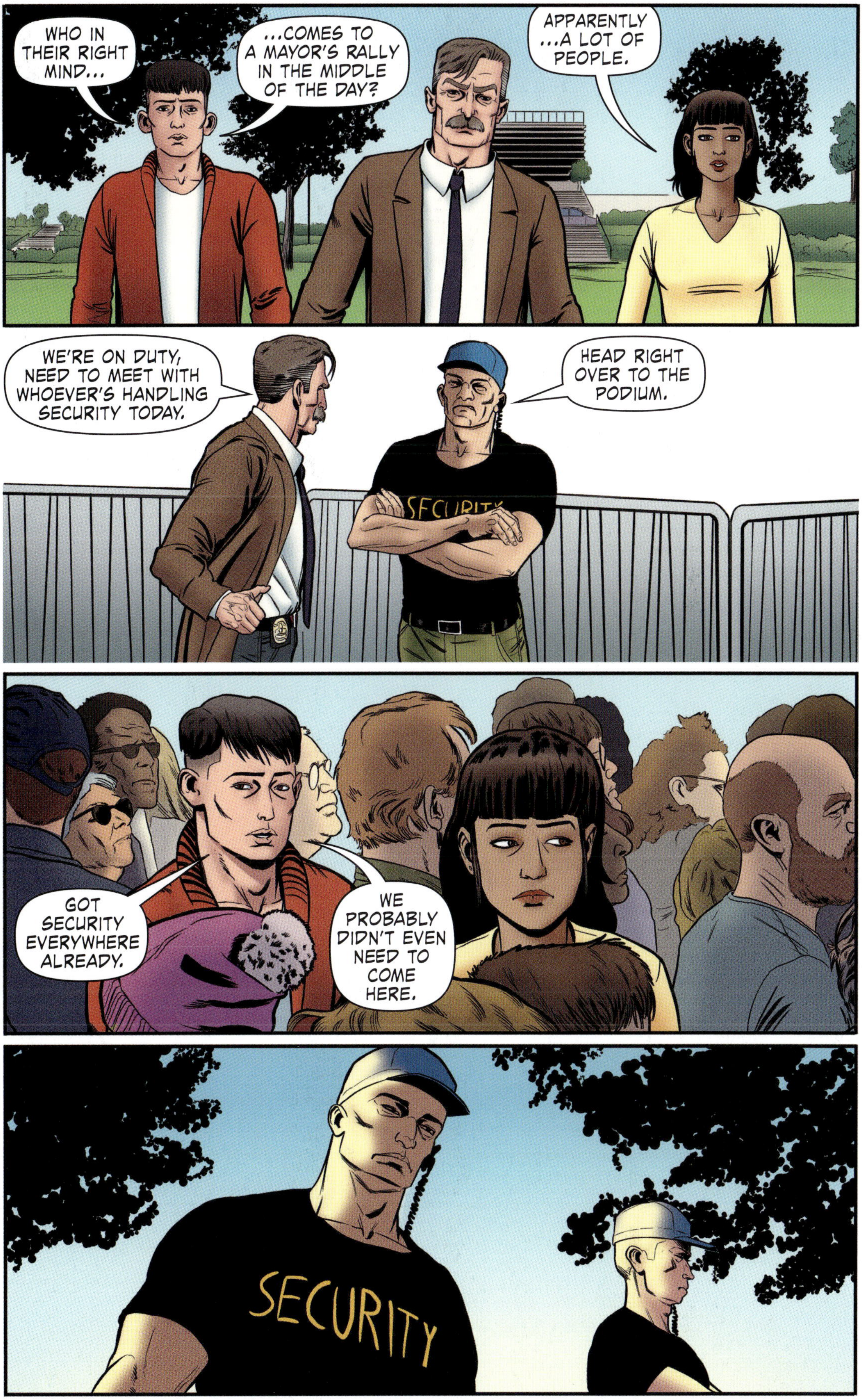
WHO IN THEIR RIGHT MIND...
...COMES TO A MAYOR'S RALLY IN THE MIDDLE OF THE DAY?
APPARENTLY ...A LOT OF PEOPLE.
WE'RE ON DUTY, NEED TO MEET WITH WHOEVER'S HANDLING SECURITY TODAY.
HEAD RIGHT OVER TO THE PODIUM.
SECURITY
GOT SECURITY EVERYWHERE ALREADY.
WE PROBABLY DIDN'T EVEN NEED TO COME HERE.
SECURITY

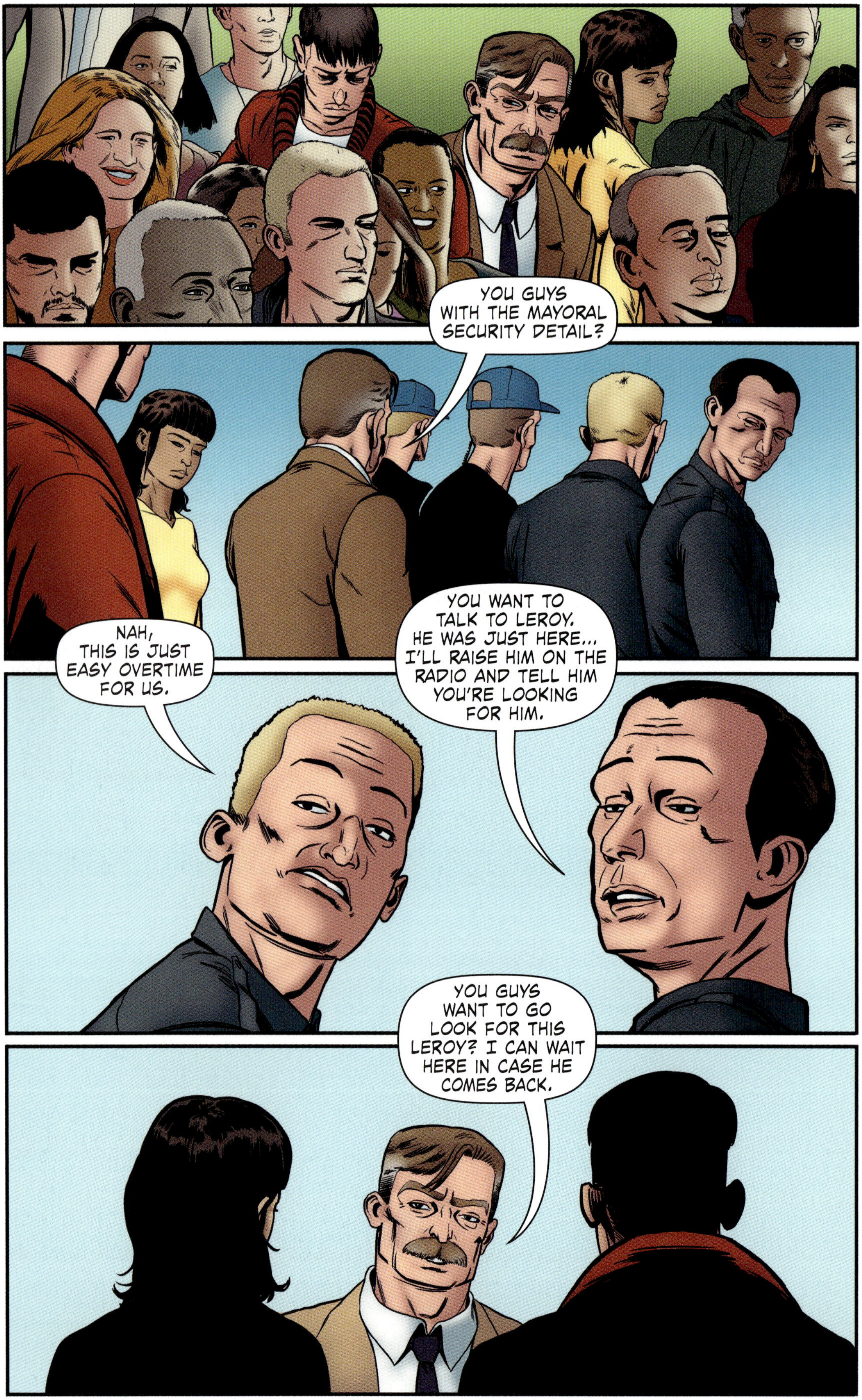
YOU GUYS WITH THE MAYORAL SECURITY DETAIL?
NAH, THIS IS JUST EASY OVERTIME FOR US.
YOU WANT TO TALK TO LEROY. HE WAS JUST HERE... I'LL RAISE HIM ON THE RADIO AND TELL HIM YOU'RE LOOKING FOR HIM.
YOU GUYS WANT TO GO LOOK FOR THIS LEROY? I CAN WAIT HERE IN CASE HE COMES BACK.

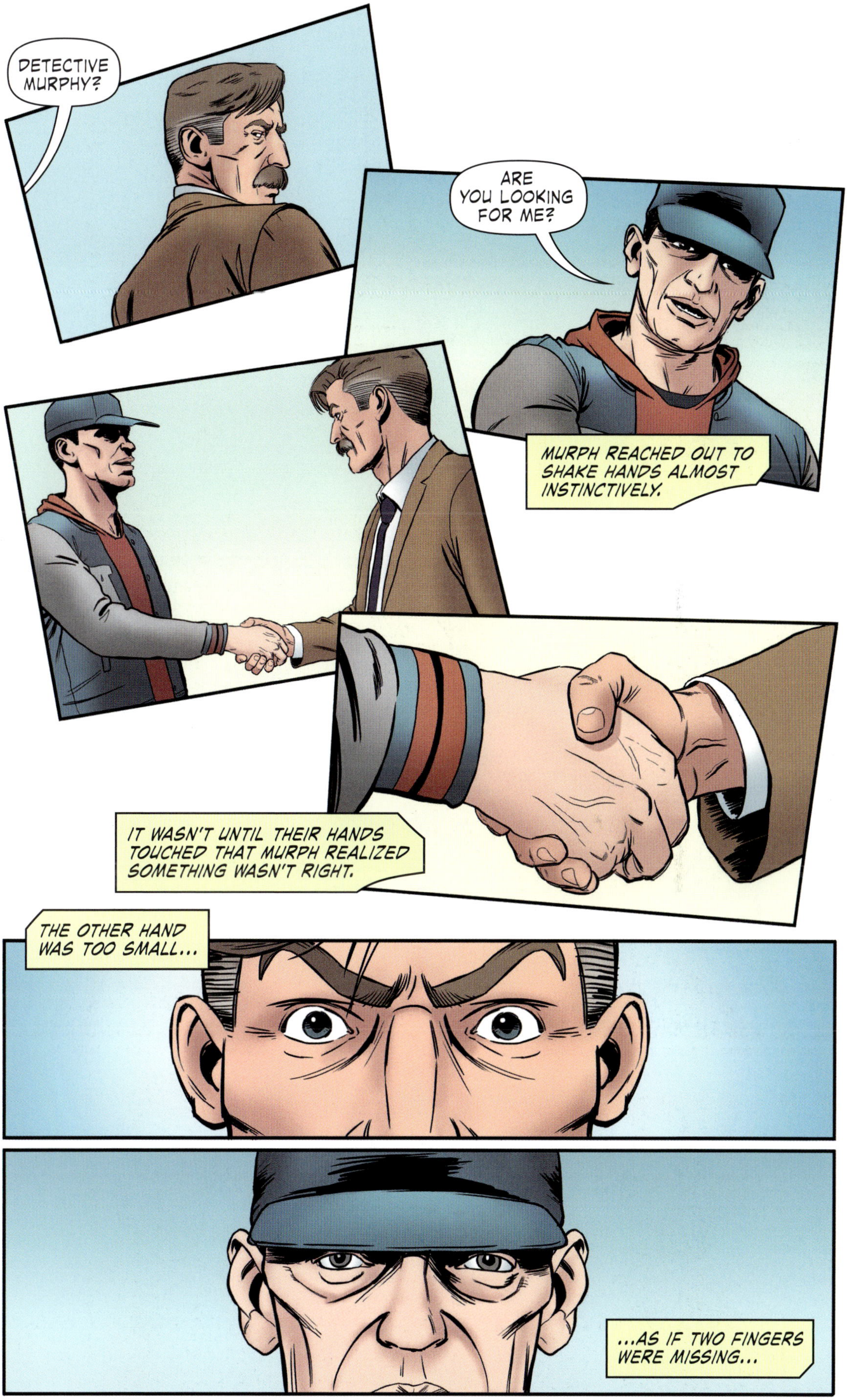
DETECTIVE MURPHY?
ARE YOU LOOKING FOR ME?
MURPH REACHED OUT TO SHAKE HANDS ALMOST INSTINCTIVELY.
IT WASN'T UNTIL THEIR HANDS TOUCHED THAT MURPH REALIZED SOMETHING WASN'T RIGHT.
THE OTHER HAND WAS TOO SMALL...
...AS IF TWO FINGERS WERE MISSING...

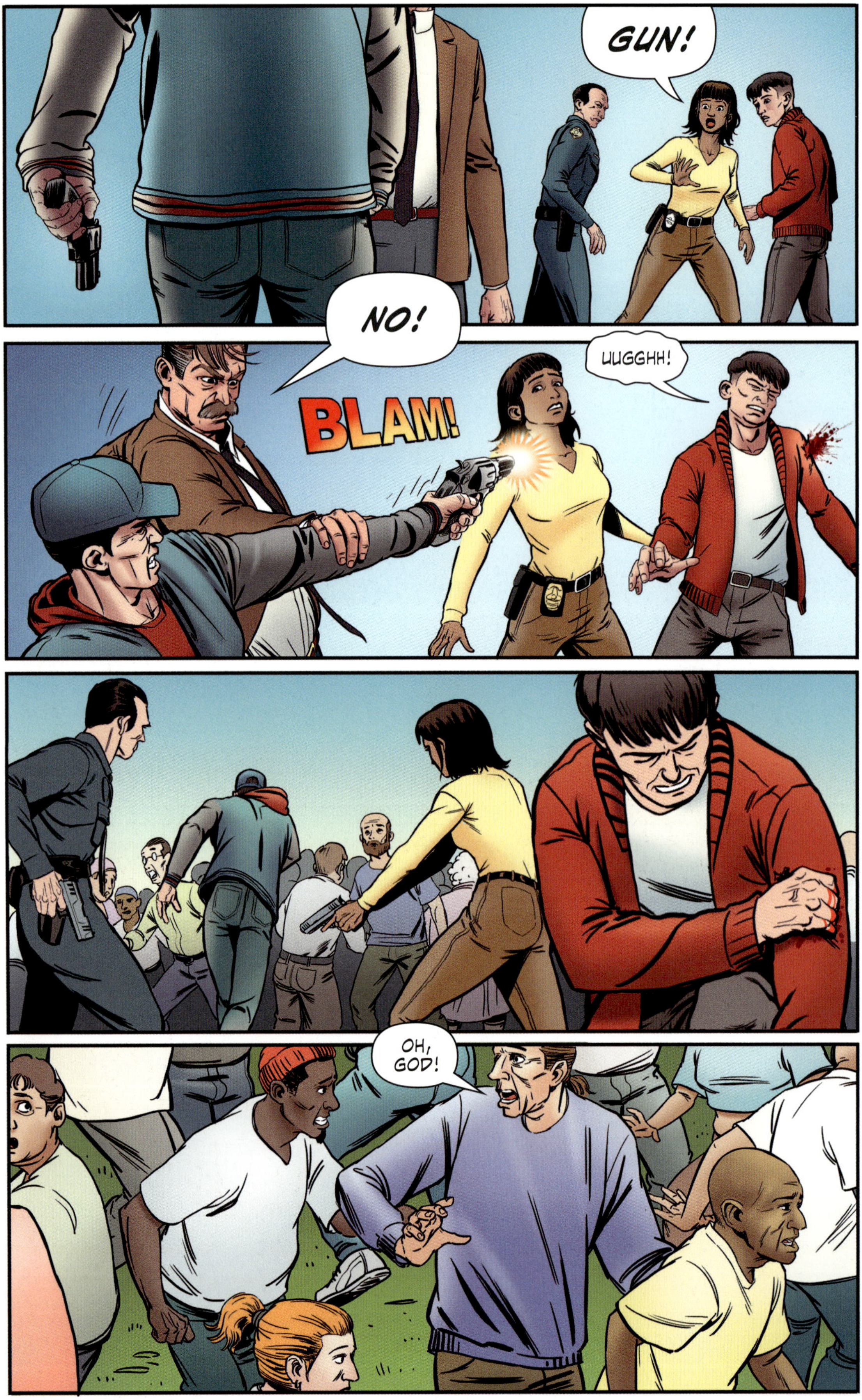
GUN!
NO!
BLAM!
UUGGHH!
OH, GOD!

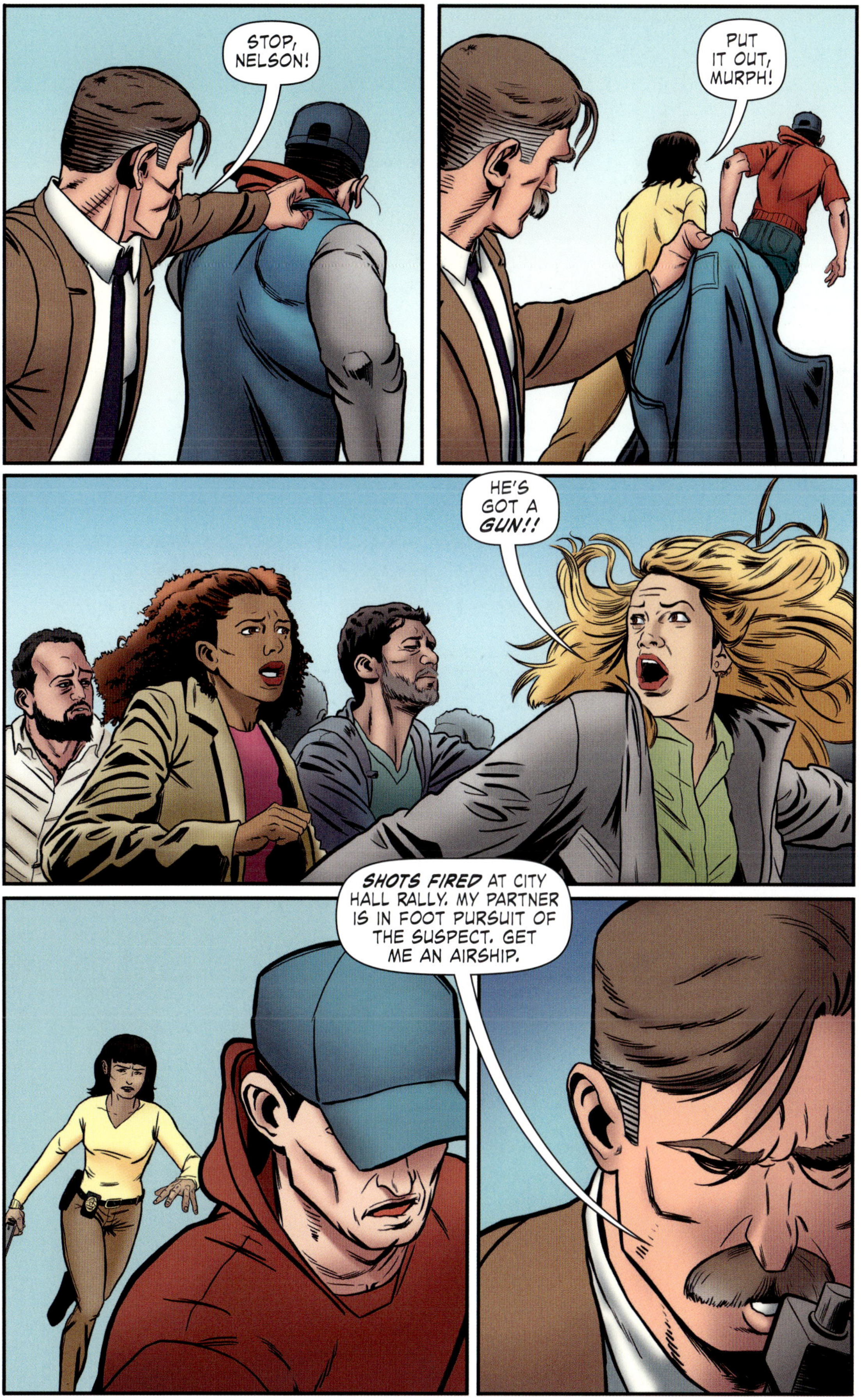
STOP, NELSON!
PUT IT OUT, MURPH!
HE'S GOT A GUN!!
SHOTS FIRED AT CITY HALL RALLY. MY PARTNER IS IN FOOT PURSUIT OF THE SUSPECT. GET ME AN AIRSHIP.

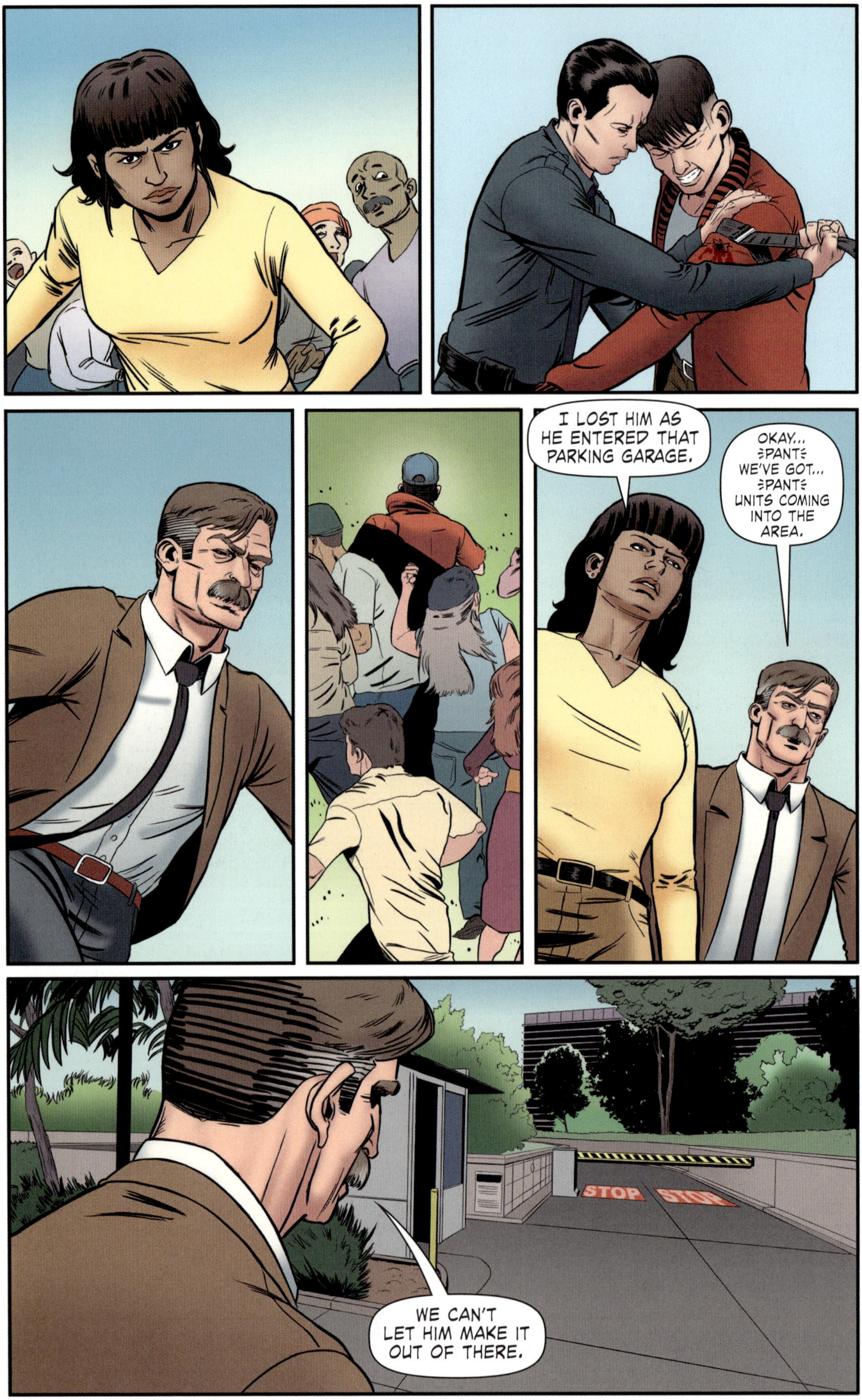
I LOST HIM AS HE ENTERED THAT PARKING GARAGE.
OKAY... ≷PANT≶ WE'VE GOT... ≷PANT≶ UNITS COMING INTO THE AREA.
STOP
STOP
WE CAN'T LET HIM MAKE IT OUT OF THERE.

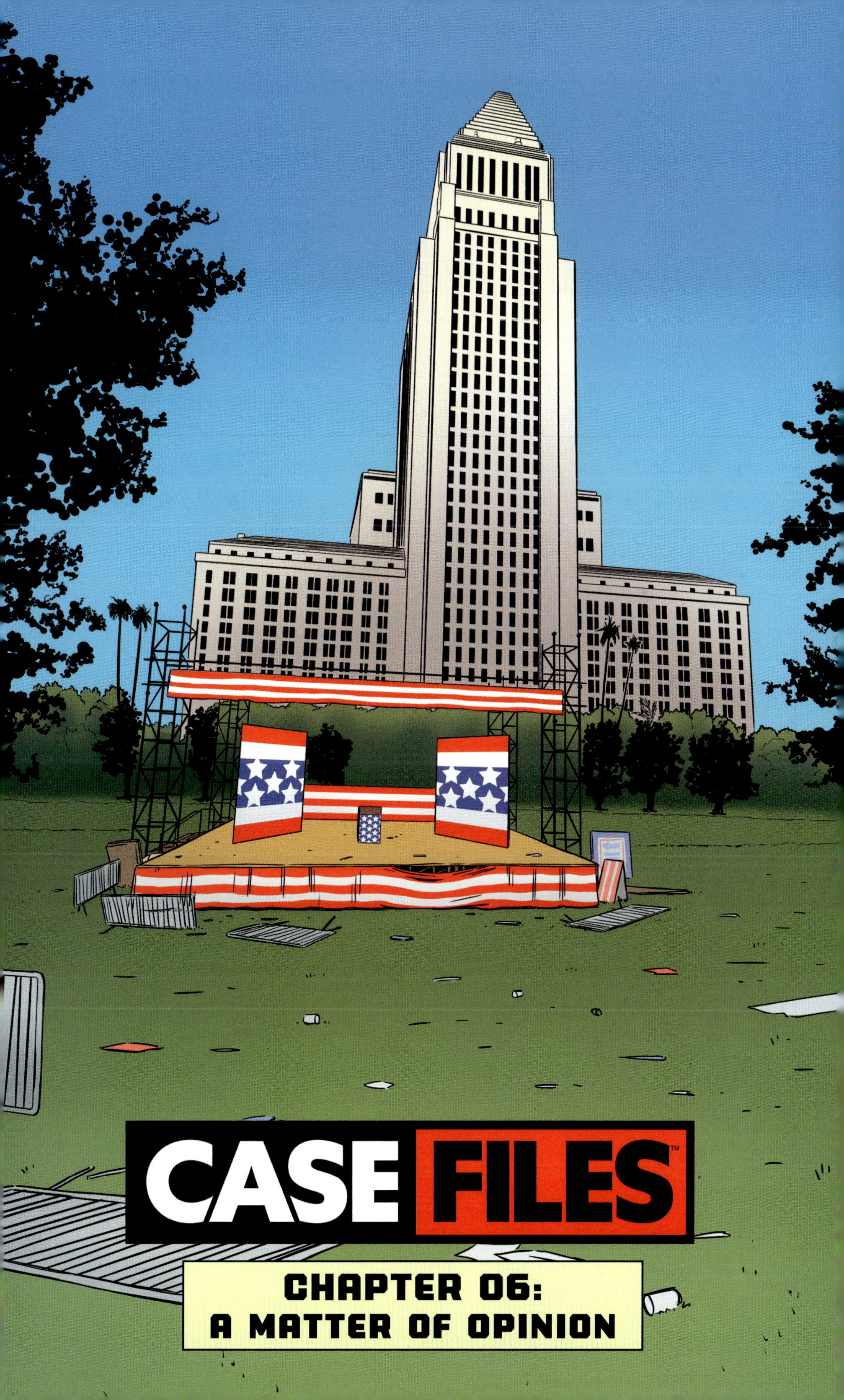
CASE FILES
CHAPTER 06:
A MATTER OF OPINION

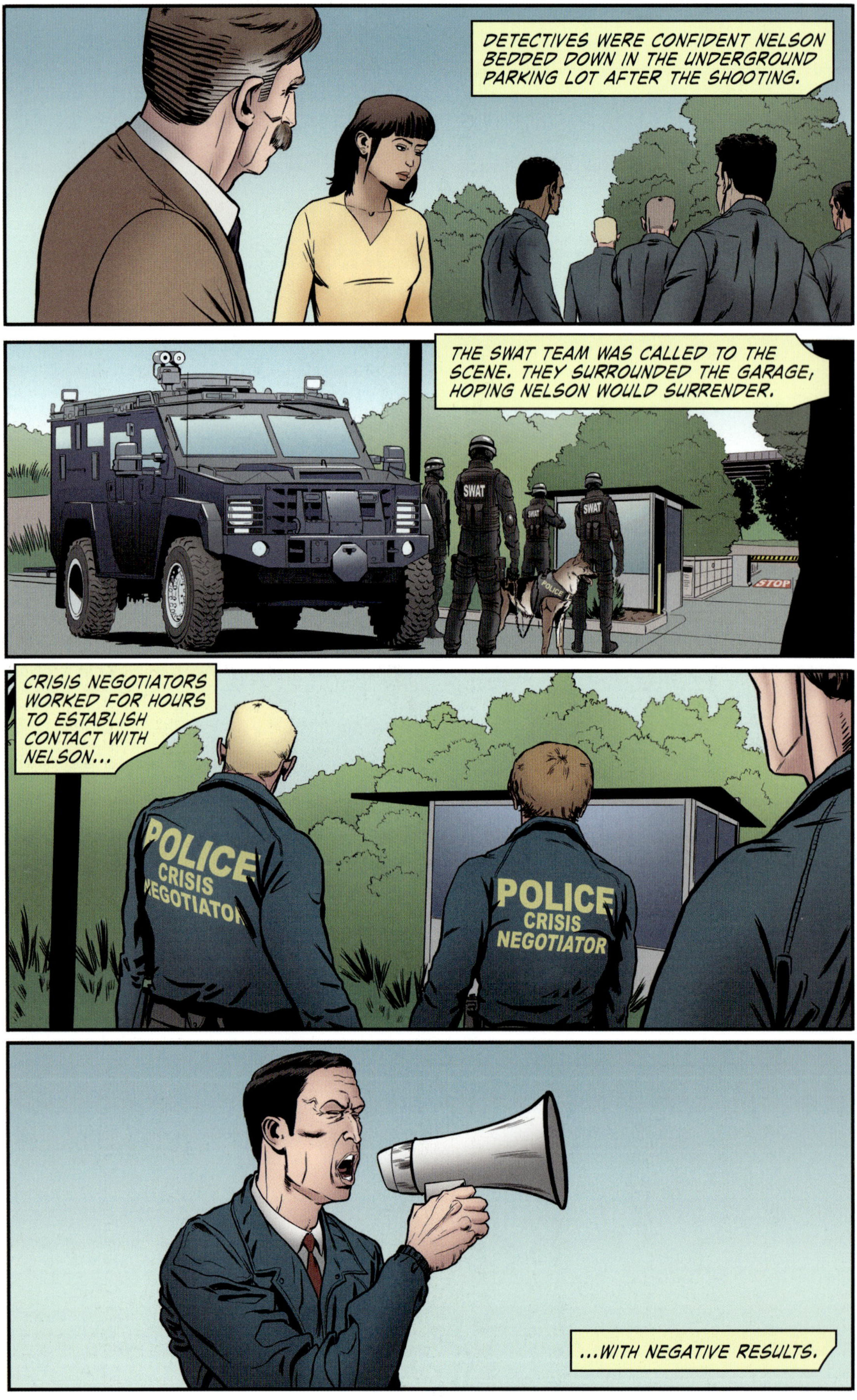
DETECTIVES WERE CONFIDENT NELSON BEDDED DOWN IN THE UNDERGROUND PARKING LOT AFTER THE SHOOTING.
THE SWAT TEAM WAS CALLED TO THE SCENE. THEY SURROUNDED THE GARAGE, HOPING NELSON WOULD SURRENDER.
SWAT
SWAT
SWAT
POLICE
STOP
CRISIS NEGOTIATORS WORKED FOR HOURS TO ESTABLISH CONTACT WITH NELSON...
POLICE CRISIS NEGOTIATOR
...WITH NEGATIVE RESULTS.

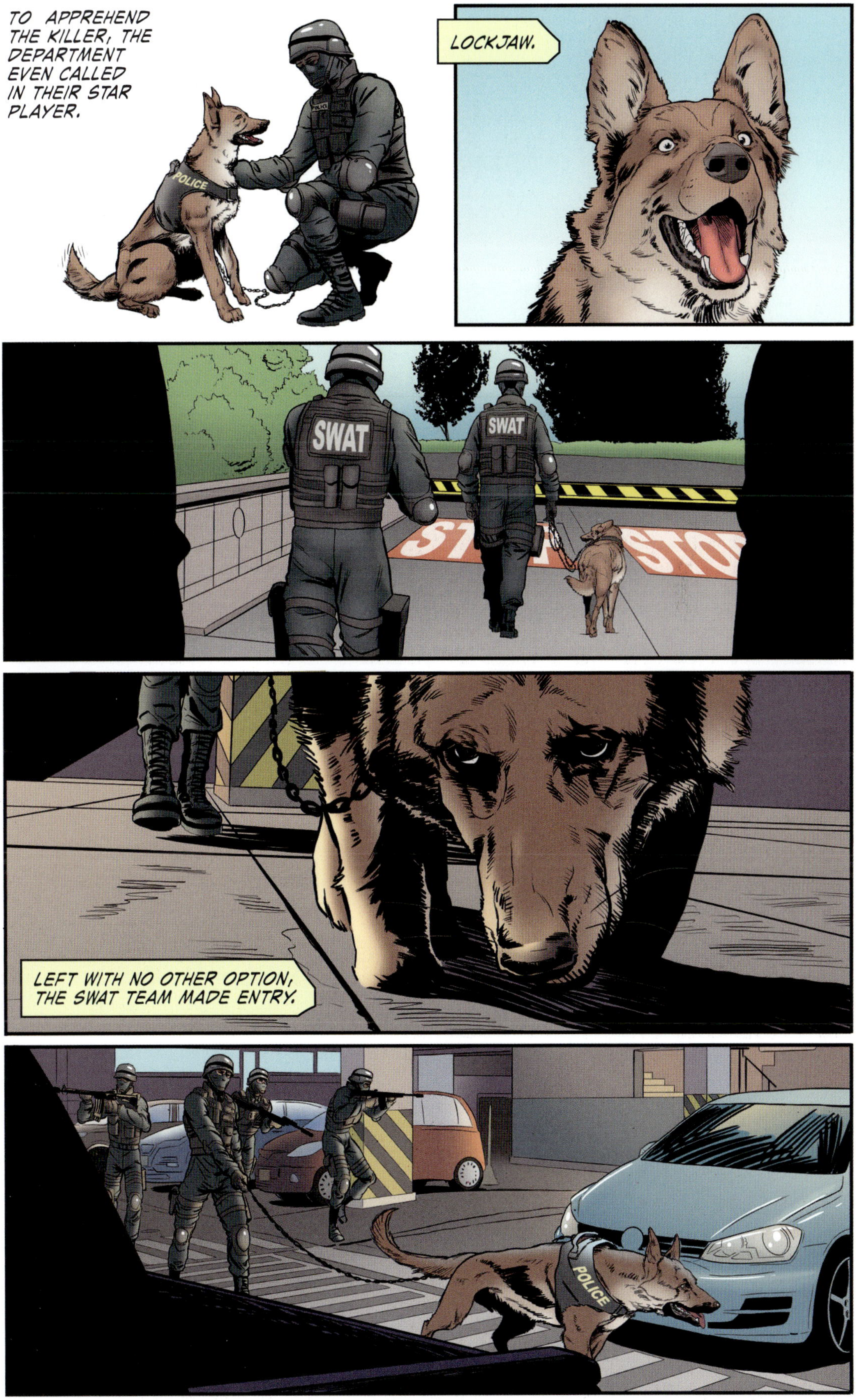
TO APPREHEND THE KILLER, THE DEPARTMENT EVEN CALLED IN THEIR STAR PLAYER.
POLICE
LOCKJAW.
SWAT
SWAT
LEFT WITH NO OTHER OPTION, THE SWAT TEAM MADE ENTRY.
POLICE

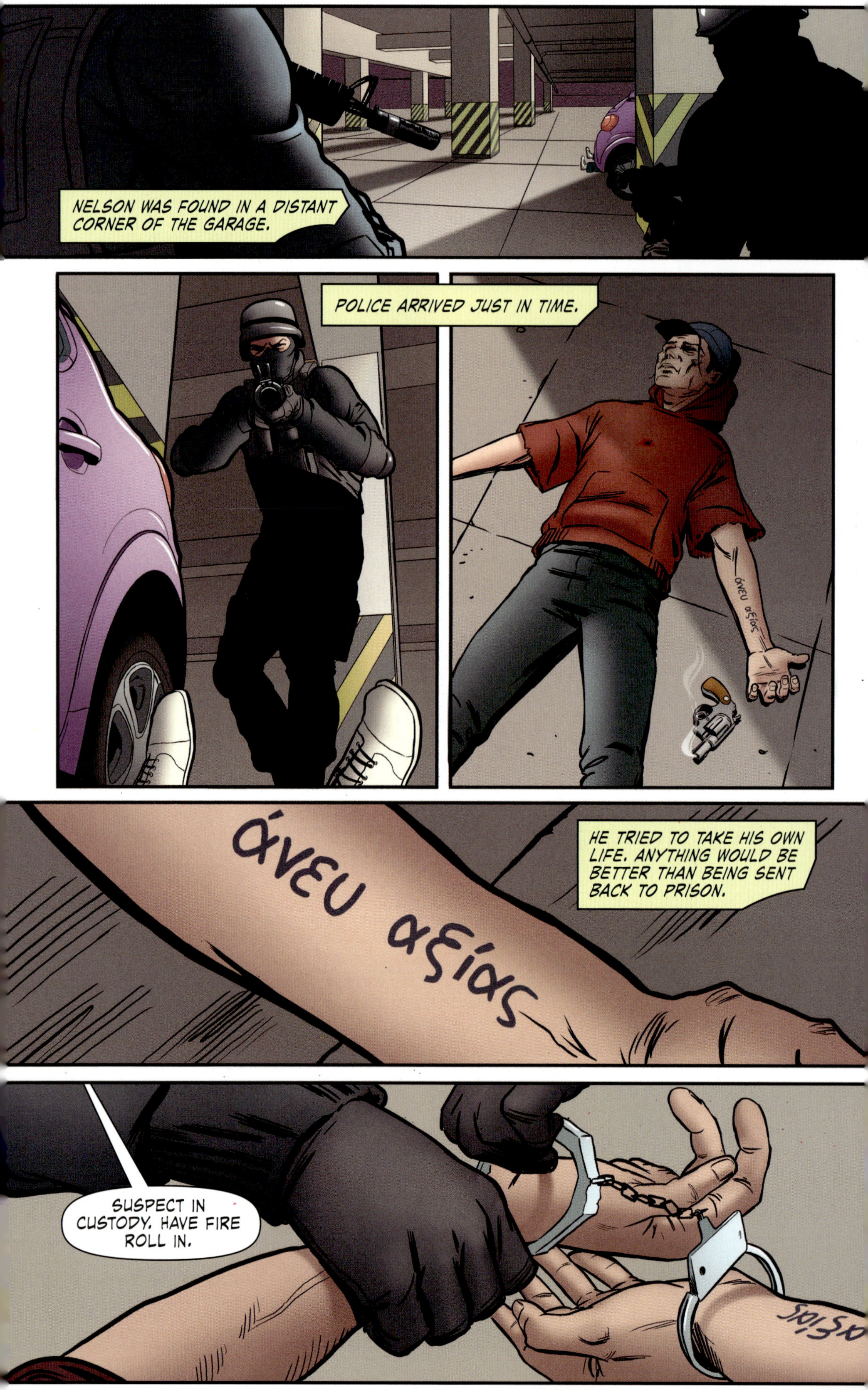
NELSON WAS FOUND IN A DISTANT CORNER OF THE GARAGE.
POLICE ARRIVED JUST IN TIME.
άνευ αξίας
HE TRIED TO TAKE HIS OWN LIFE. ANYTHING WOULD BE BETTER THAN BEING SENT BACK TO PRISON.
SUSPECT IN CUSTODY. HAVE FIRE ROLL IN.

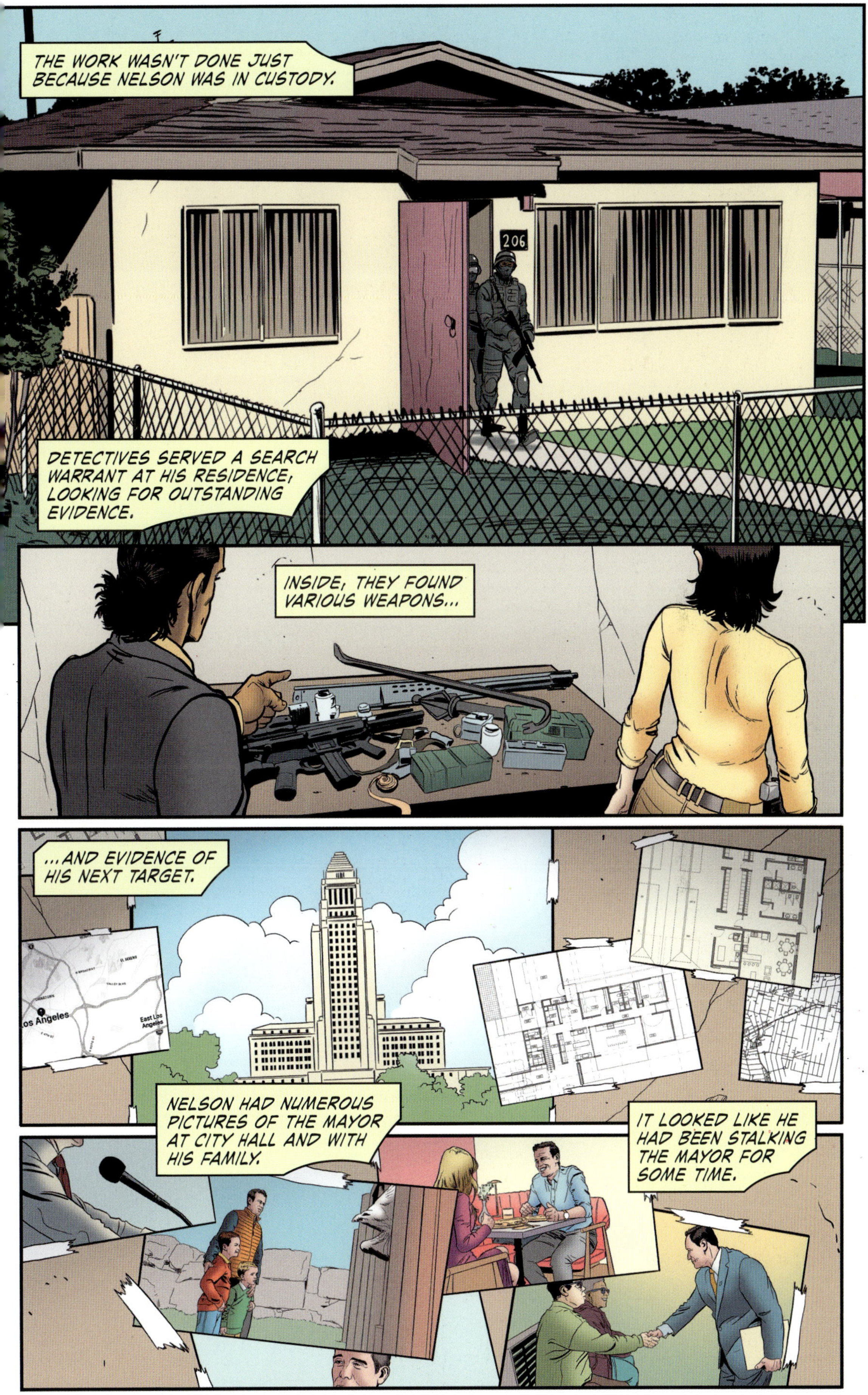
THE WORK WASN'T DONE JUST BECAUSE NELSON WAS IN CUSTODY.
206
DETECTIVES SERVED A SEARCH WARRANT AT HIS RESIDENCE, LOOKING FOR OUTSTANDING EVIDENCE.
INSIDE, THEY FOUND VARIOUS WEAPONS...
...AND EVIDENCE OF HIS NEXT TARGET.
Los Angeles
East Los Angeles
NELSON HAD NUMEROUS PICTURES OF THE MAYOR AT CITY HALL AND WITH HIS FAMILY.
IT LOOKED LIKE HE HAD BEEN STALKING THE MAYOR FOR SOME TIME.

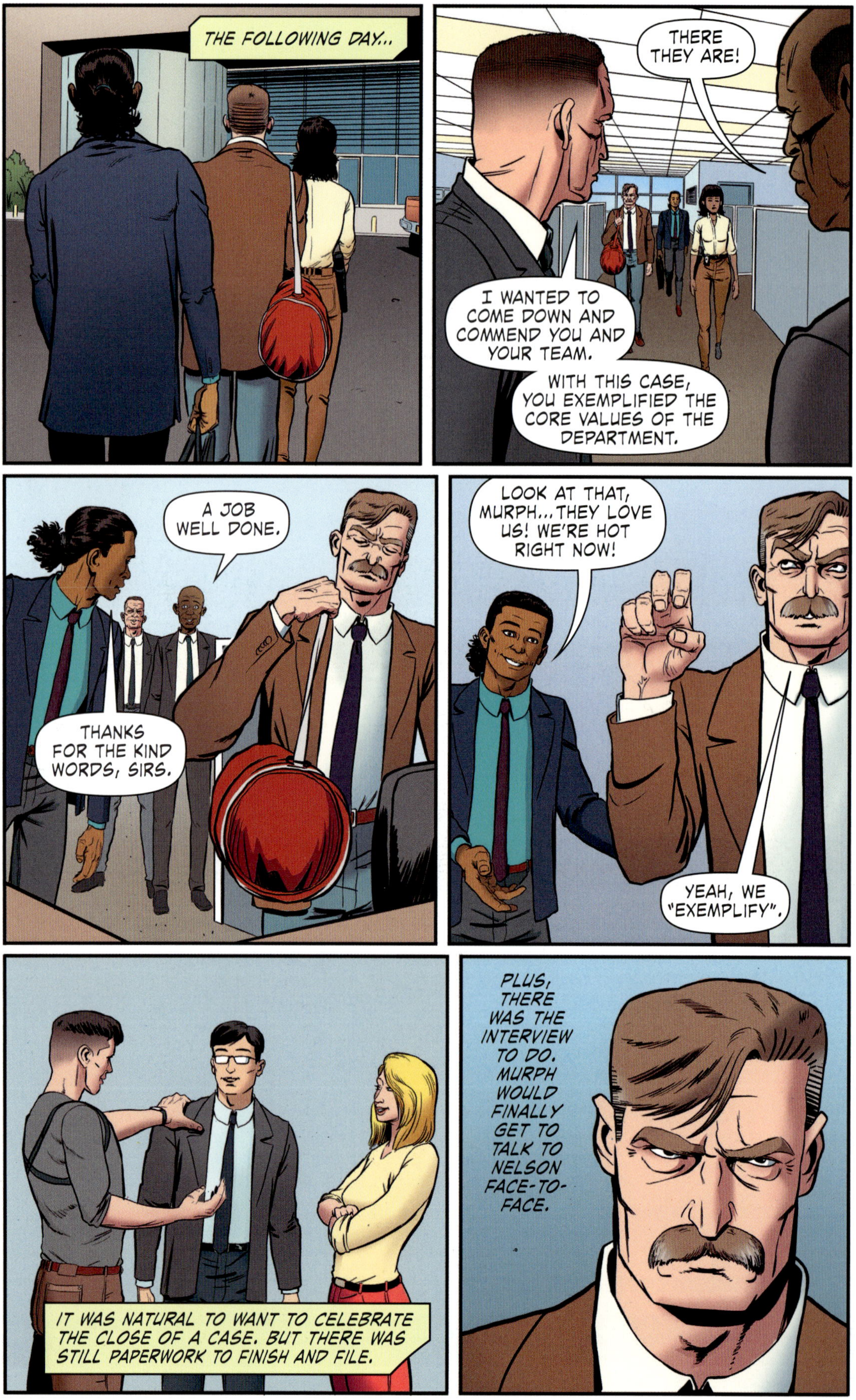
THE FOLLOWING DAY...
THERE THEY ARE!
I WANTED TO COME DOWN AND COMMEND YOU AND YOUR TEAM.
WITH THIS CASE, YOU EXEMPLIFIED THE CORE VALUES OF THE DEPARTMENT.
A JOB WELL DONE.
THANKS FOR THE KIND WORDS, SIRS.
LOOK AT THAT, MURPH...THEY LOVE US! WE'RE HOT RIGHT NOW!
YEAH, WE "EXEMPLIFY".
IT WAS NATURAL TO WANT TO CELEBRATE THE CLOSE OF A CASE. BUT THERE WAS STILL PAPERWORK TO FINISH AND FILE.
PLUS, THERE WAS THE INTERVIEW TO DO. MURPH WOULD FINALLY GET TO TALK TO NELSON FACE-TO-FACE.

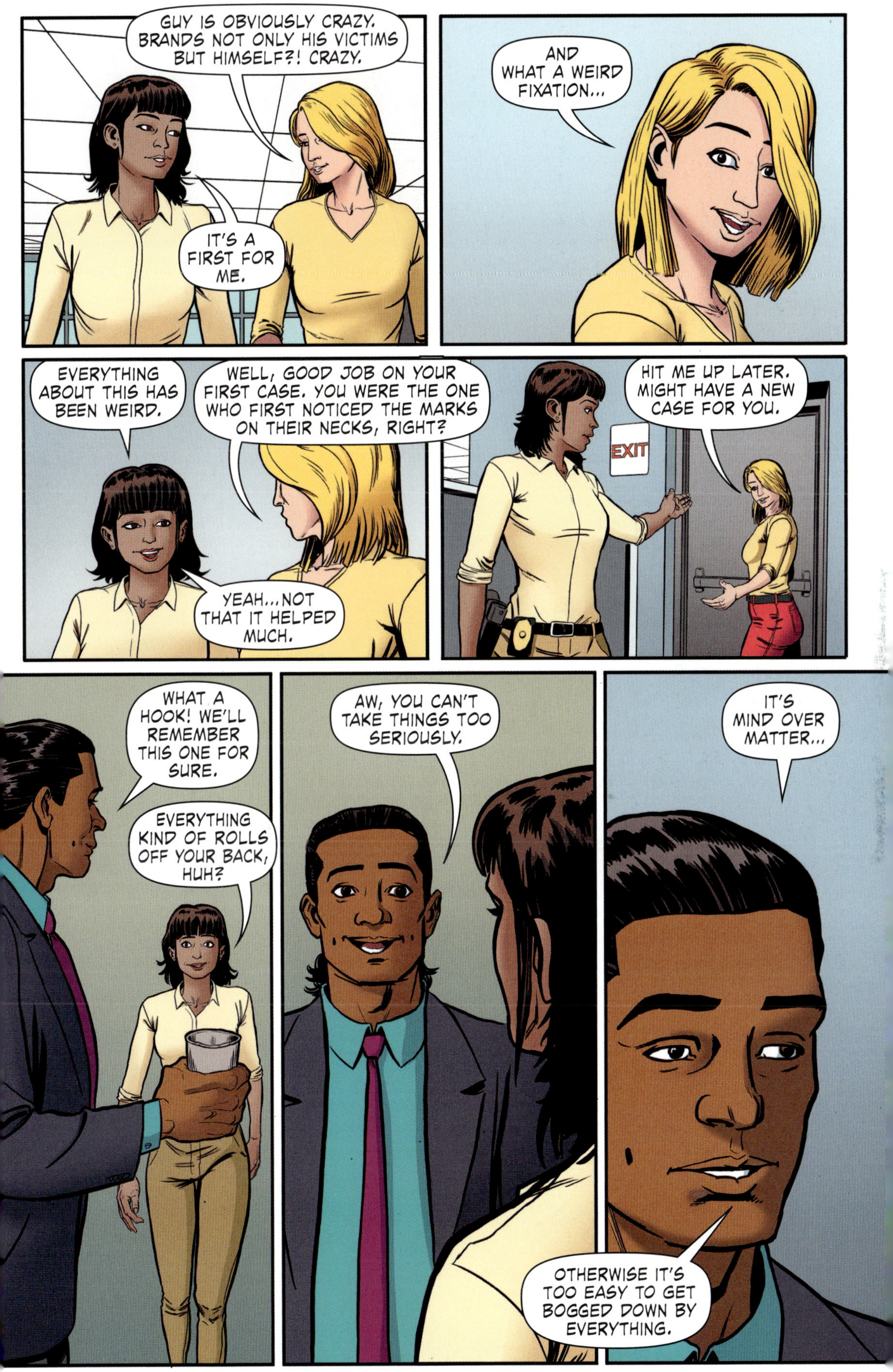
GUY IS OBVIOUSLY CRAZY. BRANDS NOT ONLY HIS VICTIMS BUT HIMSELF?! CRAZY.
IT'S A FIRST FOR ME.
AND WHAT A WEIRD FIXATION...
EVERYTHING ABOUT THIS HAS BEEN WEIRD.
WELL, GOOD JOB ON YOUR FIRST CASE. YOU WERE THE ONE WHO FIRST NOTICED THE MARKS ON THEIR NECKS, RIGHT?
YEAH...NOT THAT IT HELPED MUCH.
HIT ME UP LATER. MIGHT HAVE A NEW CASE FOR YOU.
EXIT
WHAT A HOOK! WE'LL REMEMBER THIS ONE FOR SURE.
EVERYTHING KIND OF ROLLS OFF YOUR BACK, HUH?
AW, YOU CAN'T TAKE THINGS TOO SERIOUSLY.
IT'S MIND OVER MATTER...
OTHERWISE IT'S TOO EASY TO GET BOGGED DOWN BY EVERYTHING.

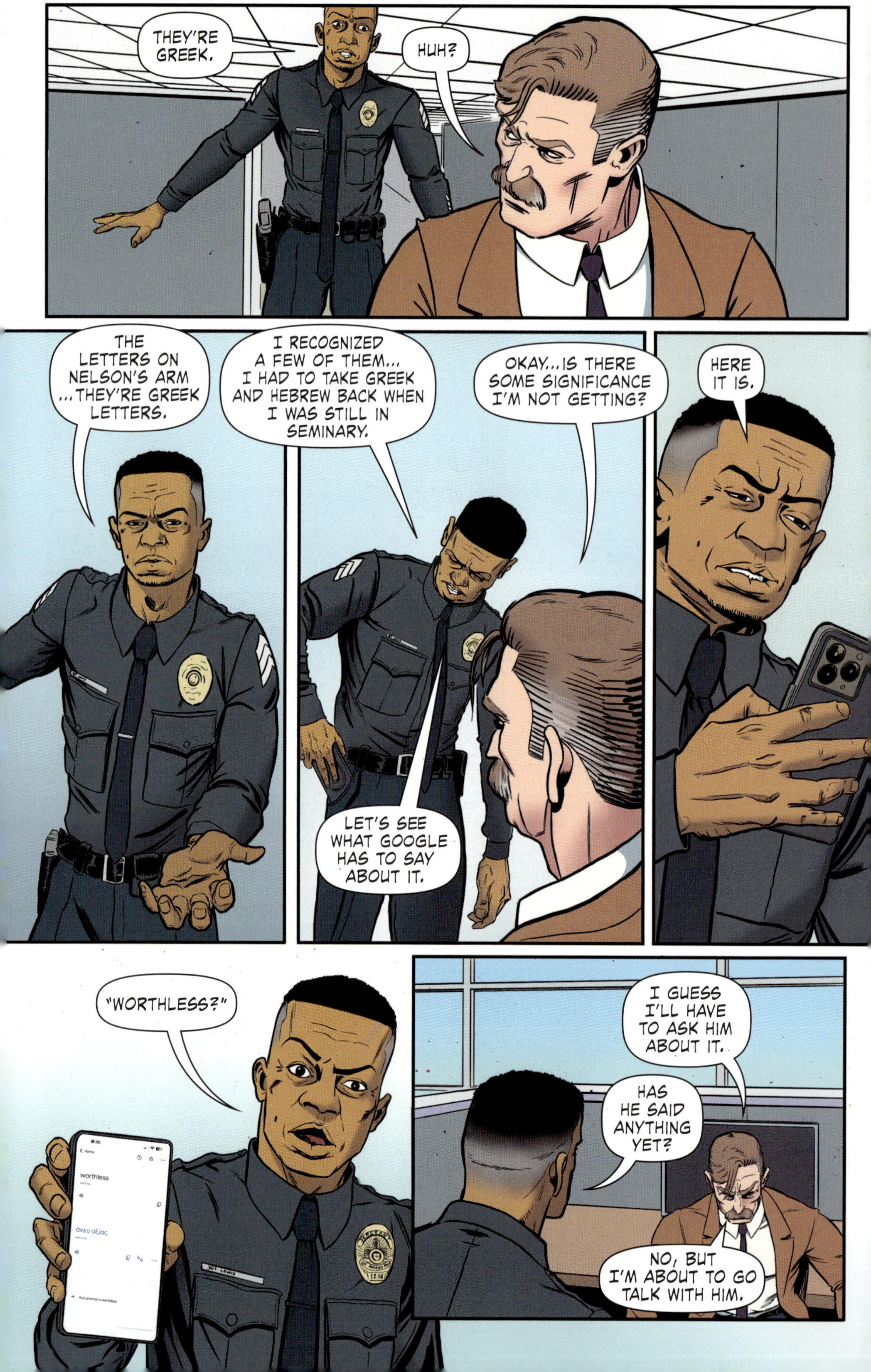
THEY'RE GREEK.
HUH?
THE LETTERS ON NELSON'S ARM ...THEY'RE GREEK LETTERS.
I RECOGNIZED A FEW OF THEM... I HAD TO TAKE GREEK AND HEBREW BACK WHEN I WAS STILL IN SEMINARY.
OKAY...IS THERE SOME SIGNIFICANCE I'M NOT GETTING?
LET'S SEE WHAT GOOGLE HAS TO SAY ABOUT IT.
HERE IT IS.
"WORTHLESS?"
worthless
άνευ αξίας
I GUESS I'LL HAVE TO ASK HIM ABOUT IT.
HAS HE SAID ANYTHING YET?
NO, BUT I'M ABOUT TO GO TALK WITH HIM.

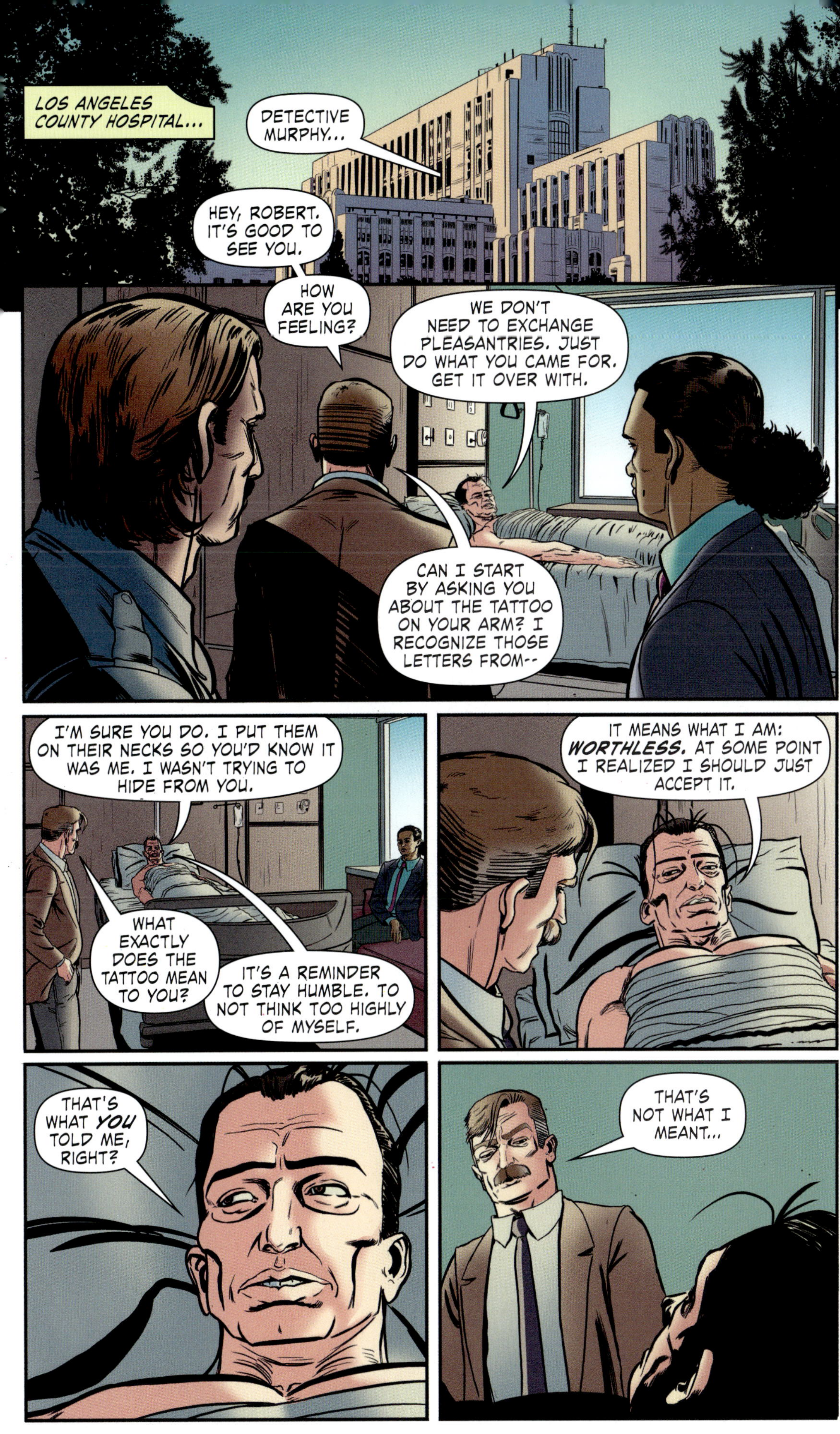
LOS ANGELES COUNTY HOSPITAL...
DETECTIVE MURPHY...
HEY, ROBERT. IT'S GOOD TO SEE YOU.
HOW ARE YOU FEELING?
WE DON'T NEED TO EXCHANGE PLEASANTRIES. JUST DO WHAT YOU CAME FOR. GET IT OVER WITH.
CAN I START BY ASKING YOU ABOUT THE TATTOO ON YOUR ARM? I RECOGNIZE THOSE LETTERS FROM--
I'M SURE YOU DO. I PUT THEM ON THEIR NECKS SO YOU'D KNOW IT WAS ME. I WASN'T TRYING TO HIDE FROM YOU.
WHAT EXACTLY DOES THE TATTOO MEAN TO YOU?
IT'S A REMINDER TO STAY HUMBLE. TO NOT THINK TOO HIGHLY OF MYSELF.
IT MEANS WHAT I AM: *WORTHLESS.* AT SOME POINT I REALIZED I SHOULD JUST ACCEPT IT.
THAT'S WHAT *YOU* TOLD ME, RIGHT?
THAT'S NOT WHAT I MEANT...

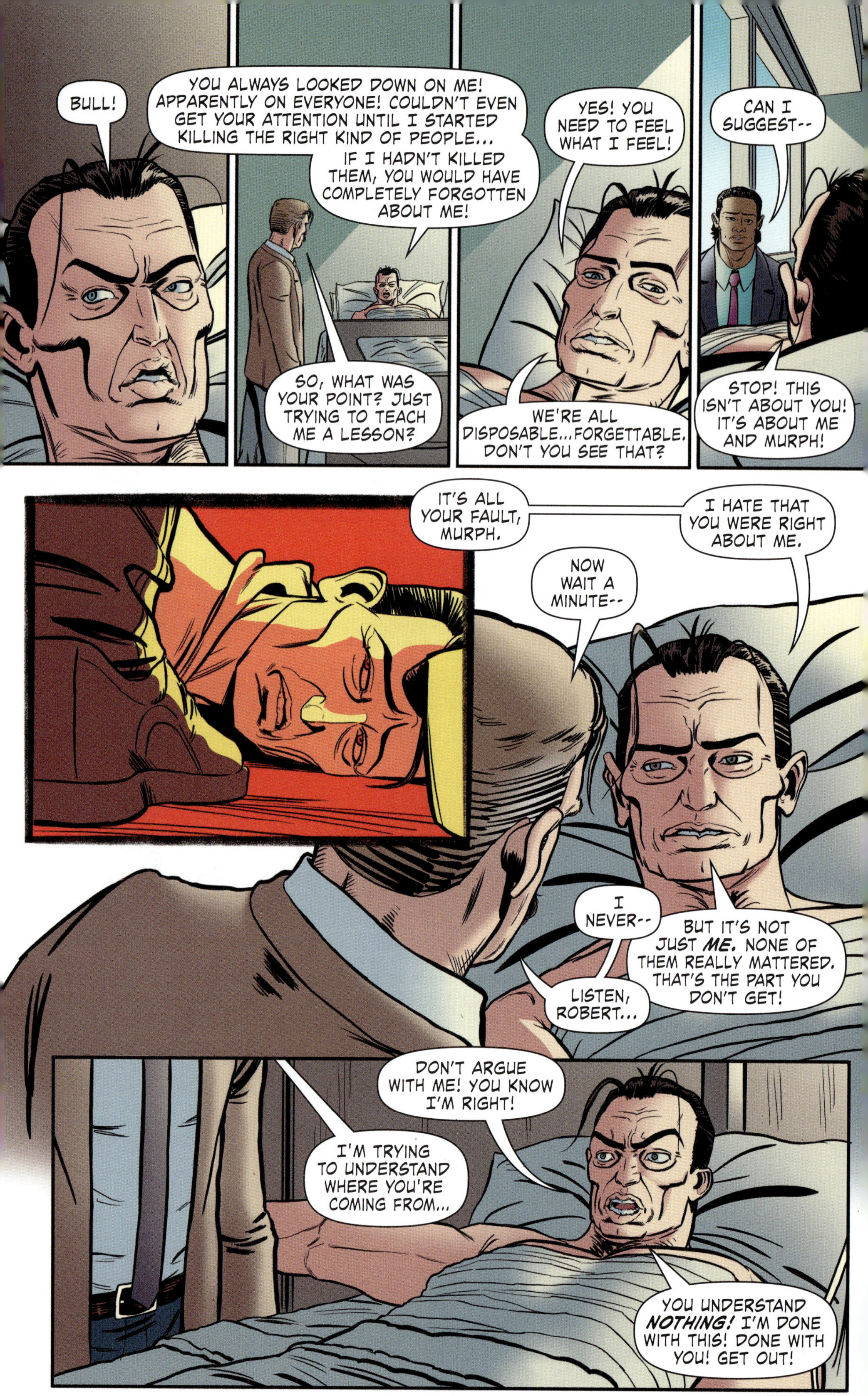
BULL!
YOU ALWAYS LOOKED DOWN ON ME! APPARENTLY ON EVERYONE! COULDN'T EVEN GET YOUR ATTENTION UNTIL I STARTED KILLING THE RIGHT KIND OF PEOPLE...
IF I HADN'T KILLED THEM, YOU WOULD HAVE COMPLETELY FORGOTTEN ABOUT ME!
SO, WHAT WAS YOUR POINT? JUST TRYING TO TEACH ME A LESSON?
YES! YOU NEED TO FEEL WHAT I FEEL!
WE'RE ALL DISPOSABLE...FORGETTABLE. DON'T YOU SEE THAT?
CAN I SUGGEST--
STOP! THIS ISN'T ABOUT YOU! IT'S ABOUT ME AND MURPH!
IT'S ALL YOUR FAULT, MURPH.
I HATE THAT YOU WERE RIGHT ABOUT ME.
NOW WAIT A MINUTE--
I NEVER--
BUT IT'S NOT JUST *ME*. NONE OF THEM REALLY MATTERED. THAT'S THE PART YOU DON'T GET!
LISTEN, ROBERT...
DON'T ARGUE WITH ME! YOU KNOW I'M RIGHT!
I'M TRYING TO UNDERSTAND WHERE YOU'RE COMING FROM...
YOU UNDERSTAND *NOTHING!* I'M DONE WITH THIS! DONE WITH YOU! GET OUT!

I'M AFRAID WE NEED TO RUN A NEW I.V. AND DO A FEW TESTS, GENTLEMEN.
WE'RE DONE ANYWAY! OUT! GET OUT, MURPH!
YOU MADE ME LIKE THIS, MURPH! I'LL NEVER FORGIVE YOU FOR THIS!
YOU'RE JUST AS MESSED UP AS I AM!
110
NELSON HAD ADMITTED HIS INVOLVEMENT IN THE SERIAL KILLINGS. A CONFESSION TO BE SURE.
MAIN ENTRANCE
EMERGEN
Main Entra
BUT TO MURPH, IT DIDN'T REALLY FEEL LIKE A SUCCESS.

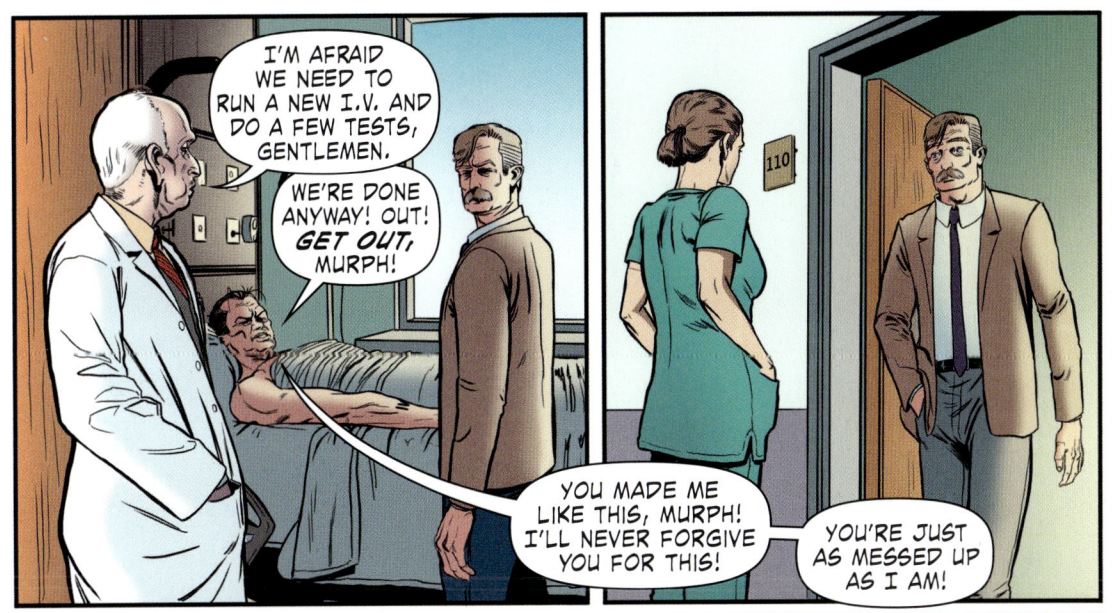

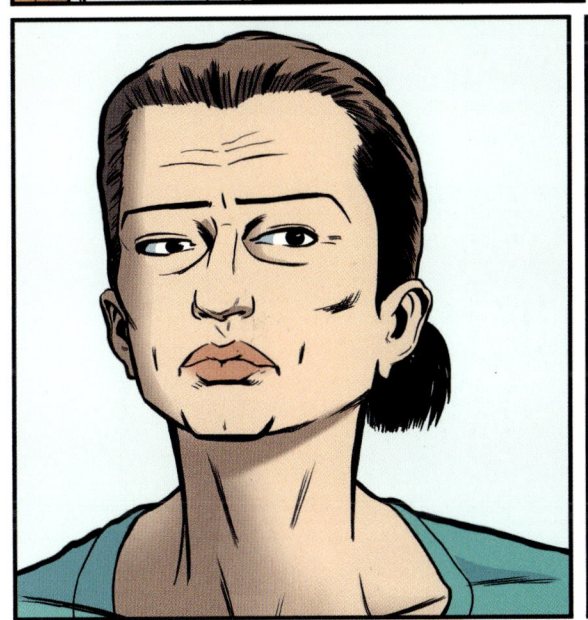

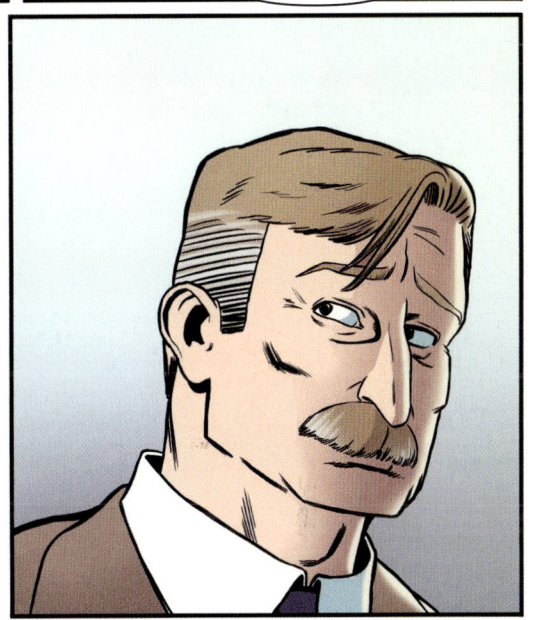

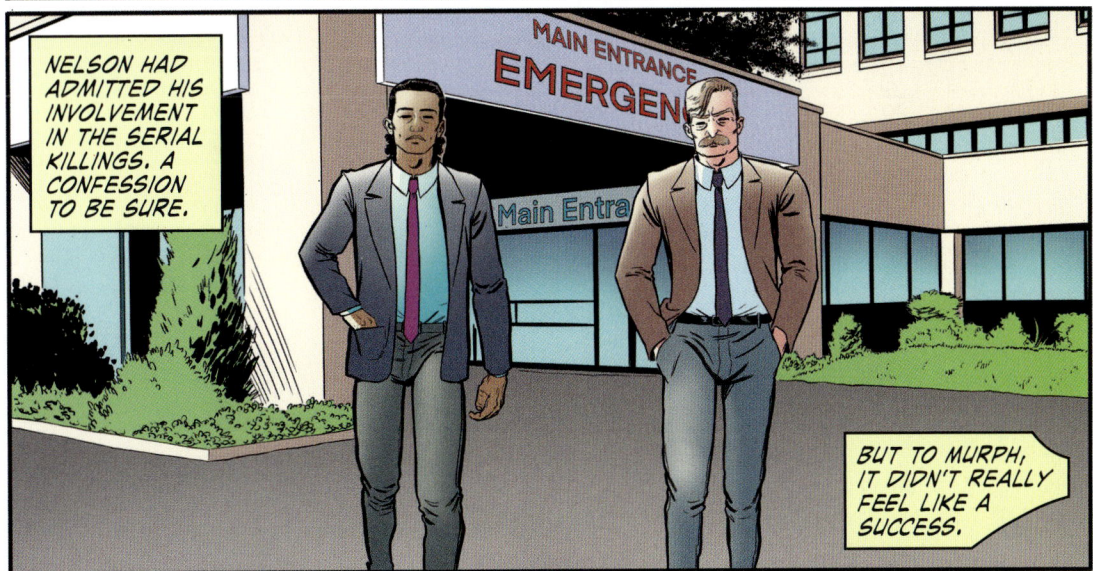

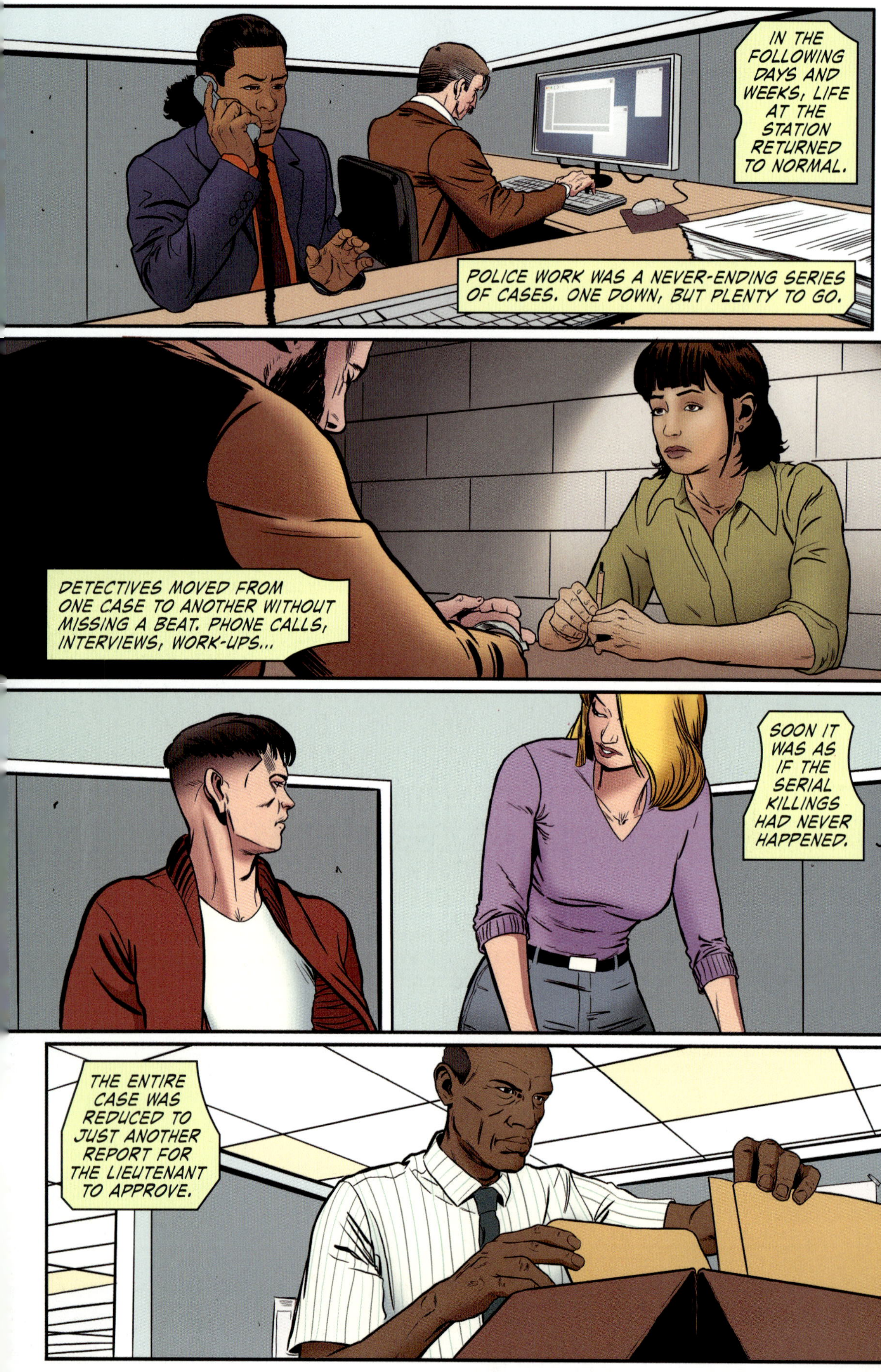
IN THE FOLLOWING DAYS AND WEEKS, LIFE AT THE STATION RETURNED TO NORMAL.
POLICE WORK WAS A NEVER-ENDING SERIES OF CASES. ONE DOWN, BUT PLENTY TO GO.
DETECTIVES MOVED FROM ONE CASE TO ANOTHER WITHOUT MISSING A BEAT. PHONE CALLS, INTERVIEWS, WORK-UPS...
SOON IT WAS AS IF THE SERIAL KILLINGS HAD NEVER HAPPENED.
THE ENTIRE CASE WAS REDUCED TO JUST ANOTHER REPORT FOR THE LIEUTENANT TO APPROVE.

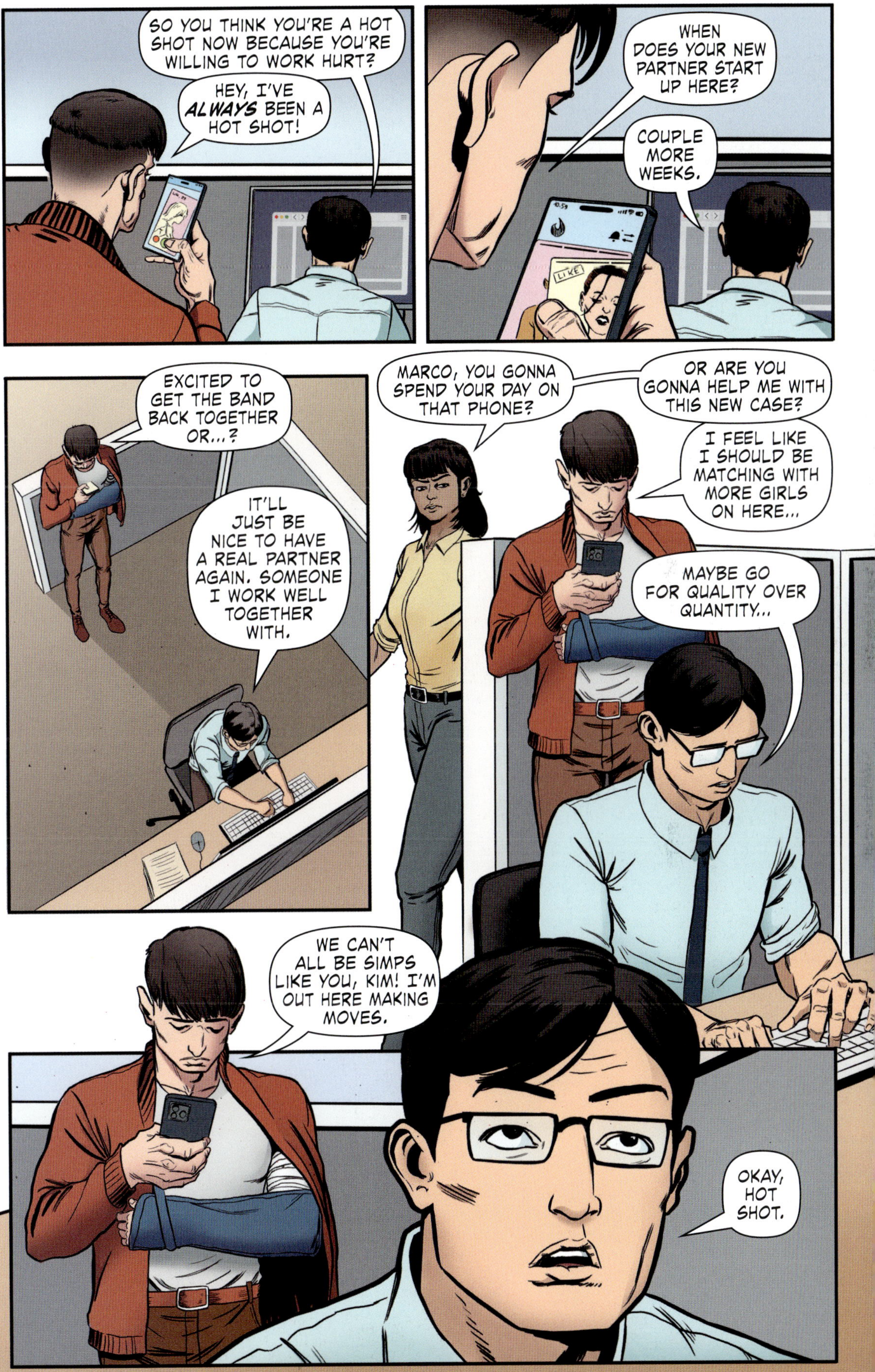
SO YOU THINK YOU'RE A HOT SHOT NOW BECAUSE YOU'RE WILLING TO WORK HURT?
HEY, I'VE *ALWAYS* BEEN A HOT SHOT!
WHEN DOES YOUR NEW PARTNER START UP HERE?
COUPLE MORE WEEKS.
EXCITED TO GET THE BAND BACK TOGETHER OR...?
IT'LL JUST BE NICE TO HAVE A REAL PARTNER AGAIN. SOMEONE I WORK WELL TOGETHER WITH.
MARCO, YOU GONNA SPEND YOUR DAY ON THAT PHONE?
OR ARE YOU GONNA HELP ME WITH THIS NEW CASE?
I FEEL LIKE I SHOULD BE MATCHING WITH MORE GIRLS ON HERE...
MAYBE GO FOR QUALITY OVER QUANTITY...
WE CAN'T ALL BE SIMPS LIKE YOU, KIM! I'M OUT HERE MAKING MOVES.
OKAY, HOT SHOT.

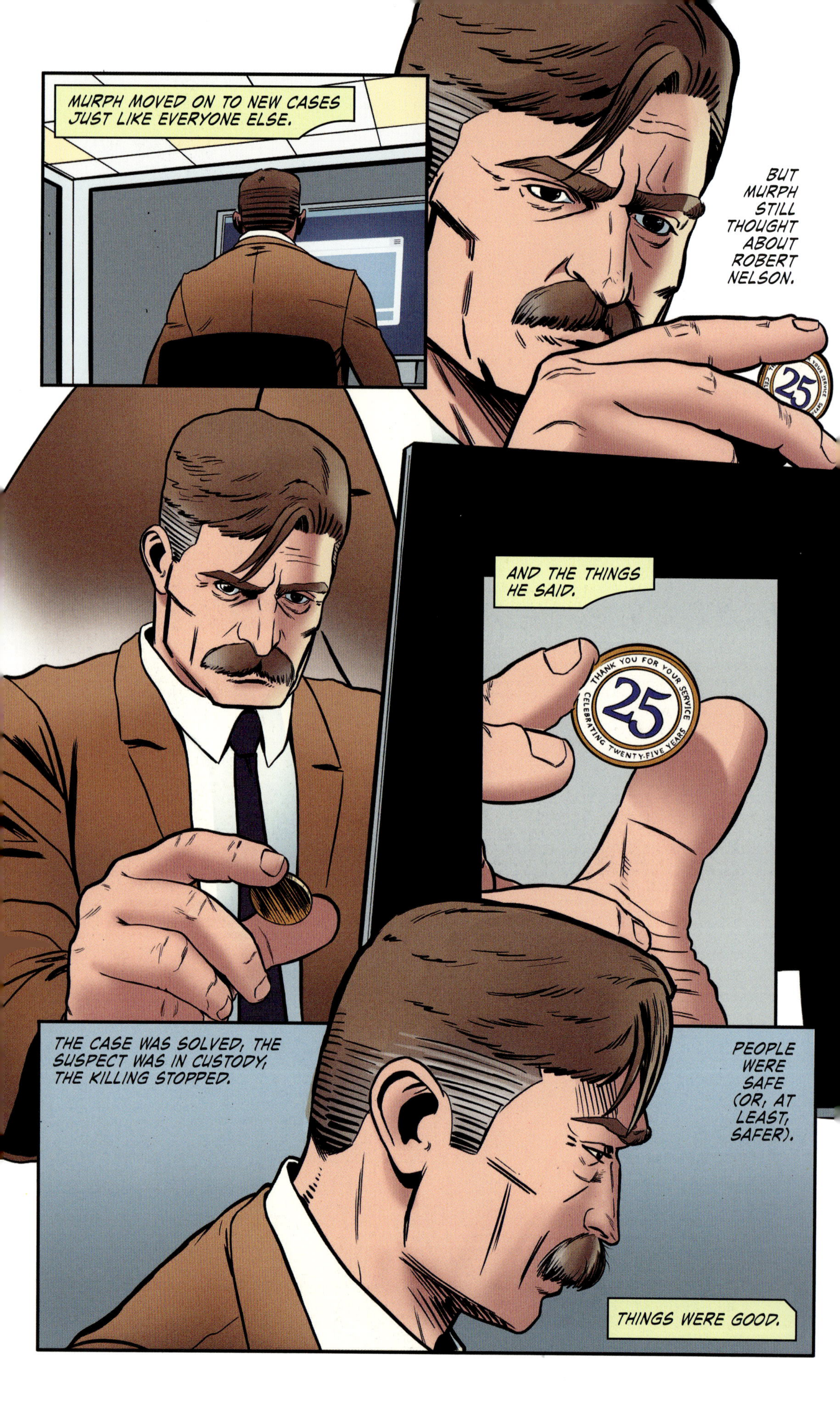
MURPH MOVED ON TO NEW CASES JUST LIKE EVERYONE ELSE.
BUT MURPH STILL THOUGHT ABOUT ROBERT NELSON.
AND THE THINGS HE SAID.
THANK YOU FOR YOUR SERVICE
25
CELEBRATING TWENTY-FIVE YEARS
THE CASE WAS SOLVED, THE SUSPECT WAS IN CUSTODY, THE KILLING STOPPED.
PEOPLE WERE SAFE (OR, AT LEAST, SAFER).
THINGS WERE GOOD.

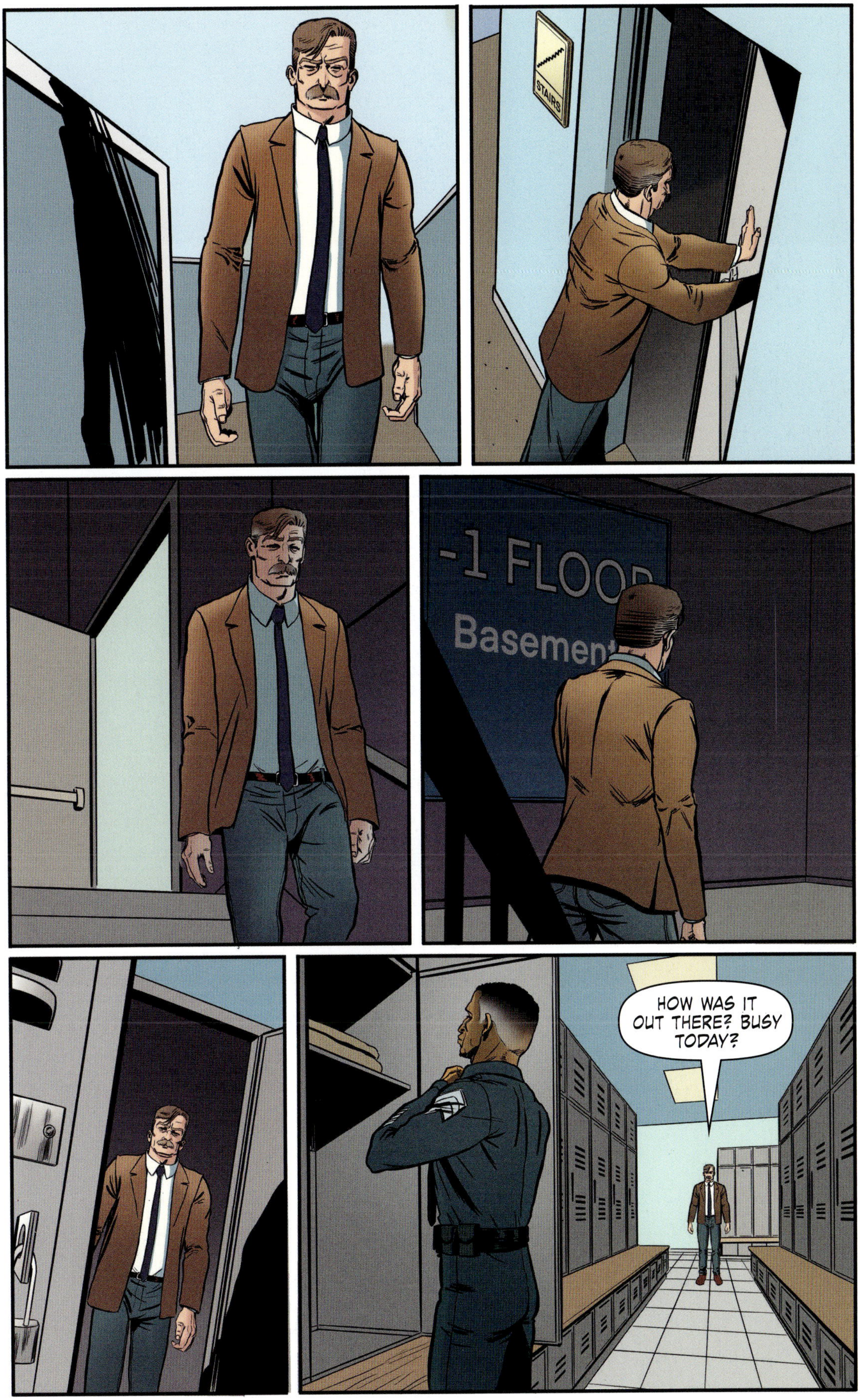
STAIRS
-1 FLOOR
Basement
HOW WAS IT OUT THERE? BUSY TODAY?

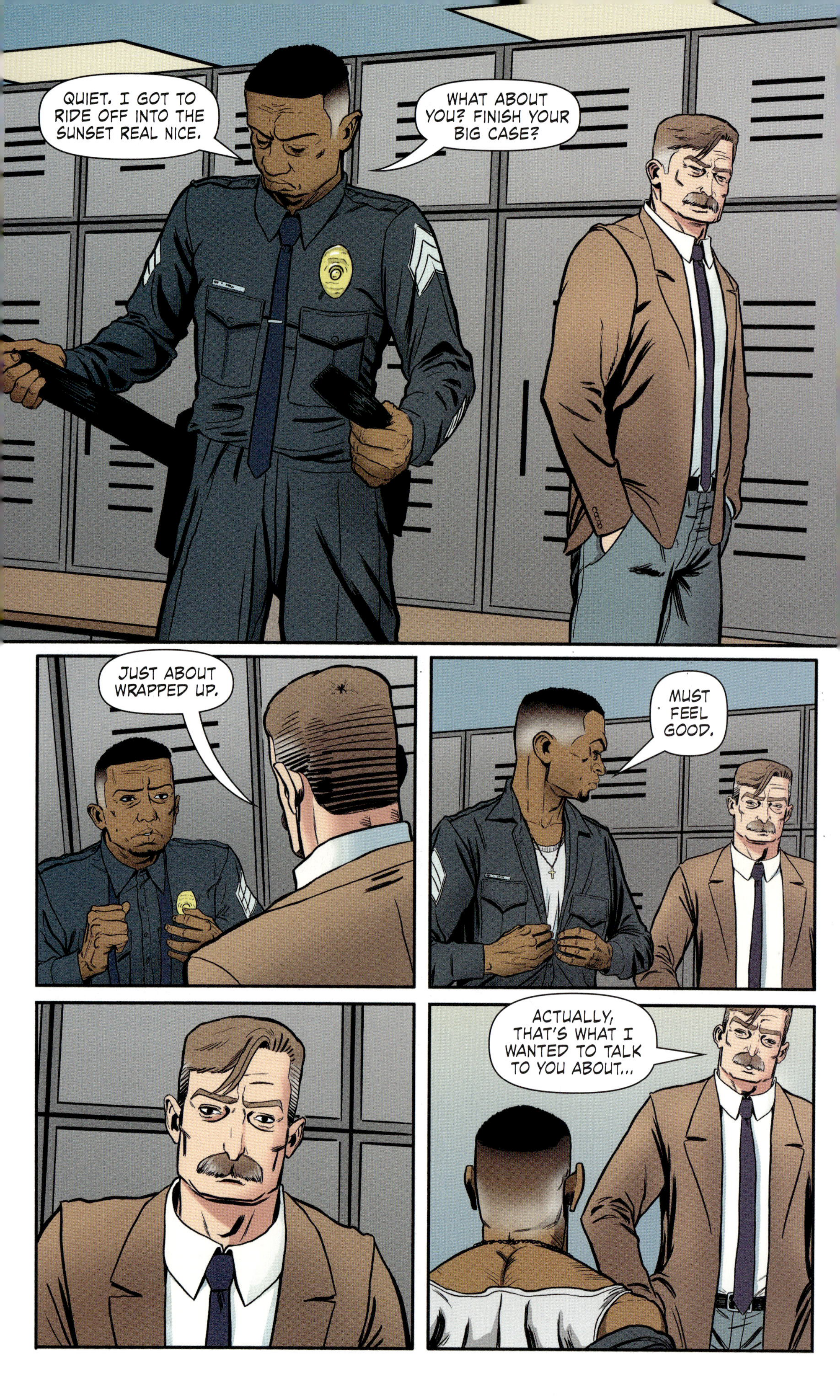
QUIET. I GOT TO RIDE OFF INTO THE SUNSET REAL NICE.
WHAT ABOUT YOU? FINISH YOUR BIG CASE?
JUST ABOUT WRAPPED UP.
MUST FEEL GOOD.
ACTUALLY, THAT'S WHAT I WANTED TO TALK TO YOU ABOUT...

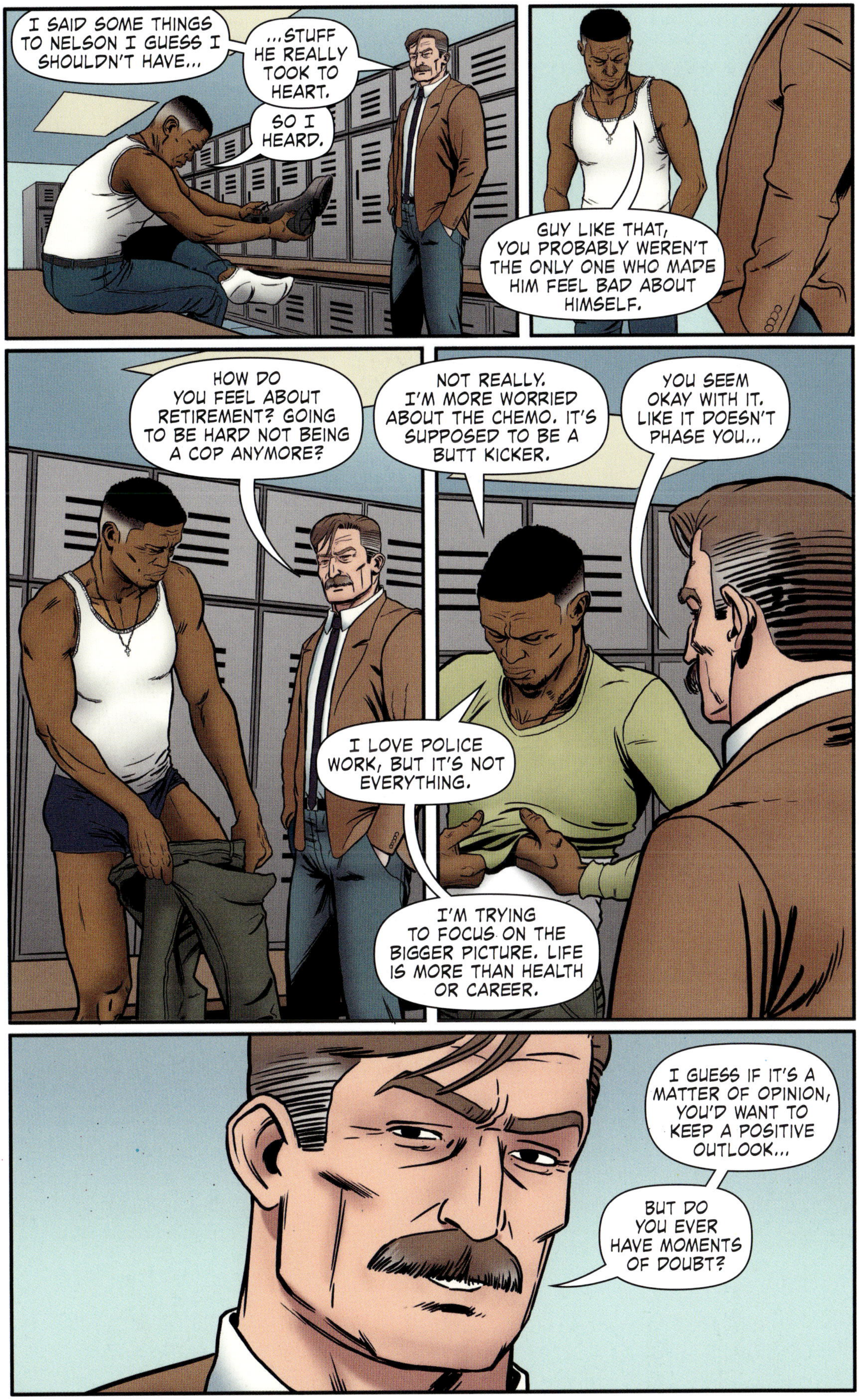

I SAID SOME THINGS TO NELSON I GUESS I SHOULDN'T HAVE...
...STUFF HE REALLY TOOK TO HEART.
SO I HEARD.
GUY LIKE THAT, YOU PROBABLY WEREN'T THE ONLY ONE WHO MADE HIM FEEL BAD ABOUT HIMSELF.
HOW DO YOU FEEL ABOUT RETIREMENT? GOING TO BE HARD NOT BEING A COP ANYMORE?
I LOVE POLICE WORK, BUT IT'S NOT EVERYTHING.
NOT REALLY. I'M MORE WORRIED ABOUT THE CHEMO. IT'S SUPPOSED TO BE A BUTT KICKER.
YOU SEEM OKAY WITH IT. LIKE IT DOESN'T PHASE YOU...
I'M TRYING TO FOCUS ON THE BIGGER PICTURE. LIFE IS MORE THAN HEALTH OR CAREER.
I GUESS IF IT'S A MATTER OF OPINION, YOU'D WANT TO KEEP A POSITIVE OUTLOOK...
BUT DO YOU EVER HAVE MOMENTS OF DOUBT?

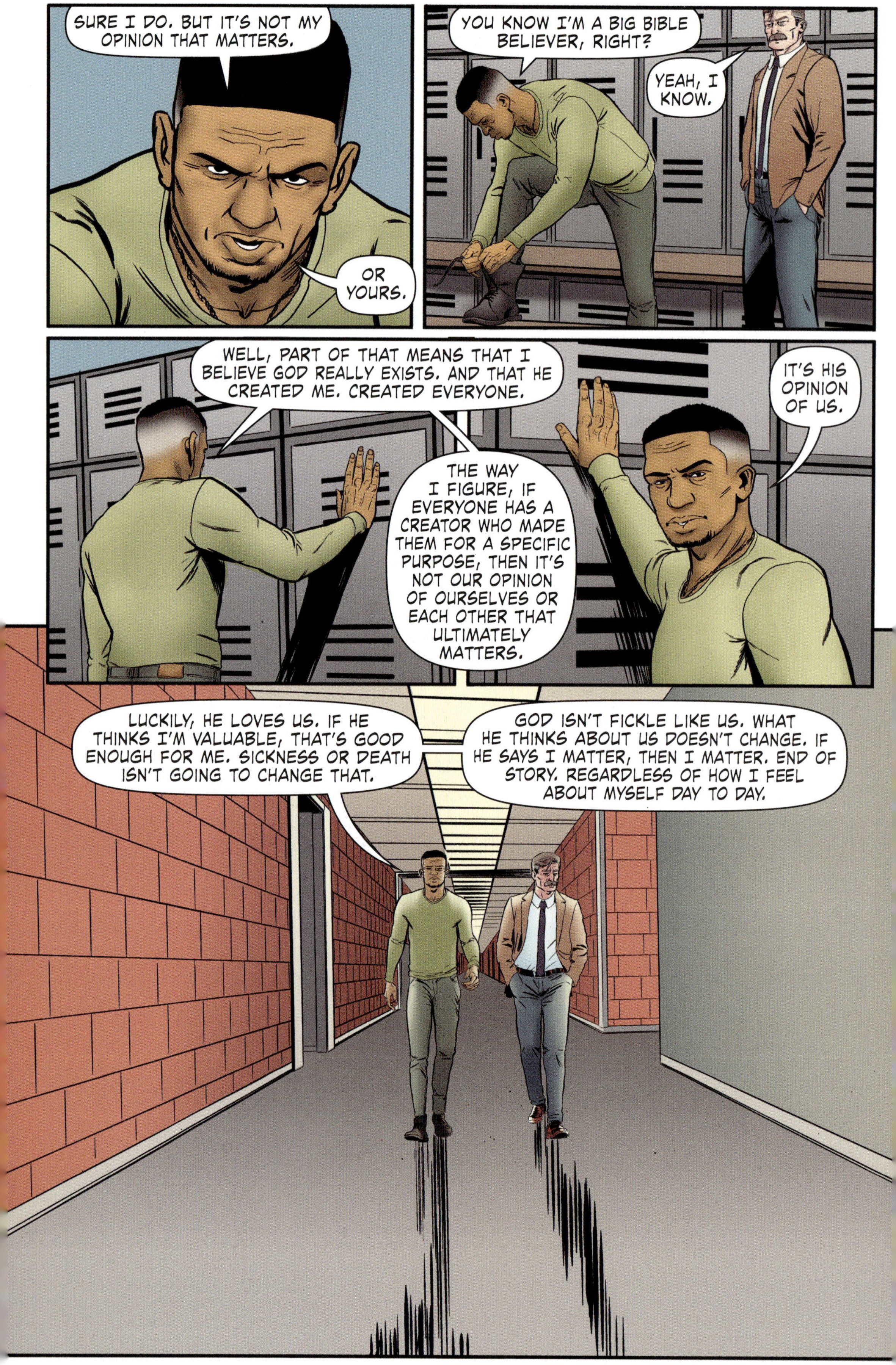
SURE I DO. BUT IT'S NOT MY OPINION THAT MATTERS.
OR YOURS.
YOU KNOW I'M A BIG BIBLE BELIEVER, RIGHT?
YEAH, I KNOW.
WELL, PART OF THAT MEANS THAT I BELIEVE GOD REALLY EXISTS. AND THAT HE CREATED ME. CREATED EVERYONE.
THE WAY I FIGURE, IF EVERYONE HAS A CREATOR WHO MADE THEM FOR A SPECIFIC PURPOSE, THEN IT'S NOT OUR OPINION OF OURSELVES OR EACH OTHER THAT ULTIMATELY MATTERS.
IT'S HIS OPINION OF US.
GOD ISN'T FICKLE LIKE US. WHAT HE THINKS ABOUT US DOESN'T CHANGE. IF HE SAYS I MATTER, THEN I MATTER. END OF STORY. REGARDLESS OF HOW I FEEL ABOUT MYSELF DAY TO DAY.
LUCKILY, HE LOVES US. IF HE THINKS I'M VALUABLE, THAT'S GOOD ENOUGH FOR ME. SICKNESS OR DEATH ISN'T GOING TO CHANGE THAT.

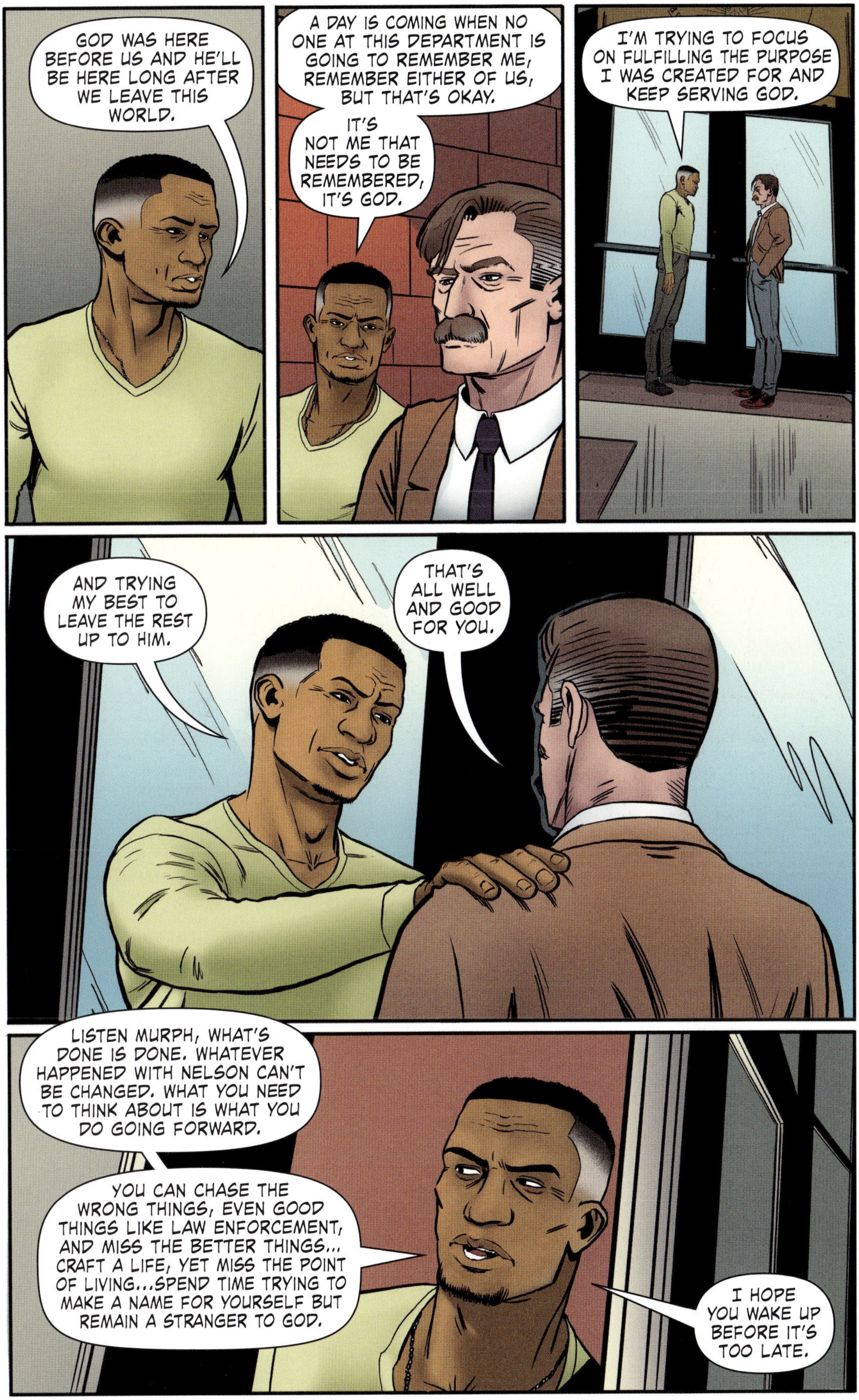
GOD WAS HERE BEFORE US AND HE'LL BE HERE LONG AFTER WE LEAVE THIS WORLD.
A DAY IS COMING WHEN NO ONE AT THIS DEPARTMENT IS GOING TO REMEMBER ME, REMEMBER EITHER OF US, BUT THAT'S OKAY.
IT'S NOT ME THAT NEEDS TO BE REMEMBERED, IT'S GOD.
I'M TRYING TO FOCUS ON FULFILLING THE PURPOSE I WAS CREATED FOR AND KEEP SERVING GOD.
AND TRYING MY BEST TO LEAVE THE REST UP TO HIM.
THAT'S ALL WELL AND GOOD FOR YOU.
LISTEN MURPH, WHAT'S DONE IS DONE. WHATEVER HAPPENED WITH NELSON CAN'T BE CHANGED. WHAT YOU NEED TO THINK ABOUT IS WHAT YOU DO GOING FORWARD.
YOU CAN CHASE THE WRONG THINGS, EVEN GOOD THINGS LIKE LAW ENFORCEMENT, AND MISS THE BETTER THINGS... CRAFT A LIFE, YET MISS THE POINT OF LIVING...SPEND TIME TRYING TO MAKE A NAME FOR YOURSELF BUT REMAIN A STRANGER TO GOD.
I HOPE YOU WAKE UP BEFORE IT'S TOO LATE.

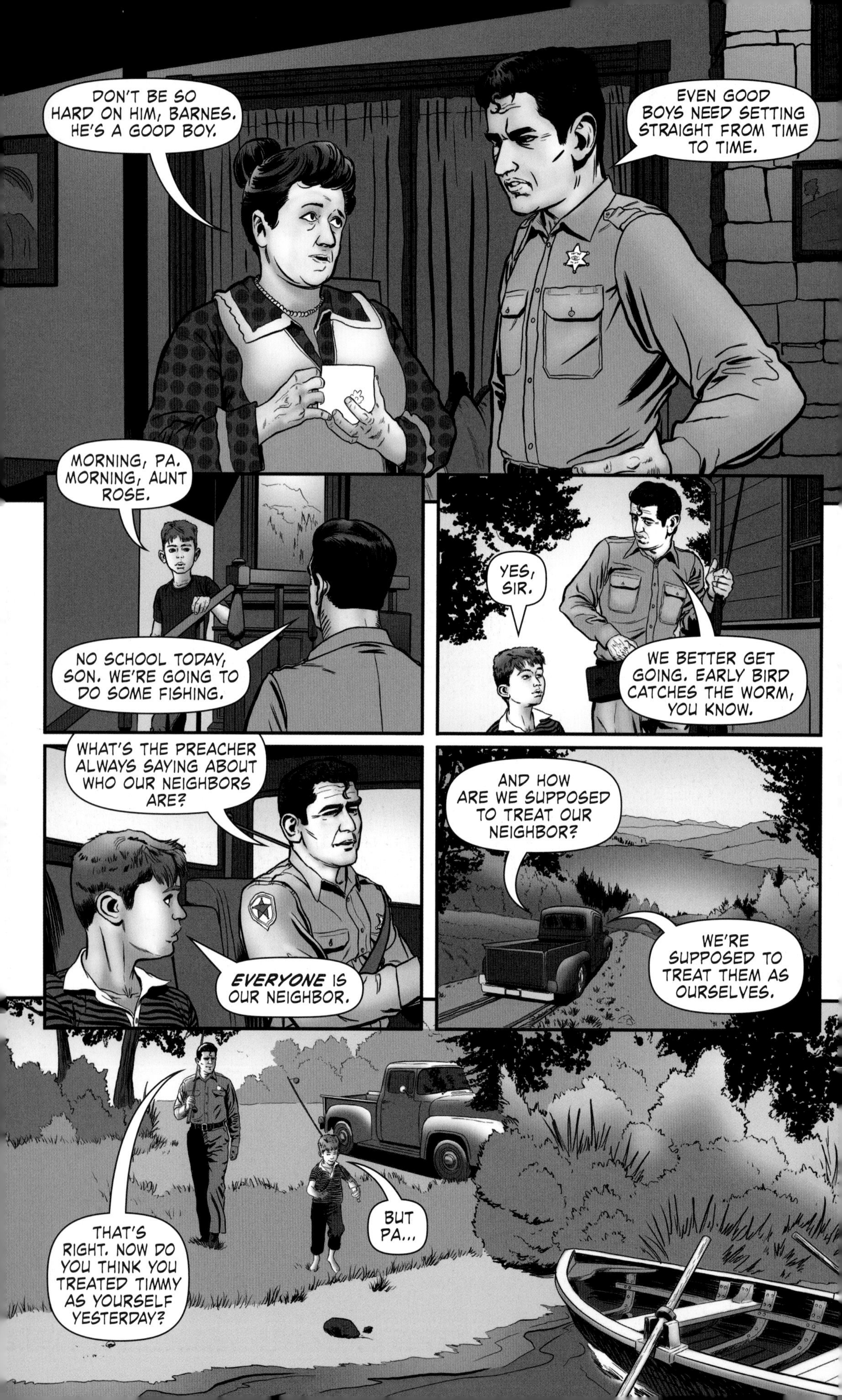
DON'T BE SO HARD ON HIM, BARNES. HE'S A GOOD BOY.
EVEN GOOD BOYS NEED SETTING STRAIGHT FROM TIME TO TIME.
MORNING, PA. MORNING, AUNT ROSE.
NO SCHOOL TODAY, SON. WE'RE GOING TO DO SOME FISHING.
YES, SIR.
WE BETTER GET GOING. EARLY BIRD CATCHES THE WORM, YOU KNOW.
WHAT'S THE PREACHER ALWAYS SAYING ABOUT WHO OUR NEIGHBORS ARE?
EVERYONE IS OUR NEIGHBOR.
AND HOW ARE WE SUPPOSED TO TREAT OUR NEIGHBOR?
WE'RE SUPPOSED TO TREAT THEM AS OURSELVES.
THAT'S RIGHT. NOW DO YOU THINK YOU TREATED TIMMY AS YOURSELF YESTERDAY?
BUT PA...

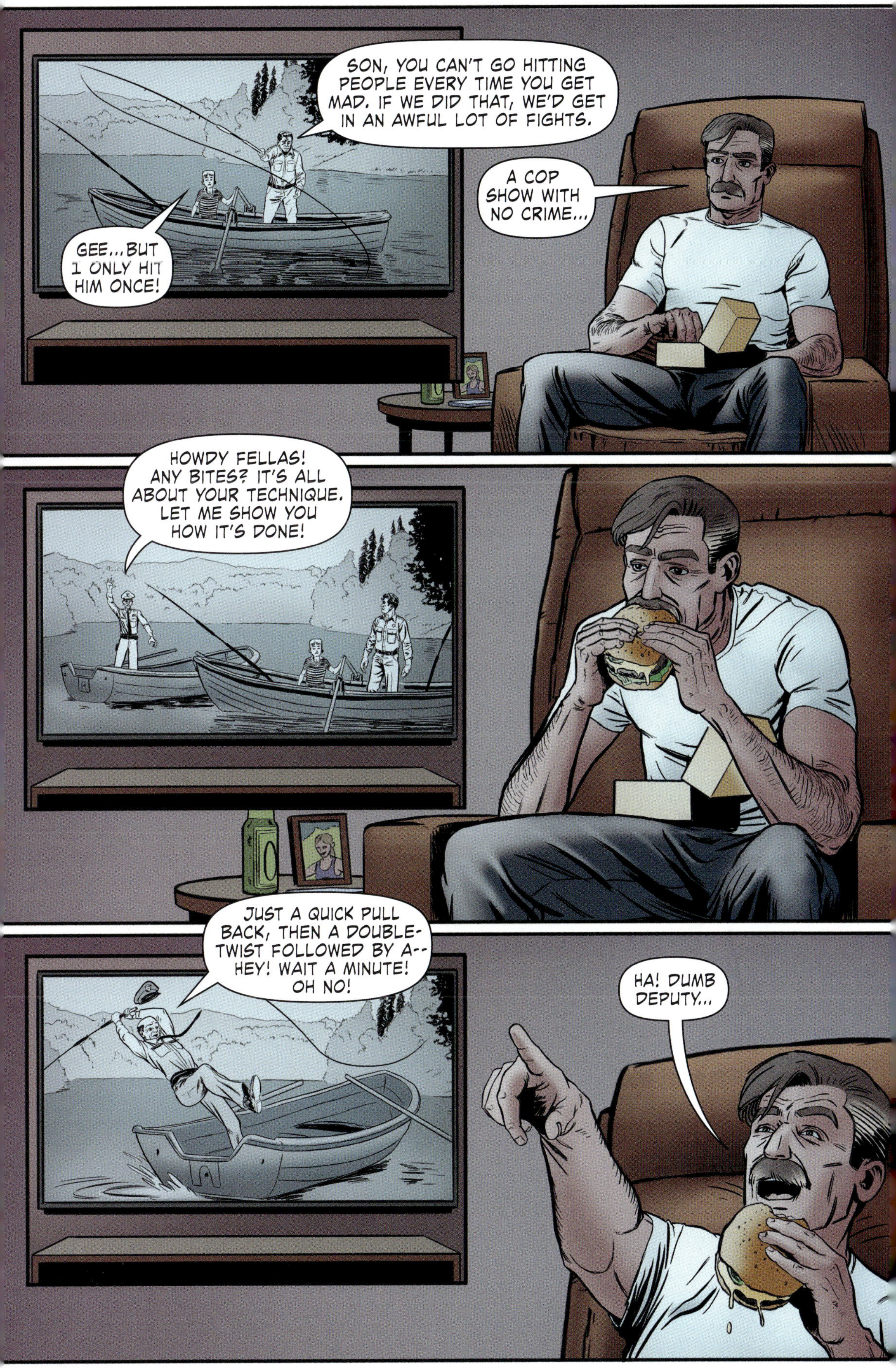
SON, YOU CAN'T GO HITTING PEOPLE EVERY TIME YOU GET MAD. IF WE DID THAT, WE'D GET IN AN AWFUL LOT OF FIGHTS.
GEE...BUT I ONLY HIT HIM ONCE!
A COP SHOW WITH NO CRIME...
HOWDY FELLAS! ANY BITES? IT'S ALL ABOUT YOUR TECHNIQUE. LET ME SHOW YOU HOW IT'S DONE!
JUST A QUICK PULL BACK, THEN A DOUBLE-TWIST FOLLOWED BY A-- HEY! WAIT A MINUTE! OH NO!
HA! DUMB DEPUTY...

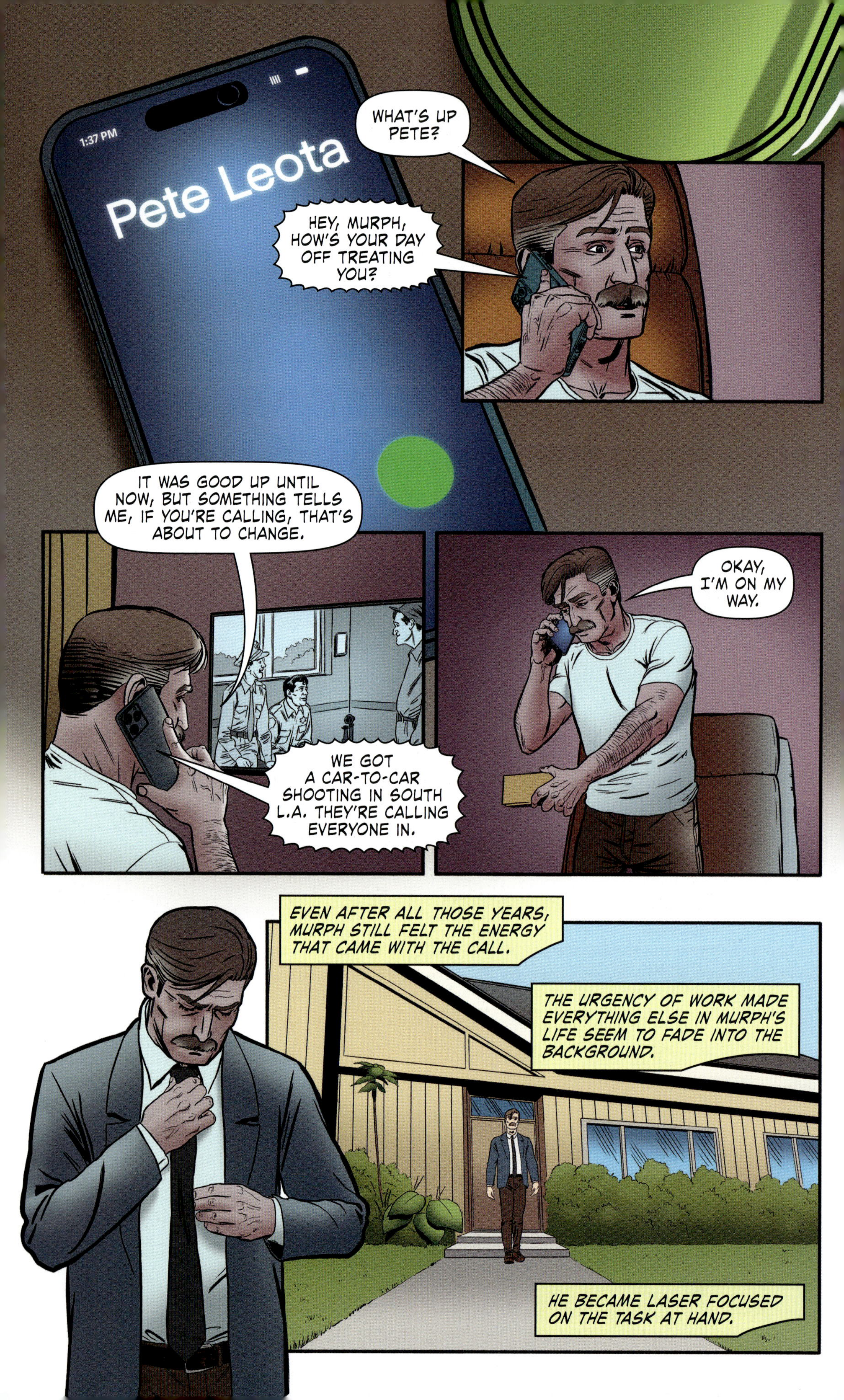
1:37 PM
Pete Leota
WHAT'S UP PETE?
HEY, MURPH, HOW'S YOUR DAY OFF TREATING YOU?
IT WAS GOOD UP UNTIL NOW, BUT SOMETHING TELLS ME, IF YOU'RE CALLING, THAT'S ABOUT TO CHANGE.
WE GOT A CAR-TO-CAR SHOOTING IN SOUTH L.A. THEY'RE CALLING EVERYONE IN.
OKAY, I'M ON MY WAY.
EVEN AFTER ALL THOSE YEARS, MURPH STILL FELT THE ENERGY THAT CAME WITH THE CALL.
THE URGENCY OF WORK MADE EVERYTHING ELSE IN MURPH'S LIFE SEEM TO FADE INTO THE BACKGROUND.
HE BECAME LASER FOCUSED ON THE TASK AT HAND.

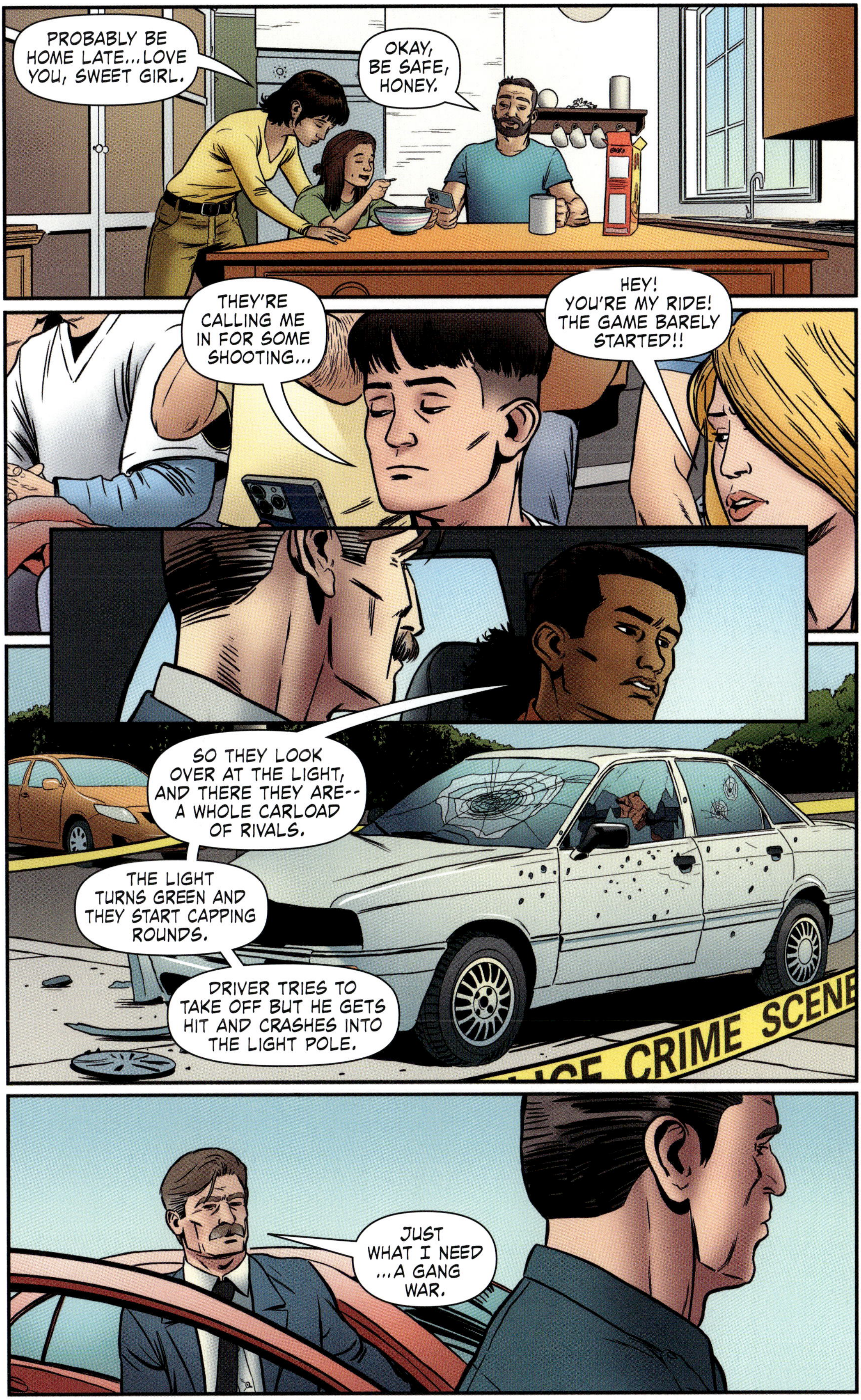
PROBABLY BE HOME LATE...LOVE YOU, SWEET GIRL.
OKAY, BE SAFE, HONEY.
THEY'RE CALLING ME IN FOR SOME SHOOTING...
HEY! YOU'RE MY RIDE! THE GAME BARELY STARTED!!
SO THEY LOOK OVER AT THE LIGHT, AND THERE THEY ARE--A WHOLE CARLOAD OF RIVALS.
THE LIGHT TURNS GREEN AND THEY START CAPPING ROUNDS.
DRIVER TRIES TO TAKE OFF BUT HE GETS HIT AND CRASHES INTO THE LIGHT POLE.
CRIME SCENE
JUST WHAT I NEED ...A GANG WAR.

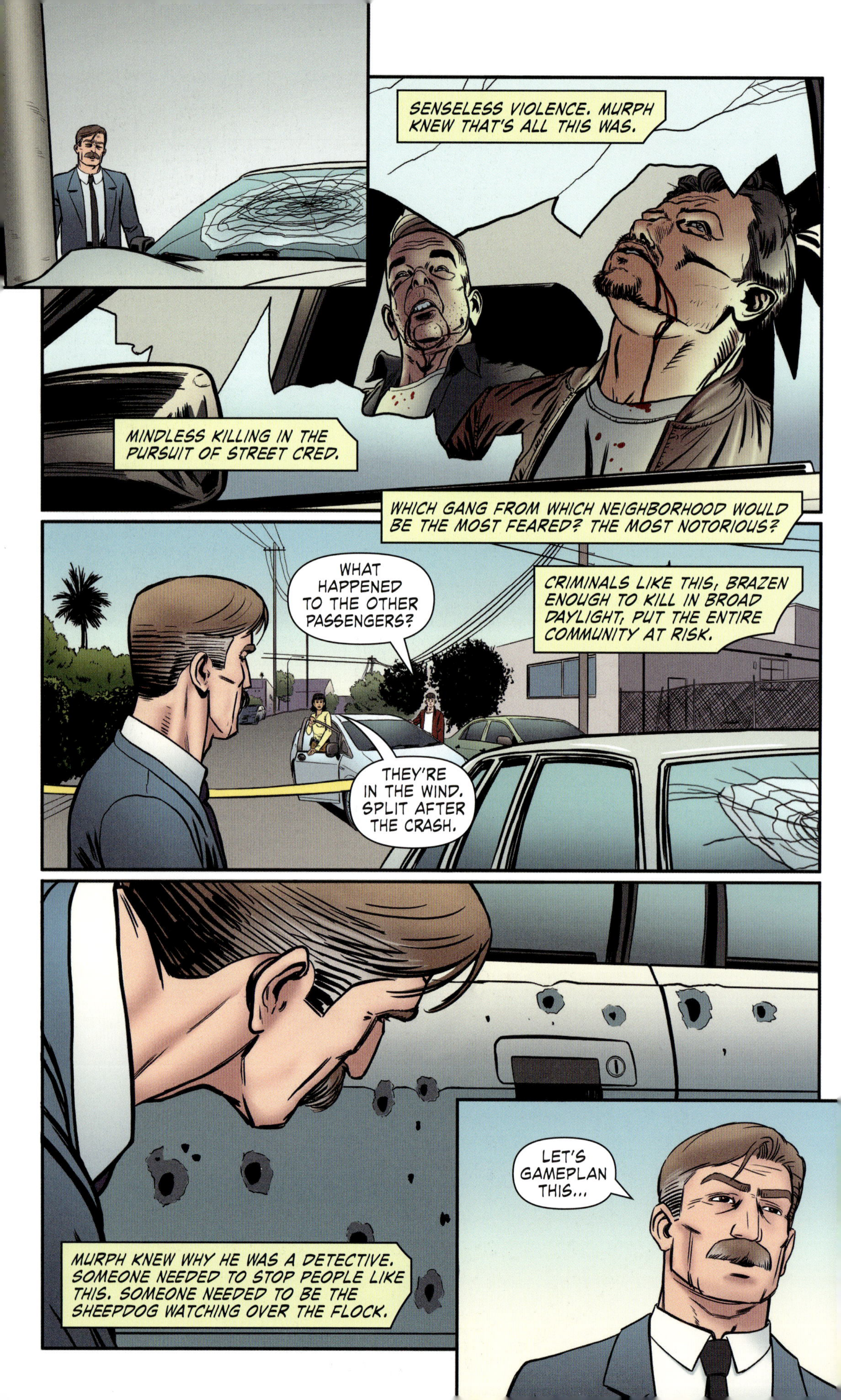
SENSELESS VIOLENCE. MURPH KNEW THAT'S ALL THIS WAS.
MINDLESS KILLING IN THE PURSUIT OF STREET CRED.
WHICH GANG FROM WHICH NEIGHBORHOOD WOULD BE THE MOST FEARED? THE MOST NOTORIOUS?
WHAT HAPPENED TO THE OTHER PASSENGERS?
CRIMINALS LIKE THIS, BRAZEN ENOUGH TO KILL IN BROAD DAYLIGHT, PUT THE ENTIRE COMMUNITY AT RISK.
THEY'RE IN THE WIND. SPLIT AFTER THE CRASH.
MURPH KNEW WHY HE WAS A DETECTIVE. SOMEONE NEEDED TO STOP PEOPLE LIKE THIS. SOMEONE NEEDED TO BE THE SHEEPDOG WATCHING OVER THE FLOCK.
LET'S GAMEPLAN THIS...

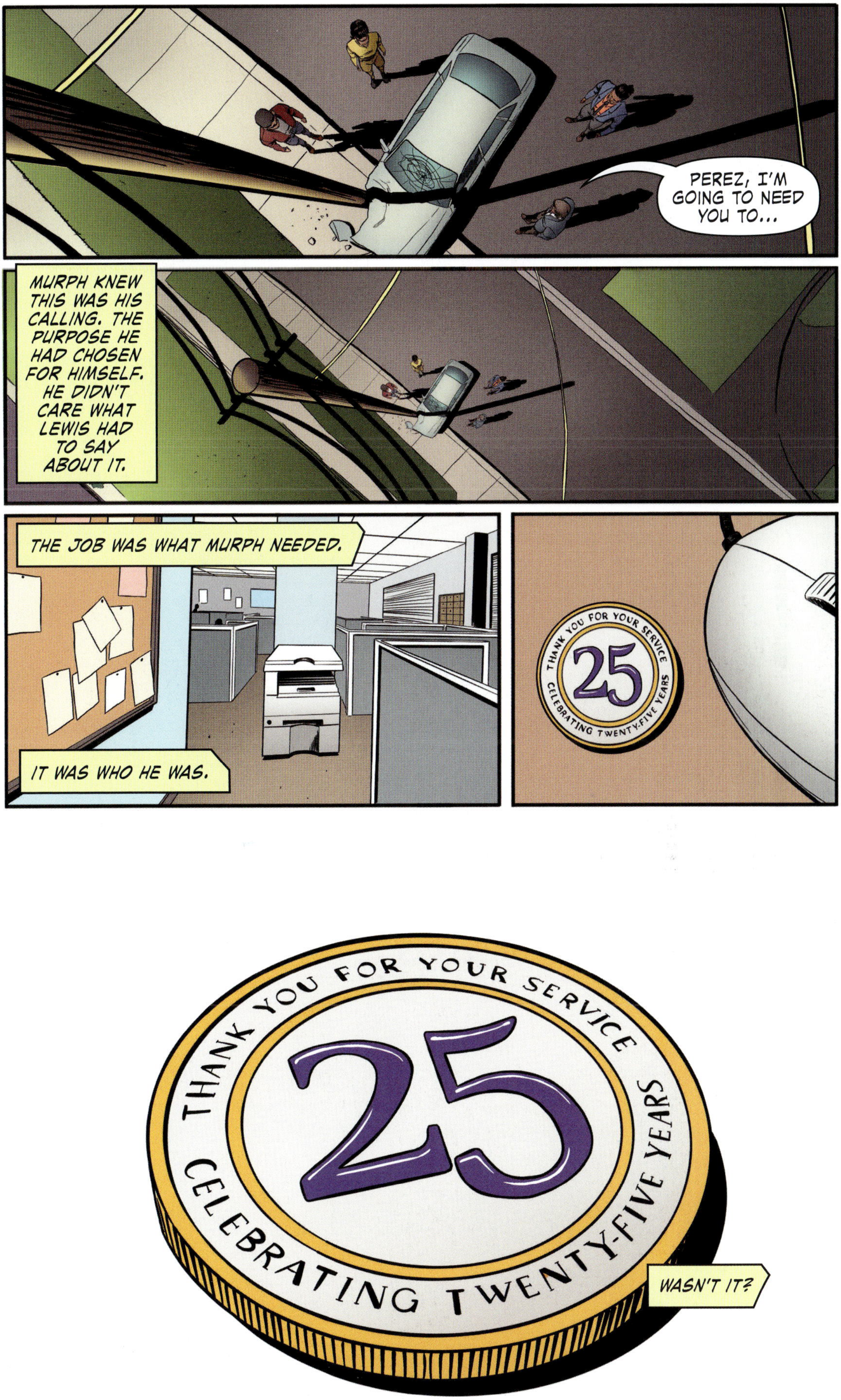
PEREZ, I'M GOING TO NEED YOU TO...
MURPH KNEW THIS WAS HIS CALLING. THE PURPOSE HE HAD CHOSEN FOR HIMSELF. HE DIDN'T CARE WHAT LEWIS HAD TO SAY ABOUT IT.
THE JOB WAS WHAT MURPH NEEDED.
IT WAS WHO HE WAS.
THANK YOU FOR YOUR SERVICE
25
CELEBRATING TWENTY-FIVE YEARS
THANK YOU FOR YOUR SERVICE
25
CELEBRATING TWENTY-FIVE YEARS
WASN'T IT?

END.